To...

Dancing in
Shadows

*With best wishes
for a bright future!
Stamford, 2-21-09*

Asian Voices
A Subseries of Asian/Pacific Perspectives
Series Editor: Mark Selden

Dancing in Shadows

Sihanouk, the Khmer Rouge, and the United Nations in Cambodia

BENNY WIDYONO

ROWMAN & LITTLEFIELD PUBLISHERS, INC.
Lanham • Boulder • New York • Toronto • Plymouth, UK

ROWMAN & LITTLEFIELD PUBLISHERS, INC.

Published in the United States of America
by Rowman & Littlefield Publishers, Inc.
A wholly owned subsidiary of The Rowman & Littlefield Publishing Group, Inc.
4501 Forbes Boulevard, Suite 200, Lanham, Maryland 20706
www.rowmanlittlefield.com

Estover Road, Plymouth PL6 7PY, United Kingdom

British Library Cataloguing in Publication Information Available

Library of Congress Cataloging-in-Publication Data
Widyono, Benny, 1936-
  Dancing in shadows : Sihanouk, the Khmer Rouge, and the United Nations in Cambodia / Benny Widyono.
      p. cm. — (Asian voices)
  Includes bibliographical references and index.
  ISBN-13: 978-0-7425-5552-5 (cloth : alk. paper)
  ISBN-10: 0-7425-5552-6 (cloth : alk. paper)
  ISBN-13: 978-0-7425-5553-2 (pbk. : alk. paper)
  ISBN-10: 0-7425-5553-4 (pbk. : alk. paper)
  1. Cambodia—Politics and government—1979- 2. United Nations—Cambodia. 3. Widyono, Benny, 1936- 4. Party of Democratic Kampuchea. 5. Norodom Sihanouk, Prince, 1922- I. Title.

Printed in the United States of America

♾️™ The paper used in this publication meets the minimum requirements of American National Standard for Information Sciences—Permanence of Paper for Printed Library Materials, ANSI/NISO Z39.48-1992.

For my wife, Francisca, and
my children, Martin, Ron, Monique, and Dan

A scholar's highest obligation, the phrase had it in the 1960s, was to speak truth to power. It turned out, however, that truth was a tragically relative term in the Cold War era. Many Americans were sent to die by the tens of thousands, while Asians, Latin Americans, and Africans were sentenced to death by the millions because U.S. officials disagreed with foreign leaders about what each believed was true in terms of the needs of their own national interests.

—*Walter LaFeber in a foreword to George McT. Kahin,* Southeast Asia: A Testament

Contents

List of Illustrations

MAPS

TABLES

Glossary of Abbreviations and Terms

ADB	Asian Development Bank.
Angkar	This was the official name of the authority in power under the Khmer Rouge. It simply means Organization.
ANKI	Armée National pour un Kampuchea Independent (National Army for an Independent Kampuchea). Formerly known as ANS.
ANS	Armée National Sihanoukienne, or Sihanouk's National Army. Changed its name in 1990 to ANKI.
ASEAN	Association of Southeast Asian Nations.
Bangbatt	Bangladesh battalion in UNTAC.
BLDP	Buddhist Liberal Democratic Party. The political party of the KPNLF.
CDC	Cambodian Development Council. The body dealing with foreign aid and foreign investment.
CDCF	Cambodian Development Cooperation Forum, a Cambodian government body established in 2007 to coordinate the annual donors meetings, replacing the CG. See CG.
CG	Consultative Group. An annual meeting organized by the World Bank to coordinate aid to Camodia. In 2007 it was replaced by the CDCF. See CDCF.

CGDK   Coalition Government of Democratic Kampuchea. A
                  government in exile consisting of the DK (Khmer
                  Rouge), FUNCINPEC, and KPNLF. Established in 1982.
                  In October 1991 it was renamed the National Govern-
                  ment of Cambodia (NGC).
CivPol   Civil Police component of UNTAC.
CPAF   Cambodian People's Armed Forces. The army of the
                  PRK/SOC.
CPP   Cambodian People's Party. The political party of the
                  PRK/SOC government.
DES   District electoral supervisor of UNTAC.
DK   Democratic Kampuchea. The official name of the Khmer
                  Rouge regime.
DNUM   Democratic National Union Movement. Established by
                  Khmer Rouge leader Ieng Sary after he defected to the
                  RGC in 1996.
ECCC   Extraordinary Chambers in the Courts of Cambodia, the
                  tribunal established to try the Khmer Rouge leaders.
Expanded Perm 5
(EP 5)   An informal but powerful body consisting of the ambas-
                  sadors of the five permanent members of the UN Security
                  Council plus Australia, Canada, Germany, India, Indone-
                  sia, Japan, and Thailand.
FUN   Front Uni National, also known as NUF (National United
                  Front). Coalition of parties established by FUNCINPEC,
                  KNP, and BLDP to fight the CPP (i.e., Hun Sen) wing of
                  the Royal Government.
FUNCINPEC   Front Uni National Pour un Cambodge Independent,
                  Neutre, Pacifique at Cooperatif (National United Front
                  for an Independent, Neutral, Peaceful and Cooperative
                  Cambodia). Movement established by Sihanouk in 1981.
                  The political party of the movement.
FUNK   Front Uni National du Kambodge (National United Front
                  of Cambodia). Established by Sihanouk in Beijing after
                  he was overthrown as head of state in 1970.

GRUNK	Gouvernement Royal d'Union Nationale du Kampuchea (Royal Government of National Union of Kampuchea). A government in exile established by Sihanouk in Beijing after his ouster as head of state in 1970.
ICORC	International Committee for the Reconstruction of Cambodia.
Indobatt	Indonesian battalion in UNTAC.
Kampuchea	Direct transliteration more faithful to the Khmer pronunciation of Cambodia, which is the English transliteration directed from the French Cambodge. Politically, Kampuchea is preferred by the Khmer Rouge and the PRK.
Khmer	Official name of the language of the country that is sometimes referred to as Cambodian. The Khmer people who take their identity from their common language are the dominant ethnic group of Cambodia. Khmer and Cambodian are used interchangeably.
KNP	Khmer Nation Party. Established by prominent opposition politician Sam Rainsy.
KPNLAF	Khmer People's National Liberation Armed Forces. Military wing of KPNLF that later split from KPNLF.
KPNLF	Khmer People's National Liberation Front. Anticommunist movement established by Son Sann in 1979 to fight the PRK/SOC and the Vietnamese forces in Cambodia. It was one of the four factions that entered into the peace process.
KR	Khmer Rouge. Loose name given by Sihanouk to the Communist Party under Pol Pot.
LDP	Liberal Democratic Party. Political Party of the KPNALF. Did not gain any seats in the UNTAC elections.
Molinaka	Mouvement de Liberation Nationale du Kampuchea (National Movement for the Liberation of Kampuchea). Name of the political party of the movement.
MovCon	Movement Control. Unit of Dutch marines who controlled UNTAC's movements by air.

NADK	National Army of Democratic Kampuchea. The army of the Khmer Rouge.
Neak Chas, or Neak Moultanh	Literally "old people," or base people, in the Khmer language. An epithet given to the peasants who lived in the rural areas "liberated" by the Khmer Rouge after the coup d'etat of 18 March 1970.
Neak Thmei	Literally means "new people" in the Khmer language. An epithet given by the Khmer Rouge to the urban people evacuated from Phnom Penh and other cities after 17 April 1975.
NGC	National Government of Cambodia (see CGDK).
NGO	Nongovernmental organization.
NUF	National United Front. See FUN.
Pakbatt	Pakistani battalion in UNTAC.
PCPB	Post Conflict Peace Building.
Perm 5	Five permanent members of the UN Security Council.
PRK	People's Republic of Kampuchea. Government established by the UFNSK in January 1979 after the overthrow of the Pol Pot regime. The PRK changed its name to the State of Cambodia (SOC) in 1989 to shed its communist image.
PRPK	The name of the Communist Party of Cambodia established by the KNUFNS in January 1979 in Phnom Penh. Changed its name to the Cambodian People's Party (CPP) in 1991.
RCAF	Royal Cambodian Armed Forces. The army of the RGC.
RGC	Royal Government of Cambodia. Coalition government between the CPP and FUNCINPEC nominally headed by King Sihanouk. Constitutionally established after the UNTAC elections in 1993.
SGRC	The UN secretary-general's representative in Cambodia.
SNC	Supreme National Council.
SOC	State of Cambodia.
SRN	Sangkom Reaster Niyom (People's Socialist Community). Political movement founded by Sihanouk that ruled the country during 1955 to 1970.

SRP   Sam Rainsy Party. Political party of opposition leader Sam Rainsy after he quit KNP.

UFNSK   United Front for the National Salvation of Kampuchea. Established in December 1978 by former Khmer Rouge and other dissident Cambodian elements to overthrow the Pol Pot regime.

UNAMIC   United Nations Advance Mission in Cambodia. Forerunner of UNTAC. Deployed in 1991 to prepare for UNTAC.

UNCHR   United Nations Center for Human Rights in Cambodia.

UNDP   United Nations Development Program.

UNHCR   United Nations High Commissioner for Refugees.

UNICEF   United Nations Children's Fund.

UNMLT   United Nations Military Liaison Team in Cambodia.

UNMO   United Nations military observers.

UNSGRC   United Nations secretary-general's representative in Cambodia.

UNSRSG   The special representative of the UN secretary-general in Cambodia.

UNTAC   United Nations Transitional Authority in Cambodia.

UNV   United Nations volunteers.

Yuon   Derogatory term for Vietnamese in the Cambodian and Thai languages.

WB   World Bank.

WFP   World Food Programs.

Foreword by Ben Kiernan

The modest, white-walled Noor Al-Ihsan mosque on the northern outskirts of Phnom Penh was one of the two oldest buildings in the Cambodian capital. When the city, supposedly founded in 1434, celebrated its 550th anniversary in 1984, few if any Phnom Penh buildings predated the nineteenth century. A sign in Arabic and Khmer above the old mosque's entrance dated its foundation to 1813. That was just a few years after Cambodia's royal court first moved south to Phnom Penh from Udong, the former capital upriver. Already living in the Phnom Penh area at the time was a community of Muslim Chams, refugees from an eighteenth-century civil war downriver in neighboring Vietnam. Sadly, this important historical site that the Chams founded in 1813 in Cambodia's modern capital has now been obliterated. Today nothing remains of the former Noor Al-Ihsan. The old mosque, whose Arabic name meant "Light of Beneficence," was bulldozed in the 1990s to make way for a shining new construction of Middle Eastern design, financed by a US$70,000 donation from a Kuwaiti group in order to foster global Islam in a Buddhist kingdom.

Even the genocidal Pol Pot regime had left this historic Cham mosque intact. But not out of any respect for indigenous Islam. When I first visited the Noor Al-Ihsan mosque in July 1980, Cambodia's Muslims were only just beginning their long recovery from the Khmer Rouge genocide that had sent about one-third of them, perhaps one hundred thousand people, to their graves from 1975 to 1979. Yet Pol Pot's regime still occupied Cambodia's seat in the United Nations, which considered "the Cambodia problem" to be the Vietnamese occupation, not the Khmer Rouge genocide it had stopped. Inside Cambodia, the country's new pro-Vietnamese government, unrecognized in New York, proclaimed that all Cambodians had suffered genocide and directed some attention to the fate of minorities like the Cham, yet most international legal scholars still paid no heed.

It is difficult in 2007 to imagine what Cambodian genocide survivors, including Cham Muslims, were up against. During 1980 and 1981, only six of the world's Islamic countries voted against the ousted Pol Pot regime's claim to retain Cambodia's UN seat: Afghanistan, Algeria, Chad, Libya, Syria, and South Yemen. Another half-dozen Muslim or Arab states—Iran, Iraq, Jordan, Lebanon, Mali, and Tunisia—abstained from casting a vote on the issue, perhaps reluctant to legitimize a defunct regime, let alone a genocidal one. Yet no fewer than twenty-one Muslim-majority countries lined up with China, the United States, and most European states (France abstained), in permitting the diplomats of the Khmer Rouge regime to represent its surviving victims. Those who voted in favor of this outcome included Indonesia and Malaysia, both members of the Association of Southeast Asian Nations (ASEAN), as well as Bahrain, Bangladesh, Djibouti, Egypt, Kuwait, Maldives, Mauritania, Morocco, Niger, Nigeria, Oman, Pakistan, Qatar, Saudi Arabia, Senegal, Sudan, Somalia, Turkey, and the United Arab Emirates.[1]

It was in this context that two unexpected foreign visitors went to meet with Cham survivors and pay their respects at the Noor Al-Ihsan mosque. I found these two men seated cross-legged on straw mats on the historic building's tiled floor, chatting to the *hakkem*, the Cham community leader, and other elders, as I stepped into the mosque that day in mid-1980. It was clear that the presence of a pair of Indonesian reporters had created something of an event. If it only temporarily relieved the trauma of Cambodian Chams, it also partially lifted their international isolation. Indeed the appearance at the mosque of leading journalists from the world's largest Muslim country achieved a small, quiet diplomatic breakthrough. The two Indonesian reporters were well-known writers for prominent Jakarta newspapers. Fikri Jufri, a Javanese Muslim, was deputy editor of the weekly magazine *Tempo*, and Sabam Siagian, a Christian Batak from Sumatra, was a distinguished reporter for the daily *Sinar Harapan*. Over a quarter-century later, *hakkem* Ali bin Mouser recalled these two "asking questions about the Pol Pot regime and how the Khmer Rouge mistreated people," and making inquiries about the state of mosques in post-genocide Cambodia.[2] After returning to Jakarta, Sabam Siagian summed up Cambodia's prospects in an influential *Sinar Harapan* article, entitled "The Remedy: Food, Religion and Culture (As Long as Peace Prevails)."[3]

The two Indonesians' unobtrusive visit to Cambodia and their subsequent reporting on the situation there helped pioneer a slow policy turnaround in Jakarta, which unfolded over the ensuing decade. That policy revision enabled Indonesia to play a major role in resolving the Cambodia conflict at the end of the 1980s. The two journalists' unofficial diplomacy also served as a precedent for their compatriot Benny Widyono, the author of this book, to make his own independent contribution to Cambodia's future in the 1990s. Indonesia's role in the regional resolution of the confrontation over Cambodia in the 1980s provided an important backdrop to this memoir and illuminates the work of its author as an international civil servant and UN official informed by his own Southeast Asian background.

Until the fall of General Suharto's dictatorship in 1998, all Indonesian journalists, whatever their views, had to operate within what in many ways was a criminal regime. In 1965–1966, Suharto's army had seized power in a massacre of over five hundred thousand suspected communists. As Fikri Jufri and Sabam Siagian visited Cambodia in 1980, Suharto's military were still exterminating East Timorese who resisted Indonesia's forced annexation of their homeland. Jakarta's official policy on Cambodia, too, was to isolate it in support of the Khmer Rouge. Yet Indonesia could never be reduced to Suharto's regime. Its cultural diversity, including seven hundred languages spoken in an archipelago of six thousand inhabited islands, has made the republic a very large, multiethnic society, with multiple flourishing literatures and traditions of syncretism and compromise.[4] Indonesia's modern culture also boasts a number of brave newspaper reporters, some of whom paid a price, yet made a difference. And so did the two journals that sent reporters to embargoed Cambodia in 1980. Two years later, the Suharto regime banned Fikri Jufri's *Tempo* and froze its license to publish, and then relented, until the government finally revoked *Tempo*'s license in 1994. In 1986, Jakarta also banned Sabam Siagian's *Sinar Harapan*. But both journals sprung up again with new names or in other formats.[5] From 1983 to 1991, Sabam served as founding editor of the *Jakarta Post*. Eventually Suharto appointed him ambassador to Australia, where in his first press conference, Sabam delighted the local press corps by referring to them colloquially if undiplomatically, as "bloody idiots."

The visit of these two independent Indonesians to Cambodia in 1980 was a breath of fresh air in a still-devastated and embargoed country, which was dependent on Vietnamese and Soviet aid for its recovery and rehabilitation. But other new developments were also in the air. Just a few months earlier, in March 1980, Suharto had met with Malaysia's prime minister in the Malaysian town of Kuantan, and the two men came up with the "Kuantan principle." The Indonesian and Malaysian leaders expressed their concern at the USSR's role in Cambodia, through its ally Vietnam, but they balanced this with their concern at China's role. The *Far Eastern Economic Review* reported that most regional countries shared their view: "Vietnam, it was generally thought, would withdraw only if there was no more Soviet aid to make the occupation viable, and if there was some guarantee that China would not leap into the breach after the withdrawal."[6] In other words, Hanoi had some legitimate concerns that were shared in Southeast Asia. Only in 1990 did Indonesia, for instance, resume diplomatic relations with China, after a twenty-five year rupture. These Southeast Asian concerns had to be addressed in negotiations. Indonesia's Armed Forces chief, Benny Murdani, made secret trips to Hanoi in 1980 and 1982 to try to mediate in the Cambodia dispute.[7]

In 1983, a new Australian foreign minister, Bill Hayden, identified the two main issues dominating the Cambodian conflict: the threat of a Khmer Rouge return to power and the need for a Vietnamese withdrawal. Hayden hoped to facilitate regional dialogue, which Indonesia encouraged. Jakarta recommended that Australia send development aid to Hanoi. Then, at the end of 1983, Indonesia began what an Australian observer termed "a fascinating coat-trailing exercise with Vietnam."[8] In February 1984, dropping his previous preference for secret diplomacy, Indonesian Armed Forces chief Benny Murdani made an official visit to Hanoi, the first senior ASEAN (Association of Southeast Asian Nations) figure to do so for three years. He concluded his third trip to Vietnam by stating that Hanoi posed no threat to Southeast Asia, and that its invasion of Cambodia had been undertaken in self-defense, "to maintain Vietnam's own existence" against Pol Pot's armed attacks. Two weeks later, the head of Indonesia's semi-official Centre for Strategic and International Studies, Jusuf Wanandi, arrived for a joint seminar in Hanoi. Wanandi surprised observers by praising "Vietnam's heroic struggle for independence," and he recommended "cooperating with Vietnam if there is a willingness on Hanoi's part jointly to seek a compromise in solving the Cambodian conflict."[9] Hanoi then made a new diplomatic proposal, which Indonesia's foreign minister, Mochtar Kusumaatmadja, called "a significant step forward." Mochtar also made two trips to Moscow, discussing Cambodia with the Soviet backers of Hanoi and Phnom Penh. Even Thailand's pro-Chinese foreign minister welcomed "new elements" in Hanoi's position.[10]

Wanandi's praise for Vietnam's "struggle for independence" implied common cause with Indonesia's own anticolonial struggle against Dutch rule— though not, of course, with the contemporary East Timorese resistance to Indonesian occupation. In 1989, Vietnam would answer Jakarta's call for a Vietnamese withdrawal from Cambodia, but East Timor had to wait another decade for Indonesia to end its brutal occupation there.

Still, the regional diplomacy on Cambodia slowly gained momentum. In 1985, Hanoi dropped its demand that the Chinese threat to Vietnam would have to end before a full Vietnamese troop withdrawal from Cambodia.[11] Australian foreign minister Hayden visited Hanoi in March 1985 and heard further Vietnamese proposals, which he termed "a considerable advance." Hayden asserted that his trip had "been quite successful and that will be proved."[12] Indonesia's Mochtar concurred that there had been another "advance in substance" in Hanoi's position.[13]

While in Vietnam, Hayden also met the new Cambodian premier, Hun Sen, becoming the first of many regional leaders to do so. Hun Sen told him: "We are ready to make concessions to Prince Sihanouk and other people if they agree to join with us to eliminate Pol Pot." Hun Sen later announced that the Vietnamese troops, rather than occupy Cambodia until 1995, would all leave by 1990, or earlier in the case of a settlement.

Vietnam now insisted only that the Khmer Rouge be prevented from returning to power. This meant that the Cambodia problem could from that point be resolved within Southeast Asia; principally by Thailand, which could cut off the Thai sanctuary and local transit of Chinese supplies that kept the Khmer Rouge alive, and by Vietnam, which could withdraw its own remaining troops. China's cooperation in a Cambodia settlement was no longer necessary. With Australian support, Indonesia had helped set the stage for a regional solution to the conflict.

On 10 April 1986, the *Far Eastern Economic Review* reported that in June, ASEAN ministers would finalize "a detailed blueprint for a settlement of the Cambodia question":

> The confidential outline attempts to satisfy Hanoi's demand that the withdrawal of its troops from Cambodia be coupled with cessation of Chinese arms supplies to the Khmer resistance by proposing to station an international peacekeeping force along Cambodia's land and sea borders. The sea border is being specified to assure Vietnam China would not be able to continue the supplies once the land routes from Thailand have been closed in the wake of a successful settlement.

China and the exiled Khmer Rouge coalition overruled this initiative. The June 1986 ASEAN foreign ministers' meeting in Manila apparently did not discuss it. But Hayden did address the question of the Khmer Rouge. At the Manila meeting, he broke new ground when he proposed the establishment of an international tribunal to try the Pol Pot leadership for its crimes. In taking up this suggestion made by Gregory Stanton, an international lawyer then on a visit to Canberra, Hayden became the first statesman to advocate legal accountability for the Khmer Rouge, two decades before the mixed UN-Cambodia tribunal began its operations in 2006.

As on related Cambodian issues, the great powers differed with the regional leaders. The U.S. Secretary of State George Shultz declined to support the Khmer Rouge tribunal idea, as did China, while Australia's pro-U.S. prime minister Bob Hawke distanced himself from his own foreign minister's prescient suggestion. Yet the Malaysian foreign minister immediately endorsed Hayden's proposal in principle, and a few weeks later the Indonesian foreign minister added his own agreement.[14] The next year, Mochtar again publicly endorsed a proposal to try the Pol Pot regime before the World Court for genocide.[15] Even Cambodia's Prince Norodom Sihanouk withdrew temporarily from the Khmer Rouge coalition. He then met with Hun Sen for the first time in December 1987 and carried to Beijing Hun Sen's proposal for the disarming of the Khmer Rouge. China rejected it, however, and Sihanouk cancelled his next round of talks with Hun Sen.

Yet Indonesia pursued its regional diplomatic initiatives on Cambodia with increasing seriousness. In July 1988, the first round of the Jakarta Informal Meetings (JIMs) convened in the Javanese hill resort of Bogor, attended by representatives of all nine ASEAN and Indochinese countries, including all the Cambodian factions. This meeting leapt a major hurdle, the refusal of the Cambodian sides to meet face-to-face, each having long insisted that it would negotiate only with the foreign backers of the other. Indonesia artfully broke the ice by having the Cambodian parties meet first, with the Southeast Asian supporters of each then joining the conference.

The "consensus statement" from the meeting, released by the new Indonesian foreign minister Ali Alatas, stressed the two problems Hayden had identified: a Vietnamese withdrawal (now promised for 1990), and prevention of "a recurrence of the genocidal policies and practices of the Pol Pot regime."[16] In April 1989, the Vietnamese advanced the projected withdrawal of their forces from Cambodia to that September. Sihanouk and Hun Sen met again, once more in Jakarta, the following month. They reached general agreement, and Sihanouk said he was prepared to go it alone without the Khmer Rouge should they prove recalcitrant.[17] However, he reneged on the undertaking immediately after leaving Jakarta.

The third Jakarta informal meeting, in February 1990, eventually broke down over the Khmer Rouge objection to use of the word "genocide" in the final communiqué. Although it had appeared in previous statements, the Khmer Rouge now opposed its inclusion, insisting instead on mention of "Vietnamese settlers" in Cambodia, to which Hun Sen and the Vietnamese foreign minister Nguyen Co Thach objected. The Australian foreign minister, Gareth Evans, then proposed placing an asterisk next to each disputed phrase, with a note that these had not been agreed upon unanimously. Hun Sen and Thach agreed to this compromise. But the Khmer Rouge refused, and the talks broke up.[18] Sihanouk and his anticommunist partner Son Sann still declined to break with the Khmer Rouge.

But meanwhile, the regional climate was changing. The policy of Thailand, the "front-line state" most threatened by Hanoi's 1979 removal of the Pol Pot regime, had also shifted in the direction pioneered by Indonesia and Australia. Thailand's first prime minister to be elected since 1976, Chatichai Choonhavon, won office in 1988 and pursued a new Cambodia policy until a short-lived military junta overthrew his government in 1991. During that three-year period, sensing advantage in the accelerating Vietnamese withdrawal from Cambodia, Bangkok had moved closer to both Hanoi and Phnom Penh, hoping to turn Indochina from "a battleground into a trading ground." In Southeast Asia, the Cambodian issue was the major one dividing the region, and the momentum developed for a settlement.[19] The regional consensus, at the Indonesian meetings and elsewhere, usually favored a settlement that would exclude both Vietnamese troops and the Khmer Rouge—which Hanoi welcomed.

The final 1991 UN Plan still catered to the Chinese and U.S. refusal to exclude the Khmer Rouge, but Indonesia, along with Australia and then Thailand, had borne the burden of the diplomatic work of regional reconciliation and practical compromise. In a different way, this important Indonesian legacy persisted in the 1990s in Benny Widyono's independent role as a UN official in Cambodia, lucidly described here in his historic memoir. Hopefully common regional interests in Cambodian peace and development have finally outlasted the effects of local genocide and great-power geopolitics.

Now gone forever, in its final decades the historic Noor Al-Ihsan mosque played a modest but important role in the renaissance of Cambodia and of its minority Cham community. It was in the old mosque that key Indonesian journalists first met with leading survivors of Cambodia's Muslims. It was there that Chams began to make their voices heard in the Islamic world and to help foster change in the regional and finally the international understanding of the Khmer Rouge genocide. During the 1980s, the "Light of Beneficence" shone one last time. How well the gleaming new mosque which now bears that name will serve Cambodian Muslims is another question. Thanks to the contribution of many people like Benny Widyono, as well as the efforts of other regional actors and the Cambodian people themselves, their country is now guided by its own lights, beneficent or otherwise.

NOTES

1. See Anthony Barnett and John Pilger, *Aftermath: The Struggle of Cambodia and Vietnam*, London: New Statesman, 1982.

2. Sorya Sim kindly consulted the *hakkem* on my behalf. Personal communication, 16 and 17 January 2007.

3. Sabam Siagian, "Resepnya: Pangan, Agama dan Seni Budaya (Asal Tetap Aman)," *Sinar Harapan*, n.d. 1981.

4. See e.g., Ben Kiernan, "What We Can Learn from Indonesian Islam," in T. N. Srinavasan, ed., *The Future of Secularism*, New Delhi, Oxford: 2006, 181–85.

5. See for instance Janet Steele, *Wars Within: The Story of* Tempo, *an Independent Magazine in Soeharto's Indonesia* (Jakarta, Equinox, 2005). *Sinar Harapan* reemerged in 1987 as *Suara Pembaruan*.

6. *Far Eastern Economic Review, Asia 1981 Yearbook* (Hong Kong, 1981), 191.

7. Nayan Chanda, *Brother Enemy* (New York, 1986), 393.

8. Marian Wilkinson, "Kampuchea: A Whiff of Change," *National Times* (Australia), 6–12 April 1984, 12–17, at 13.

9. *Age* (Melbourne), 16 March 1984; Wilkinson, "Kampuchea: a Whiff," *National Times*, 6–12 April 1984.

10. *Age*, 16, 19 and 27 March 1984.

11. Hanoi hinted at a new policy in late 1984. A November *Nhan Dan* article stated that Vietnam would withdraw from Cambodia "when the Chinese threat and the danger of Pol Pot's return have been removed and when the security of Kampuchea is fully ensured," but unveiled Hanoi's bottom line: "To discard the Pol Pot remnants, rather than calling for Vietnam to unilaterally withdraw troops from Kampuchea, is a crucial and imperative demand of peace in the region." *Age* (Melbourne), 29 December 1984.

12. Ben Kiernan, "Kampuchea: Hayden is Vindicated," *Australian Society*, 4:8, August 1985, 20–23.

13. *Age*, 21 March 1985.

14. *Sydney Morning Herald*, 27 June 1986, and Mochtar's press conference in Jakarta on 8 August 1986 reported in *Indonesia Times*.

15. *Christian Science Monitor*, 17 June 1987. Two thousand Cambodians living abroad signed a petition to Australian prime minister Bob Hawke (and leaders of other governments) asking for action against the Pol Pot regime in the World Court (*Far Eastern Economic Review*, 14 July 1988). Hawke refused, but the Australian opposition leader Andrew Peacock and the Australian section of the International Commission of Jurists supported the idea.

16. *Far Eastern Economic Review*, 11 August 1988, 29.

17. "Sihanouk to Return as Cambodia's Head of State," and "Move to Dump Khmer Rouge," *Sydney Morning Herald*, 3 and 4 May 1989.

18. Roy Eccleston, "Evans Plan Stumbles over an Ugly Word," *Australian*, 2 March 1990.

19. For the background to this regional feeling in the common postwar anticolonial struggles, see Ben Kiernan, "ASEAN and Indochina: Asian Drama Unfolds," *Inside Asia 5* (September–October 1985), 17–19.

Preface

This book tells the story of the five critical years in Cambodian history that I witnessed firsthand in two different capacities. My first assignment, in 1992–1993, was as a peacekeeper in the United Nations Transitional Authority in Cambodia (UNTAC), a multifunctional peacekeeping operation entrusted to implement the Paris Peace Agreements on Cambodia.[1] During my UNTAC posting, I served as the provincial director, or "shadow governor," in the province of Siem Reap. After UNTAC left, in 1994 I returned to Cambodia as the UN Secretary-General's Political Representative, or personal envoy, to the new government of Cambodia. I served in that capacity in Phnom Penh, the capital, until 1997.

This book has been a long time in the making. Meanwhile a great number of other books appeared on Cambodia. The early ones that came out right after UNTAC left all hailed the UNTAC elections and the formation of the new government of Cambodia as a model for future peacekeeping operations. However, after the peace process unraveled, culminating in a violent clash between the two coalition partners in Phnom Penh in July 1997, new books appeared that were more critical of UNTAC and its contribution to solving the Cambodian tragedy. UNTAC dropped out of sight from the UN inventory of success stories. My book goes beyond the second category in its critical assessment of the involvement of international actors in shaping and perpetuating the Cambodian tragedy.

I wrote these memoirs in the hope of filling a void. Most of the other books were written by Western journalists and scholars with a Western perspective on events. But I believe it's important to have more Asian accounts by people better positioned to reflect on the cultural dimensions of the tragedy. Coming from neighboring Indonesia, I hope to offer a fresh perspective. These memoirs are unique in that I tell my own story and offer personal reflections on events that I witnessed firsthand.

While writing these memoirs I debated with myself how frank I should be when describing people I had contact with in Cambodia. Often, however, I felt that straightforwardness was required to paint a full and honest picture. I wish to beg forgiveness if I have hurt anyone's feelings and wish to assure them that my intentions were solely to provide a wider understanding of Cambodian events.

I wrote wearing three pairs of lenses. The first pair was that of a personal observer. Practically everybody I met in Cambodia had lost loved ones during the Khmer Rouge's reign of terror. Every day in my five years there I breathed the smells of Cambodia, ate its food, observed its sights, and listened to its sounds—of exploding rockets mixed with the laughter of children and adults slowly coming back to life. As I interacted with the people of Cambodia—literally from prince to pauper—I was impressed by the strength and perseverance of the common people.

My second pair of lenses was that of a career United Nations civil servant. I had been with the United Nations since 1963 and posted in New York since 1981. In New York I witnessed firsthand and with dismay the diplomatic maneuverings that allowed the genocidal Khmer Rouge to represent Cambodia in the UN for more than ten years after their ouster from power in 1979.

Through my third pair of lenses—that of an academic—I was able to better understand the roots of the Cambodian tragedy. From March 2003 to May 2006, I was a visiting scholar at the Kahin Center for Advanced Research in Southeast Asian Studies at Cornell University. My intellectual perspective on Cambodia was considerably enhanced by the scholarly research I conducted at Cornell and by my interactions with faculty and students there, particularly in the Southeast Asia program. It was in the quiet atmosphere of the Kahin Center, housed in a historic building, surrounded by magnificent red bud forests where deer roamed freely,[2] and down the hill from the Southeast Asian library—one of the best in the world—that I wrote this story.

I was born in Indonesia in 1936 in Magelang, near the Borobudur temple in Central Java.[3] My father, an ethnic Chinese, was a tobacco merchant. When the regime of President Suharto came to power in Indonesia after the aborted coup d'etat in 1965, it instituted many laws against ethnic Chinese and Chinese culture, so I was forcefully persuaded to change my name from Oei Hong Lan to Benny Widyono.

After receiving my PhD in economics from the University of Texas in Austin in 1963, I joined the United Nations. I have been a UN international civil servant throughout my working life. However, until my appointment with UNTAC in Cambodia in 1992, I had dealt primarily with economic and social issues in UN offices in Bangkok, Geneva, Santiago, and New York. The UNTAC appointment changed my life. After years in the economic and social realms, I entered the world of politics. As it turned out, my five-year posting in Cambodia became the highlight of my career.

NOTES

1. UN document A/46/608-S/23177, later issued as United Nations, "Agreement on a Comprehensive Political Settlement of the Cambodia Conflict," Paris, 23 October 1991. United Nations: New York, January 1992. Hereinafter cited as UN, The Paris Agreements.

2. Unfortunately, at the time of this writing this splendid forest was razed to make way for a parking lot.

3. Built at the end of the eighth or early ninth century, Borobudur is world-class, inviting comparison with Angkor Wat in Cambodia.

Acknowledgments

I wish to acknowledge the institutions and the many friends and scholars whose helpful assistance, thoughts, advice, writings, and experiences have made this book possible. First and foremost, I wish to express my gratitude to the people of Cambodia who generously and patiently gave me their time, kindness, hospitality, and thoughts during my five happy years in Cambodia and beyond. I also wish to thank members of the foreign community in Cambodia, many of whom tremendously improved the depth of my analysis.

At the top of the list of individuals who helped me is Audrey Kahin, who generously, patiently, and selflessly oversaw the editing of this manuscript. Without her constant encouragement, this book would never have been completed. Audrey is a great scholar on Asia. After a long conversation, she took an interest in my project, which was inspired by her husband, the late George Kahin, the cofounder of Cornell's Southeast Asia program that made Cornell a leading institute on Southeast Asian studies. I had first met Professor Kahin while doing research on Indonesia in the Cornell library in 1961. I am indebted to the Southeast Asia program and its director, Thak Chaloemtiarana, for enabling me through my appointment as a visiting scholar at the Kahin Center to write these memoirs. I also wish to thank the members of Telluride House, an all-scholarship honors dormitory, for having lovingly accepted me as a faculty guest during the difficult final year of writing at Cornell.

I wish to express my deepest gratitude to Ben Kiernan for writing such a great foreword for this book and to Mark Selden for his guidance and his help in finding a publisher. I wish furthermore to single out Adriane Smith, who did the major substantive editing on the book in a competent, helpful, and experienced manner. I would like to express my gratitude to Shashi Tharoor, Under-Secretary-General of the UN for Communications and Public Information, who has encouraged me to write these memoirs and has generously provided me with photographs and maps of the UNTAC period. I owe a particular debt to my daughter Monique, who read and skillfully edited earlier drafts.

Other friends and scholars who offered helpful thoughts, comments, and suggestions on various parts of the book are too numerous to list in full, but they include Amitav Acharya, Rafeeudin Ahmed, Nicole Americanos, Ben Anderson, Maureen Aung-Thwin, Allan Beaulieu, Jay Carter, Barbara Crossette, Stephen Heder, Helen Jarvis, Raoul Jennar, Ben Kiernan, Audrey Kubota, Doreen Lee, Paul Matthews, Lois de Menil, Ngo Manh Lanh, Sorpong Peu, Claudia Rizzi, Paul Reddicliffe, Tim Carney, and Michael Vickery as well as Tom Wells who did the professional editing of the book. Finally, my deep sense of gratitude goes to my wife, Francisca, who patiently stood by me throughout this entire project.

Needless to say, the opinions and judgments expressed in these memoirs, as well as its shortcomings, are entirely my own responsibility.

I

THE VIEW FROM
THE FIELD, 1992–1993

1

When the World "Invaded" Cambodia

When I first arrived in Cambodia in April 1992, I was greeted by faces resigned to suffering, almost as if war and genocide had become part and parcel of the Cambodian way of life. Coming from the hallowed halls of the United Nations in New York, where Cambodia was prominent on the agenda during the 1980s, I became ever more convinced that Cambodia had, due to its geopolitical location, seen itself subjugated in the ongoing power struggles for hegemony in Southeast Asia. The result was a tragedy of enormous proportions that for more than twenty years prior to our arrival had plunged Cambodia— a victim of both Cold War and post–Cold War diplomatic maneuverings— into chaos, turmoil, civil war, and deep despair.[1]

I have attempted to place at the center of the story of this book, my experiences in Siem Reap, Angkor, and Phnom Penh as the basis for unfolding a larger story about Cambodia's changing polity and society in the years of my two missions. Three actors played a dominant role in this story: Sihanouk, the Khmer Rouge, and the United Nations. Their interactions run like a common thread interwoven throughout the book. They were like dancing in shadows in shaping the destiny of Cambodia.

Sihanouk has dominated Cambodian modern history since his coronation by the French in 1941. He had ruled Cambodia as king, prince, head of state, prime minister, head of the main political movement, head of the Khmer Rouge government, chairman of the Coalition Government of Democratic

Kampuchea, head of the Supreme National Council, and finally back as king again in 1993 until he retired in 2004. During this long period, he was undoubtedly considered the father of Cambodia by the bulk of Cambodia's people.

Then there is the Khmer Rouge, under whose vastly destructive rule around 1.7 million Cambodians—nearly one-third of the population—had lost their lives. Most other Cambodians were traumatized in ways not yet fully comprehended.[2] As will be seen in chapter 2, the heavy bombardments of Cambodia by the United States and Chinese support played a role in the meteoric rise of this movement. Because of diplomatic maneuverings in the UN, the Khmer Rouge continued to play its destructive rule during the five years covered by this book.

Finally there is the United Nations, which was both part of the problem and the solution of the Cambodian tragedy. The ouster of the genocidal Khmer Rouge regime by Vietnamese forces and a Cambodian rebel force in January 1979 did not end the tragedy. In New York, accusing the Vietnamese of having invaded Cambodia, the United States, China, and ASEAN spearheaded annual UN resolutions to continue to recognize the Khmer Rouge regime as representing Cambodia rather than the People's Republic of Kampuchea (PRK) established by the rebel Cambodians, which soon became the de facto government of the country. The Soviet Union, its allies, and some other countries including India recognized the PRK. This stalemate continued throughout the 1980s during which Cambodia was treated like a pariah state as the West banned all aid to the country—thereby prolonging the suffering of its people for another decade. It was only resolved with the signing of the Paris Peace Agreements on 23 October 1991,[3] which stipulated that the UN itself take control of the governance of Cambodia until elections were held. The United Nations Transitional Authority on Cambodia (UNTAC) was established to implement the Paris Agreements.

I came as part of UNTAC. UNTAC was at the time also the largest and most integrated one the United Nations had ever undertaken. It brought together 20,600 military, police, and civilian personnel from more than one hundred countries.[4] It had a multidimensional mandate: to organize and carry out free and fair elections for a National Assembly, disarm the previously warring parties, verify the withdrawal of foreign forces, repatriate Cambodian refugees, begin the process of restoring human rights, and supervise and control the Cambodian police forces.[5]

IN A NEW YORK RESTROOM

For me it all started in New York. "Huh? You want to go to Siem Reap?" asked an aghast Yasushi Akashi, the UN Under-Secretary-General for Disarmament Affairs. It was 4 p.m. on the 22nd of January in 1992, and we were in the men's room, of all places, on the thirty-first floor of the UN headquarters on First Avenue in New York City. Both of our offices were on that floor; Akashi headed the large Department of Disarmament while I directed a small office as the New York representative of the five Regional Economic and Social Commissions of the United Nations, covering all five regions of the world.[6] Akashi had just been appointed head of UNTAC.

After congratulating Akashi on his appointment, I asked whether I could go with him and be stationed in Siem Reap, a province in northwest Cambodia near the Thai border. "Huh, that is the most troublesome province," he replied, with some agitation. "You can only go there by helicopter. The Khmer Rouge is still there in large numbers, larger than elsewhere. The other resistance forces also have their bases there, and their refugee camps are across the border in Thailand. It also has Angkor Wat with all its complications for financial control and conservation."

"Yes, I would like to be sent to Siem Reap," I responded. I did not want to be stationed in the capital, where I would be one of many senior directors, nor in Sihanoukville, for that matter, the idyllic seaside resort where there was very little action. There had been little action there even during the days of the Khmer Rouge.

"Okay, then, you will go to Siem Reap," Akashi decided. "You will be one of the twenty-one provincial directors of UNTAC." None of the provincial directors, including myself, had any experience with governance or Cambodia. Such was the reality of United Nations peacekeeping. I found out later that Siem Reap was a much-coveted post. I felt lucky to land this coveted post.

My introduction to the Cambodian tragedy had actually started during my posting with the United Nations Economic and Social Commission for Asia and the Pacific (ESCAP) in Bangkok in the 1970s. From that vantage point, one could not help but note the tragedy unfolding to the east, especially following the ouster of the Khmer Rouge in January 1979. Cambodian refugees in rags, fleeing the country by the tens of thousands, often emaciated and barely able to walk, seemingly unable to speak or smile, reached hastily erected refugee camps in Thailand. I visited one such camp, Khao I Daeng, when it was first constructed and could only surmise the misery these refugees had endured. The horrible atrocities of the Khmer Rouge, finally exposed to the world, stared coldly at us from our televisions, newspapers, and magazines.

I had known Yasushi Akashi for years. In New York we both commuted by train from the suburbs, he from Scarsdale in Westchester County where many Japanese live, and I from Stamford, Connecticut. Although he is a few years older than me, he often overtook me walking from Grand Central Station to the UN headquarters about six blocks away. He always walked briskly and reprimanded me for my slower pace. The walk to the station was part of his exercise regimen, he said. Later in Cambodia, he was famous for his brisk pace and his short, staccato way of speaking.

Akashi's appointment as head of UNTAC had surprised everyone. The speculation in the corridors of the UN in New York had been that Rafeeudin Ahmed, the UN point man on Cambodia throughout the 1980s, would get the job. When Ahmed declined for personal reasons, the Secretary-General, Boutros Boutros-Ghali, had appointed Akashi instead, apparently with support from Tokyo.[7] As a fellow Asian who understood the Asian mind and culture, he was deemed capable of dealing with the dynamic personalities in Cambodia. It also helped that he was Japanese, as Japan was slated to play a key role in the long-overdue process of reconstruction and rehabilitation in Cambodia.

I took a long flight from New York to Bangkok, the gateway to Cambodia. There I checked in at the Ambassador Hotel on Sukhumvit Road, which had been transformed into a staging area for UNTAC personnel coming from all over the world. The lobby was full of glittery military and police uniforms in a panorama of colors, from all parts of the world, an unusual sight even in cosmopolitan Bangkok. They all had one thing in common: the blue helmet identifying them as United Nations peacekeepers.

The next day, 20 April 1992, I boarded a military Hercules 130, leased by UNTAC from Indonesia, which took me to Phnom Penh in less than an hour. All of the signs in the plane were in my native Indonesian. The plane was packed with military types and police, along with some stray civilians like myself, all headed for UNTAC duty. UNTAC controlled the airport, so there was no immigration or customs processing.

After landing at the airport, I was whisked away to the Cambodia Inn, next to Phnom Penh's only luxury hotel, the four-star Cambodiana where many

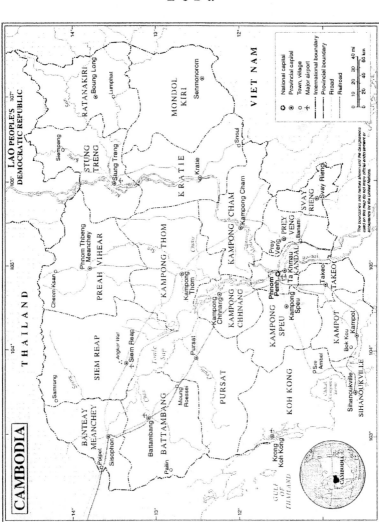

Map 1.1. Cambodia at the time of my arrival in March 1992. United Nations, Cartographic Section, UN map no. 3860R4.

top brass of UNTAC stayed. I was pleasantly surprised to find that the Inn, a less than two-star affair, had air-conditioning. But, alas, it barely worked.[8]

Driving into town I was distressed by the contrast between the "Asian miracle" then taking place in Thailand and other Association of Southeast Asian (ASEAN) countries and Cambodian reality.[9] Per capita income in the ASEAN region had been growing at 10 percent or more annually for decades. But that had been far from the case in Cambodia though in the early 1960s under Prince Norodom Sihanouk's *Sangkom Reastr Niyom* (People's Socialist Community) Government, Cambodia's per capita income reportedly had been higher than Thailand's.[10]

Everywhere I went in Phnom Penh, evidence of the Khmer Rouge's reign of terror abounded. Obviously, the efforts of the State of Cambodia (SOC) government to start reconstruction and development had been severely handicapped by Cambodia's continuing political ostracism and economic isolation imposed by the West and the United Nations during the 1980s. That had left the Soviet Union as Cambodia's single major donor during those years. The economic disintegration of the country had become quite acute after the collapse of the Soviet Union in 1989, which stopped aid to Cambodia. There were no telephones, and broken bridges and highways full of potholes highlighted the battered infrastructure.

Whenever I arrive in a new town, I head straight to the market in order to feel the city's pulse. At five, the morning after arriving in Phnom Penh, as I struggled to recover from jet lag, I took a *moto dop*, or motorcycle taxi—it was the most common form of transportation—riding tandem, to the *Psar Thmei* (new market) of Phnom Penh. *Psar Thmei*, a massive yellow art deco structure, was octagonal in shape; the grid of streets around it was completed in 1937 by the French town planner Ernest Hebrard.[11]

The driver of the *moto dop* sped along the wide, French colonial–style, paved grand boulevards shaded with rows of coconut palms. Phnom Penh's layout was a leftover from colonial times, when King Sihanouk had tried to make sure that the city would serve as the capital of an independent nation rather than an appendix to Saigon, the city the French apparently preferred. Many impressive buildings with stone facades and arched windows lined the boulevards. All of them were dark yellow ocher in color, including the royal palace, government offices, hotels, and theaters. And all, except the royal palace, showed signs of decay. The SOC government, in anticipation of the return of Prince Sihanouk as head of the Supreme National Council, had renovated the palace. SOC saw the advantage of turning Sihanouk into a king rather than simply the leader of the National United Front for an Independent, Neutral, Peaceful and Cooperative Cambodia (FUNCINPEC), the Royalist resistance faction.

When they had emptied Phnom Penh and forced the people into the countryside in April 1975, the Khmer Rouge had left these yellow ocher buildings intact, except for the Catholic cathedral and Central Bank. The cathedral had been dismantled stone by stone, the bank blown up; they had been deemed symbols of "reactionary religion" and "decadent capitalism." Throughout the Khmer Rouge's rule, Phnom Penh and other cities had remained empty and largely abandoned. To the best of my knowledge, never in the history of the world had entire cities been completely emptied of their inhabitants.

But the center of Phnom Penh was now once again the hub of life in the city. That morning before sunrise the market was pitch dark, as electricity was scarce. UNTAC had plenty of electricity in the luxurious hotels and offices, but the Cambodians suffered in darkness. Yet at that hour they still went about their daily business in a cheerful way, cutting ice, slicing slabs of pork, unloading fresh fruit and vegetables, and so on. Right then and there I predicted that Cambodia's recovery would be quick once it started. After all, despite its poverty, Cambodia was part of Southeast Asia, with its prominent work ethic.

When daylight broke, little stalls selling everything from the ubiquitous imported cans of beer and soda, to flowers and produce, to watches and slabs of pork started opening up. At the edge were the ever-present glass-encased cubicles of the money changers; the dollar and the Thai baht circulated freely. Even bananas could be bought with dollars, with the change given in local riels. Like in neighboring Thailand, Buddhist monks were doing their morning rounds begging for food. Buddhism had been abolished under the Khmer Rouge but apparently revived by the People's Republic of Cambodia, which nominally was also communist.

In *Psar Thmei* the only person selling lobsters and big shrimps initially refused to sell to me as she thought I was Cambodian. I only sell to "rich" UNTAC, she gruffly proclaimed. After some time in *Psar Thmei*, I headed back to town by cyclo, a three-wheeled pedicab, another prevalent form of transportation. Everywhere I went I encountered people, ex-soldiers and civilians, staggering about in makeshift wheelchairs or crutches as Cambodia was among the most heavily mined countries in the world.

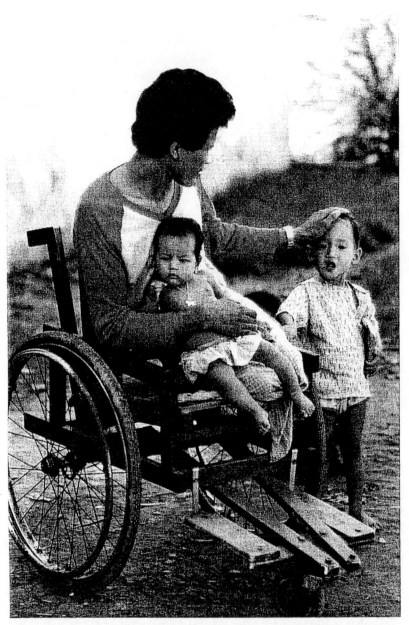

Photo 1.1. Mine victim in wheelchair: an everyday scene during UNTAC times. Credit: UN Photo 120696/J. Ralph.

On my third day in Phnom Penh, I visited Tuol Sleng, the infamous S-21 interrogation center of the Khmer Rouge. The Phnom Penh government had converted it into a museum. In January 1979, two Vietnamese journalists who were embedded in the Vietnamese army, driven by the incredible stench of decomposing corpses, had discovered S-21, just as American GIs had stumbled upon Auschwitz in Nazi Germany after World War II. Formerly a high school, S-21 had functioned under the Khmer Rouge as a ghastly prison, where twenty thousand prisoners died from torture and execution.

I was overwhelmed by a sense of immense tragedy that has haunted me ever since. I entered a former classroom in which a complex of prison cells—cubical enclosures made of thin brick and mud-plaster walls—was built. I stepped into one of the cells, which were about three feet wide and five feet long—not long enough to sleep flat on the floor. Then there was Building A, which contained a series of stark, grim rooms lit only by meager sunlight, each containing a rusty bed frame, a pair of leg shackles, an ammunition box for urine and feces, and a large black-and-white photo of the prisoner who had been found there. These rooms were for high-level prisoners who deserved a private room! When the Vietnamese journalists entered the prison, they encountered the victims shackled to iron beds and left to rot and die.

I next entered S-21's torture chambers where prisoners were tortured and forced to make "confessions" to implicate anybody they could think of, including their friends, neighbors, and relatives. The people they named were then brought in to be tortured themselves, forced to confess to crimes they had never committed. It was said that Pol Pot's main entertainment, at night, was to read these confessions, many of them extracted from old friends and comrades of his who had been accused of "treason." In fact, most of the prisoners were fellow Khmer Rouge soldiers, mainly from the east zone, accused of being Cambodian bodies with Vietnamese minds.

While in the prison, I pondered why Pol Pot and his cronies had been allowed to occupy Cambodia's seat in the United Nations throughout the 1980s instead of standing trial in an international criminal court. It struck me as adding insult to injury to allow these butchers to become one of the four legitimate Cambodian factions now facing UNTAC.

UNTAC'S "INVASION"

But there was a glimmer of hope in the faces of the Cambodians that greeted UNTAC peacekeepers as we descended upon their country. We were like a peaceful invading army.[12] Dubbed UNTACists by Prince Sihanouk, we all wore blue helmets, blue berets, or blue baseball caps. Although the media in Cambodia at that time was in a rudimentary stage, people knew from word of mouth that we had come to help bring peace. They invited us to join them for tea and cakes everywhere we went. Finally, after twenty years of civil strife and turmoil, Cambodians saw light at the end of the tunnel. Peace appeared within their grasp.

There were smiles everywhere as they anticipated how these strange people—speaking Hungarian, Indonesian, Spanish, and English in various accents, and many other languages—would become a familiar sight in even the most remote corners of their country. In distant Ratanakiri province, for instance, where the Uruguayans were stationed, many children and young people started speaking Spanish in no time. In Kompong Thom, where an Indonesian battalion was keeping the peace, Indonesian was spoken. Everywhere, naked toddlers would greet me with "Hello UNTAC, hello UNTAC," while dogs barked ferociously as I passed by. Although as an Indonesian I looked like a Cambodian, I was apparently too well fed to pass for a local, even among the dogs.

UNTACists drove around in flashy and fully air-conditioned white Toyota land cruisers, white pickups, white minibuses, and white trucks, while white helicopters and white airplanes filled the sky and white patrol boats plied the waters, all with the giant letters "UN" splashed on in black. Hence we were dubbed "the invasion of the white cars." Because these land cruisers all looked alike, to ordinary Cambodians it often appeared as if these vehicles were just driving around in circles.

After twenty years of isolation, the invasion of the white cars must have been quite a spectacle to Cambodians, like a permanent circus coming to town. Soon, however, the white cars were a familiar sight, except in those areas controlled by the Khmer Rouge. Most of the other vehicles seen on the road at that time, apart from the ubiquitous *moto dops*, were old Russian- and Chinese-made trucks and stolen compact cars from Thailand easily identifiable by their right-hand steering wheel common in Thailand, but ill adapted to Cambodia, where motorists are required to drive on the right-hand side of the road.[13]

Conspicuously absent were white tanks and white artillery pieces common in peace-enforcing operations in places like East Timor in the late 1990s. The

Photo 1.2. UNTAC staffer fixing a safety reflector on a cyclo. Credit: UN Photo 137772/P. Sudhakaran.

United Nations Transitory Authority in East Timor had been a Chapter VII peace-enforcing operation, while UNTAC was a Chapter VI peacekeeping operation. The former allowed the use of force, the latter did not. UNTAC was only in Cambodia to keep the peace, not enforce it.[14] The Khmer Rouge would later take advantage of the mission's peaceful nature. They considered us a paper tiger.

Even in their white cars, travel for UNTACists was difficult. The road between Phnom Penh and Siem Reap, for instance, a distance of 310 kilometers, had been heavily mined by all factions during the civil war, and the Khmer Rouge and other unidentified rogue elements were purportedly lurking behind every tree and bend. It was ruled that UNTAC personnel in Siem Reap and other far-flung provinces could only travel to and from Phnom Penh by military helicopter or fixed-wing aircraft.[15]

As a result, I had to remain for several weeks in Phnom Penh before being deployed to Siem Reap. The massive M26 helicopters, the biggest in the world, which could carry three vehicles at a time and which the UN leased from the notorious Soviet airline Aeroflot, were late in arriving. Furthermore, the old, poorly maintained Russian helicopters seemed infinitely more dangerous than the New York subway at night. My life seemed in danger every time I boarded one of these machines to fly to Phnom Penh and back for monthly directors' meetings. I was not sure whether it would have been better to travel overland on the road infested with Khmer Rouge, bandits, and land mines had we been allowed to.

On one of these helicopter trips later, the Russian pilot suddenly descended in the deep jungle and landed in the middle of nowhere. He brushed off my concern and said he had to check something in the engine. After fifteen or so minutes he laconically took off again. On another occasion, in Siem Reap, I watched with horror as one of these helicopters, carrying fifteen journalists, spiraled rapidly downward, damaging it beyond repair. Fortunately, nobody was seriously injured.

UNTAC'S INTERNAL MACHINERY
While waiting to be deployed to Siem Reap, I was getting to know the UNTAC senior staff. UNTAC headquarters was located in the palace of the former

Photo 1.3.   A giant Soviet-made MI-26 helicopter finally took me and my vehicle to Siem Reap. Credit: UN Photo 73480/P. Sudhakaran.

French governor general, or proconsul, in front of Wat Phnom, a temple on a hill considered the center of Phnom Penh. It was a very impressive structure with high ceilings and about twenty big rooms, but obviously not the ideal habitat for the headquarters of a multibillion-dollar operation involving seven components and twenty-two thousand personnel. As Phnom Penh did not have office buildings that could be rented or secured for a large headquarters, UNTAC's components were later spread out all over town in private buildings rented from the public or the SOC.

The UNTAC organization in Phnom Penh was every bit as complex, if not more, than the Cambodian governmental structure.[16] It consisted of directors who were either experienced in political and bureaucratic maneuverings in the UN that had little to do with governing a country or came straight from their governments, like Gerard Porcell, my immediate boss,[17] who did not have the faintest clue as to how a UN organization should function.[18] With all of them thrown together in one building where there was a shortage of everything from paper clips to toilet paper, one could almost breathe the tension in the air. Yet a sense of excitement engulfed me every day as I awoke.

My first task was to report for duty to Yasushi Akashi. He was pleased to see me again and relieved that at least two of the twenty-one provincial directors had arrived. The other was my friend Vladimir Yulin, a Russian also from the UN in New York who would be provincial director in nearby Kompong Speu province. UNTAC's Civil Administration was particularly slow to deploy its personnel. "The deployment of UNTAC in the provinces is very important," Akashi confided in me. "We must make our presence felt everywhere in Cambodia, even in Khmer Rouge controlled areas." He was right. I found out later that on many occasions our mere presence helped prevent human rights abuses and impunities of the worst kind. After talking to Akashi, I went next door to see Deputy SRSG Behrooz Sadry, an Iranian who had been in the UN Secretariat in New York for ages and whom I knew very well. I used to meet him often for drinks at the Delegates Lounge in New York headquarters.

My next stop was a courtesy call to Lieutenant General John Sanderson, the force commander and head of UNTAC's Military Component. A burly, efficient, and no-nonsense Australian, he supervised all the military units. Sanderson had good political instincts and was very close to Akashi, with whom he had arrived on 15 March. He managed UNTAC's twelve battalion commanders from many cultures and countries quite successfully while maintaining working relations with the Cambodian armies, except the Khmer Rouge.[19]

The French had wanted one of their own to fill Sanderson's post, but the United States did not want one of the five permanent UN Security Council members to play such an important role.[20] As a compromise, the French Brigadier General Jean Michel Loridon was made deputy commander. He had previously served as commander of UNTAC's precursor, UNAMIC (United Nations Advance Mission in Cambodia). UNAMIC had been established to supervise Phase I of the military plan, i.e., the implementation of the cease-fire between the four warring Cambodian armies. Colleagues knew him as something of a loose cannon, and he would resign in July 1992, after his proposal advocating the use of force against the Khmer Rouge was rejected.

The UN in New York decided that both English and French would be official languages of UNTAC, although the overwhelming majority of personnel used English. The language problem surfaced as soon as UNAMIC was established at the beginning of 1990. At that time the French wanted the entire mission to be comprised exclusively of Francophone personnel, which was unreasonable considering the majority of personnel came from Asia and spoke little, if any, French. The other four permanent members of the Security Council raised strong objections, as did the ASEAN countries, all of which were Anglophone.

The battle between English and French hit home for me when I called on Gerard Porcell, director and head of the Civil Administration component who was my direct boss. Porcell looked like an artist from the Left Bank of Paris with wildly flowing silver hair. He was a judge by profession and lacked any United Nations experience. Porcell was shocked that I did not have a fluent command of French. With no experience in the UN, where either English *or* French was required of senior officials, he made his own rule that all senior UN personnel must speak French. English was the working language in the UN in New York as well as in UNTAC, but he still insisted that all people at my level should speak French. Thus he would conduct the monthly coordination meetings of provincial directors in French. Vladimir Yulin, who also did not speak French, and I complained to Akashi, but Porcell did not budge. The meetings of all the other component heads as well as of Akashi's senior staff were conducted in English.

As cochairman of the Paris conferences on Cambodia in 1989 and 1991, France had gotten Porcell's post, which was supposed to carry out the crucial task of controlling "existing administrative structures" of Cambodia to ensure "a neutral political environment." Indonesia, the other cochairman, only got two provincial directors serving under Porcell: Achmad Padang, who was provincial director of Takeo, and me.

I was not sure whether France as a matter of policy was biased against the Khmer Rouge, but Porcell was irritated at UNTAC's weakness toward them. I personally got into trouble with him on this issue. Because of the shortage of space at that time, Porcell, with his deputy and secretaries, occupied a suite that Yulin and I also shared.

One day Khmer Rouge delegates from the General Assembly in New York arrived at UNTAC headquarters. As I had been stationed in New York and frequently attended UN meetings and diplomatic receptions, I jovially offered a diplomatic handshake to one of them, Thep Kunnal. This was a normal multilateral diplomatic practice in New York. But one of Porcell's assistants saw that handshake and immediately reported to Porcell, who changed his attitude toward me and promptly ordered Vladimir and me out of his office. Henceforth we had to work from our hotels, pending deployment to the provinces.

Porcell then complained at a meeting of ambassadors of the Expanded Perm Five (EP5) group of countries[21] that Widyono was very intimate with the Khmer Rouge and more or less demanded my removal. The Indonesian ambassador, Taufik Soedarbo, reminded Porcell that the Khmer Rouge was a signatory to the Paris Agreement and was therefore technically not an enemy of UNTAC. Our job, Soedarbo pointed out, was to work with all four Cambodian factions. Much later, in February 1993, Porcell offered his resignation because of a lack of UNTAC enforcement powers, especially in dealing with the Khmer Rouge, though he later agreed to stay on until the May 1993 elections.

Thus we had two senior Frenchmen, Loridon and Porcell, who resigned because UNTAC was too soft on the Khmer Rouge. Porcell was certainly one of the most disorganized of the directors. As I was to coordinate the work of the components in Siem Reap, I made it a point to get to know the other component heads as well. In most books on UNTAC, the Civil Police component, along with Civil Administration, has borne the brunt of criticism of UNTAC.[22]

Among the outstanding directors I should single out Tim Carney, who was seconded from the U.S. government and was head of the Information Division. This division had the best complement of international staff fluent in Khmer; they were drawn from the UK, Australia, Germany, Canada, the United States, and even the former Soviet Union. Fourteen of the division's forty-five international staff members were experts and scholars on Cambodia who spoke and read Khmer and had at least some experience in the country.[23] If the other UNTAC components including Civil Administration had followed in their footsteps and hired more people who spoke and read Khmer, the mission could have been more successful.

UNTAC's slow deployment caused a great deal of harm to the mission. When Akashi arrived in Phnom Penh in March, he was accompanied by only a small complement of advisory staff. It took until July for the Civil Administration component (to which I belonged) to finally establish offices in every province.[24] Logistical problems hindered operations throughout the whole UNTAC period. A UN report recommended that due to the lack of facilities in Cambodia, basically everything from pencils to computers to prefab buildings be imported.[25] It also advised using all-terrain vehicles, small or medium-size trucks, and buses. UNTAC's deployment therefore included 1,109 Toyota jeeps, 852 minibuses, 3,260 double-cabin pickups, and additional vehicles costing an astronomical sum of $88.7 million.[26]

Since UNTAC personnel could not yet travel to their posts, a huge area was marked off in Phnom Penh where all these shiny vehicles were parked awaiting deployment. Passing by this giant car lot, impoverished Cambodians, most of whom barely owned a bicycle, wondered what in the world UNTAC was up to. Also, the almost complete absence of a communications network necessitated that UNTAC import a communications system worth $35 million capable of providing telephone, facsimile, data, and courier communications at the provincial and district levels.[27]

On the human resources side, every one of us recruited internationally, including car mechanics, received $145 a day in a Mission Subsistence Allowance. With a budget of $1.7 billion, UNTAC's was by far the most costly peacekeeping operation ever mounted at the time.[28]

As I continued to wait for my deployment to Siem Reap, Vladimir Yulin and I tried to press Porcell on his views on the scope of control over Civil Administration in the provinces. We were repeatedly told that he was quite busy and that we should not bother him. He would deal with that matter later—much later. Porcell and his special assistant, whom he brought from France, were more interested at the time in finishing a new penal code for Cambodia based on the French model. While this was important, it was performed at the expense of the more pressing issue of conceptualizing the complex problem of control over Civil Administration. That, after all, was the main mandate of our component as stipulated by paragraph 6 of the Paris Agreements. Porcell's mismanagement and delay in tackling this important issue was one of the main reasons Civil Administration's control function failed. By the time Porcell finally realized its significance, it was too late.

NOTES

1. See chapter 2 for a short summary of the twenty years prior to UNTAC's arrival.

2. Estimates of the number of lives lost continue to be debated today. The noted Cambodian scholar Ben Kiernan consistently estimates the number of deaths to be around 1.7 million. For a summary of recent debate on this issue, see Kiernan, "The Demography of Genocide in Southeast Asia," *Bulletin of Critical Asian Studies*, vol. 35, no. 4, 2003, 585–97. See also Patrick Heuveline, "Between One and Three Million: Towards the Demographic Reconstruction of a Decade of Cambodian History, 1970–1979," *Population Studies*, London, vol. 52, no. 1, March 1998, 49–65. In another estimate, Stephen Heder calculated deaths at 2.2 million, of which between five hundred thousand and one million Cambodians were executed outright while others died of starvation and disease as a result of inhuman and cruel policies. See Heder with Brian D. Titlemore, *Seven Candidates for Prosecution*, Washington: War Crimes Research Office, American University, 2001, 7.

3. UN Paris Agreements. The Federal Republic of Germany also joined and signed the Paris Peace Agreements on 28 April 1994 as the eighteenth signatory nation.

4. See appendix 1. Deployment of UNTAC.

5. As these are my memoirs, they do not provide a comprehensive evaluation of UNTAC. For such an evaluation, a great number of books on both UNTAC and the post-UNTAC period can be consulted. The earlier books on UNTAC praised it as a success story and a model for future peacekeeping operations. See Jamie Frederic Metzl, "The Many Faces of UNTAC: A Review Article," in *Contemporary Southeast Asia*, vol. 17, no. 1, June 1995, which reviewed four books on UNTAC: Trevor Findlay, *Cambodia, The Legacy and Lessons of UNTAC*, Oxford; Jarat Chopra, *United*

Nations Authority in Cambodia, Institute for International Studies; United Nations Research Institute for Social Development, *Between Hope and Insecurity;* and the United Nations Bluebook Series, *The United Nations and Cambodia.* See also Michael W. Doyle, "UN Peacekeeping in Cambodia: UNTAC's Civil Mandate," Occasional Papers Series, International Peace Academy (Boulder, CO: Lynne Rienner, 1995); and Stephen Ratner, *The New United Nations Peacekeeping: Building Peace in Lands of Conflict after the Cold War* (New York: St. Martin's Press, 1995). Books and articles published after the unraveling of the peace process that culminated in violent clashes in 1997 are more tentative in praising UNTAC. See, for example, McAlister Brown and Joseph J. Zasloff, *Cambodia Confounds the Peacekeepers, 1979–1998*, Ithaca, NY and London: Cornell University Press, 1998; Marrack Goulding, "Cambodia," in *Peace Monger*, London: John Murray, 2002; and Richard H. Solomon, *Exiting Indochina*, Washington, DC: U.S. Institute for Peace, 2000.

6. The Regional Commissions are the regional arms of the United Nations's work in economic and social areas. Their headquarters are in Santiago, Chile (for Latin America and the Caribbean), Bangkok (for Asia and the Pacific), Beirut (for the Middle East), Addis Ababa (for Africa), and Geneva (for Europe).

7. Barbara Warner, "Japan Views Leadership Opportunities through the United Nations." *Japan Economic Institute Report*, no. 10A, 13 March 1992.

8. In the post-UNTAC period, the Cambodia Inn was razed and a luxurious Singapore-owned Mi Casa apartment building erected in its place. With the boom in tourism in post-UNTAC Cambodia, the luxurious Cambodiana now has many competitors in the four-star category, including the refurbished colonial-era Hotel le Royal, which played an important role in the life of journalists during the Lon Nol period, as depicted in the movie *The Killing Fields.*

9. ASEAN at the time consisted of six countries: Brunei Darussalam, Indonesia, Malaysia, the Philippines, Singapore, and Thailand.

10. Unpublished communication from Andy Flatt, director of Statistics, Economic and Social Commission for Asia and the Pacific, "Table on Per Capita GDP in Cambodia and Thailand," extracted and processed from UN, ECAFE, *Statistical Yearbook for Asia and the Far East.* Mr. Flatt cautioned about the difficulties of making such comparisons, including the use of the exchange rates employed by ECAFE: the Cambodian riel was fixed at thirty-five to the U.S. dollar, whereas the Thai Baht was floating.

11. Michel Igout, *Phnom Penh Then and Now*, Bangkok: White Lotus, 1993, 147.

12. The 15,996 soldiers came from thirty-four countries, whereas the 3,359 civilian police came from thirty-two countries. See United Nations, *The United Nations in Cambodia*, New York, 1995, 27. Hereinafter referred to as the *Blue Book*.

13. The problem of stolen cars from Thailand was tackled in 2003 when Cambodia vowed to arrest the owners of right-hand-driven cars who could not provide ownership documents. Yuwadee Tunyasari, "Automobile Theft," *Bangkok Post*, 24 May 2003.

14. Chapters VI and VII refer to chapters in the Charter of the United Nations.

15. When I returned to Cambodia in January 2005, regular buses, air-conditioned ones for a $6 fare and non-air-conditioned ones for $4, plied this road regularly, full of Western and Japanese backpackers and NGP workers exploring Cambodia, as the Lonely Planet travel book series had finally discovered one of the most closely guarded secrets in Southeast Asia.

16. For details of UNTAC's deployment, please see appendix 1.

17. There was a controversy, which was never resolved in Phnom Penh, whether as provincial "governor" I was a little Akashi, the chief administrator of UNTAC, in Siem Reap, or a little Porcell, the director of Civil Administration. See chapter 4 on this controversy.

18. For details see the second part of appendix 1.

19. Sanderson was officially appointed UNTAC force commander on 9 March 1992, two days before deploying to Cambodia. However, he had already been involved in the planning of the UNTAC mission earlier in New York, funded by the Australian government, but without an official position. A military engineer, he had seen active service in East Malaysia in 1966 and South Vietnam in 1970–1971. See Peter Bartu, "The Fifth Faction: The United Nations Transitional Authority in Cambodia 1991–93," PhD dissertation, Monash University, 1998, 1.

20. Janet E. Heininger, *Peacekeeping in Transition: The United Nations in Cambodia*, New York: The Twentieth Century Fund Press, 1994, 37.

21. Countries that played a major role in the negotiations leading to the Paris Agreements included the five permanent members of the Security Council—the United States, the United Kingdom, France, the Soviet Union, and China—and Australia, Indonesia, Japan, and Thailand.

22. See for instance (proceedings of a seminar in Singapore on UNTAC which I attended), Nasserine Azimi, ed., *The UN Transitional Authority in Cambodia (UNTAC), Debriefing and Lessons*, London: Kluwer International, 1996, 17.

23. They included, among others, Stephen Heder, Judith Lidgerwood, Christopher Preschool, Vladimir Sourkov, Ali Kistanov, Penny Edwards, Jay Jordan, Kate Frieson, and John Marston. Many later became the small core of Cambodian experts in the academic world in the English-speaking West to which I myself now belong.

24. UN document S/24578, *Second Progress Report of the Secretary-General on UNTAC*, 21 September 1992.

25. UN document S/24578, 6.

26. UN document A/46/903, *Financing of the United Nations Advance Mission in Cambodia and Financing of the United Nations Transitional Authority in Cambodia*, 38. This is an important document as it contains the entire deployment plan of UNTAC by personnel and finance. Together with the UNTAC *Handbook*, it provides an overview of the planning of UNTAC. Hereinafter cited as *UNTAC Planning and Financing*.

27. UN document A/46/903, *UNTAC Planning and Financing*, 46.

28. UN document A/46/903, 46.

A Glimpse into the Past

At this point I feel a strong urge to interrupt my memoir by providing an account of Cambodia's recent horrendous past to help both the readers and myself to better understand the events I saw unfolding before my eyes.

THREE PHASES IN CAMBODIA'S TRAGEDY

The catastrophic twenty years before UNTAC's arrival in Cambodia can be divided into three phases. The first took place from the 1960s to 1975. It is useful to compare Cambodia's situation to Indonesia's during this period, as both countries were victims of U.S. policy during the Cold War. During the 1960s at home both President Sukarno of Indonesia and Prince Norodom Sihanouk of Cambodia, who were very close friends and called each other brothers, tried to maintain a political balance between a right-wing military and a growing communist movement—and were forced to turn to the left as a result. Both incurred the wrath of the Americans by charting an independent foreign policy. And both were overthrown by anticommunist militarist elements that the United States covertly supported.

But Sihanouk proved more resilient than Sukarno, who died under house arrest ordered by his successor, Suharto, the anticommunist general who would rule Indonesia for the next thirty-two years. The regime change from Sukarno to Suharto had been accompanied by a massacre of some seven hundred thousand to eight hundred thousand suspected communists, many of them innocent peasants and workers who were members of labor and peasant mass organizations, fronts of the Communist Party of Indonesia.[1] This was one of the largest forgotten massacres in recent history.

Sihanouk, on the other hand, survived and continued to govern in various capacities despite Cambodia's tumultuous history. In 1941 he had first fooled the French, who had thought he would turn out like Bao Dai, the playboy king of Vietnam. "The French thought I was a lamb, but instead I am a tiger," he often cackled. He had guided Cambodia into independence in 1953. However, bored with being a mere ceremonial king, he had abdicated in 1955 in favor of his father, King Norodom Suramarit, so that he could enter politics as an executive head of state. He established the *Sangkom Reastr Niyom* (People's Socialist Community) that ruled the country for fifteen years. In the years 1955 to 1965, Sukarno and Sihanouk visited each other's country five times.

At a lunch during the Asian-African conference of 1955 held at Bandung, Indonesia, Chinese Premier Zhou Enlai had assured him that China respected Cambodia's neutrality.[2] However, neutrality had not been acceptable to President Eisenhower of the United States and leading U.S. intelligence services, including the CIA, who were determined to support any anticommunist Khmer they could find.[3] Initially, Sihanouk persecuted Cambodia's embryonic communist movement, which he dubbed the Khmer Rouge.[4] When the United States escalated the Vietnam War in 1964–1965, neutrality became impossible for Cambodia to sustain. Sihanouk was unable to stop North Vietnam from building sanctuaries in the northeast of Cambodia, which the North Vietnamese needed to pass across Cambodia from North to South Vietnam via the so-called Ho Chi Minh trail. This upset the United States, and relations between the two countries continued to deteriorate.

Two U.S. actions—one overt, the other covert—indirectly fed the meteoric rise of the Khmer Rouge: U.S. President Richard Nixon's massive bombardment of Cambodia and the ouster of Sihanouk by pro-American right-wing General Lon Nol. Nixon authorized massive secret bombings of Cambodia beginning on 18 March 1969. In total, more than five hundred thousand tons of bombs were dropped in the four years of U.S. air raids. It was estimated that the bombardments killed somewhere between fifty thousand and one hundred fifty thousand people, most of them civilians.[5] Recently, however, new data became available that indicated 2,756,941 tons of bombs were dropped into Cambodia. To put this into perspective, the Allies dropped just over two million tons of bombs during all of World War II. Cambodia may be the most heavily bombed country in history.[6] The bombings unleashed a huge flow of refugees into the cities, radicalized the youth in the rural areas, and drove many people into the ranks of the Khmer Rouge.

On 18 March 1970, Sihanouk was overthrown by Lon Nol. Lon Nol's coup seemed to be patterned after what Suharto had done in Indonesia in 1965 and included training of Cambodian military forces by American Green Berets in Bandung, Indonesia.[7] Enraged by the coup, Sihanouk accused the United States of orchestrating it.[8] He formed a front and a government in exile in Beijing. The prince embraced Pol Pot, and the Khmer Rouge soon became the dominant force in both the front and the government in exile. Encouraged by Sihanouk's call for Cambodians "to struggle against the U.S. imperialists who have invaded our Indochina and are oppressing its peoples and breeding injustice, war and all kinds of calamities, hostility and disunity, troubles, crimes and misery among our three peoples—Khmers, Vietnamese and Laotians,"[9] thousands of young men and women joined the Khmer Rouge now aligned with the popular prince. The ties between the prince and Pol Pot also meant that a massive flow of weapons from China and North Vietnam went to the Khmer Rouge, as China was no longer bound by the neutrality pledge made in Bandung, Indonesia. As a result, the Khmer Rouge grew from about three thousand guerrillas fighting Sihanouk to around thirty thousand guerrillas allied to him. It was a turning point in Cambodian history.

The U.S. incursion of Cambodia in 1970 shortly after the coup, involving thirty thousand U.S. and over forty thousand South Vietnamese troops, also fueled the rise of the Khmer Rouge and Cambodia's decline. The stated purpose of the incursion was to find the Central Office of South Vietnam (COSVN), the headquarters of South Vietnamese communists. That headquarters was never found.

A full-scale civil war erupted in Cambodia from 1970 to 1975 between Lon Nol's Khmer Republic and the Khmer Rouge. In April–May 1970, a massive contingent of North Vietnamese forces entered Cambodia, joining the North Vietnamese and Vietcong troops who were already in the country to fight alongside the Khmer Rouge against Lon Nol. Relations between Pol Pot and the North Vietnamese leaders were then warm.[10] But the Khmer Rouge army grew steadily stronger and started to turn against the Vietnamese while refusing their further support. Corrupt and weak, the Lon Nol regime found itself increasingly isolated.

On 17 April 1975, the Khmer Rouge army triumphed and started the second phase of Cambodia's earlier history. Simply put, Cambodia descended into hell during this period. During the Khmer Rouge rule that lasted three years, eight months, and twenty days, the Khmer Rouge abolished private property, personal possessions, money, leisure, socializing, marriage (except in cadre-approved cases), religion, and all personal liberties.

Cambodia became a land of totalitarian rural communes. The nation's cities were evacuated, hospitals emptied, schools closed, factories deserted, money and wages abolished, monasteries emptied, and libraries scattered. Freedom of the press, movement, worship, organization, association, and discussion all completely disappeared for nearly four years. So did daily family life. In the countryside, people slaved and starved to grow rice that went to China and hauled buckets of earth to build dams without engineers or technicians.

At first, Sihanouk became the nominal head of the Khmer Rouge regime. He was soon abruptly "retired," however, and placed under virtual house arrest, where he remained for the rest of the Khmer Rouge era. The real leader of the Khmer Rouge remained the secretive Pol Pot, who had led the party since the mid-1960s. Collectively, the party and its leaders identified themselves only as *Angkar* (the organization).

Pol Pot had studied the overnight collapse of the Communist Party of Indonesia (PKI) following an abortive coup by some leftist elements on 30 September 1965. At the time he was in Beijing, and he concluded along with the Chinese leaders that despite the PKI's emergence as one of the four main parties during democratic elections in Indonesia in 1955, its strategy of aligning with Sukarno and trying to take over the country through democratic means had been disastrous.

Pol Pot resolved that *Angkar* would not come to the same end, and he ensured that the Khmer Rouge's strength would be its army (the PKI did not have one). Pol Pot also decided that the Khmer Rouge should not align itself too closely with Sihanouk, as the PKI's dependence on Sukarno had not saved it from total annihilation by Suharto.[11] Claiming that the country was "four to ten years ahead" of other Asian communist states, Pol Pot initiated a "super great leap" toward "socialist society right away."[12] He aimed to introduce the purest and most thorough Marxist-Leninist movement in history. No other regime had ever attempted such rapid and radical change.[13] Though Cambodia was a closed society, media coverage of Pol Pot's atrocities increased markedly after the 1978 publication of Father Ponchaud's book on Cambodia.[14]

In the end, the Khmer Rouge's arrogance proved to be their undoing. They launched increasingly vicious attacks against Vietnam—their erstwhile strong supporter—slaughtering thousands of Vietnamese villagers in Tay Ninh province in 1977. Pol Pot's paranoia subsequently caused him to turn against his own soldiers, especially those in the eastern zone bordering Vietnam. He accused them of behaving like "Khmer bodies with Vietnamese minds." He killed at least one hundred thousand during the period of May to July 1978.[15]

To escape these purges, many Khmer Rouge soldiers, especially from the eastern zone, fled to Vietnam, where their leaders, Heng Samrin and Hun Sen, raised a rebel army and formed a government in exile, the *Renaksei Samaki Sangkruoh Cheat Kampuchea*, or United Front for the National Salvation of Kampuchea (UFNSK), also known as the Salvation Front. The front vowed that it would "unite the entire people to topple the Pol Pot/Ieng Sary gang of dictators" and establish a people's regime to make Kampuchea a peaceful, democratic, and nonaligned country advancing to socialism.[16]

The UFNSK consisted of three groups: Khmer Rouge defectors from the eastern zone of Cambodia, including Heng Samrin, Hun Sen, and Chea Sim; the so-called Khmer-Vietminh, Cambodian communists who had fled to Vietnam after the 1954 Geneva Conference and stayed there, including Penn Sovan; and representatives of the former intelligentsia, including Hor Nam Hong.[17]

On 25 December 1978, twelve Vietnamese divisions, totaling one hundred thousand troops, together with the UFNSK's rebel army of twenty thousand, entered Cambodia and then overthrew the Pol Pot regime. The UFNSK established the People's Republic of Kampuchea (PRK) led by Heng Samrin and Hun Sen. This ushered in the third phase of Cambodia's earlier history. The phase lasted until 1991, when the Cambodian tragedy became internationalized and the battle shifted to the corridors of the United Nations in New York.

Vietnam's intervention in Cambodia proved critical in removing the Khmer Rouge regime. No other country was then willing or ready to take on the Khmer Rouge. Certainly not the United States, which had just been defeated by the Vietnamese. U.S. Senator McGovern called this the ultimate irony: "After all those years of predictions of dominoes falling and Communist

conspiracies, it was Vietnam that went in and stopped Pol Pot's slaughter. . . .
They should have gotten the Nobel Peace Prize." Andrew Young, the U.S. Ambassador to the UN, argued that although it was almost always wrong to trans-
gress another country, "in the case of Cambodia I am not so terribly upset
. . . it is a country that has killed so many of its own people."[18]

But the United States had a different agenda in the United Nations. Intense
lobbying by the United States, China, and ASEAN portrayed the ouster of the
Khmer Rouge as an act of aggression by Vietnam, and the PRK was condemned. A resolution to continue seating the Khmer Rouge as the legitimate
representatives of Cambodia passed in the UN General Assembly year after
year until October 1991. Meanwhile, the de facto government of the PRK went
unrecognized, and in the field a civil war continued to rage. Now the war was
between two communist forces: the Khmer Rouge backed by China versus the
People's Republic of Kampuchea backed by Vietnam and the Soviet Union.

As I was then stationed in New York, I witnessed firsthand the bizarre
events in the United Nations with dismay. The United States sided with China
in opposing the Soviet Union's support of the PRK.[19] Although the Tianan-
men massacre of 4 June 1989 complicated relations between the United States
and China, the two countries continued to work together on Cambodia.

Here's what happened: In 1979 representatives of the two Cambodian governments, the Khmer Rouge and the PRK, jockeyed for Cambodia's UN seat.[20]
As the Security Council debated which government to seat, a very tense Sihanouk was flown in from Beijing, and he spoke emotionally on behalf of the
Khmer Rouge, demanding the withdrawal of all foreign troops. It was clear,
however, that his sympathies were divided. In a press conference he even labeled Pol Pot a butcher.[21] Sihanouk also slipped a note to his American security detail requesting asylum from the U.S. government. The United States did
not give him asylum, but it did spring him from his Khmer Rouge minders
and sent him to France. He was persuaded by Chinese leader Deng Xiao Ping
not to defect.[22]

When the UN General Assembly convened in September 1979, Vietnam
challenged the credentials of the Khmer Rouge delegation, which it claimed
"did not represent anybody."[23] The president of the General Assembly, Salim
Salim from Tanzania, then convened the Credentials Committee, a little
known nine-member subcommittee of the General Assembly. After heated debate, and under intense U.S. pressure, the Committee voted on a resolution

6–3 to award the UN credentials to the Khmer Rouge. They did this without even reviewing the credentials of the PRK that had been duly submitted by head of state Heng Samrin in accordance with the Rules of Procedure of the General Assembly.[24] This resolution was then sent to the full General Assembly for voting.

Robert Rosenstock, the U.S. delegate, revealed later, "I was told to engineer the results of the Credentials Committee, so I engineered the results."[25] The person happiest with the results was Ieng Sary, the Khmer Rouge's chief representative. He came up to Rosenstock after the tally and extended his hand. "Thank you so much for everything you have done for us," he said. Rosenstock shook his hand—and then told a colleague, "I think I know how Pontius Pilate must have felt."[26]

In the General Assembly, Indian Ambassador Mishra introduced an amendment to the resolution of the Credentials Committee that would have left the Cambodian seat vacant.[27] He argued that this was in conformity with the decision of the Sixth Summit of Heads of State or Government of the Non-Aligned countries in Havana held just prior to the General Assembly session. The Non-Aligned movement represented the weak and nonaligned countries in the United Nations, which commanded a majority in the Assembly. Normally, an amendment to a resolution had to be voted on first, and India's amendment to keep the Cambodian seat open would have had a strong chance of success.[28] But Mishra's amendment was not even considered. Ambassador Tommy Koh of Singapore, a staunch supporter of the United States, cleverly argued that India's amendment was a new resolution, not an amendment. Koh proposed that the Credentials Committee's resolution to seat the Khmer Rouge be discussed first.[29]

After intense debate, with charges and countercharges hurled back and forth, the General Assembly voted 71 to 35, with 34 abstentions and 12 absentees, to approve the resolution of the Credentials Committee. It thereby continued to recognize the genocidal Khmer Rouge government in exile as the legitimate representative of the Cambodian people.[30] The sophisticated diplomatic maneuverings in the corridors of the UN had a harsh impact on ordinary Cambodians. The political ostracism and economic isolation imposed on Cambodia by the General Assembly's decision led to another ten years of suffering by the Cambodian people after the ouster of the Khmer Rouge. This despite the fact that the decision was widely condemned internationally in the press and by NGOs (nongovernmental organizations) as a policy to "punish the poor."[31]

In deciding which way to vote, the United States was in all likelihood influenced by its continuing vendetta against the Vietnamese, who in 1975 had ousted American forces from their country. There is also U.S. fondness for China that remained the prime military and economic backer of Pol Pot.[32] Both the United States and ASEAN, as well as many other countries, faced a moral dilemma: Which was the lesser evil? A regime that slaughtered two million of its own people or a Soviet-backed communist regime that occupied a foreign nation? This dilemma was underscored by Ambassador Tommy Koh in the General Assembly.[33]

Koh's argument and the ensuing UN vote should be contrasted with the silence of the UN when Tanzanian troops invaded Uganda—also in 1979—and forced the murderous Idi Amin into exile. Amin, like the Khmer Rouge, was responsible for the deaths of hundreds of thousands of people. As David Malone stated, "Obviously double standards [in the Security Council] abound. Order does not necessarily equate to fairness. In the Council the powerful impose what they can, the weak endure what they must."[34]

Meanwhile, the Soviet bloc and its allies viewed the conflict in Cambodia as rooted in a domestic power struggle among opposing Cambodian factions. The regime change, they contended, was the result not of Vietnam's invasion but of a truly popular uprising of the Kampuchean people. They also claimed that Vietnam's deployment of substantial troops was justified under the terms of the 1979 security treaty between Vietnam and the PRK.

Despite an initial international outcry against the General Assembly's vote, and strong public opinion (including in Western media) against supporting the Khmer Rouge, the criticism was quickly swept under the carpet. The relevant powers simply ignored the Khmer Rouge's role in the horrendous events that had befallen Cambodia. For example, Kishore Mahbubani, a Singaporean intellectual and former foreign office official, argued, "In short, what these Cambodians did in working with Pol Pot was what Churchill did in working with Stalin, work with a genocidal ruler for national survival."[35] Of course, his comparison of the PRK to Hitler and Pol Pot to Stalin raised eyebrows: normally it was Pol Pot, not the PRK, who was likened to Hitler.

In 1982, ASEAN, supported by the United States and China, pressed strongly for the formation of a Coalition Government of Democratic Kampuchea (CGDK) consisting of the Khmer Rouge and two hastily established anti- or noncommunist contra-type resistance movements: the National United Front for an Independent, Neutral, Peaceful and Cooperative Cambodia (known by its French acronym FUNCINPEC) established by Sihanouk in 1981 and the Khmer People's National Liberation Front (KPNLF) led by former Prime Minister Son Sann and made up mainly of remnants of Lon Nol's regime. ASEAN, the United States, and China pushed for a coalition government partly because it became clear that the PRK could not be destroyed; they were also responding to criticism they took for legitimizing the Khmer Rouge with a UN seat.

It was like draping the wolf in sheep's clothes. It was a mostly superficial maneuver, as the UN seat still was held by Democratic Kampuchea (the official name of the Khmer Rouge). The Khmer Rouge flag continued to fly outside the UN Secretariat until 1991, offering a constant affront to the millions of Cambodian people who had had no voice in the negotiations.[36] The cosmetic nature of the coalition was readily apparent; the three factions' mutual hatred was only exceeded by their common hatred of Vietnam. In 1990 Sihanouk announced that the Coalition Government of Democratic Kampuchea, which was neither a coalition nor a government, would henceforth be called the National Government of Cambodia (NGC), another cosmetic move.

As a by-product of the UN's decision, the defeated Khmer Rouge was resuscitated by the generous military and other assistance it received from China through Thailand. It was thus given the means to grow politically and militarily for another twelve years. During this period, the Khmer Rouge used its UN seat to great advantage, lobbying the General Assembly for additional material and political aid to oppose Vietnam and the PRK. The PRK was also opposed by the small noncommunist armies of FUNCINPEC and the KPNLF, who received substantial assistance from the West. U.S. aid was confined to these two resistance forces, as the United States was strictly banned by congressional legislation from providing aid to the Khmer Rouge.[37]

Chinese supplies to Khmer Rouge sanctuaries were allowed to pass through Thailand after Beijing offered Thailand a commission on arms transfers, cessation of aid to the Thai Communist Party, and oil and weapons at cut-rate prices.[38] Thus was born the "Deng Xiao Ping Trail" through which Chinese ships delivered arms and ammunition to the Thai ports of Sathahip and

Klong Yai. From these ports the Thai army transported the materials to Khmer Rouge camps and later to noncommunist resistance groups along the Thai-Cambodian border.[39]

Meanwhile, the United States provided aid to the Khmer Rouge's noncommunist partners while it "winked, semi publicly" and encouraged China and Thailand to give the Khmer Rouge direct aid to fight against the Vietnamese occupation.[40] Zbigniew Brzezinski, U.S. President Carter's national security adviser, advised Carter to go easy when China invaded Vietnam in 1980 in order to teach Hanoi a lesson for its invasion of Cambodia. He recommended that a condemnation of the Chinese invasion be coupled with a condemnation of Vietnam's invasion of Cambodia.[41]

In the field, the end of the Khmer Rouge regime had revealed to the world the extent of the disaster engulfing Cambodia. Initially, despite attempts by the U.S. government to discredit the PRK, Western governments donated substantial amounts of funds to Phnom Penh channeled through UN agencies and nongovernmental organizations (NGOs). This assistance, combined with aid from the Soviet bloc and Vietnam, did much to stave off the massive famine predicted by Western aid agencies. For a while, such aid enabled the Cambodian people to begin a process of recovery.[42]

In 1983, however, UN member states declared the Cambodian emergency over, and in conformity with the UN's nonrecognition of the PRK, imposed a period of economic isolation and political ostracism on the country. The UN agencies were forced to ban "development" aid as distinct from "humanitarian" aid to Phnom Penh. Thus, only UN agencies with an emergency-relief mandate, such as the World Food Program (WFP), UNICEF, and the UN High Commissioner for Refugees (UNHCR), were allowed to implement certain projects in Cambodia. The ban was extended to the entire UN family, including the Economic and Social Commission for Asia and the Pacific (ESCAP) based in Bangkok, where the Khmer Rouge flag continued flying throughout the 1980s.

In addition, Western donors led by the United States imposed a ban on bilateral aid to the PRK. The PRK continued to receive limited help from the Soviet Union and its Eastern bloc, with the Soviets providing aid amounting to $100 million a year. NGOs were very active in trying to fill the gap, but the overall level of assistance remained totally inadequate.[43]

THE PARIS AGREEMENTS: A FLAWED SOLUTION

Given the international political divisions, it is not surprising that it took more than twelve years to bring the various Cambodian factions to the negotiating table. International meddling, outside the control of Cambodians, left them in a quagmire for much of the 1980s. The enormous suffering of the Cambodian people failed to generate the necessary urgency to break the deadlock. China and the United States both actively discouraged reconciliation with the PRK, perpetuating the status quo.

The UN Secretariat had been trying to help solve the Cambodian conflict from the beginning and continued to do so until the Paris Agreements were signed in October 1991. In addition to the UN and the four Cambodian factions, the SOC and the three resistance factions Khmer Rouge, FUNCINPEC, and KPNLF, the peace process engaged all five original ASEAN countries plus Vietnam and Laos, the five permanent members of the Security Council, Japan, and Australia. Each of these countries had entertained a relationship with one or more of the factions.

A real breakthrough only became possible when the Cambodians judged themselves ready for it. In 1987, Sihanouk and Hun Sen, leaders of the two opposing forces, the CGDK and the SOC, came together for two historic meetings near Paris that finally broke the stalemate.[44] After that, a confluence of favorable factors, including the collapse of the Cold War, brought a solution closer to reality.

Vietnamese troops completed the final stage of their withdrawal from Cambodia that same year. To shed its communist image, the People's Republic of Kampuchea subsequently renamed itself the State of Cambodia (SOC). In 1991, its political party, the Kampuchean People's Revolutionary Party (KPRK), adopted a new platform, renounced communism, adopted free market policies, and changed its name to the Cambodian People's Party (CPP).[45]

The Sihanouk-Hun Sen rapprochement enabled the six noncommunist countries of the Association of Southeast Asian Nations (ASEAN) to play a key role in helping to achieve a comprehensive settlement of the Cambodian conflict. In this connection, I agree fully with Ben Kiernan who convincingly argued in the foreword of this book that Indonesia in particular played a crucial role in the solution of the Cambodia problem. Throughout the 1980s, although Indonesia continued to show its solidarity with frontline state

Thailand, it began to see the prolongation of the war in Cambodia, the "bleeding Vietnam and Cambodia white" strategy, as not being in its or the region's interests. Although never retreating from ASEAN's central demand of Vietnamese withdrawal from Cambodia and Cambodian self-determination, Indonesia actively sought to engage the Cambodians and Vietnamese and their external sponsors. By 1984, Indonesia was given the formal role of "interlocutor" in the Cambodian situation.[46] The breakthrough came in July 1987, in the Mochtar Kusumaatmadja-Nguyen Co Thach (Indonesia's and Vietnam's ministers of foreign affairs respectively) communiqué in which Vietnam accepted the idea of an informal meeting between the Khmer parties, to which other concerned countries would be invited. This was the so-called "cocktail party" formula. In a cocktail party people attending do not have to recognize each other.

It came therefore as no surprise that it was the Jakarta informal meetings (JIMs) of July 1988, February and May 1989 that brought together—for the first time—all four Cambodian factions, who were not talking to each other, in a neutral setting. The JIMs were chaired by internationally acclaimed Indonesian foreign minister Ali Alatas who skillfully steered the tense negotiations in the right direction for maximum results. These JIMs and other meetings elsewhere in the region, including Bangkok, Tokyo, and Pattaya, Thailand, prepared the ground for the Paris Conference of 30 July to 30 August 1989 that was convened and cochaired by foreign ministers Ali Alatas from Indonesia and Roland E. Dumas from France. Two of the principal obstacles in the negotiations were the power-sharing formula and the future participation of the genocidal Khmer Rouge. Ultimately, the rapidly changing world situation between 1989 and 1991 enabled a framework document to emerge.[47] This document, which was agreed upon by the five permanent members of the Security Council, was to become the Paris Agreements.[48]

According to an idea of Sihanouk and U.S. congressman Stephen Solarz and officially proposed by the Australian Minister of Foreign Affairs Gareth Evans, the UN itself would take control of the administration of Cambodia until it had successfully conducted elections for a new government.[49] However, since the UN was banned by Article 78 of its charter from placing a sovereign member state under trusteeship, on 9–10 September 1990, a Supreme National Council (SNC) was established to serve as "the unique legitimate body and source of authority" in Cambodia throughout the transition period.

It consisted of thirteen members, including six representatives of the SOC and two each from the Khmer Rouge, FUNCINPEC, and KPNLF.[50] The Paris Agreements therefore stipulated that the SNC delegate all powers necessary to UNTAC to implement the agreements. It was envisaged that the SNC would serve largely as a symbolic body, a forum for reconciliation and some very minimal powers of governance. Both UNTAC and the SNC were novel concepts in international law.[51]

The Paris Agreements were signed on 23 October 1991 by the four warring factions of Cambodia and seventeen other nations; they had signed in the presence of the United Nations Secretary-General.[52] The agreements and UNTAC were convenient vehicles for the big powers to extricate themselves from the Cambodian proxy war when the Cold War was over. Even though the agreements—including the formation of two new legal entities, UNTAC and the SNC—were hailed as a great breakthrough, they were essentially fragile and flawed on at least two scores. One was the inclusion of Khmer Rouge in the peace process. They should have been put on trial in a tribunal like the ones organized for perpetrators of the massacres in Rwanda and the former Yugoslavia. Flowing from this flaw, the UN's continued coddling of the Khmer Rouge throughout the UNTAC process was also a big mistake, with far-reaching consequences for the new Cambodia. The second flaw was the downgrading of the SOC—who had ruled Cambodia for more than ten years—to become simply one of four "existing administrative structures." That belied reality.

I am not suggesting that giving executive powers to the United Nations was not a brilliant idea. It certainly was. However, other policies could have had a profoundly different and perhaps superior impact on the course of events in Cambodia. For instance, if the Cambodian seat in the UN had been left empty throughout the 1980s, as advocated by the nonaligned countries and proposed by India in the General Assembly, humanitarian aid could have flowed to both sides rather than only to the CGDK partners. Ironically, even Sihanouk favored keeping the seat open.[53] And leaving the seat vacant could have encouraged implementation of other solutions much earlier. Michael Vickery has argued that by 1988 there was reason to believe that changes in geopolitics, particularly in Sino-Soviet relations, had caused China's interest in the Khmer Rouge to decrease. One or another Western country, perhaps Australia or France, he maintained, could have broken ranks and recognized the PRK.

Vickery quoted Sihanouk as saying at the time that "Washington should be realistic" and "flexible," taking into account the real situation in Cambodia.[54] Vickery concluded that by the late 1980s the real leader of the anti-PRK vendetta was not China but the United States.

Finally, in 1991, when Sihanouk returned to Cambodia triumphantly, there had been talk of a deal between Hun Sen and Sihanouk, but realpolitik had dictated otherwise. The powers that be had rejected an under-the-table rapprochement between Sihanouk and Hun Sen's SOC that would have left the Khmer Rouge and their allies out in the cold. Cambodia had had to go through the whole ritualistic process of the UNTAC elections in order to establish legitimacy as a Western-style liberal democracy.

NOTES

1. An extensive literature exists on this episode. On the coup and its aftermath, see, for instance, Benedict R. Anderson and Ruth T. McVey, *A Preliminary Analysis of the October 1, 1965 Coup in Indonesia*, Ithaca, NY: Cornell University, 1971; Harold Crouch, "Another Look at the Indonesian Coup," *Indonesia*, Cornell University, April 1972; and Robert Cribb, "The Indonesian Killings of 1965–1966," Centre of Southeast Asian Studies, Monash University, Clayton, Victoria, Australia, 1990. On Suharto's prolonged rule, see, among other sources, Adam Schwarz, *A Nation in Waiting*, Boulder, CO: Westview Press, second edition, 2000; and Hal Hil, ed., *Indonesia's New Order*, St. Leonards, NSW Australia: Allen and Unwin, 1994.

2. George McT. Kahin, *Southeast Asia: A Testament*, London and New York: Routledge Curzon, 2003, 260–61.

3. David Chandler, *The Tragedy of Cambodian History: Politics, War and Revolution Since 1945*, New Haven: Yale University Press, 1991, 81.

4. During their brutal reign of terror in 1975–1979 and afterwards, the Khmer Rouge regime called itself Democratic Kampuchea (DK). Unless otherwise indicated, and in order to reduce the confusion, the term Khmer Rouge will be used throughout this book.

5. Ben Kiernan, "The American Bombardment of Cambodia," *Vietnam Generation*, vol. 1, no. 1 (winter 1989), 32.

6. Taylor Owen and Ben Kiernan, "Bombs over Cambodia," *The Walrus* (Canada), October 2006, 62–69.

7. For a well-documented and detailed account of U.S. involvement in Sihanouk's ouster, see McTurnan Kahin, *Southeast Asia*, 279–99.

8. Norodom Sihanouk, as related to Wilfred Burchett, *My War with the CIA*, New York: Pantheon Books, 1972.

9. "Message and Solemn Declaration by H. E. Samdech Norodom Sihanouk, Cambodian Head of Nation," Beijing, 23 March 1970. Available in Cornell University's John Echols collection.

10. Dmitry Mosyakov, "The Khmer Rouge and the Vietnamese Communists: A History of Their Relations as Told in the Soviet Union," in Susan E. Cook, ed., *Genocide in Cambodia and Rwanda: New Perspectives*, Yale Center for International and Area Studies, Genocide Studies Program Monograph Series no. 1, 2004, 55.

11. See Ben Kiernan, *How Pol Pot Came to Power*, London: Verso, 1985, 222.

12. Ben Kiernan, *The Pol Pot Regime*, New Haven: Yale University Press, 1996, 26, footnote 88.

13. David P. Chandler, *Brother Number One: A Political Biography of Pol Pot*, St. Leonards, Australia: Allen and Unwin, 1992, 5.

14. Francois Ponchaud, *Cambodia Annee Zero*, Paris: Julliard. Translated into English by Nancy Amphoux, *Cambodia Year Zero*, New York: Holt, Rinehart & Winston, 1978.

15. Nayan Chanda, *Brother Enemy*, New York: Collier Books, 1986, 252–54.

16. Central Committee of the UFNSK, "Declaration of the Kampuchea National United Front for National Salvation," Kampuchean Liberated Zone, 2 December 1978. A copy is available in Cornell's Echols collection.

17. On the composition of the front, see Stephen Heder, "From Pol Pot to Pen Sovan to the Villages," Institute of Asian Studies, Bangkok, quoted in Kimmo Kiljunen, ed., *Kampuchea: Decade of the Genocide*, London: Zed Books, 1984, 25–26. Hor Nam Hong was a prominent member of the Khmer Rouge intelligentsia, having returned from abroad to serve the regime. He became separated from the Pol Pot group who escaped Cambodia just prior to the Vietnamese invasion and joined the UFNSK. The new government of Cambodia that resulted from the July 2003 elections was finally formed in July 2004; he remains foreign minister in the new cabinet today.

18. Samantha Power, *A Problem from Hell: America and the Age of Genocide*, New York: Basic Books, 2002, 146.

19. John Esterline, "Vietnam in 1986: An Uncertain Tiger," *Asian Survey*, vol. 27, no. 1, January 1987, 100.

20. It should be noted that the Khmer Rouge had been seated in the UN from the time it ousted the Lon Nol government in 1975. UN sources.

21. Nayan Chanda, *Brother Enemy: The War after the War*, New York: Harcourt Brace Jovanovich, 1986, 364.

22. Nayan Chanda, *Brother Enemy*, 366–68.

23. Ironically, the Cambodian UN seat held by right-wing General Lon Nol had been challenged in December 1973 and 1974, though unsuccessfully, on behalf of Sihanouk's revolutionary government in exile in Beijing, which included the Khmer Rouge, supported by Vietnam.

24. UN document A/34/500, *First Report of the Credentials Committee of the General Assembly*, New York: 34th session, September 1979. The letter from Heng Samrin is contained in UN document A/34/472.

25. Samantha Powers, *A Problem*, 150.

26. UN document A/34/500, 150.

27. UN documents A/34/PV3 and A/34/PV4, and Cor.1, *Official Records of the United Nations General Assembly*, 34th session, vol. 1, 3rd and 4th plenary meetings, United Nations: 21 September 1979.

28. It is worth noting that unlike in the United Nations, subsequent summits of the Non-Aligned movement—in New Delhi (1983), Harare (1986), and Belgrade (1989)—upheld the Havana decision to keep the seat of Cambodia empty. NAM makes its decisions by consensus rather than by voting. The NAM resolutions appealed for a peaceful solution of the Cambodian problem without outside interference. See Op Paliwal, *Cambodia Past and Present*, New Delhi: Lancer International, 1991, 49.

29. For the same reason a counter draft resolution (A/34/L.2) that Ambassador Yankov of Bulgaria had introduced before the Credentials Committee's resolution had been put to a vote, proposing that the delegation of the Heng Samrin government be seated as Cambodia's representatives, was not voted on either.

30. UN documents A/34/PV.3 and A/34/PV.4, and Cor.1, *Official Records.*

31. Eva Miesliwiec, *Punishing the Poor: The International Isolation of Cambodia,* Oxford: Oxfam, 1988.

32. Samantha Powers, *A Problem,* 147.

33. UN document A/34/PV3, 21.

34. David Malone, ed., *The UN Security Council: From the Cold War to the 21st Century,* Project of the International Peace Academy, Boulder, CO: Lynne Rienner Publishers, 2004, 617.

35. Kishore Mahbubani, "Pol Pot: The Paradox of Moral Correctness," in *Can Asians Think?,* Singapore: Times Books International, second edition, 2002, 80.

36. Every modern government of Cambodia has had a different flag although all featured the famous Angkor Wat temple, the national symbol of Cambodia. In 1990 the CGDK was renamed the National Government of Cambodia, and finally the flag flying outside the UN was replaced by the old flag of Sihanouk's regime, ostensibly discarding its connection to the Khmer Rouge, but the seat continued to be occupied by the Khmer Rouge ambassador, Thioun Prasidh.

37. 1 June 2005, e-mail from Lee Twentyman, deputy director of U.S. AID in Thailand, 1984–1988, and director of U.S. AID in Cambodia, 1991–1995. The legislation remained in force during his two postings.

38. William Shawcross, *The Quality of Mercy,* New York: Simon and Schuster, 1984, 126.

39. Nayan Chanda, *Brother Enemy,* 381.

40. Elisabeth Becker, *When the War Was Over,* New York: Public Affairs, second edition, 1998, 435.

41. Zbigniew Brzezinski, *Power and Principle,* New York: Farrar, Straus, and Giroux, 1982, 411 and following.

42. Miesliwiec, *Punishing,* 15.

43. Miesliwiec, *Punishing,* 81.

44. Personal communication from Hun Sen.

45. K. Viviane Prings, "The Cambodian People's Party and Sihanouk," *Journal of Contemporary Asia,* vol. 25, no. 3, 1994.

46. Special meeting of ASEAN Foreign Ministers in Jakarta. UN document
A/40/492, 17 July 1985.

47. UN document A/45/472-S/21689, letter from the Permanent Five members
transmitting a statement and framework document adopted by their representatives
at a meeting in New York, 27–28 August 1990.

48. UN, *Paris Agreements.*

49. See Government of Australia, *Cambodia: An Australian Peace Proposal,*
Canberra: Commonwealth of Australia, 1990.

50. In 1990 it was renamed the National Government of Cambodia (NGC).

51. Stephen R. Ratner, "The Cambodia Settlement Agreements," *American Journal of
International Law*, vol. 87, no. 1, January 1993, 9. Actually the SNC was created by
the Cambodian factions prior to Paris, but the concept was endorsed by Paris.

52. UN Paris Agreements. The Federal Republic of Germany also joined and signed
the Paris Peace Agreements on 28 April 1994, as the eighteenth signatory nation.

53. Norodom Sihanouk, "Open Letter to the Member States of the UN," in Peter
Schier and Manola Oum-Schier, *Prince Sihanouk on Cambodia: Interviews and Talks
with Prince Norodom Sihanouk*, Hamburg: Institut fur Asienkunde, 1985, 75–80.

54. Michael Vickery, "Cambodia: A Political Survey," Discussion Paper no. 14,
Research School of Pacific Studies, Australian National University, 1994, quoting
Michael Vickery, "The Campaign Against Cambodia: 1990–1991," *Indochina Issues*,
no. 93, August 1991.

The Intricate Dance of Governance

WHO IS REALLY IN CHARGE HERE?

While still waiting in Phnom Penh, I soon found out over beers with UNTAC colleagues that of the two governing entities created by the Paris Agreements, neither UNTAC nor the SNC really held day-to-day power. That lay in the hands of the State of Cambodia (SOC) government, even though it continued to go unrecognized by the United Nations.

The Paris Agreements were deliberately vague on the issue of sovereignty. The word *government* was not mentioned in them. As a "transitional authority," UNTAC had selective—and we need to stress the word *selective*—"proconsul" functions of sovereignty in Cambodia.[1]

SNC's own status as the unique authority of Cambodia was quite ambiguous. Sihanouk supposedly served as a neutral chairman. To assure his neutrality, he officially resigned from FUNCINPEC. Yet there was widespread suspicion that, informally, Sihanouk continued to be the grand old man of FUNCINPEC and the power behind it. This problem would be a headache to UNTAC and plague Cambodia long after UNTAC left. UNTAC's reach was an issue throughout its stay in Cambodia.

SNC's two sides—Hun Sen's SOC on the one hand and the three resistance factions on the other—continued to refuse to recognize each other, although their representatives sat at the same table during SNC meetings. The Khmer Rouge of course took the SNC seriously and repeatedly demanded that SNC

Photo 3.1.   The two "rulers" of Cambodia during UNTAC: Akashi, head of UNTAC, and Sihanouk, head of SNC. Credit: UN Photo 875/P. Sudhakaran.

branches should be established at all levels of government, including at the provincial and district levels; UNTAC and of course the SOC disagreed.

The SOC government, led by Hun Sen, which, with the exception of the slivers of land near the Thai border and the refugee camps in Thailand, had controlled about 90 percent of the land and even more of the people of the country. SOC controlled the capital, all major cities and provincial capitals, and most of the 1,400 districts, that is, the bulk of the population. SOC was the only authority with ministries, departments, a police force and public security apparatus, a media and communications network, a financial system, and levels of government from the central level all the way down to the village level. However, in the Paris Agreements it became just one of four existing administrative structures. The creation of the four existing administrative structures was an ostrich-like arrangement, and UNTAC had to deal with the actual power of these four entities on the ground. The other three were members of the CGDK (Coalition Government of Cambodia)—the Khmer Rouge, FUNCINPEC, and the KPNLF—the wolf draped in sheep's clothes. After this strange creature had fulfilled its role of keeping the PRK from being recognized by the UN during the 1980s, the Paris Agreements had disassembled it and reconstituted its three components to be granted equal status to the PRK.

From my hotel room in Phnom Penh, and later in Siem Reap, I was fascinated by how Akashi, Sihanouk, and Hun Sen, heads of the three governing entities, were engaged in an intricate dance of governance with Pol Pot, the Khmer Rouge chief, disrupting everything from his jungle redoubts. Although the SOC was only one component of the SNC, in reality Hun Sen was the real power in this hide-and-seek game and political dance. This dominates the story in part I of this book.

But that was not all. Always lurking in the background in Phnom Penh was another powerful institution with a robust advisory role: the Expanded Perm 5 (EP5) group whom we have already met. The EP5 was the Phnom Penh counterpart of a similar body in New York called the Core Group. In Phnom Penh the individual ambassadors maintained constant contact with their New York counterparts to ensure their continued control over UNTAC.

To summarize: Akashi reported to his boss, Secretary-General Boutros Boutros-Ghali, who reported to his boss, the UN Security Council, where power lies in the hands of the five permanent members with veto power: the United States, the United Kingdom, the Soviet Union, China, and France. And the Khmer Rouge had its own links to powerful Perm Five members, both politically and literally, through its official ambassador. Thiounn Prasith, the intellectual Khmer Rouge diplomat, actively and suavely walked the diplomatic cocktail circuit in the UN to lobby for continued Khmer Rouge recognition. The intricate ballet between these actors would have a profound impact on Cambodian events.

Some countries, notably the United States, argued that the SOC smacked of totalitarianism and should be taught democratic principles and the rule of law. These proponents of strict control argued that Cambodia had recently emerged from a centrally planned structure with certain behavior patterns not compatible with the principles enshrined in the Paris Agreements. The agreements stipulated that "Cambodia would follow a system of liberal democracy, on the basis of pluralism."[2]

It was generally believed that Washington was keen to ensure that the two noncommunist Cambodian factions, FUNCINPEC and KPNLF, would gain control in post-UNTAC Cambodia. The outside powers who sought to bring democracy to the country wanted to have their cake and eat it too. On the one hand, they wished to extricate themselves from Cambodia as expeditiously as possible; on the other hand, they wanted UNTAC to fully control and undermine SOC, or, if possible, to transform SOC into a democratic administration.

In addition to having their eyes and ears in Phnom Penh, powerful governments exerted influence on UNTAC through the United Nations Secretariat in New York, direct access to UNTAC officials, and actual secondments to the organization, including Tim Carney from the U.S. State Department.

ASEAN, which in general was united on the need to cooperate with UNTAC, was deprived of any senior posts, however. This contrasted with UNTAG (the United Nations Transition Advisory Group) in Namibia, for example, where Africans were well represented. Yet the role of ASEAN as a provider of troops and police was quite significant. Vietnam was completely left out of the UNTAC process. Starkly, the peacekeeping force from one hundred countries included not one Vietnamese.

MY ARRIVAL IN SIEM REAP

My sense of the key players would shift once I moved out to Siem Reap province. Because of the lack of communications, the political intrigues that I saw in Phnom Penh now seemed far away. Stationed in isolated Siem Reap, there was really no SNC. The Khmer Rouge, of course, continued to insist that the SNC replace the SOC everywhere, but nobody listened to them. Thus, on a day-to-day basis, our interaction in the field was with the SOC, and control over "existing administrative structures" meant control over the SOC. And since Siem Reap had the dubious distinction of being the place most frequently attacked by the Khmer Rouge, I had to spend a great deal of time dealing with the Khmer Rouge. Finally, I had to deal with fellow UNTACists. My relations with these three entities formed the main story of my UNTAC years.

Almost two months after my arrival in Cambodia, I had finally secured room for my newly acquired Toyota land cruiser on a giant M-26 helicopter, so on 15 June 1992 I was able to fly out to take up my duties as provincial director, or UNTAC's "shadow governor," in Siem Reap. Two other vehicles boarded the same flight, on which I was accompanied by two of my staff: my personal assistant, Genevieve Merceur, a French woman who had come to UNTAC from the World Food Program in Rome, and Eugenio Polizzi, an Italian human rights lawyer who would serve as the Human Rights officer for the province.

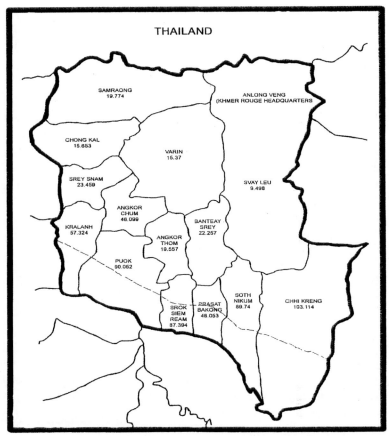

SIEM REAP PROVINCE; POPULATION BY DISTRICTS

Map 3.1. Administrative map of Siem Reap province showing population by districts. Author's personal collection.

Siem Reap was the name of the province as well as its capital. The province is 15,270 square kilometers; 50 percent was forested when I was there. Some 642,359 inhabitants were living in 914 *phums* (villages), 108 *khums* (communes), and 14 *sroks* (districts). In the northeast part of the province was the village of An Long Veng, site of one of the two remaining Khmer Rouge strongholds in the country (see map 3.1).[3]

The town of Siem Reap resembles a cross: a north-south artery runs from the temple complex of Angkor Wat six kilometers north of town to the Tonle Sap lake in the south, and an east-west road leads through the city of Sisophon to Aranyapradet, Thailand, to the west through the province of Kompong Thom, and eventually to Phnom Penh to the east. At the time of my arrival, the provincial capital was inhabited by seventy thousand people.

It was encouraging to see that although the Khmer Rouge had destroyed the entire education and health systems during its reign, the SOC government had been modestly successful in rebuilding these services. When we arrived, there were 30 nurseries, 320 primary schools, and 19 high schools including 4 lyceums in the province, with a total school population of 84,430 (or only 15 percent of the total population). The province's only hospital was located at Siem Reap. It was a pitiful, filthy, and dilapidated structure with 240 beds, 9 doctors, 7 health officers, and 88 nurses. UNTAC established a field hospital run by Indian military physicians; it was meant for UNTAC casualties in flare-ups but also provided daily free services to Khmer civilians. For them it was a welcome contribution to the quality of life in Siem Reap.

Upon arriving in the province, I realized that for the next year and a half I would be isolated there, only able to travel to Phnom Penh by air. Being stationed far from Phnom Penh was a double-edged sword. The provincial directors who were stationed near Phnom Penh or within motor-vehicle distance often showed up at headquarters in the capital to get the latest political buzz and to lobby for administrative or political advantages. On the other hand, my posting in remote and troubled Siem Reap meant that Akashi and others in Phnom Penh had to depend on me, so I was given a much better opportunity to prove my worth.

My colleagues included daring people such as Per Sander Skarvik, a Norwegian UN volunteer who ignored the rules and drove his four-wheeler from Phnom Penh to Siem Reap and back. Per was a member of the Advanced Electoral Planning Unit (AEPU), which had been deployed in Siem Reap since February 1992. The unit successfully carried out a countrywide demographic and cartographic survey in preparation for the elections.

Per and the four hundred UN volunteers like him were the unsung heroes of UNTAC. They came to Cambodia out of sheer dedication and contributed greatly to the success of UNTAC's elections. Living in very simple accommodations and taking great risks to visit remote areas without police or military protection, they recruited local staff and organized voter registration. They received less than $1,000 a month, far less than the $4,350 earned by UNTAC's "international" staff. By contrast, Cambodians participated in UNTAC only as local staff with a salary of between $300 and $500 a month. But this was a king's ransom by local standards where the nearly bankrupt SOC paid teachers only $6 a month and judges only $20, and where soldiers turned to banditry to augment their meager $13 monthly wage.

Cambodians did not assume high positions in UNTAC. They were only employed as interpreters in UNTAC internal meetings when needed. Though Cambodians had recently emerged from a period of isolation, they learned quickly, however, and toward the end of the mission many had taken on increased responsibilities comparable to so-called local international staff (i.e., international staff who were car mechanics, clerks, and secretaries in UN agencies in New York, Bangkok, Geneva, or Rome). The local staff were aware of the huge difference between their salaries and those of the UN "invaders," but they took the humiliation in stride because of UNTAC's peacekeeping mission.

Military observers were the first to be deployed to Cambodia. They monitored the cease-fire and gathered military intelligence for UNTAC. Among the military observers who greeted me on my first trip to Siem Reap was a Major Wu from China. An intriguing and open-minded person, he was not at all the inflexible, dour officer one might expect from the People's Army of China or from a country that had been deeply involved with the Khmer Rouge in the past. Major Wu was able to obtain valuable intelligence from the local ethnic Chinese about the Khmer Rouge and their intentions in the province. Using his contacts, he had already discovered the best Chinese restaurant in Siem Reap, where in spite of the scarcity of important ingredients the ninety-year-old cook, who had survived the Khmer Rouge and memorized the old recipes from the 1960s, whipped up for us a superb meal worthy of the best Chinese restaurants anywhere.

U.S. Colonel Jay Carter, who later became one of my best friends, brought in the provincial team for Siem Reap and Banteay Meanchey. It consisted of some thirty-two observers from China, Russia, the United States, the UK, France, and Japan. (This was the first time Japan had ever provided military officers in a peacekeeping operation.) The team was once seized by the omnipresent Khmer Rouge in the province, who threatened and then released them. The attitude of the Khmer Rouge toward UNTAC was ambivalent, sometimes aggressive and at other times conciliatory. Carter and his staff member Major Rustam Saliakov of Russia became the biggest of buddies. Rustam's father had been a colonel in the Soviet Strategic Rocket Forces, and Carter's had been a counterintelligence spy!

Later, when the deployment of a whole Bangladeshi battalion (Bangbatt) in the province was completed, I became close friends with Colonel Kamaluzaman, affectionately called Colonel Kamal Commander of Bangbatt. A graduate of the U.S. Army Ranger School, he was a decent soldier, competent and hard working, often into the early hours of the morning. This was important as Siem Reap province was frequently attacked by the Khmer Rouge, and the two of us had to cooperate in assessing the situation from military and political standpoints. Sometimes, in other provinces, the provincial director and the military commander did not even talk to each other, as there was some degree of rivalry between the military and civilian components of UNTAC.

One evening, at the beginning of my stay in Siem Reap, I was at Angkor Wat with my intrepid Norwegian colleague Per Sanders Skavrik and two visitors from his country. They were touring the vast Angkor complex while I stood by my vehicle, a four-by-four Toyota land cruiser. Per had the keys to the car. I waited as it gradually became dark. Suddenly, six young men in civilian clothes appeared and engaged me in conversation. As I had just arrived, my capacity in the Khmer language was nonexistent. I suddenly realized that I was in the midst of a civil war, with frequent cease-fire violations, especially by the Khmer Rouge. My anxiety and fear exceeded description. My body froze as I managed a weak smile. I worried that these young men suspected me of being a Khmer Rouge spy and therefore the enemy, or worse still, that they themselves might be Khmer Rouge. After what seemed like an eternity, Per arrived to rescue me. He later told me that the six young men were actually plain-clothes policemen of the SOC government. It turned out that my proverbial white car had told them that I was with UNTAC, and that they were there to protect me!

I was obviously still trying to figure out the political terrain.

ITH KOTHARA

During my first six months I stayed in the run-down Grand Hotel. It was literally falling to pieces. In pre–Khmer Rouge times the Grand had been the proud centerpiece of French-dominated tourism. Now it was completely dilapidated and anything but grand. To enter the elevator one had to step into an iron cage and risk the danger of never reappearing. It reminded me of old cheap hotels in Paris where I stayed near the Arc de Triomphe.[4] The rooms were huge but suffered from years of neglect.

As I was the shadow "governor," my wife and I asked the manager, Herr Rudolf Knochel from Switzerland, whether we could have a refrigerator. He delivered one to my room, but it caused a big uproar—he had taken it from the bar. Apparently there were only two refrigerators, one in the kitchen and one in the bar, where in the evening hundreds of UNTAC soldiers and police from everywhere in the world congregated to drink beer at one dollar a bottle, the only recreation available in the city at the time. The crisis was resolved when I persuaded Herr Rudolf to buy another refrigerator, which could easily be imported from Thailand, for the bar. As the coordinator of UNTAC in the province, I had to conserve my energy for fighting the other SOC governor and the Khmer Rouge in the jungle and did not want to clash with UNTAC's powerful military and police components.

Just to the right of the Grand Hotel was the Minefield Bar, run by an adventurous and enterprising New Zealander, Graham Robert Cleghorn. He was a burly and ruthless fellow, afraid of nobody, not even the Khmer Rouge, whom he befriended. Every evening his bar was packed with UNTAC military and police types along with civilians, downing those one-dollar cans of cold beer. He boasted that because of his contacts with the Khmer Rouge, they spared his bar when they attacked Siem Reap one night. After UNTAC'S departure, Cleghorn closed his bar for lack of customers and instead became a guide for tourists coming to see Angkor Wat.[5]

The refrigerator incident highlighted the situation UNTACists found ourselves in Siem Reap. Here were highly paid officials from sophisticated capitals of the world forced to live without essentials. The city as a whole was dilapidated with little or no entertainment, no TVs, and no radios; communications with Phnom Penh were sporadic at best. Moreover, the threat of the Khmer Rouge and other unidentified armed groups was constantly hanging over our heads. We lived in a warlike atmosphere not present in Phnom Penh or Sihanoukville.

In order to stay close to the common people of Siem Reap, I declined an offer from the SOC governor, Nuo Som, to rent from him a huge mansion at a preferential rate. I felt this would have compromised my work. My colleague

Enrique Aguilar from Mexico, UNTAC's "shadow governor" in neighboring Battambang, one day proudly showed me the lavish quarters in the government guesthouse offered him at a special rate by the notorious SOC Governor Um Samy of Battambang. Enrique, while accepting this offer, remained critical of Um Samy, who was suspected of corruption. Later, as the elections approached, UNTAC even demanded the governor's removal, suspecting him of being behind the many violent attacks there on opposition parties.

Instead of renting the mansion, I moved in August from the Grand into the modest home of Mrs. Lom Ang Sin and her three daughters—Ith Kothara, a schoolteacher, whom we all called Phat; Lom Iet; and A Lin. Lin lived in a separate modest bamboo structure in the back of the compound with her husband and two children, Rada and Radet.[6] Mrs. Lom Ang Sin's husband, Ith Sarin, a school administrator during Lon Nol times, had emigrated to California with his two sons after the overthrow of the Khmer Rouge regime, leaving the rest of the family behind.

Ith Kothara, the family's eldest daughter, was eager to learn English, and we taught each other English and Khmer. She and her family became important sources of information for me on the Khmer Rouge era and how people suffered then. In the early 1970s, Ith Sarin had joined the Khmer Rouge movement after becoming disillusioned with Lon Nol and the Khmer Republic. He then left the party and returned to Phnom Penh after nine months underground. In 1973 he wrote one of the earliest and most detailed accounts of life under the Khmer Rouge before they took over the country: *Sranaoh Pralung Khmer (Regrets for the Khmer Soul)*.

Phat told me that the main hardship under the Khmer Rouge was the all-pervasive and constant hunger, which coupled with the long working hours led to the deaths of many older people. Those who survived were deprived of all forms of liberty, including the choice of place of residence or work, and faced the constant threat of detention and possibly torture and death. Her life was completely controlled by *Angkar*, the organization. The worst command one could hear, Phat recalled, was young Khmer Rouge soldiers saying that *Angkar* wanted to speak with you. Many of her friends were taken into the jungle after hearing that simple sentence and never seen again. Their crime may have been nothing more than uprooting a tomato from their own compound to complement their meager diet of rice porridge. Such an act was considered stealing from the property of the nation.[7]

Phat and her family were able to return to their old compound when the Khmer Rouge was ousted in 1979, and they rebuilt their destroyed home stone by stone.[8] They occupied the downstairs area of the home; I had the upstairs. This was an honor for me, as the upstairs is the center of the typical Cambodian home. The downstairs, which is usually open, is where cooking takes place, and the animals roam freely. Taking out a loan from relatives, Phat and her family built for me a private Western-style bathroom according to my specifications. They built simple quarters for themselves.

Despite my comforts, living with Phat's family reminded me of Cambodia's lingering struggles. With the withdrawal of Soviet aid, the government could not always finance infrastructure nor electricity. One day I bought a simple hot-water heater from Singapore that was admired by the whole neighborhood. The only such device they had seen was in a newly constructed two-star hotel that housed UNTAC personnel. Electricity was scarce, but my position as provincial "governor" brought concessions from Governor Nuo Som, who installed a cable for extra electricity from the city. Nevertheless, the bankrupt SOC government could only provide electricity for a few hours every night, and there was always a moment of suspense in the evening when we waited in the dark with candles burning and tried to predict whether the municipal electricity would come on that night. Ordinary Cambodians paid only a token fee for their electricity, but the government charged about ten to twenty times that to members of UNTAC. I even installed an air conditioner, but the current was very weak and it never worked well. So we decided on a fan instead.

Cooking my meals was the highlight of the landlady's day. She turned out to be an excellent cook. Despite years of starvation and deprivation under the Khmer Rouge, she remembered all the age-old recipes of favorite Cambodian dishes, which she proudly rediscovered and concocted for me, in spite of shortages in the Siem Reap market. Delicacies included fried sparrows, *somlor mechou* (sour soup with bitter lemon), and *ban chiau* (stuffed pancakes). But she considered it improper for a high-ranking dignitary to eat breakfast at home. So she would never cook breakfast, which even ordinary Cambodians normally eat outside in local noodle shops. Even cyclo drivers would start the day with a bowl of *bobo sat chrouk* (porridge with slivers of pig intestines and one poor-looking shrimp) at a Chinese noodle stall. I met the local governor and his entourage most mornings at breakfast at my favorite noodle shop, where we would take turns paying for the noodle soup, U.S. 30 cents each. A lot of business got done that way before daybreak, although my limited Khmer language impeded really serious discussions.

One day my landlady bought two small piglets. They were fattened in no time. When I asked Phat at our English lesson why these pigs suddenly appeared in the house, she smiled and said, "Because *Loke* Benny (Mr. Benny) has so much garbage." In the absence of garbage disposal services in the city, the pigs became my personal garbage disposal. In Phnom Penh garbage disposal was a big problem, and it was only solved when Paris, France, donated shiny new garbage trucks, which were admired by everyone. The family also acquired two puppies, one brown and the other black, who were promptly named Un and Tac.

One evening, in our English class, I told Phat that her counterparts, teachers in Thailand, earned such good salaries that they could buy cars on installment. With her $6 monthly salary, she said that she would never be that lucky. She was very conscientious and hardworking, and when I later became the UN secretary-general's representative in Phnom Penh, I hired her as a research assistant. Eventually, after I left Cambodia, her father, Ith Sarin, invited her to join him in California. She was flown there and as a donut salesperson, was able to own a car, like the teachers in Thailand.

NOTES

1. UNTAC's interim role was unique in UN history. UNTEA (UN Temporary Executive Authority) had assumed such functions in West Irian (Papua), Indonesia, in 1962–1963, but then it did not exert authority over a sovereign nation, as it took over the executive powers from the Netherlands until a referendum could be held on the status of the territory. Also, UNTEA was a very small operation and as Ratner stated, was little more than a face-saving device for the Netherlands. Stephen R. Ratner, "The Cambodian settlements agreements," *American Journal of International Law*, vol. 87, no. 1 (January 1993), 13. The United Nations's executive powers in Cambodia, though much broader, were also quite limited compared with its role much later in Kosovo and East Timor. In those two cases, UNMIK (United Nations Mission in Kosovo) and UNTAET (the United Nations Transitional Authority in East Timor), both UN Peacekeeping Operations created in 1999, effectively assumed all government functions in the two regions respectively. UNMIK and UNTAET ran the gamut of tasks, from responsibility over policing, elections, executive power, and legislative to judicial power. See table 1 of International Peace Academy "You the

People: Transitional Administration, State-Building and the United Nations?" Conference Report, New York: International Peace Academy, 2002, 4.

2. United Nations, Paris Agreements, "*Final Act of the Paris Conference on Cambodia*," Part VII, Annex 5, Article 4.

3. The other remaining Khmer Rouge stronghold was Pailin in Battambang province.

4. In 1997, just when I left Cambodia for the second time, the Grand Hotel was reopened as a five-star hotel operated by Raffles hotel of Singapore. The caged elevator was kept intact as a tourist attraction.

5. In February 2004, a Cambodian court sentenced Cleghorn to twenty years in prison for raping five mostly underage girls, while his twenty-six-year-old Cambodian wife was convicted for assisting in the crimes.

6. By January 2005, when my wife returned to Siem Reap, Lin and her husband had made a modest fortune from the booming tourist industry. They built a mansion where the bamboo structure had stood and rented it out to the vice governor. They built a second house for themselves.

7. Many volumes on the Khmer Rouge's atrocities have appeared in the Western press, and it is not my intention to summarize them here. Among the interesting personal accounts is one written by a young survivor of the Khmer Rouge regime: Loung Ung, *First They Killed My Father: A Daughter of Cambodia Remembers*, New York: Harper Collins, 2000. Of the scholarly works, I highly recommend Ben Kiernan's *The Pol Pot Regime: Race, Power and Genocide in Cambodia under the Khmer Rouge, 1975–1979*, New Haven: Yale University Press, 1996. It is based on very extensive interviews with Cambodian survivors as well as documentary records, particularly from the Khmer Rouge apparatus.

8. It was not clear why the Khmer Rouge destroyed their house, as usually they used such dwellings for storing grain or their own use.

4

We Stared at Each Other and I Blinked

THE SECOND PRINCE FROM JAVA

"I wish to thank you, Excellency Mr. Yasushi Akashi, for sending another prince from Java to help bring peace to Cambodia," quipped Sihanouk, referring to me. We were at the official inauguration of the provincial headquarters of UNTAC in Siem Reap in August 1992.[1] Sihanouk knew me from the lavish receptions he used to hold in the Helmsley Hotel in New York to promote the cause of the Coalition Government of Democratic Kampuchea (CGDK). He was ably assisted in this task by Thiounn Prasith, the Khmer Rouge ambassador. Now, as chairman of SNC, he spoke on behalf of all Cambodians. The ceremony was in the front garden of my new office as provincial director, a two-story rented house.

The inauguration was being held in conjunction with a meeting of the SNC in Siem Reap; the SNC normally met in Phnom Penh. Apart from Sihanouk and Akashi, the SNC meeting and inauguration were attended by the entire SNC membership, diplomats, all the senior staff of UNTAC including the component heads, and all the provincial authorities of SOC. As Siem Reap could for all practical purposes only be reached by air from Phnom Penh, this event was a logistical nightmare and a big challenge for all of us, the still incomplete staff of UNTAC at Siem Reap. It was fortunate that the whole delegation went back to Phnom Penh that same evening as hotel space was still very limited in Siem Reap.

That day, the reservoir of goodwill and spirit of cooperation that had developed among UNTAC units and between UNTAC and the local SOC authorities was tested in a dramatic way. The various components supplied the fifteen land cruisers and two buses we needed. The local government provided the red carpet laid down in front of my office to properly receive Sihanouk. UNTAC provided lunch (although the huge bill was only paid three or four months later), while a Bangladeshi band played 1960s American pop music to entertain the guests. After lunch, UNTAC's French engineering regiment in Siem Reap provided paratroopers for a brief air show to the delight of local children and adults alike, who had never seen such a demonstration.

Sihanouk's joke baptizing me as the second prince of Java had its origin way back in the year AD 802, when a solemn ceremony was performed at Mahendraparvata, now known as Phnom Kulen, a sacred mountaintop not far from where we gathered that day. At that ceremony, Prince Jayavarman II was proclaimed a universal monarch (*Kamraten jagat ta Raja* in Cambodian), or God King (*Deva Raja* in Sanskrit). According to some sources, King Jayavarman II had resided for some time in Java during the reign of the mighty Sailendras, or Lords of the Mountain.[2] Hence the concept of *Deva Raja*, or God King (still often applied to Sihanouk), was ostensibly imported from Java.[3] This ceremony was also meant to free King Jayavarman II from the overlordship of the Sailendras of Java.[4] At that time, the Sailendras allegedly ruled over Java, Sumatra, the Malay Peninsula, and parts of modern Cambodia.[5]

Jayavarman II's inauguration in the year AD 802 gave birth to the Angkor period, a glorious Khmer civilization that dominated mainland Southeast Asia with ebbs and flows for the next six centuries. It ended when the armies of Sukhotai of Thailand sacked Angkor, its capital, in 1531. The capital remained in the Siem Reap area until it was moved to the Phnom Penh area that year. The suffix "varman," meaning protected, was applied to Jayavarman as a reflection of his omnipotence, a tradition which continues today, as Varman is one of Sihanouk's titles.

When Sihanouk jokingly baptized me the second prince from Java, he touched upon an unusual coincidence, as I was born near the sprawling Javanese Mahayana Buddhist temple complex of Borobudur located in Central Java. Borobudur was built at the height of the mighty Indonesian empire of the Sailendras.

Even after Cambodia's capital was permanently moved to the Phnom Penh area, Siem Reap continued to play an important cultural and political role in the country. Culturally, the people of the area are descendants of the Khmer Angkor and are distinct from the people of the Khmer Kandal, or Central Khmer, in Phnom Penh. Siem Reap was often the center of opposition against Phnom Penh.

For Sihanouk, Siem Reap had great personal significance. Whenever he felt slighted or otherwise unhappy with the situation in Phnom Penh, he would seek refuge in Siem Reap, where he had maintained a palace since the 1960s. If he was very unhappy, he would either go to Beijing for medical treatment or to North Korea for rest and recreation.

The magnificent Angkor Wat is located six kilometers from where we gathered that day for the inauguration.[6] With its five central towers, Angkor Wat is the greatest manifestation of a tradition of temple patronage and construction practiced by many Cambodian kings of the Angkor period. Dedicated to the Hindu God Vishnu, this temple was built by Cambodia's King Suryavarman II in the twelfth century. How lucky I considered myself that I could visit these temples every day while others had to spend a fortune to come as tourists for two or three days. During my stay, the remote parts of the temple complex were still heavily mined and rife with Khmer Rouge elements and bandits. Military personnel warned me repeatedly not to go too far astray. Angkor Wat is best seen at sunrise, because unlike most Hindu funerary temples that open to the west, it opens to the east, while the beauty of the Bayon, another magnificent temple six kilometers away, can best be appreciated at sunset.

Every afternoon when I finished work, I would send my driver home and drive to the sprawling Angkor Wat or imposing Bayon. I spent numerous hours alone waiting for the sunset over Bayon, reviewing the day's work and thinking of what tomorrow would bring. Waiting for sunrise at Angkor Wat was hardly a daily ritual, but I tried to make it once in a while. After all, as Somerset Maugham wrote in 1930, the world "needs the glow of sunset or the white brilliance of the moon to give it a loveliness that touches the heart."[7]

WHY I BLINKED

I was wearing two hats in Siem Reap. In one of them, as part of UNTAC's Civil Administration component, and as the "shadow governor," I was to control the "existing administrative structures," which, again, for all practical purposes meant the SOC provincial government. I was to "produce a neutral environment for the elections." In this function, I was a "little Porcell," the head of Civil Administration. Wearing my second hat, I was to coordinate all the components of UNTAC in the province, including through monthly meetings. In this role, I was a "little Akashi," the head of UNTAC. My two functions were, of course, intertwined. In order to deal with the SOC government effectively, we had to speak with one voice.

Wearing my first hat, the day after my arrival in Siem Reap I presented my credentials to the SOC governor of the province, Nuo Som, who was flanked by his four deputies, including First Deputy Leng Vy, with whom we were to have the most dealings in the future. The ceremony was a solemn affair. I was accompanied by representatives of the other components of UNTAC already deployed to Siem Reap.

We were seated in the governor's office, facing Nuo Som and his entourage. All of us sat in old-fashioned oversized sofas in a very large room with high ceilings; the room had obviously seen better days when the country was at peace in the 1960s. Large ceiling fans whirled overhead, and tea was served.

This first meeting was no more than a polite exchange of courtesies. I felt as if I were in a strange kind of poker game as we sized each other up. I held my cards close to my chest, while knowing that Nuo Som, as the governor of the de facto administration since 7 January 1979, held powerful cards. On the other hand, he did not have the faintest clue what my cards were. While I could easily find out the strength of the SOC under Nuo Som's command, he did not know which of the various UNTAC units represented in the meeting had executive functions and thus would be directly controlling his apparatus. He could only guess which units would be doing what and how far we would go in asserting control. I was in no condition to bluff, however, as frankly we UNTACists were not sure ourselves what we were supposed to do with our powers and received no directives from Porcell, who was busy doing something else. But I and the other UNTAC representatives looked quite impressive in colorful military uniforms from Bangladesh, the United States, France, and Indonesia.

I later told the journalist William Shawcross what happened that day: "He stared at me. I stared at him. We stared at each other, and I blinked first." I was referring to control over Civil Administration as prescribed by the Paris Agreements. From this statement, Shawcross concluded: "The idea that a small group of foreign civil servants could take over and supplant a well entrenched communist regime was absurd. The Khmer Rouge could well claim that their mortal enemy, the Phnom Penh government, had survived Paris intact and that UNTAC had not met its obligations."[8] As stated before, our failure to exert control can be traced to the flaws in the Paris Agreements.[9]

In Siem Reap, the SOC was represented by Nuo Som and in military matters by General Long So Pheap, an extremely intelligent, likeable, and witty general who spoke six languages. He headed SOC's fourth army. While technically he was Colonel Kamal's counterpart, we got along very well, as Long So Pheap, like me, enjoyed a drink or two, whereas Colonel Kamal was constrained on this score by his religion. The Khmer Rouge never allowed us to enter its territory, and Governor Nuo Som complained bitterly to me that while we were concentrating our efforts on controlling him, the Khmer Rouge was completely ignoring UNTAC.

The confusing question was how to interpret UNTAC's powers of direct supervision and control. The Paris Agreements gave UNTAC a mandate, which precisely specified its powers of control. In order to create a neutral political environment for the elections, the agreements stated, five areas should be subject to the strictest level of scrutiny and control: defense, public security, information, finance, and foreign affairs.[10] But while the Paris Agreements spelled out UNTAC's mandate in detail, they did not specify UNTAC's structure. Rather, a UN document that I will conveniently call the UN "Handbook" discussed the structure.[11] The discrepancy between these two documents, especially with regard to Civil Administration, was considerable. While the Paris Agreements gave Akashi sweeping powers of control over the "existing administrative structures," for instance, the Handbook allocated only two hundred staff members to Civil Administration entrusted with control, a hopelessly inadequate number for performing the comprehensive tasks prescribed by the Paris Agreements. By way of contrast, the SOC consisted of a well-entrenched and monolithic civil service estimated at 140,000 to 200,000 persons.[12]

I asked myself whether the United Nations Secretariat, in preparing the Handbook, deliberately understaffed the Civil Administration because they realized that control was utterly unattainable. Or did some believe that the mandate of control over Civil Administration was not equitable, given that only one of the four factions had substantial administrative control? Whatever it was, I felt like the proverbial emperor with no clothes.

My conclusion, after seeing Hedi Annabi, a senior UN official who had participated in the UN fact-finding mission to Cambodia in April–May 1990, was that the UN Secretariat never intended UNTAC to exercise full control over SOC, which would have required tens of thousands of staff.[13] Annabi argued in 1993 that there was much confusion in the press about what the United Nations was expected to do: "It was never intended for the United Nations to have been mandated to practically take over the administration of Cambodia. This is not the case. It has never been considered and is obviously not possible."[14] In an interview in 2005, Annabi reiterated this point to me.

On top of these ambiguities, there was Porcell's lackadaisical attitude toward control, which considerably damaged our credibility and performance. Not able to cope with his task, and blaming his component's shortcomings on slow recruitment procedures, Porcell asked other component heads to exercise the mandate of direct control in their areas.[15]

The conventional explanation for UNTAC's control problems in most books on UNTAC, be they written by journalists or academics, was that SOC

Photo 4.1.   Akashi addresses monthy meeting of provincial directors in Phnom Penh. To his left is Gerald Porcell, director of Civil Administration. Credit: UN Photo 137773/P. Sudhakaran.

was increasingly resisting UNTAC's efforts at control because UNTAC did not have access to Khmer Rouge territories. While this was true, I would go one step further. Even if UNTAC had been given access to Khmer Rouge areas, the whole arrangement would have continued to be unfair to SOC, as the Khmer Rouge's administration of its limited territory could not be compared to the fully functioning SOC administration covering over 90 percent of the country.

Wearing my second hat, starting in June 1992 I began to hold monthly coordination meetings. These meetings would bring together the representatives of all UNTAC units plus those of other UN agencies and NGOs in the province. Most, if not all, units were represented by their chiefs. These monthly meetings supplied important opportunities to exchange information on the Khmer Rouge and other threats, and the participants eagerly awaited them.

I had asked Colonel Kamal, commander of Bangbatt, to cochair these meetings. Technically, our territories did not completely overlap. As map 3.1 in chapter 3 shows, Bangbatt's eight hundred fifty soldiers, tasked with demobilization of the Cambodian People's Armed Forces (CPAF), were deployed in an area that coincided with CPAF's military sector two deployment under General Long So Pheap, which also covered the province of Banteay Meanchey. Colonel Kamal's command area therefore covered the southern half of Siem Reap province plus the adjacent Banteay Meanchey province. The northern part of Siem Reap province was the responsibility of the Pakistani army, located at the district capital of Samrong. The Pakistani battalion in UNTAC (Pakbatt) had never cooperated effectively with me partly because their commander felt awkward visiting me in Siem Reap—then the territory of the Bangladeshi battalion—and partly because he did not have the faintest idea what a provincial director did.

I did visit him in Samrong at his headquarters twice. The first time I was kept waiting in a tent about half a kilometer away, after which he finally decided that he would see me. This small incident reflected the ignorance of most military personnel with the role of civilians in UNTAC. In previous peacekeeping operations, the military component reigned supreme and the only civilians present were finance and logistics personnel. Problems of turf would surface now and again, except with Colonels Jay Carter and Kamal, who understood my role quite well.

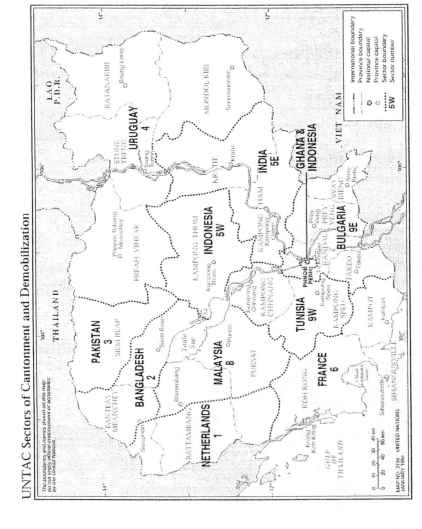

UNTAC Sectors of Cantonment and Demobilization

Map 4.1. Deployment of UN-TAC military for cantonment and demobilization. United Nations, Cartographic Section, UN map no. 3736.

THE MYTH OF CONTROL

Let's take a look at how we in the field in Siem Reap attempted to exert control over three of the five areas stipulated by the Paris Agreements: finance, public security, and information. Foreign affairs was mainly applicable to the only international airport at Phnom Penh, but we in Siem Reap did manage UNTAC border control posts at border towns with Thailand.[16]

In the area of finance, control was to ensure that SOC did not finance campaigning by its political party, the Cambodian People's Party (CPP), the renamed Communist Party of Cambodia. But because of the flaws in the Paris Agreements, control was basically a myth. At best, UNTAC achieved some token success in this area, mainly because the functions were transferred, at Porcell's request, from his office to American Roger Lawrence, Akashi's economic adviser.

Meanwhile, my staff member Simos Ogouma, an ex-ambassador of Benin to the UN, who was responsible for control over finance, got busy right away and provided weekly reports on his efforts, which were ahead of those in other provinces. Of course, although Ogouma did not meet any resistance from the SOC administration, it was absurd to think that one person could control the secretive finances of the SOC. I learned from my interpreters that the bureaucrats laughed loudly as soon as my controller departed their offices. The communist bureaucracy was as adept as any multinational corporation at concealing the real figures from outsiders. But this was neither Ogouma's nor Lawrence's fault.

A case in point was control over the revenues derived from Angkor Wat: Ogouma was given the runaround and got many different figures from different offices on them. I was immediately confronted with the sensitive issue of whether we should control the management of revenue from tourists coming to Angkor Wat, rather than just recording the size of the revenues. Some ten thousand tourists had trickled in in 1992, mostly backpackers.

The backpackers often tried to get away with paying nothing to see the wonders of Angkor Wat. However, they were often caught at Siem Reap airport upon their departure—if they had not already been caught at the temples—and forced to pay high fees. These fees ranged from $80 for a one-day tour to $160 for two days to $258 for three days. Sometimes they got buttonholed while waiting for their flight out of the country.[17]

Some improvements in collecting fees were introduced on our recommendation. European backpackers often approached UNTAC civil police at the airport to ask for help in evading payment of the $100 demanded by the SOC police, as this was in UNTAC's mandate. UNTAC police invariably protected the tourist and told the local police to sort of melt away. In November 1992, the local governments erected three tollgates at the approaches to Angkor Wat where fees were to be collected. A new fee schedule was introduced. This procedure would replace the post-visit collection of fees at the airport where backpackers were protected by UNTAC CivPol (civil police component of UNTAC) and was a vast improvement.[18]

In retrospect, it is doubtful whether UNTAC police, who had the mandate of controlling security and assisting in the establishment of human rights in Cambodia, should have meddled by preventing SOC from collecting tourist fees at the Siem Reap airport. To the cash-strapped SOC government the handful of tourists was a lucrative source of income. Angkor Wat was a national treasure, and I considered our efforts to meddle in this area, especially our effort to protect foreign backpackers from Austria or Britain from being charged high fees to visit Angkor, to be a deviation from our mandate. Whose human rights were UNTAC police protecting? However, I did not have the power to stop our CivPol from chasing away SOC police in order to allow tourists to fly away without paying anything.

The failure of UNTAC's rehabilitation function had a direct impact on SOC's finances far beyond our feeble efforts to control them. Indeed, SOC's already precarious financial position was dealt an almost fatal blow by UNTAC's failure to implement its rehabilitation mandate. In 1991 United Nations Secretary-General Perez de Cuellar appealed to the international community to support Cambodia's rehabilitation efforts. This resulted in pledges totaling $880 million at the first conference on the Rehabilitation of Cambodia in June 1992. Alas, although the UNTAC-led peace process opened the gate for unprecedented aid being pledged to Cambodia, the actual disbursement of that aid was severely constrained by several factors.

In the first place, rehabilitation was derailed by none other than the SNC. Here is what happened: large aid projects had to be approved by the SNC, which is a rare way in which this ineffectual body exhibited real power. At SNC meetings, the three opposition factions, led by the Khmer Rouge, repeatedly vetoed rehabilitation projects. The three factions argued that rehabilitation programs directly strengthened the hands of the incumbent SOC government and should be stopped. One would have expected that the United Nations would have paid top priority to rehabilitation when the pledges were made in Tokyo. Not so. To appease the Khmer Rouge and its allies, and to avoid supporting only the SOC, these unfortunate vetoes were upheld.

Secondly, even though in the Paris peace process there was a special declaration on rehabilitation, this component was largely ignored, both in Phnom Penh and the provinces.[19] It was reasoned that UNTAC's main goal was to bring elections and that rehabilitation could wait. Thirdly, donors were reluctant to authorize large aid projects in insecure conditions. That frustrated Akashi, who openly complained about it. Fourth, the SOC administrative structure was unable to absorb aid projects. And, most unfortunately, the resignation from UNTAC of Berndt Bernander, an able administrator from the United Nations Development Program (UNDP), due to disagreement with Akashi in October 1992, seriously disrupted rehabilitation. He was replaced by Roger Lawrence, who then had to wear two hats. The upshot of these actions was that once again the plight of the common people was being sacrificed in order to satisfy political and bureaucratic ends.

In contrast, there were the commendable efforts of the nonpolitical UNDP. In an attempt to circumvent the ban imposed by the United Nations on aid to Cambodia because the SOC was not a recognized government, William Draper, the UNDP administrator, took several innovative steps during the UNTAC transition period to help Cambodia. In 1990 he assigned a number of UNDP staff in Bangkok to Cambodia to prepare for the resumption of major development programs there. Eduardo Wattez, a Frenchman, headed this group,[20] which was effectively working for the Hun Sen government.[21]

As for control over public security, CivPol was tasked with supervising or controlling the local civil police and thereby ensuring that law and order was maintained and that human rights and fundamental freedoms were respected. UNTAC's 3,600-person CivPol was faced with 45,000 SOC police who were well trained in the suppression of dissent and political opposition. Although UNTAC's mandate on public security was spelled out extensively in the Paris Agreements, they did not specify how the civil police were to carry it out. The UN Handbook did not help much either and only spoke in general terms of the civil police's supervisory role. And, as in the case of Civil Administration, there was bad or insufficient planning by the leadership.[22]

In conversations with some police from developing countries, I was told that they had to pay a bribe to be sent to Cambodia. Like the rest of us civilian personnel, the civil police received $145 a day in a Mission Subsistence Allowance, which was a princely sum particularly for people from countries where police were normally paid between $100 and $250 a month.

Given these odds, I must say that in Siem Reap our achievements in the areas of public security and human rights were quite remarkable. To a great degree this was a result of the excellent cooperation between the head of CivPol, Superintendent Joe Dowling, an extremely hardworking Irish policeman; his counterpart in the SOC, Colonel Lay Sopheap; and my Human Rights officer, Eugenio Polizzi. Joe Dowling did a great job leading his contingent of 132 police from thirteen countries. He did so by setting an example of hard work, impartiality, and strict discipline. He was particularly harsh toward his own Irish police, thereby forcing others to comply. Lay Sopheap was reform-minded and very cooperative, even proposing that Joe Dowling station UN-TAC CivPol officers in his office.

As for our human rights mandate, one would have expected that UNTAC would have paid special attention to abuses by the Khmer Rouge. But, sadly, that was not the case. UNTAC treated the Khmer Rouge gently. The word "genocide," which the Khmer Rouge had committed during 1975–1979, gradually disappeared from texts. At the first Jakarta Informal Meeting on 28 July 1988, Indonesian chairman and interlocutor for ASEAN Ali Alatas's final communiqué had noted a Southeast Asian consensus on preventing a return to "the genocidal policies and practices of the Pol Pot regime."[23] This statement was progressively watered down in the diplomatic process until it reached the Permanent Five of the UN Security Council, where the Khmer Rouge enjoyed strong support from China. As a result the so-called framework document, which later became the Paris Agreements, merely referred to "policies and practices of the recent past."[24]

That vague phrase could not become the foundation for a strong UNTAC-led human rights regime that would ensure that the horrific past would never reoccur. So widely used was the euphemism that not many UNTACists, who were mainly foreigners with little knowledge of Cambodian history or culture, were even aware that "practices of the recent past" represented the deaths of millions at the hands of the Khmer Rouge.

Siem Reap, Battambang, and Kompong Cham were the three most volatile provinces, which meant that Eugenio Polizzi and the civil police had their hands full investigating human rights abuses and reforming the judicial and prison systems. Eugenio's work was hampered by the CivPol themselves, coming as some did from countries where human rights abuses were rampant. Not only were they untrained in human rights, but they also possessed no inclination to do their job. But Eugenio and Commander Dowling took the lead in implementing reforms.

On 10 September 1992, we discovered an undisclosed detention center where a large number of prisoners were incarcerated. They were all shackled to the ground. Eugenio had interviewed top CPAF generals of the fourth military region a few days earlier who had denied the existence of the detention center. He then proceeded to investigate and found that the detention center was absolutely filthy, with prisoners shackled and wallowing in squalor. Eugenio secured promises from the SOC police that the detainees would be treated humanely. Ten days later, however, nothing had changed. Once again he approached General Mon Neam, who now promised to transfer the prisoners to a civilian prison, which he did after several meetings. Although this was a relatively minor affair, it kept our limited staff fully occupied for weeks. We were trying to change an entire country one step at a time. That was the magnitude of our task.

Porcell's lack of interest in the provincial structure of UNTAC changed abruptly in December 1992. In response to a dramatic increase in politically motivated intimidation and violence, UNTAC concluded that, relatively speaking, the SOC ministries in Phnom Penh were empty shells of control, and that the Cambodian People's Party, which had its own channels to the provinces, continued to be the nucleus of decision-making. The Ministry for National Security, which was supposed to be controlled by UNTAC, was particularly notorious for being an empty shell. It was headed by the unsavory General Sin Song, who was later accused by UNTAC of instigating criminal irregularities in the 1993 elections and was sacked upon UNTAC's recommendation. At the provincial and local levels, authority was exercised through familial and personal ties to the governor.[25]

UNTAC therefore decided that it was necessary to more closely monitor the provincial SOC offices. Secret multidisciplinary control teams, known as Hush Hush teams, consisting of UNTAC personnel were established in January 1993 and secretly dropped from helicopters at provincial capitals. Ostensibly, these mobile teams were meant to verify if the local administration was being conducted in a politically neutral manner during preparations for the elections at the provincial and district levels. The teams paid surprise visits to the SOC's provincial offices, demanding to see all their documents. One member of the teams later told me that they would rapidly enter the SOC offices and cover all exits in the building, like Elliot Ness and the Untouchables during the U.S. prohibition period, opening any books and correspondence that they pleased. In Phnom Penh UNTAC gloated over the "success" of these early teams, which had uncovered secret documents outlining plans to subvert cooperation with UNTAC and intimidate opposition parties.[26] Of course, it was obvious that the element of surprise had dissipated after the first two or three visits to various provincial capitals. Later I found out that Hun Sen had been extremely unhappy with these surprise control teams and had sent a letter to Akashi stating that UNTAC's method of control was so intrusive that it resembled the activities of Pol Pot.[27] Without informing us in the provinces, Akashi decided to discontinue the Hush Hush teams, another sign of UNTAC's weakness.

In Phnom Penh, control over Information had been handed over, at Porcell's request, to Tim Carney's efficient Information Division. Creating and using a Media Working Group, which included the Cambodian parties, the Information Division also ran Radio UNTAC, a unique concept in UN peacekeeping. It embarked with live broadcasts from Phnom Penh. Radio UNTAC gained instant popularity everywhere because it gave equal time to all political parties, including FUNCINPEC and the Buddhist Liberal Democratic Party, BLDP (as members of the resistance, they had been considered the enemy during the PRK/SOC period). It also had a control unit that carried out UNTAC's mandate for control and supervision of the Cambodian media. And its Analysis/Assessment Unit produced indispensable information for internal UNTAC use on political trends, including by interpreting Khmer Rouge radio.

In the absence of media in the provinces, there was no budgetary allocation for information officers there. Nevertheless, we in Siem Reap created our own information road shows, which became important tools for informing the population of the objectives of the elections and the value of human rights. Genevieve from my office coordinated these road shows with our colleagues from CivPol. Our effort was later emulated in other provinces. These shows usually involved ten to fifteen UNTAC personnel; we used a moving generator as a power source. On one occasion we even held such a road show in a Khmer Rouge village.

Photo 4.2.   Listening to Radio UNTAC was a favorite pastime everywhere in Cambodia. Credit: UN Photo 121633/P. Sudhakaran.

Photo 4.3.   An UNTAC Information Education Team travels by boat to a Cambodian island to publicize the elections. Credit: UN Photo 137769/P. Sudhakaran.

Another road show took us to Svay Leu district, a heavily contested area that frequently changed hands between the SOC and the Khmer Rouge. We traveled by helicopter and once there did not waste any time, for we were not keen on getting caught in the cross fire. The Bangladeshi soldiers secured the immediate areas of the hamlet (as much as possible, that is) since soldiers in this part of the world were just as likely to be in mufti as in fatigues. The town seemed abandoned; those people who remained looked fearful. Everyone seemed to be waiting for something. Shops were shut. The food and drink stalls—always part and parcel of Cambodian life—were nowhere to be seen. The only sign of life was one shack stuffed with elderly Khmer men who appeared to be intent on just one thing: getting inebriated on locally brewed liquor.

In fact, everyone there was in purgatory. Some locals told me that the continuous fighting between the Khmer Rouge and CPAF made people wary of settling into secure patterns of everyday life. Hence the lack of food stalls. Fortunately we had packed our lunch boxes. After lunch, Major Tarek, who was Colonel Kamal's trusted aide, and I were sitting under a banyan tree when a group of soldiers sauntered over from the other side of the one-street town. As usual for such groups of Cambodian armed bands, they wore mixed uniforms and carried an odd assortment of weaponry: AK47s, RPGs (rocket-propelled grenades), and B40s. Major Tarek, who studied the uniforms of Cambodia as part of his training, suddenly looked fearful when he realized that one of the soldiers wore an unmistakably Khmer Rouge uniform. We questioned him about his loyalties. The man lackadaisically answered, "Well, my own uniform was very old and when I killed this Khmer Rouge soldier, I just took his uniform and his gun, and these are now my only set of clothes and my only gun."

This was a problem we encountered everywhere. Military observers and battalions often reported that a group of attacking soldiers was wearing "mixed uniforms." Thus, it could not always be ascertained whether the attackers were Khmer Rouge forces. They were more like roving groups of bandits, soldiers who had not been paid for months. Moreover, their uniforms were probably their only serviceable clothes.

GENERAL LONG SO PHEAP IN ACTION

The financial problems of the SOC administration were the consequence of the economic and political isolation of Cambodia during the 1980s. The bleeding to death of the SOC's finances, of course, affected day-to-day life in the country. General Long So Pheap in Siem Reap took unique measures to lessen the deprivation.

One night we were offered a particularly sumptuous feast of roast pork and rice (this dish is popular in Vietnamese restaurants in the United States) with plenty of beer and Scotch. The next day, UNTAC Chief of CivPol Superintendent Dowling received a complaint from a civilian whose truck full of pigs had been hijacked, ostensibly by Long So Pheap's troops. When confronted, General Long So Pheap retorted that the pigs were destined for the Khmer Rouge anyway and that the confiscation was legitimate because the Khmer Rouge was violating the cease-fire. After a well-timed pause, he asked, "Did Dowling and the other UNTACists enjoy their pork dinner last night?"

The general, whose major weakness was Johnny Walker Black Label Scotch and who would eventually die of liver complications, loved parties where a contingent of prostitutes danced to a military band playing Cambodian songs and American standards (including an endless rendering of "Lambada"). The liaison officers from the three resistance forces were always invited to the parties, and whenever my wife, who is broadminded and a good dancer, was in Siem Reap, she had to take turns dancing the lambada and jiving with Khmer Rouge generals and colonels from FUNCINPEC and KPNLF (after first being swept onto the floor by Long So Pheap, an avid dancer). Noblesse oblige.

On another occasion Long So Pheap decided to inspect the lucrative road traffic from Poi Pet at the Thai border, through Banteay Meanchey and Battambang provinces, and on to Phnom Penh. The relative peace prevailing since UNTAC's arrival allowed huge Thai lorries to travel the road, filled with Thai merchandise ranging from videocassettes and bicycles to soap and clothes destined for Phnom Penh. Underpaid soldiers would hold up these lorries for illegal levies before allowing them to pass.

I accompanied Long So Pheap, both of us traveling incognito, at stops at these illegal checkpoints and asked, "Hey soldier, whom do you work for?" When the soldiers answered, "I work for General Long So Pheap," the general announced, "I am General Long So Pheap" and angrily ordered the soldiers, who were armed with AK-47s, to go home. The soldiers would salute and leave, but Long So Pheap would chuckle and say that they would be back, as this was the only way to feed their hungry families. These underpaid soldiers, who officially received $13 a month, often went for months without pay whenever their commanders decided to withhold their wages. At one point the man manning the checkpoint, when asked, replied that he was not a soldier. Long So Pheap angrily demanded to know why he was carrying an AK-47 to which he laconically replied: "I rented it for $3 a day from that soldier," pointing to a soldier dozing off in a hammock. The entrepreneurial spirit was obviously not fully destroyed by the Khmer Rouge. The gun truly ruled, and the AK-47 was the only tool they had to augment their meager incomes, as Long So Pheap recognized.

NOTES

1. Audiotape of the inauguration ceremony from my private collection.

2. Actually, some sources trace Javanese influence over Kambuja from the beginning of the eighth century during the reign of King Sanjaya of Java over the Sailendra Empire. The Javanese influence over Kambuja was mentioned in his inscription dated AD 732. See Ramesh C. Majumdar, *Suvarnadvipa, Ancient Indian Colonies in the Far East*, vol. II, part II, "Cultural History," chapter 1, as quoted in Ramesh C. Majumdar, *Kambuja Desa, An Ancient Hindu Colony in Cambodia, Sir Williams Meyer Lectures, 1942–43*, Madras: University of Madras, 1944, reprinted by Philadelphia: Institute for the Study of Human Issues, 1980, 73 ff.

3. Majumdar, *Suvarnadvipa*, 77, footnote 3. According to an eleventh century inscription, the cult was known as *kamraten jagat ta raja* in Khmer (universal monarch) or *devaraja* in Sanskrit. G. Coedes and P. Dupont, "L'inscription de Sdok Kak Thom," *Bulletin de l'Ecole francaise d'Extreme Orient (BEFEO)*, 43 (1943–1946), 57–134.

4. G. Coedes, *The Indianized States of Southeast Asia*, Honolulu: The East West Press of Hawaii, 1968, 97. Original French version: Paris: E. de Boccard, 1964. See also G. Coedes, *The Making of South East Asia*, Berkeley: Berkeley University of California Press, 1964, 97. Original French version: *Les Peuples de la Peninsule Indochinoise*, Paris: Dunod, 1962.

5. *Columbia Encyclopedia*, New York: Columbia Univerity Press, 2001–2005. Other sources do not make clear whether Java was the island Java or some other place in Southeast Asia. See for instance David Chandler, *A History of Cambodia*, Chieng Mai, Thailand: Silkworm Press, 1993, 35. The name Sailendra (which means King of the Mountain) was probably chosen because it was the title of the Kings of Funan (old Cambodia) from whom the royal family of the Sailendra Dynasty claimed descent. Coedes, *The Indianized States*, 89.

6. The only written description of Angkor at the height of its splendor is to be found in *Notes on the Customs of Cambodia* by a Chinese traveler, Chou Ta Kuan (Zhou Daguan), who traveled to Cambodia in 1296. Chou vividly described life in Cambodia in those days, including in the walled city of Angkor Thom. Chou Ta Kuan (Zhou Daguan), *The Customs of Cambodia*, Bangkok: The Siam Society, second edition, 1992. Translated by J. Gillan d'Arcy Paul. From the French, Paul Pelliot, *Memoirs sur les Coutomes du Cambodge de Tseou Ta-kuan*, Paris: Liraite d'Amerique et d' Orient, 1957.

7. Somerset Maugham, *The Gentleman in the Parlour*, Garden City, NY: Doubleday, Doran and Company, 1930.

8. William Shawcross, *Deliver Us from Evil*, 75.

9. See chapter 2.

10. UN, Paris Agreements.

11. UN Handbook.

12. The United States General Accounting Office, in *UN Peacekeeping: Lessons Learned in Managing Recent Missions*, gave the figure of 140,000 (see p. 36). Michael Doyle, *UN Peacekeeping in Cambodia: UNTAC's Civil Mandate*, New York: International Peace Academy, 42, cited the figure of 200,000.

13. See unpublished confidential UN report, *Report of the United Nations Fact-Finding Mission on Present Structures and Practices of Administration in Cambodia, 24 April to 9 May 1990*, New York, June 1990.

14. Hedi Annabi, "The United Nations Plan for Cambodia," in Ben Kiernan, ed., *Genocide and Democracy in Cambodia*, New Haven: Yale University Press, 1993, Appendix I, 286.

15. Roger Lawrence had direct control over finance, Force Commander Sanderson over defense, CivPol Commander Brig Gen. Klaas Roos over security/police, and Information Division Chief Tim Carney over media/information. Personal interview with Tim Carney, December 2006.

16. The other two fields, defense and foreign affairs, were mainly controlled in Phnom Penh.

17. Angkor Tourism Company of Siem Reap Province, "The Confidential Package Tour for Accommodation at Siem Reap Province," unpublished document signed by Koy Sang, director of Angkor tourism, May 1993.

18. When I visited Angkor Wat in January 2005 the more than one million tourists had to pay $20 for a whole-day visit to the temples. I met some local authorities, whom I knew from UNTAC days, who were smiling broadly.

19. Paris Agreements, "Declaration on the Rehabilitation and Reconstruction of Cambodia."

20. Wattez later became the first UNDP resident representative in Phnom Penh and my colleague after the elections.

21. UNDP had in reserve a huge Indicative Planning Figure (IPF) that had accumulated for Cambodia since 1975, nearly US$100 million. After the conclusion of the Peace Accord in the fall of 1991 and the return of the king, UNDP and the other UN development agencies that progressively returned to Cambodia undertook huge development projects there such as CARERE. The interlocutor with the arrival of UNTAC and Akashi formally became UNTAC itself, but in reality UNDP continued to work at the technical assistance level with the Hun Sen government. When UNTAC departed, the UNDP office became the office of the resident coordinator/UNDP representative coordinating other UN development agencies, as in any other "normal" country. Wattez e-mail to author.

22. In most books on UNTAC, the Civil Police component, along with Civil Administration, has borne the brunt of criticism of UNTAC. This was also the case at the Singapore seminar I attended. See, Nassarine Azimi, ed., *The UN Transitional Authority in Cambodia (UNTAC), Debriefing and Lessons*, London: Kluwer International, 1996, 17.

23. *Far Eastern Economic Review*, 11 August 1988, 29. This was a chairman statement, not a joint declaration of the Southeast Asian countries present.

24. UN document A/45/472-S/b21689, 31 August 1990, containing the so-called framework document of the five permanent members of the Security Council, Section 4, paragraph 24.

25. Porcell, "The Case of the Empty Shells."

26. In retrospect, all this reminded me of the search in 2003 for weapons of mass destruction in Iraq.

27. Yasushi Akashi, "The Challenges Facing UNTAC," 192.

5

The Khmer Rouge
Derail Demobilization

DEMOBILIZATION COMMENCES

On 13 June 1992, Phase II of UNTAC's military mandate—the demobilization of 70 percent of the four Cambodian armies—was set to commence as scheduled, even though not all UNTAC troops had yet been deployed.[1] It was to be concluded within four weeks, prior to voter registration for the elections. The troop strength of the four armies as reported to the United Nations was as shown in table 5.1.

It was obvious that the Cambodian People's Armed Forces (CPAF) was the dominant force and was able to maintain SOC's control over the country after the Vietnamese army left completely in 1989. Of the three resistance forces, the Khmer Rouge army was well disciplined and better trained and posed a continuing threat during UNTAC times.

In the southern part of Siem Reap province, Bangbatt, the Bangladeshi battalion, was well prepared. I accompanied Colonel Kamal on a survey of all of Bangbatt's regroupment sites. He showed me the sheds his battalion had to build—complete with secure padlocks—to store arms to be collected from CPAF. In the northern part of the province, the Pakistani troops did the same. The Pakistanis had the additional task of disarming FUNCINPEC troops—a smaller operation. Their plan to demobilize the Khmer Rouge in An Long Veng never materialized.

Table 5.1.   Troop strength of the four armies as reported to the United Nations.

The Four Armies	Number of Soldiers	Militia	Weapons	Heavy Weapons	Ammunition
CPAF (SOC)	126,000	220,290	273,343	877	79,205,175
NADK (Khmer Rouge)	27,000		20,000	176	516,000
ANKI (FUNCINPEC)	17,500		13,500		742,000
KPNLF	27,800		13,600		266,000
Total	198,300	220,290	320,443	1,053	80,729,175

Source: UN Military Survey Mission to Cambodia, 17 November, 16 December, 24 December 1991.

During Phase II, Colonel Kamal invited me to witness the disarmament process taking place at Bangladesh military headquarters in Siem Reap city. General Long So Pheap, Colonel Kamal, and myself sat on a dais while the soldiers to be disarmed stood in front of us in troop formation. A CPAF video camera recorded the ceremony. General Long So Pheap ordered his soldiers one by one to hand over their weapons to the Bangladeshi soldiers, who registered and handed out receipts for them. The Bangladeshi soldiers then proceeded to the shed and locked away the weapons, which were to be kept under constant surveillance. I noticed grins on the faces of the Bangladeshis. The Cambodian soldiers also smirked. This puzzled me. I assumed the Bangladeshi and Cambodian soldiers shared an inside military joke. Later Colonel Kamal showed me two or three examples of the weapons handed in. They were rusty museum pieces, no longer serviceable. The better weapons were all still kept hidden away by the CPAF, and UNTAC had no way of checking their garrisons or their homes.

General Long So Pheap informed us that these CPAF soldiers would now take agricultural leave to help their families harvest the rice crop. Noticing my perplexed look—according to the UNTAC Standard Operating Procedures (SOP), the soldiers were supposed to gather in cantonment areas built by the Bangladeshi battalion and remain in these areas until demobilization or the new Cambodian government accepted responsibility for them—Colonel Kamal explained that in practice, feeding these cantoned troops had become a problem, as it was not the responsibility of UNTAC. The noncooperation of the Khmer Rouge also contributed to the cantonment problem. As CPAF soldiers normally would take agricultural leave at harvest time anyway, UNTAC could do nothing but allow the leave. Those taking leave were supposed to be on two weeks notice to report to their cantonment areas before the process of demobilization would begin.

THE BAMBOO POLE INCIDENT AND DEMOBILIZATION

Meanwhile, in what would become known as the bamboo pole incident, the Khmer Rouge gave UNTAC the finger. On 30 May 1992, two months after their arrival, Yasushi Akashi and General John Sanderson visited Pailin, the major Khmer Rouge stronghold in Battambang province, adjacent to Thailand. From Pailin the two were to travel west through Khmer Rouge territory to the Thai border to meet with Dutch marines who were tasked with demobilizing the Khmer Rouge soldiers in that area and were awaiting deployment to the Khmer Rouge zone. Upon leaving Pailin, Akashi's party was prevented from proceeding farther by a simple roadblock when several young, unarmed Khmer Rouge soldiers refused to lift a single bamboo pole over the road through their territory, which led to Thailand.[2]

Under the Paris Agreements, UNTAC could have insisted on entering the zone under the protection of UNTAC soldiers. Many felt that it should have called the Khmer Rouge's bluff and sent UN troops into the area at once. However, Akashi and Sanderson decided against it. Their party turned back. The Khmer Rouge concluded that UNTAC was merely a paper tiger. This was a defining moment: UNTAC had blinked again. The incident was publicized all over the world, and Akashi seemed completely devastated.

Meanwhile, the very impressive Dutch marines at the Thai border were refused entry into the territory completely and were redeployed to Sisophon, the capital of the SOC province of Banteay Meanchey.[3] Subsequently, on 9 June, the Khmer Rouge told Akashi in a letter that it would not allow UNTAC to deploy in its areas.[4] UNTAC complied.

General Sanderson argued that strong pressure against the Khmer Rouge would cause an escalation of hostilities and that many of the countries contributing troops would not tolerate it. He also reminded his superiors that UNTAC had no enforcement power since it was a peacekeeping, and not a peace enforcement operation. Sanderson's outspoken Deputy Force Commander, the French General Loridon, estimated that the tough policy against the Khmer Rouge that he advocated would cause two hundred UNTAC casualties (he counted himself among them). But Akashi felt that a military plan costing two hundred lives would be a failure for the entire United Nations peacekeeping operation. And after all, according to the flawed Paris Agreements, the Khmer Rouge was one of the four legitimate partners and not an enemy at all.

We in Siem Reap province experienced our own "bamboo pole incident" at around the same time. In northern Siem Reap province, poorly maintained and heavily mined roads hampered the movements of the Pakistani battalion (Pakbatt), headquartered in the SOC-administered town of Samrong. Bamboo poles and teenage soldiers also blocked its entry into the adjacent Khmer Rouge territory of An Long Veng.

The nonparticipation of the Khmer Rouge military led to the complete abandonment of demobilization. Naturally, CPAF, and to a lesser extent the two small resistance factions, refused to proceed with a process that would leave them vulnerable to attacks by an intact Khmer Rouge army. By 10 September 1992, when demobilization halted, UNTAC had cantoned only a paltry 50,000 soldiers, that is, CPAF: 42,368; FUNCINPEC: 3,445; KPNLF: 6,479; and Khmer Rouge: nil.[5]

Photo 5.1.   Soldiers of the Cambodian People's Armed Forces (CPAF), being demobilized. Credit: UN Photo 137762/P. Sudhakaran.

The SOC was furious. It claimed that UNTAC was biased in implementing the peace process. Governor Nuo Som asked me several times in Siem Reap when I would start getting tough on the Khmer Rouge. Now both the Khmer Rouge and the SOC despised UNTAC, and only the two small factions supported it. After all, they had nothing to lose but their slivers of land.

As a result of its failure to demobilize the armies, UNTAC had to completely overhaul its entire strategy for deploying its military component. UNTAC's military would henceforth be charged with providing security for the elections. This meant that instead of the phased withdrawal outlined in the original operation plan, all military battalions had to stay until the end of the UNTAC mandate, at a considerably higher cost to the United Nations.[6]

And now troops had to be redeployed to positions corresponding to UNTAC's civilian administrations rather than according to the deployment of the CPAF's military sectors. (Compare map 4.1 in chapter 4 to map 5.1 that follows.) For Siem Reap, the consequence of the redeployment was that Bangbatt was now responsible for the entire province of Siem Reap, relegating Pakbatt to the underdeveloped and insignificant province of Preah Vihear next door. This change recognized the professionalism of Colonel Kamal and his Bangbatt troops. My excellent personal relations with him ensured that coordination at our provincial level was much better than in most provinces. The monthly interagency meetings, which we cochaired, often ended with a shared beer in my house.

In Siem Reap, with the Bangladeshi battalion now providing security for the elections and deploying in nineteen rather than seventeen locations, an interesting problem arose: Colonel Kamal complained to General Sanderson that he did not have enough cooks! Sanderson laughed heartily, as he thought such a complaint would come from the French, not the Bangladeshis.

I accompanied Colonel Kamal on many of his inspection tours throughout the province by helicopter. We had to deliver whole sides of lamb, imported from New Zealand, to the military outposts, as lamb curry was the Bangladeshis' main staple. As these huge carcasses were unloaded, the local population, especially hungry children, gathered and stared in amazement, but they were shooed away by gruff Bangladeshi soldiers. None of the meat was for the local population: it was to feed UNTAC. During this overnight trip, we had Bangladeshi gourmet curries for breakfast, lunch, and dinner.

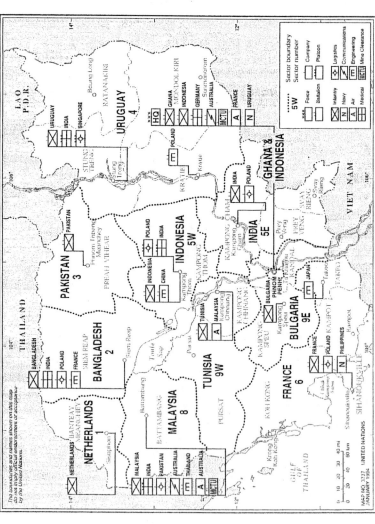

UNTAC Military Deployment for Electoral Support

Map 5.1. Military deployment for electoral support after demobilization failed. United Nations, Cartographic Section, UN Map no. 3737.

Photo 5.2.   UN Military Observer from the United States plays with baby from the Krung-Brau tribe. Credit: UN Photo 137770/John Isaac.

On another of these trips, we stayed overnight at Banteay Mean Rith, a border village controlled by General Dien Del of the KPNLF. He had a pleasant bungalow and was celebrating his son's birthday on 31 October, which coincided with Sihanouk's birthday. A band was brought in from adjacent Thailand and played late into the night, long after the boy was asleep. I was invited to share a military tent with Colonel Kamal. Just like a British officer, he had a batboy take off his boots and help him change into pajamas.

The Khmer Rouge meanwhile escalated their strategy of noncooperation by launching incessant attacks on UNTAC, SOC, and the Vietnamese, especially in Siem Reap province. Their rejection of the peace process culminated in their boycott of the elections. They subsequently returned to their jungle redoubts, which due to the United Nations' persistent latitude had grown considerably since the arrival in 1991 of the United Nations Advance Mission in Cambodia (UNAMIC), UNTAC's predecessor.[7]

A BLESSING IN DISGUISE

The same rights and obligations accorded the Khmer Rouge as the other three factions included full membership in the Supreme National Council (SNC), participation in the UNTAC elections, and inclusion in the resultant government. For the Khmer Rouge this was not a bad deal at all considering that this genocidal movement had been ousted from power in January 1979. The obligations included observing the cease-fire, allowing UNTAC to enter its territory and monitor its administrative structures and military activities, and, most importantly, disarming and demobilizing its army.

Except for repatriation of refugees under its control, the Khmer Rouge violated virtually all of its obligations. Its disregard started with many cease-fire violations as soon as UNAMIC was deployed in November 1991. Apart from declaring their zones of control off-limits to UNTAC, the Khmer Rouge failed to provide information on their troops and material, and left unmarked the minefields in their zones. Their obstructionism culminated in September 1992 when they sabotaged disarmament and demobilization.

There were two interpretations of the recalcitrant attitude that Khmer Rouge leader Pol Pot adopted after the Paris Agreements. One—advanced by Cambodia experts Roger Normand, Ben Kiernan, and others—held that Pol Pot made a serious miscalculation in signing the agreements, which he thought would give his army breathing space. According to this interpretation, Pol Pot intended to use the time bought by the agreements to let his army regroup so that the Khmer Rouge could once again take control of the country.[8] In other words, Pol Pot never had any intention of complying with the Paris Agreements.

The other interpretation was advanced in an internal briefing by UNTAC staffer Stephen Heder, an expert on the Khmer Rouge in his own right. Using copies which UNTAC had secured of Pol Pot speeches dating from February 1992, along with Khmer Rouge documents from the 1980s, Heder argued that Pol Pot had indeed supported the change from a military to a parliamentary struggle as provided by the Paris Agreements.[9] In his speeches Pot seemed sincere in wanting his cadres to implement the agreements, and he accused UNTAC of not complying with the mandate stipulated in them.[10]

The truth was probably somewhere in the middle. Although Pol Pot continued to dream of taking power again, the Khmer Rouge's loss of support (both materially and diplomatically) had weakened them considerably, and

Pol Pot knew that they never posed a real military threat to the SOC. And, pivotally, he had been told by the Chinese after the agreements were signed that the Khmer Rouge should comply with them and seek the parliamentary road to power.

If Pol Pot indeed sought to comply with the agreements, then the Khmer Rouge's subsequent rejection of the UNTAC process and criticism of UNTAC might have been genuinely sparked by perceived UNTAC partiality in implementing them. Harangues against my leadership in Siem Reap by the Khmer Rouge liaison officer, Brigadier General Nop Socheat, and radio broadcasts attacking Akashi support this interpretation.

The Khmer Rouge offered three assertions to justify their refusal to cooperate with the peace process. First, they argued that under the Paris Agreements the Supreme National Council (SNC) had not been authorized to be the sole source of power in Cambodia. Second, they held that UNTAC had failed to exercise its mandate to control SOC administration in five areas as stipulated in the agreements. Third, they claimed that Vietnamese forces were still present in Cambodia. Though their first two arguments were valid, UNTAC found no evidence of Vietnamese troops remaining in Cambodia, despite painstaking investigation.[11] As a result the United Nations repeatedly declared that it had found no foreign troops in Cambodia and asked the Khmer Rouge for proof of its allegations. None was ever offered. Vietnam reaffirmed on 10 June 1992 that it had withdrawn all of its troops, weapons, and equipment by September 1989.[12]

The Khmer Rouge deliberately confused the issue by lumping together the alleged presence of Vietnamese troops with that of Vietnamese residents and immigrants in Cambodia. It was true that many thousands of Vietnamese had illegally entered Cambodia during the UNTAC boom, including construction workers, farmers, traders, and prostitutes. It was true too that many construction workers were ex-soldiers who sought their fortune in Cambodia. But UNTAC ascertained that they could not be considered an army in disguise, for the construction boom needed skilled workers.[13]

Unfortunately, the Paris Agreements had no provisions for noncompliance with UNTAC by the Cambodian factions. They had been drawn up in good faith with the optimistic assumption that all four factions would cooperate. The architects of the agreements had assumed that the factions would consider the making of contingency plans for noncompliance an act of bad faith by the United Nations, one which could undermine the UN's precarious position in Cambodia.

Discussions at the diplomatic level at the United Nations in New York and elsewhere vacillated between imposing sanctions on the Khmer Rouge and trying gentle persuasion. In the end, the UN imposed some forms of sanctions, including a ban on supplying the Khmer Rouge petroleum products (which was difficult to enforce, as UNTAC could not enter Khmer Rouge territory). A personal appeal from Boutros Boutros-Ghali to Khmer Rouge leader Khieu Samphan went unheeded, and the United Nations' efforts simply fell on deaf ears.

Any appeasement of the Khmer Rouge elicited a strong reaction from none other than Norodom Sihanouk, the Khmer Rouge's former ally. In July 1992 he reversed course and recommended a tough policy of isolating the Khmer Rouge and excluding them from the peace process.[14] Sihanouk said that Pol Pot had not changed his colors and still sought to rule Cambodia again, sincerely believing that "in Cambodian history one never had the fortune of having a more brilliant regime."[15] In Jakarta at the Summit of the Non Aligned Countries on 3 September 1992, Sihanouk repeated his call for UNTAC to abandon the Khmer Rouge.[16]

But owing to political realities, UNTAC was not sure how far exclusion of the Khmer Rouge should go. Should the top leaders be tried in a tribunal while allowing the rank and file to participate in reconciliation? Although the Khmer Rouge's eventual withdrawal from the Paris Agreements regrettably disenfranchised many of the ordinary people who made up its rank and file, legitimizing the organization's leaders would have been a greater travesty of justice. Thus I consider their withdrawal from the peace process a blessing in disguise.

A BANQUET HOSTED BY THE KHMER ROUGE

After Sihanouk's return from the summit in Jakarta and the second SNC meeting in Siem Reap in September, he used Siem Reap as a base to make trips by helicopter to the headquarters of the three resistance factions to see how preparations for the elections were going. Contrary to some predictions, the completion of the Vietnamese troop withdrawal in 1989 had not brought a significant change in the military balance in Cambodia: SOC continued to control all provincial capitals. In late 1989 the Khmer Rouge did manage to capture the resource-rich logging center of Pailin in Battambang province, and Khmer People's National Liberation Front (KPNLF) captured Thmar Pouk and Banteay Min Rith in Banteay Meanchey province. Sihanouk now decided to visit both Pailin and Thmar Pouk, also planning trips to FUNCIN-PEC's headquarters at Phum Khu. Because he was using UNTAC helicopters, Sihanouk requested that a senior UNTAC person accompany him. I had the privilege of being his escort and the extraordinary experience of witnessing his trip to the heartland of a resistance movement that he formerly had headed as President of the CGDK. It also gave me a rare opportunity to experience life in the Khmer Rouge zone firsthand.

We boarded a small six-seater French military helicopter in Siem Reap. To avoid provoking the Khmer Rouge, the Prince and Princess Monique traveled accompanied only by three aides and myself. My wife in Siem Reap was quite worried. Indeed, during the short flight I too was apprehensive. Even though the Khmer Rouge had shed its murderous image, we were headed for their lair, and I could not drive images of their atrocities from my mind. The royal couple, however, seemed completely at ease.

We arrived at the Khmer Rouge's main stronghold of Pailin, where Sihanouk received a thunderous welcome from the populace who were brought in from surrounding villages by trucks. They were attired in colorful new dresses all imported from Thailand just eighteen kilometers away and looked relatively wealthy compared with the poverty-stricken people in Siem Reap. Encouraged by cheerleaders with bullhorns, they lined the one-kilometer-long road, from where the helicopter landed to the royal guesthouse. Sihanouk and Princess Monique walked all the way to the royal guesthouse and obviously reveled in this warm welcome.

The little children all waved the SNC flag, which I never saw anywhere else, neither in SOC territory nor in that controlled by the other factions. The flag had a light blue background on which a map of Cambodia was depicted in white, with the inscription in Khmer of the word Kampuchea. When we touched down at the headquarters of the other factions, it was like going to different countries, for we were greeted by each of their flags. But the Khmer Rouge wanted to show that they took the concept of the SNC as a ruling government seriously.

The plan was for the French helicopter to take me back from Pailin to Siem Reap, and we would pick up the Prince the next day when his visit was over. I reminded the pilot in my poor French to wait for me before I accompanied the prince into town. But the pilot left without me—he was obviously in a hurry to leave Pailin. I now had to stay in Khmer Rouge territory until another helicopter could retrieve me. I discovered that there was one UNTAC post in town (the only one in Khmer Rouge territory), staffed by British, United States, and Irish military observers along with Australian communication personnel. Its presence was not generally known. I asked the Australian communication unit to call UNTAC transportation headquarters at Battambang, but they were unable to send a helicopter. As I had no telephone, I asked Battambang to inform my wife in Siem Reap that I would be staying overnight, but they never did. I later discovered that my wife did not get a wink of sleep that night.

A group of Thai and Western journalists had come from Thailand to cover Sihanouk's visit at the invitation of the Khmer Rouge command. Since they were to return the next day for a ceremony attended by Akashi and General Sanderson, they offered me a ride back to Bangkok. The Khmer Rouge protocol officer would not agree, however. He said that I was accompanying Sihanouk and was their official guest as well, and that my trip to Thailand would be risky, as there were many "Vietnamese lurking in the jungle who could harm me." A sudden chill came over me. I decided to stay put rather than risk an ambush on the road to Thailand. Losing face is an affront for Asians, and the Khmer Rouge was no exception. The protocol officer assured me that my unplanned overnight stay had gone to the highest authorities (probably meaning Pol Pot himself) for approval, and soon I would be accompanied to my quarters.

I learned from observation that the UNTAC soldiers in Pailin were practically prisoners of the Khmer Rouge soldiers, who threatened to shoot down any helicopter that came to take them away. Only supply helicopters were not attacked. The movements of the UNTAC soldiers were restricted to a small radius. They played Ping-Pong and drank a lot of beer all day and into the night. They had Khmer servants, supplied by the Khmer Rouge, who would go to the market, and a Thai cook to cook their meals. As I spoke Thai, the cook told me that that evening there was going to be a party in Pailin. She did not know the details. I was kept in suspense until later in the evening. Because I accompanied the Prince, the protocol man would not hear of me spending the night at the UNTAC military compound. As an official guest, he argued, I would have found it uncomfortable to spend the night with Ping-Pong-playing, radio-blaring, and beer-drinking twenty-year-old soldiers. I agreed: I was quite a bit older.

I made quite a hit in one of the stores by offering SOC riel banknotes to buy a roll of film. They had never seen these banknotes and called what must have been the entire village to look and laugh at this silly man with his strange "Hun Sen money." I was lucky not to be arrested as a Hun Sen spy! The medium of exchange in Khmer Rouge territory was the Thai baht. Fortunately, I had some U.S. dollars with me, which were circulating freely in Siem Reap but not here. At a very disadvantageous rate I was able to buy film and shoot some interesting pictures, including one of young Khmer Rouge soldiers in Chinese uniforms. Unfortunately, when I went back to Siem Reap, I developed my films in the only photo shop in town, and three days later the shop owner apologetically informed me that he could not find one of the films. It had most probably been confiscated by the SOC authorities for further study.

The town of Pailin had gem mines and lumber, two lucrative sources of foreign exchange for the Khmer Rouge that funded their mischief. The Khmer Rouge in Pailin, unlike their brothers in An Long Veng in Siem Reap province, were quite wealthy, earning tens of millions of dollars from their businesses. The mines were operated by unscrupulous Thai companies and controlled ostensibly by Thai regional military commanders, whose huge trucks I saw carrying logs and dirt containing gems toward Thailand. As in Indonesia, the army operated quite independently of the civilian authorities.

These trucks traveled the same eighteen-kilometer road to Thailand on which Akashi and Sanderson had been stopped by the famous bamboo pole and the Dutch marines had been halted on the Thai side. Thus UNTAC top commanders and Dutch marines were refused entry, but Thai businesses and people had no problem traveling back and forth. It was a heavily traveled road and not at all typical of a Khmer Rouge guerrilla base. The trucks rumbled on feverishly around the clock as if gem mining and logging were going out of fashion. The Thais made foreign investment contracts with the Khmer Rouge and were probably afraid that, with peace coming, the newly elected government of Cambodia might declare contracts with the Khmer Rouge null and void. Also, there were talks in the United Nations Security Council of slapping sanctions on the uncooperative Khmer Rouge, including a ban on gems and logging exports.

I went back to the compound where Sihanouk was housed. At lunchtime I was invited to join a banquet of Khmer Rouge top brass in honor of the royal couple. Khieu Sampan, Son Sann and his wife, Dr. and Mrs. Thioun Munn,[17] and I flanked the Prince and Princess; Pol Pot was conspicuously absent. Ieng

Sary's daughter, who studied in London, prepared a sumptuous lunch: Khmer nouvelle cuisine, including fine eggshells delicately filled with fluffy dried fish, chicken curry in individual bowls for each guest with bread, and Cambodian sour soup with dried fish, all washed down with Mouton Cadet, a Sihanouk favorite.

From my vantage point at the end of the table, I was able to observe first-hand the bizarre relationship between Sihanouk and these butchers. Their strange conversation centered on the concept of the immaculate conception of the Virgin Mary and Friday the 13th as a Western superstition. The Khmer Rouge top brass continuously teased Sihanouk that he had stopped his amorous escapades after he had found Princess Monique, his sixth official wife. Sihanouk turned to me and confirmed with his inimitable cackle that Princess Monique kept him in chains and would not let him ever again look at other women. Princess Monique, who in November 1993 would be crowned Queen Norodom Monineath, had married the prince on 5 March 1955 and had faithfully stood by his side through decades of turmoil, including during his house arrest by the Khmer Rouge in Phnom Penh. It was rumored that she was his closest and most trusted counsel. Together they seemed relaxed and at ease. Their visible enjoyment of the meal posed a marked contrast to a grim photograph I once saw of them taken at another dinner held by the Khmer Rouge in Phnom Penh in 1975, in the days when they were virtually kept prisoners in the palace.

Around 4 p.m., the protocol officer announced that my overnight stay in Pailin had been approved (ostensibly by Pol Pot himself). I was escorted to the only public guesthouse in town and allotted an oversized room with three huge beds and two ceiling fans whirling away. The prince and princess, of course, stayed in the colonial mansion reserved for dignitaries, which was presumably also the house in which the Khmer Rouge top brass stayed. A large basket of fruit from Chantaburi, Thailand, famous for its fruit, was kept nice and cold next to my bed. In contrast to the conditions at Siem Reap, electricity was plentiful and on twenty-four hours a day.

That night I had dinner with Sihanouk's entourage: Madame Khek Sysoda, who was his aide de camp; Truong Mealy, who later became the ambassador to Japan; and Dr. Than Sina, who was in the SNC secretariat and later became the deputy mayor of Phnom Penh. The menu was Japanese-style sukiyaki with excellent beef imported from New Zealand by way of Bangkok.

In the late afternoon I walked along the main road of town, which was filled with cafés selling Thai-style roast chicken, Thai beer, and whiskey. The whole atmosphere was Thai, punctuated by glaring Thai disco music. At the end of the road I continued into the dark. When the protocol officer appeared from nowhere, it dawned on me that I was under twenty-four-hour surveillance. He immediately admonished me, saying that it was dangerous to stray into the darkness, as I could get killed by the proverbial Vietnamese lurking everywhere (meaning in SOC territory). Back at the main plaza, the festive activities, including families taking pictures and laughing merrily in a park in front of the prince's guesthouse, went on until 2 a.m. Truong Mealy and Tan Sina joined me in the park. In all likelihood, the people that day had been ordered to show a happy and peaceful face for the king.

The British military observers in town said that this relaxed party was unusual, although the Thai-style chicken with blaring music and whiskey and beer were normal. That evening I met many Thai white-collar personnel and workers and even some girls from Myanmar who had come to work in the local electric company, attracted by the high wages. Imagine that: migrant workers flocking to Khmer Rouge territory in search of better wages!

While lying awake at night and munching on the lavish fruits courtesy of the Khmer Rouge, I started thinking about the whole Khmer Rouge issue. My immediate impression was that the Khmer Rouge territory was better organized and its soldiers better disciplined than SOC soldiers in Siem Reap. This was, of course, relatively prosperous territory, where rich resources and the porous Thai border had raised the standard of living higher than in Siem Reap. My visit confirmed that the civilian population under the Khmer Rouge was more comfortable than civilians in adjacent SOC territories, which suffered from a decade of unjust sanctions imposed by the United Nations. These people had no intention of escaping to SOC territory. Even the Khmer Rouge soldiers, who were given every chance to defect, refused to go. The rank-and-file Khmer Rouge deserved to be incorporated into the new Cambodia and should have been given a chance to participate in the elections. Their leaders, however, continued to obstruct all aspects of the Paris Agreements. In the end, the zone continued to be isolated.

The next day at 9 a.m., there was a mass rally addressed by Sihanouk and Khieu Samphan. Yasushi Akashi, General Sanderson, and a few more UNTAC dignitaries from Phnom Penh showed up in a helicopter but left that same evening. The contingent of journalists from Bangkok was back, and they were happily surprised to see me alive and well, what with all the stories of Khmer Rouge atrocities still circulating.

The reception for Akashi was cold and there were no cheering people. This was no surprise, given the anti-Akashi and anti-UNTAC propaganda barrage launched by Khmer Rouge radio. Again the podium was bedecked with SNC flags, and the people all waved small ones.

A group of Buddhist monks opened the rally with their chants to demonstrate that religion was no longer prohibited in the Khmer Rouge zone. Sihanouk told the crowd how happy he was to be in Pailin where people were joyful and relatively prosperous. He said that the previous night at midnight he had gone out onto the balcony of his room and seen people in the plaza in front of his guesthouse still taking pictures with their families and laughing. The gist of Samphan's speech was that the Khmer Rouge was paying homage to the prince. He emphasized in particular the forthcoming seventieth birthday of Sihanouk on 31 October.

In the afternoon the French helicopter came to take us away. The Khmer Rouge obviously wanted to show that they were completely reformed and were taking good care of their territory and people.

Sihanouk continued his survey by visiting the headquarters of the other two factions, FUNCINPEC and KPNLF. The next day our helicopter took a day trip to Phum Ku in Oddar Meanchey in the northern part of Siem Reap province, headquarters of FUNCINPEC. We were welcomed by Sihanouk's son, Prince Ranariddh, and his wife, Princess Marie, descendants of the Chams (Cambodian Moslems), and by the FUNCINPEC flag, which had been the flag of Cambodia during the 1960s and would later become the flag of the Royal Government again in 1993. We were received in a much more subdued manner by the people and the sophisticated Royalists, with a guard of honor and an official marching band.

Lunch was at the residence of Prince Ranariddh and Princess Marie. I did not recognize the wine, but it was not Mouton Cadet. Although Sihanouk had become the neutral head of SNC, in his rally in Phum Ku he emphasized that FUNCINPEC and ANKI (its armed wing) had "adhered to a correct policy, now and in the future," and were "firmly united and strong." Later in his election campaign speeches, Prince Ranariddh would unfairly identify FUNCINPEC and himself closely with Sihanouk. It was a ploy, as Sihanouk was supposed to be neutral, but it appeared to be very effective in handing the electoral victory to FUNCINPEC. Ranariddh also implied that the SOC did not fully support Sihanouk, which was untrue.[18]

Finally Sihanouk visited Thmar Pouk and Banteay Min Rith, respectively the civilian and military capitals of the KPNLF. The two wings had split, with Son Sann heading the civilian wing and General Sak Sudsakorn the military wing. Sihanouk drove in a motorcade from Thmar Pouk to Banteay Min Rith, so I was not asked to come along.

Although the Khmer Rouge controlled some territories in between the two towns, they did not bother the prince's motorcade. The flag of the KPNLF was evident everywhere throughout the region. Thmar Pouk, with a population of seventy-eight thousand, suffered a high incidence of serious crime; it was inhabited by many returnees from the refugee camps in Thailand. But the Khmer Rouge lived quite peacefully next to the KPNLF. This was probably the only region where Australian UNTAC CivPol managed to convince Khmer Rouge and KPNLF police to sit together at a training course for police.

This trip convinced me even more that, in reality, the only two viable armies confronting each other were the SOC's CPAF and the National Army of Democratic Kampuchea (NADK) of the Khmer Rouge. The other two factions, FUNCINPEC and KPNLF, had token armies in their respective bits and pieces of land; they were moving in and out of border refugee camps in Thailand while occasionally blowing up bridges or government outposts with little military or political consequence. With noncooperation from the Khmer Rouge, demobilization was really aimed at the CPAF.

HOW DID THE CAMBODIANS VIEW THE KHMER ROUGE?

The trip with Sihanouk to Pailin had a big influence on my views of the Khmer Rouge. But what was the attitude of ordinary Cambodians toward them? The Cambodian rank and file never use the term "Khmer Rouge," which was coined by Sihanouk and later used in speeches by leaders such as Hun Sen. The common people still refer to the Khmer Rouge regime as "Pol Pot," as if Pol Pot himself was personally responsible for all their woes. This belief was undoubtedly fostered by the SOC, whose manifesto in the jungle had hailed the liberation of Cambodia by the Khmer Rouge in 1975, before betrayal by the Pol Pot/Ieng Sary clique.

Many Cambodians I spoke with wanted the Khmer Rouge to be put on trial. Not for revenge, but for justice for the victims and to deter future leaders from repeating such brutal acts. The question of "why" haunted them: how could the Khmer Rouge have committed massacres against their own people? In the United Nations–imposed "safe area" of the SOC regime, most expressed surprise that the UN had seated the Khmer Rouge as the legitimate representative of Cambodia instead of placing them before a criminal tribunal. They were equally stunned that after fighting the SOC the Khmer Rouge was allowed to participate in the SNC in Phnom Penh.

And although no Khmer Rouge flag fluttered over the house of the liaison officers in Siem Reap, as it had once flown above the Manhattan and Bangkok skylines, people still expressed shock that Khmer Rouge liaison officers resided in the provincial capital in a government-provided home. I tried to explain as best I could that the politics playing out in New York shaped events in Siem Reap. But with no television and international news limited by the government-controlled radio, the compromises of New York seemed worlds away. The people with whom I spoke were straightforward: the Khmer Rouge should be tried.

Most of our interpreters held slightly different views of the Khmer Rouge. They were not adamant about trials. They were chiefly former refugees in Thailand, because the pre-1989 ban on teaching foreign languages other than Vietnamese and Russian meant there were few English-speaking people in the SOC-controlled territory. The refugees, including our interpreters, were mostly sympathetic to the noncommunist resistance movements FUNCIN-PEC and KPNLF. While they abhorred the Khmer Rouge, many were critical of the SOC as well, claiming that it was totalitarian and controlled by Vietnamese advisers.

Phat, my landlady's daughter, along with my interpreters and all the people working with UNTAC and the local SOC civil service, belonged to the middle class who had suffered most under the Khmer Rouge. During the Khmer Rouge rule, they had been labeled *neak thmei* (new people) and driven from their city homes to live in the villages occupied by the *neak moultanh* (base people), the poorest among the poor, who became their masters. The "new people" had to beg the "base people" to build simple lean-tos for shelter during rains before they could build their own little shacks. They hated the Khmer Rouge.

The Khmer Rouge was initially popular among the "base people," the poor peasants who formed a majority of the country's population. The genocide of

1975–1979 had mainly targeted the new people, middle-class urban residents, and later during Pol Pot's paranoid purges, the Khmer Rouge's own cadres, especially in the east zone. The Khmer Rouge *yothea*, or soldiers, were teenagers recruited from among the "base people" and indoctrinated to be loyal only to *Angkar*, the organization. They enjoyed their power over life and death. Indeed, it was common for children to turn in their parents, whom they considered the enemy, to *Angkar* for punishment, including death for small infractions.

Under UNTAC's stewardship the pro-peasant attitude of the Khmer Rouge continued as they stayed close to their peasant support base. They gave land to the peasants and helped farmers. The country was dotted with numerous Khmer Rouge bases, mostly in forested areas, which continued to cause problems for UNTAC and SOC.

NOTES

1. Paris Agreements, Annex 2, Article V, paragraph 1.

2. Personal notes.

3. Dr. D. C. I. Schoonoord, *The Koningklijke Marine in Actie voor de Verenigde Naties: Mariniers in Cambodia, 1992–1993*, The Hague: Ministerie van Defensie, 1993.

4. United Nations document S/24090, *Special Report of the Secretary-General on UNTAC and Phase II of the Cease Fire*, 12 June 1992, 3.

5. Source: United Nations document S/24578, *Second Progress Report of the Secretary-General on UNTAC*, 21 September 1992.

6. According to the original UNTAC plan, a maximum of twelve infantry battalions would be deployed to engage in the active phase of demobilization and cantonment, to begin in June 1992. If all had gone well, this would have been reduced to six battalions for the electoral phase and three for the post-electoral phase. UNTAC Handbook, UN document S/23613, 26 February 1992. See also Annex tables 2 and 3.

7. United Nations official maps. See Ben Kiernan, *Genocide and Democracy in Cambodia*, 214–15.

8. Allegedly in 1988 Pol Pot in secret speeches revealed plans to "delay the elections" until Khmer Rouge forces could "control all the country," while his officials would "lead the balloting work." Roger Normand obtained copies of these secret speeches from defecting Khmer Rouge commanders in 1990. Ben Kiernan, "The Inclusion of the Khmer Rouge in the Cambodian Peace Process: Causes and Consequences," in

Kiernan, ed., *Genocide and Democracy in Cambodia*, New Haven: Yale University Southeast Asia Studies, 203, quoting Roger Normand, fieldwork editor of the *Harvard Human Rights Journal*. See also Normand, "The Teachings of Chairman Pot," *Nation*, 3 September 1990.

9. Policy paper of the National Army of Democratic Cambodia (Khmer Rouge), *Minutes on Clarification of Certain Principled Views to Act as the Basis of Our Views and Stance*, 6 February 1992.

10. See Stephen Heder and Judy Ledgewood, eds., *Propaganda, Politics and Violence in Cambodia: Democratic Transition under United Nations Peacekeeping*, New York: M. E. Sharpe, 1996, 74. Heder obtained further evidence in support of this view when he interviewed a number of self-demobilized soldiers of the Khmer Rouge.

11. Inter alia, UNTAC deployed checkpoints along the borders of Vietnam, Laos, and Thailand to verify the nonpresence and nonreturn of foreign forces and deployed Strategic Investigation Teams (SITs) to investigate allegations of the presence of foreign forces. Akashi presented the plan for the SITs to the SNC on 20 October 1992. UNTAC also checked personnel lists of Phnom Penh government ministries to determine whether any Vietnamese advisers remained.

12. UN document S/24982, Note verbale dated 10 June 1992 from Vietnam transmitting two notes dated 30 May 1992 sent to UNTAC by the Ministry of Foreign Affairs of Vietnam.

13. Yet the staunchly anti-Vietnamese KPNLF leaders, Son Sann and Ieng Mouly, echoed the Khmer Rouge in claiming that Vietnamese troops continued to be present disguised as civilians.

14. Nayan Chanda, " 'Isolate Khmer Rouge' Sihanouk Chides UNTAC for Feeble Response," *Far Eastern Economic Review*, 30 July 1992, 18.

15. Chanda, "Isolate Khmer Rouge."

16. *New York Times*, 3 September 1992.

17. A medical doctor, Thiounn Munn was one of four Thiounn brothers, all intellectual supporters of the Khmer Rouge. Another brother, as we have seen, is Thiounn Prasith, who was the Khmer Rouge ambassador in the United Nations in New York during the 1980s.

18. UNTAC Information/Education Division, FUNCINPEC broadcast news, 16–30 September 1992.

The Rocky Road to Elections

ONLY "CAMBODIANS" CAN VOTE

Despite the setbacks faced by UNTAC in its attempt to create a neutral political environment, however, and despite deteriorating security with the failure of demobilization, UNTAC was determined to go ahead with the elections—with or without the Khmer Rouge. Unlike UNTAC's haphazard activities in the field of civil administration, preparations for the elections were systematic and started as early as October 1991. The electoral law was promulgated by Akashi on 12 August 1992.[1]

UNTAC's mandate on the elections was straightforward: it was the only authority authorized to conduct all aspects of the elections, including the legal ones. This was unprecedented in the history of United Nations peacekeeping operations. Not even in Namibia, where the United Nations was heavily involved, did it get such sweeping powers.

After sabotaging demobilization, the Khmer Rouge took advantage of their continuous coddling by the UN to employ a variety of tactics to destabilize the country. As members of the Supreme National Council (SNC), they were able to disrupt the SNC in various ways, rendering it practically powerless. The most blatant way was to attempt to introduce selective racism into the electoral law, which delayed its adoption and had other harmful consequences.

While Akashi possessed total authority to promulgate the law, he wanted to consult the Cambodian factions as much as possible. The main problem was the insistence of the Khmer Rouge and other resistance factions that ethnic Vietnamese—including those who had lived in Cambodia for generations—should be excluded from the electorate. The representatives of the factions in the SNC deliberately did not talk of a Khmer race. Rather, they insisted that only "Cambodians" could vote. The Khmer race is the largest ethnic group in Cambodia; it constitutes 90 percent of the population and speaks Khmer. If the representatives had used the term "Khmer race," they would have been excluding from the electorate the other minorities, the Chinese and Cham, too.[2] It was politically motivated racism.

Naturally, UNTAC opposed it. But to appease the resistance factions, who wanted an ethnically defined electorate, Article 3 of the electoral law emphasized "Cambodianness" in the elections and defined "Cambodian persons" as follows: (1) a person born in Cambodia, at least one of whose parents was born in Cambodia, or (2) a person, wherever born, at least one of whose parents is or was a Cambodian person within the meaning of stipulation 1.[3]

A HORRIBLE ECHO OF THE PAST

On 10 March 1993, the Khmer Rouge harked back to its bloody past by attacking the Vietnamese floating village Chong Kneas on the banks of the Tonle Sap Lake in Siem Reap province. The raid was the single bloodiest incident during UNTAC's tenure. The attackers did not discriminate along any line other than race: 124 ethnic Vietnamese whose families had lived in Cambodia for generations were killed.[4]

It is sad to recount that we in Siem Reap had been forewarned of the Chong Kneas attack more than a month before it took place. Our British naval military observers did a good job of detecting and probably delaying the planned massacre. On 9 February, I had joined a reconnaissance trip to a Khmer village near Chong Kneas. Traveling in two very rapid French helicopters designed for flying low over troubled areas, we landed in the village and through our interpreters started to interview the villagers. They said that the Khmer Rouge had come to the village a few days previously and held a town meeting. The Khmer Rouge had said that they were going to attack the Vietnamese spies and murderers in nearby Chong Kneas. The Khmer Rouge commonly issued such forewarnings before their attacks.

Omens had continued to appear up until the day before the massacre. As if preparing the Cambodian people for the attack, the Khmer Rouge accused the

Vietnamese in the Tonle Sap district of organizing into Vietnamese communist party cells.

Yet, in spite of all these forewarnings, neither SOC nor UNTAC were prepared. SOC was fully alerted but did not interfere, as the government was, after all, in "cease-fire mode." Bangbatt was already overstretched in their new task of defending UNTAC electoral positions, and they did not consider it within UNTAC's mandate to defend the Vietnamese, or local Cambodians for that matter. Thus Bangbatt did not have any posts in the area of the attack, and the poor Vietnamese villagers were left completely defenseless. We reported our findings to Phnom Penh, but we were told that we could not do anything. John Sanderson, the force commander, explained weakly to journalists in Siem Reap two days after the attack that "we are here on a peace-keeping . . . not internal security mission."[5] It was enormously frustrating to see such an attack unfolding but not be able to do anything about it.

Neither Sihanouk nor UNTAC officials were willing to respond to the Chong Kneas massacre. The prince stated that he could no longer "be responsible" for the security of Vietnamese civilians in Cambodia and encouraged them to return to Vietnam. FUNCINPEC just kept silent. UNTAC was also mostly silent, except for feeble excuses that we were not responsible for the security of the country. John Sanderson was quite emphatic: "Brute force is not my interpretation of peacekeeping."[6]

Despite opposing overt selective racism, UNTAC's attitude toward the Vietnamese was ambivalent at best. The Paris Agreements made no mention of the ethnic Vietnamese question. Some powerful UNTAC officials felt that we should stay out of what was perceived as an internal matter. But UNTAC had assumed responsibility for all aspects of the elections. When it came to making crucial decisions, UNTAC chose to bury its head in the sand. Despite all that the Khmer Rouge had done to thwart us, UNTAC still hoped that they would cooperate. To appear to help the ethnic Vietnamese, the thinking went at senior levels, would jeopardize the chances of Khmer Rouge participation in elections.[7] The ethnic Vietnamese were to be sacrificed—a small wrong for a greater good. The dead were to pay the price for UNTAC's flawed thinking.

The head of UNTAC's Human Rights component supplied the sole exception to this ostrichlike policy. New Zealander Dennis McNamara considered the plight of the Vietnamese to be within UNTAC's ambit. Since neither UNTAC nor CPAF/SOC would protect them, we accompanied Dennis on visits to

Chong Kneas after the massacre to arrange for the evacuation of ethnic Vietnamese from the entire area. The majority subsequently fled farther toward the Vietnamese border, where they did not participate in the elections. By the end of April 1993, more than twenty-one thousand ethnic Vietnamese, many of them second- and third-generation residents of Cambodia, had fled their homes.[8] Thus, what the Khmer Rouge could not do through the SNC they had accomplished through their bloody attack at Chong Kneas. If the attack was meant to scare these hapless people into fleeing the country rather than voting, to a large extent it succeeded.

VIOLENCE LEADING UP TO THE ELECTIONS

While UNTAC continued to prepare for the elections, including through voter registration, registration of political parties, and political campaigning, violence escalated everywhere. According to UNTAC figures, between the beginning of April and the middle of May, 100 Cambodians were killed and 179 wounded. Casualties included members of all four factions as well as members of UNTAC itself.[9]

The Khmer Rouge effectively ignored the warnings of the Security Council and stepped up its aggression toward UNTAC in the hope of derailing the elections and scaring, if not shooting, UNTAC out of Cambodia. Its tactics included direct attacks and taking UNTAC officials hostage. The Khmer Rouge also continued to violate the cease-fire by attacking SOC positions. Things came to a head when the Khmer Rouge closed their office in Phnom Penh on 13 April 1993. Khieu Samphan, the Khmer Rouge representative in SNC, complained to Sihanouk that "we have seen that we do not have enough security to continue our work with the SNC in Phnom Penh."[10] Though the Khmer Rouge called the withdrawal temporary, they completely abandoned their compound. We feared that this might be the prelude to fierce attacks. Our fear was realized in Siem Reap province, which carried the brunt of increasingly violent Khmer Rouge tactics.

Siem Reap continued to hold the dubious distinction of being the main trouble spot. Other provincial "shadow governors" were not so "lucky" as to be stationed in so lively a sector and were often envious of my position. Siem Reap had earned notorious distinction in many respects: it experienced the largest massacre of ethnic Vietnamese; it suffered the most attacks from Khmer Rouge and unidentified forces; it was the first province in which UNTAC officials were killed in a Khmer Rouge attack—the list could go on.

Photo 6.1. Khmer Rouge soldier in a zone controlled by the faction. Credit: UN Photo 137765/J. Bleibtreu.

The Khmer Rouge was not the only culprit in the escalating violence. A great deal of the violence was related to the forthcoming election and involved other factions. The means employed were not subtle. Harassment of political opponents included verbal threats and petty vandalism of political posters. In Siem Reap, newly established offices of resistance political parties, approved by me as provincial director, were bombed, workers were attacked, and sometimes even party leaders were kidnapped.

There were also nonpolitical reasons for the violence against UNTAC. These included Cambodian anger and accusations that UNTAC personnel seduced Cambodian women and behaved disrespectfully toward local culture and customs. Cambodians also complained of the blatancy with which UNTACists flaunted their wealth in an atmosphere of extreme poverty. Wealth and perceived disrespect provoked a lot of attacks on UNTAC premises, sometimes simply to steal. In the absence of banks, UNTACists in Siem Reap kept large amounts of cash at home. They also had valuable personal items, as their fabulous daily allowance enabled them to purchase jewelry in Bangkok and duty-free stereo sets in Singapore. We traveled for free on UNTAC flights to these places for shopping and rest and recreation. We did not worry about customs since Pochentong airport was controlled by UNTAC.

Many UNTACists, regardless of nationality, did look down on Cambodians. A number of UNTAC troops, police, and civilians were guilty of sexual harassment, weapons smuggling, and causing numerous Cambodian fatalities through reckless driving. In Siem Reap, a ghastly example close to home illustrated this insensitivity toward the Cambodian population. Driving from a farewell party for a departing UNTAC police contingent at Puok District on 26 January 1993, an Indian civil police officer, too inebriated to drive on the right side of the road, hit and killed a Cambodian cyclist. His only punishment was transfer to another province. This problem of UN peacekeepers' immunity would continue to plague UN peacekeeping operations in the future.

Naturally, such incidents angered the Cambodians and poisoned the atmosphere, and the Khmer Rouge and others took revenge in whatever ways they could. A striking example was the point-blank murder of Bulgarian officers in Kompong Speu by Khmer Rouge officers during a dinner hosted by the officers. The killings were allegedly in retaliation for several incidents of sexual harassment and humiliation perpetrated by the Bulgarians. It was general knowledge that the first Bulgarian battalion sent to Cambodia had been recruited from ex-criminals and was causing the largest number of incidents.[11]

Needless to say, I spent a great deal of time dealing with security problems. I relied heavily on cooperation from Colonel Kamal of Bangbatt, Irish Superintendent Dowling (Head of of CivPol), and U.S. Colonel Jay Carter, later replaced by U.S. Colonel O'Toole, who headed the military observers group in the province. Coordination for security purposes had an entirely different meaning to us than it did to staffers in Phnom Penh and in other more peaceful provinces.

We were there before the boom in mobile phones that took Cambodia and Southeast Asia as a whole by storm a few years later. We were equipped with a $750 two-way transmitter with a limited range of fifty kilometers, just enough to cover the troublesome Angkor Chum district. Each of us on the international staff was given a call sign based on the international alphabet for two-way communications. My call sign was P9, pronounced Papa Niner in universally accepted lingo for military communications. We operated on a certain frequency and could only hear the chatter on that frequency. The Bangladesh battalion brought their own communications system and communicated to each other in Bengali.

My handheld transmitter and Papa Niner call sign became regular parts of my life. Although I did not know the difference between an AK-47 and an RPG (rocket-propelled grenade) before I came to Cambodia, these items became old hat too, as every day uniformed soldiers and unidentified individuals passed by my house and office carrying their prized possessions, like others would carry their backpacks.

Weapons were everywhere. The main arteries of the province were regularly mined. The war between the Cambodian People's Armed Forces (CPAF) and the Khmer Rouge continued incessantly, with the latter making inroads toward Siem Reap. Strategic villages and hamlets changed hands several times. All district capitals except Kralanh, Chongkal, and the capital city were now within mortar or rocket range of the Khmer Rouge. There was even an attack on an UNTAC helicopter in Varin, which had to make a forced landing. The Aeroflot pilot had made the mistake of trying to land in Khmer Rouge territory instead of in an SOC-controlled portion of Varin.

With his new mandate of protecting UNTAC's personnel as they prepared for the elections, Colonel Kamal often worked until 2 or 3 a.m., conscientiously trying to draw up the best plans. The ambush and murder of Nakata

Atsuhito, a Japanese District Electoral Supervisor (DES), and his interpreter, Lay Sok Pheap, in April 1993 by unknown perpetrators in neighboring Kompong Tom province heightened concern over security measures in Siem Reap. The DESs were UN volunteers who played a major role in the elections. The murders were first attributed to the Khmer Rouge, but it was later determined that an angry young man who had been refused employment in UNTAC by Atsuhito was the culprit. In response to the killings, about sixty DESs decided to leave the country, but in Siem Reap confidence in Bangbatt's security provisions was fairly high and only fifteen of the forty-five DESs in the province left before the elections.

The military and police components of UNTAC completely revamped security and polling stations in response to the escalating violence. The new procedures included provisions for UNTAC personnel in the districts to travel with armed escorts or in convoys, and to stay at night in guarded Bangbatt compounds, which were located in twelve of the fourteen districts. These compounds had bunkers and gun positions and were surrounded by a double fence. They had an "open fire" policy: unauthorized people were told that if they came within the fence they would be shot. If conditions worsened further, UNTAC civilian personnel, including me, were to move our offices and sleeping quarters into the military compounds. Colonel Kamal had frequently asked me to move into air-conditioned quarters in his compound, but I declined, preferring to stay in my own residence, though I never declined offers of delicious Bangladeshi food.

During the tumultuous period between April and the elections in 1993, I was only evacuated for one night to my office compound, when Siem Reap town was attacked. My continuous presence in the house was appreciated by my Cambodian landlady and, indeed, by the entire population, who watched my every move. It added to the sense of confidence in many UNTACists, some of whom continued to be badly shaken by the often-violent attacks. In fact, almost nightly we heard the incessant sounds of incoming and outgoing artillery fire. One night it was very quiet and I could not sleep—I had grown so used to counting explosions rather than sheep.

Colonel Kamal and I observed the electoral preparations at the district level, where the tension was quite high in the run-up to the elections. Many young UN volunteers, including Carlo Accame and his partner, Lorella D'Apporto, from Italy decided to stay nevertheless.

Siem Reap province witnessed a number of spectacular attacks against UN-TAC, most but not all of which were attributed to the Khmer Rouge. At nine one morning that November, my transmitters told me that an UNTAC pick-up truck had struck a powerful antitank mine thirty kilometers outside Angkor Chum on the road to Siem Reap. Two Tunisian civil police were wounded. An hour later, radio chatter indicated that another truck had hit a mine nearby. This time two Indonesians were hurt; one, Major Hendro, was injured badly. The previous week Hendro had dined in my house in Siem Reap. He had requested and received a transfer to Siem Reap from Takeo province, where nothing ever happened. Prior to the mine incident, the adventuresome Hendro had been in the helicopter attacked near Varin.

At UNTAC's Indian hospital in Siem Reap, the doctors recommended immediate amputation for Major Hendro. I asked him in Indonesian if he wanted the amputation. "No, no amputation!" he screamed. In that case, the Indian doctors said, I could transport him to Phnom Penh, but they emphasized that I would be responsible should he die on the helicopter. An Indian doctor and I then accompanied Hendro and one of the Tunisians who was also seriously wounded to Phnom Penh. That one-hour helicopter ride was one of the most anxious hours in my life. We observed the tremendous loss of blood by the two wounded policemen with horror. After we arrived at the German UNTAC hospital in Phnom Penh, which was much bigger and better equipped than Siem Reap's hospital, the Germans sent Hendro on another one-hour flight to Bangkok, where the hospitals met international standards. Unfortunately, one of Hendro's legs did have to be amputated.

In late December 1992, heavy shelling over Christmas and New Year's Eve forced UNTAC's units to abandon Svay Leu district, adjacent to the Khmer Rouge stronghold of An Long Veng. It was the first major evacuation of UNTAC units due to a direct attack by Khmer Rouge forces. Then, on 12 January 1993, heavy shelling and small-arms fire at Angkron in Siem Reap district, twenty-five kilometers east of Siem Reap town, claimed the lives of two UNTAC electoral employees. These were the first deaths of UNTAC personnel from a direct attack. The civilian casualties included a five-year-old girl.

The next day, Colonel Kamal and I went with the liaison officers of the three resistance forces from Phnom Penh to the scene of the attack. It was clear that UNTAC had been the target. All three liaison officers denied being involved. But General Nop Socheat of the Khmer Rouge, while denying

Khmer Rouge involvement, said that "the people"—the Khmer Rouge always spoke as representatives of "the people"—were angry because of the immoral behavior both of UNTAC officers and the Cambodian women working for UNTAC. He alleged that UNTAC civil police slept with female electoral workers. That was why "the people" had shot two such women dead, he said.

The attack on Angkron was the harbinger of a new level of violence. A major attack on Siem Reap town by the Khmer Rouge erupted on 3 May. It was the largest Khmer Rouge attack during the entire UNTAC period and was intended to destabilize Cambodia and stop the elections. We had known it was coming. Khmer Rouge troops had been taking up positions around the city for many months. And yet, when it finally came, it was a very unpleasant surprise.

The attack came between 4 and 5 a.m. when four large groups of Khmer Rouge soldiers advanced into the town. They totaled three hundred to four hundred men. They unleashed rocket launchers, machine guns, grenades, and, of course, AK-47s. The attack lasted about six hours, until around 11 a.m., when the last group finally withdrew.

Listening to the UN military observers (UNMOs) chatter on my transmitter, it was clear that they were puzzled about two things. In spite of the heavy shelling for six hours, there was little damage done or heavy casualties. Even more puzzling, when CPAF reinforcements came from the east, they allowed the Khmer Rouge troops to leave the city through a southern corridor. Perhaps they did so to avoid casualties.

Although the military observers advised me to stay home during the attack, I drove my land cruiser as dawn emerged about 5:30 a.m. toward my office in the provincial headquarters. When I reached the bridge at the end of my road, I was stopped by armed men in civilian clothes. My heart was pounding. Could they be Khmer Rouge? After all, in physical appearance the Khmer Rouge were identical to all other Cambodians. As far as uniforms were concerned, they wore anything they wanted. But I suddenly recognized one of them as an SOC policeman, and he smiled and waved me on. I then went to the only phone in town that provided long-distance services, located near my office in the Australian communications unit, and called my wife in Stamford, Connecticut, about the attack.[12] As I was speaking to my wife, an Australian soldier shouted at me to lie down: I was exposed to attack.

After a radio conference call among senior staff, we decided, in conformity with United Nations standard operating procedures during attacks, to temporarily evacuate our prefab offices. They were in the middle of the war zone in the city. We would go to the heavily protected Bangbatt garrison away from the fighting. Colonel Kamal and his two senior deputies were in Phnom Penh on official business. Some civilians, journalists, and tourists later criticized our evacuation; they had been caught in the battle and did not know where they should go. They claimed we had relinquished our responsibility.

To allay their fears, the able UNMOs, the French foreign legionnaires, and CivPol patrolled the town searching for stray foreign civilians as well as UN-TAC personnel stranded in their homes. Of course, if the main objective of the attack had been to create panic and fear, the attackers had been extremely successful. The attack killed tourism in one fell swoop. Ten hotels were now empty. Thus ended the short-lived tourist boom in Siem Reap.

On Sunday, 16 May, the troubled district of Angkor Chum was attacked again. Once more faced with matters of life and death, Commander Kamal and I had to decide whether to evacuate the district capital. When the CPAF promised reinforcements, we decided not to evacuate. The two blonde Scandinavian DESs stationed there, Kathrin and Guri, declined an offer of evacuation out of solidarity with the military units. The next morning at 6 a.m., I raised the call signs of Kathrin and Guri on my transmitter. Nobody answered. Fearing the worst, I kept repeating the calls. Still there was no response. Finally, at 7 a.m., they replied, sleepily scolding me for waking them up: they had not gone to bed until 2 a.m. But I had never felt so relieved in my life.

The raiders never bothered Kathrin and Guri, even though the two women lived in a remote area and the attack was definitely directed against UNTAC. Instead, the attackers ransacked and looted the civil police houses belonging to Nepalese CivPol. The Nepalese were targeted because they allegedly hosted pornographic shows with videos they imported from Bangkok while trying to seduce local girls by flashing their dollar bills. In contrast, Kathrin and Guri, who were low-paid UN volunteers, rented a small, modest, Cambodian-style wooden house and just did their work. Whoever attacked UNTAC that night knew and respected the Scandinavian women. Once again morality had come into play.

According to Colonel Kamal, a ballistic survey of the bullets used in the attack indicated that it could have come from the CPAF garrison rather than the more remote Khmer Rouge location. The Phnom Penh team who came to investigate the attack shrugged off his assessment, however, arguing that we had enough trouble with the Khmer Rouge and should not also provoke the CPAF and SOC! So it will forever remain a mystery who had attacked UNTAC's position.

WHO WAS RESPONSIBLE FOR SECURITY?

The attacks on Angkor Chum, Siem Reap, and the ethnic Vietnamese village of Chong Kneas revealed another basic flaw in the Paris Agreements. Visiting Siem Reap after one of the major Khmer Rouge attacks, the SOC Defense Minister Tea Banh reminded me that the agreements did not provide for protection of UNTAC positions by CPAF. He was right. After all, technically all four Cambodian armies, including CPAF, were supposed to be in cease-fire mode.

So the important unanswered question, which would surface again and again, for instance in East Timor in 1999 was: who was responsible for security in the country during peacekeeping operations? Most critics of UNTAC argue that the agreements had not assigned responsibility for security and defense in the case of serious attacks by the Khmer Rouge or others against civilians and UNTAC. I would, however, go one step further. The flaw is not the absence of such a provision but the concept of demobilization itself. If demobilization had succeeded, who was to provide security up to and through the elections? Certainly the sixteen thousand five hundred peacekeeping troops were totally inadequate for defending the entire county from the Khmer Rouge. Nor was it their duty under the Paris Agreements, which did not address this problem.

The assumption of the Paris Agreements was that the four armies had the political will to embark upon all aspects of the peace process. The sequence of demobilization followed by elections had indeed been successfully applied, among other places, in Mozambique. But, of course, RENAMO, the resistance in Mozambique, was not the Khmer Rouge. Assuming that the Khmer Rouge would cooperate was a mistake. Because the UN had continued to recognize the CGDK as the legitimate government of the country throughout the 1980s, we were all lulled into thinking that, in gratitude, the Khmer Rouge would shed its spots, repent its sins, and behave like nice boys in the peace process.

Since this did not occur, it stands to reason that we would have faced even more serious problems if demobilization had succeeded and the other factions, especially CPAF, had turned in their weapons. If I saw CPAF handing in rusty weapons to Bangbatt while keeping the best ones for a rainy day, I thought to myself, what would have prevented the Khmer Rouge, which banned UNTAC from entering their jungle redoubts, from hiding huge arsenals? What was important was not the process, but the political will of the factions, all four of them. And the Khmer Rouge obviously lacked the political will.

This flaw in the Paris Agreements was indirectly addressed much later by Hun Sen at a conference in Phnom Penh celebrating the tenth anniversary of the agreements. I represented the United Nations at the conference. Hun Sen recalled that Akashi had asked him during the lead-up to the elections to quell the Khmer Rouge's onslaught. But, he had responded, the CPAF was supposed to be in a cease-fire mode. Hun Sen also recalled that in the volatile preelection period, he had asked for a change in policy—in essence, for UNTAC to assume the Chapter VII function of peace enforcement—but that UNTAC had turned a deaf ear to his proposals. Of course, UNTAC would have had to go to the Security Council for that policy change, and Akashi and Sanderson had already rejected this proposal by the French General Lorridon. When the Khmer Rouge were about to attack Siem Reap in 1992–1993, Hun Sen continued, Akashi had asked the SOC to protect Siem Reap, even though the cease-fire agreement only called for warding off attacks in self-defense.[13] In retrospect, I consider the failure of demobilization a blessing in disguise, as I got protected by CPAF forces who chased out the Khmer Rouge when they attacked Siem Reap town in May 1993.

NOTES

1. Michael Malley, "Reflections on the Electoral Process in Cambodia," in Hugh Smith, ed., *International Peace Keeping: Building on the Cambodian Experience*, Canberra: Australian Defense Studies Center, 1994. The continuity of staffing throughout the electoral process ensured the smooth working of this component.

2. The ethnic Chinese were also persecuted during the Khmer Rouge period as part of the class struggle. But they were not persecuted on the basis of race because of the close ties between the Khmer Rouge and China. Unlike in Indonesia, in Cambodia the Chinese are fully assimilated and many high-ranking officials today are ethnic Chinese. The Cham are descendants from refugees from the old Champak kingdom in Vietnam, which was overrun by the Vietnamese. The Cham are Muslims and were also persecuted by the Khmer Rouge; many were forced to assimilate. They speak a Malayo-Polynesian language.

3. United Nations, *Electoral Law of Cambodia*, UNTAC, August 1992.

4. UNTAC internal document.

5. "UNMOs Powerless to Protect Ethnic Vietnamese," *Phnom Penh Post*, 26 March–8 April 1993. UNTAC's mandate was subject to interpretation, especially since we had responsibility for overall security in Cambodia, particularly for the elections. Action is also dependent on a sense of moral obligation.

6. "John Sanderson the Peace General," in Marje Prior and Heide Smith, *Shooting at the Moon*, Australia: Ainslie Act, 1994.

7. United Nations, *Blue Book*, 42.

8. United Nations, *Blue Book*, 41.

9. United Nations sources.

10. *Bangkok Post*, 15 April 1993.

11. William Branigin, "Bulgarians Put a Crimp in Peacekeeping," *Washington Post*, 29 October 1993, A33.

12. This was in a phone booth provided by an Australian company, Telstra, which later monopolized long distance services in the country.

13. Address by Prime Minister Hun Sen to the closing session of the national conference: "Peace, National Reconciliation and Democracy Building: Ten Years After the Paris Peace Agreement," 22 October 2001, excerpted in *Cambodia New Vision*, issue 45, October 2001.

7

A Vote for Peace?

Let's talk now about UNTAC's successes. Its two major triumphs were refugee repatriation and the elections. But it also fostered a freer exchange of ideas, liberated the media, and embedded the concept of human rights in the Cambodian vocabulary. Moreover, civil society grew rapidly, and the economy finally began to recover. By the time of the elections in May of 1993, Cambodia was on the mend.

GOING HOME AT LAST

The first wave of refugees had fled to Thailand from Cambodia when the Khmer Rouge regime had been ousted in January 1979. Suddenly, the gates of the nationwide concentration camp were wide open and people had been able to move freely. By far the largest stream had gone to Thailand in the fall of 1979, when the failure of Cambodia's rice crop had driven the hungry and exhausted to seek food, medicine, and shelter across the border. Crisscrossing the country by the tens of thousands, many had settled in the refugee camps, which had sprung up like mushrooms. But initially the Thais did not like the refugees and turned many back to Cambodia.

UNTAC's repatriation of the refugees was one of its most solid achievements. Coming from refugee camps in Thailand controlled by the Khmer Rouge, FUNCINPEC, or KPNLF, more than half of all returnees chose to be resettled in the northwestern provinces, including Siem Reap, because it was

Photo 7.1.   Cambodians returning from refugee camps in Thailand. Credit: UN Photo 137763/P. Sudhakaran.

located near the Thai border. Marion Roche, the local head of UNTAC's repatriation component who hailed from the United Nations High Commissioner for Refugees (UNHCR), and her assistant, Sivanka Dhanapalan, were personal friends. We often discussed Cambodia and the refugees over beers.

UNTAC dispensed enough rice and other essentials donated by the World Food Program to refugees for four hundred days (two hundred if they resettled in Phnom Penh). Programs managed jointly with United Nations Development Program (UNDP) helped repatriates reintegrate into their societies. As a result of these efforts, 362,209 displaced Cambodians from nine border camps in Thailand were able to return home after thirteen to fourteen years in the camps. That was a laudable humanitarian achievement.[1]

Several factors contributed to the success of UNTAC's repatriation effort. The efficient UNHCR, under the highly acclaimed leadership of Ms. Sagato Ogata from Japan, had begun planning as early as 1989. Later UNHCR activities to repatriate refugees were simply incorporated into UNTAC (though UNHCR's administration remained independent). In Siem Reap, I used to run to Marion Roche's office for news from Phnom Penh, as she already had an embryonic e-mail system that allowed her to exchange instant messages with the capital. But with UNTAC I had trouble even sending faxes or using the long-distance telephone, as the young Australian soldiers manning our communications system did not have the faintest clue what a provincial director of UNTAC was.

Eventually the late Sergio de Mello, the head of the repatriation component of UNTAC in Cambodia, was able to convince the four Cambodian factions that repatriation was basically a humanitarian rather than a political affair. This was not entirely acceptable to SOC, and I think SOC was right, as repatriation did have a political dimension tied to the elections. To the SOC government, the refugee camps, each governed by one of the three resistance factions, seemed like breeding grounds for rebel armies. And SOC worried that the returning refugees would all vote for the resistance parties. But Sergio persuaded the SOC that their return was desirable.

Repatriation started early, on 30 March 1992, barely two weeks after Akashi had arrived in Cambodia.[2] There were some miscalculations in the planning, though. The most important one was the idea of allotting two hectares of arable land to each returning family. This was, unfortunately, wishful thinking. After twenty years of civil war, Cambodia was heavily mined, and any arable lands not yet cultivated were unsuitable for planting. It was unrealistic to expect people to hand over all the mine-free arable land to returnees from border camps from which their armies had attacked Cambodia throughout the 1980s. UNTAC's demining efforts were only a drop in the bucket, as Cambodia remained one of the world's most heavily mined countries, with about nine million mines still in the fields after UNTAC left.

Another problem was that, although most of the refugees had originally been farmers, after living in the refugee camps for a long time, farming was not a ready option. Many refugees (those twelve years and younger) had been born in a camp and never seen Cambodia. More than half had never seen a rice paddy. When some youngsters were asked during a school test at a camp, "Where does rice come from?" they answered, "From the WFP [World Food Program] truck!" UNHCR therefore pursued other options, such as giving refugees cash and offering them employment with UNTAC.

In Siem Reap, when the first convoy arrived at the UNHCR Reception Center, Marion Roche, Colonel Kamal, and I headed the reception committee. The returnees came in very brightly colored Thai buses and trucks chartered by UNHCR and brought all their prized possessions from the border camps with

Cambodia Repatriation: final destination of returnees by province

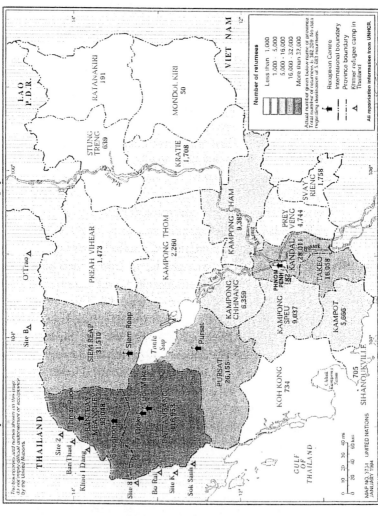

Map 7.1. Cambodia repatriation; final destination of returnees. United Nations, Cartographic Section, UN Map no. 3734.

them. I remember a little girl clutching her two dogs while she was helped off the truck. The adults clutched plastic bags. Some came home relatively wealthy, even with stereos and electric fans, for their enterprising spirit had made them successful businesspeople in the sprawling refugee camps.

It was a very touching scene. Repatriates entered Siem Reap as if they had just been released from thirteen years in a concentration camp. The Thai government had not allowed them to leave the nine fenced-in camps in Thailand, some of which spread for miles and housed as many as 160,000 refugees. But as soon as they stepped on Cambodian soil, they were free to travel anywhere they liked, after staying between two and seven days in reception centers.

The returnees appeared well fed and well clothed. Their encounters with friends and relatives who had stayed behind in Cambodia were emotional. Many relatives who had not seen each other for decades hugged and spent days without sleep talking to each other. The colorful Thai trucks and buses stayed overnight near the Grand Hotel and were unusual sights for the local people, who were accustomed to seeing only old and ugly Russian-made trucks or white UNTAC vehicles.

Relatively speaking, the refugees were also well educated. Schools had opened in the camps, and thousands of young volunteers from the United States, Europe, and Japan had flocked to them to teach everything from English and French to computers. UNTAC had recruited many of its interpreters and other Cambodian staff from the camps.

By 20 January, 260,000 refugees had been repatriated. But ten days before the end of the voter registration process, approximately 120,000 refugees were still in Thailand. Anxious to ensure that all refugees were given a chance to vote, UNTAC registration teams were sent to the camps.

REGAINING THEIR DIGNITY

We had assumed that the elections would be held in a peaceful environment. They were not. Civic education, voter registration, political campaigning, polling, and ballot counting all took place under different circumstances than envisaged in the Paris Agreements. As violence and acts of intimidation escalated, electoral officials in some provinces received death threats almost daily—and from just about every faction.

Despite the obstacles, however, UNTAC members of the Advanced Electoral Planning Unit (AEPU), including my friend Per in Siem Reap, generated detailed information on the population distribution and estimated the eligible voter population; UN volunteer cartographers located people's homes (existing maps were twenty years out of date). The District Electoral Supervisors (DESs) played a major role in the voter registration process, as did the 450 UN volunteers (UNVs), who also helped organize polling. I came to know personally all of those stationed in Siem Reap province—young men and women who lived in appalling conditions in the district capitals. They were, in essence, living like Cambodians, with no electricity at night and no running water (Bangbatt provided them drinkable water).

A Cambodian electoral staff of four thousand was recruited to help with the registration process. They issued the registration cards, conducted civic education programs, and ran the polls. More people registered than anticipated. At election time, another fifty thousand Cambodians actually manned the polling booths. These dedicated young Cambodians instilled confidence in their fellow countrymen that the voting would be free and secret.

Cambodians were very proud of possessing the high-tech laminated voter identification cards with their pictures. They had regained their dignity in a

Photo 7.2.   Cambodian proudly displays his registration card against background of UNTAC billboard on the elections. Credit: UN Photo 7132 /P. Sudhakaran.

society where, during the brutal regime of the Khmer Rouge, they had been forced to destroy their identity cards and were treated like animals. Many carried their identity cards with them all the time.

I remember very well the first day of registration in Siem Reap. The morning started slowly, with a few curious Cambodians trickling in to the registration centers. They later emerged triumphantly, displaying their forgery-proof cards. "They don't even charge for this," one lady marveled. By the end of the registration process, on 31 January 1993, 4.7 million Cambodians nationwide had registered, representing about 96 percent of the estimated eligible voters, including those in Khmer Rouge–held areas.[3]

Reports soon began to circulate that the Cambodian People's Party (CPP) of the SOC government as well as the Khmer Rouge were confiscating registration cards.[4] But Sok An, the deputy interior minister and head of the SOC electoral organization, assured everyone that the purpose was to collect the names of potential voters and determine who had not yet registered in order to persuade them to do so. The cards collected by the SOC were later returned.[5]

As violence escalated with the approaching elections, UNTAC decided to reduce the number of polling stations from 1,800 to 1,561, thereby increasing the average distance a voter had to travel to reach the nearest station. Of course, by transporting voters to the polling sites (some of which were five miles or more away) and temporarily taking custody of their registration cards, the SOC hoped that they would vote for the CPP.

The Khmer Rouge actually permanently confiscated cards from people in the areas they controlled or in adjacent areas. But they did so to no avail. The electoral law and UNTAC's preparations made it possible for people to vote even if they had lost their registration cards. In the provinces, we sent all data on registered voters to Phnom Penh, where it was entered into a giant computer equipped with the Khmer script. People who had lost their cards could thereby vote through tendered ballots, which were sent to Phnom Penh for verification.

TOWARD A MULTIPARTY SOCIETY

UNTAC continued laying the groundwork for pluralism in a society that had been dominated by a single party for so long. And, personally, I finally enjoyed real executive authority in matters like the establishment of political parties and approval of campaign rallies. For once, I became the real governor of the province, not just a shadow governor.

Provisional registration of political parties had begun in August of 1992, four days after the promulgation of the electoral law. Three of the Cambodian factions established four major political parties: the Cambodian People's Party; the FUNCINPEC (the Royalist party); the Buddhist Liberal Democratic Party (BLDP) led by Son Sann; and the Liberal Democratic Party (LDP) led by Sak Sudsakorn. The Khmer Rouge had already decided to boycott the elections and so registered no parties. A variety of smaller parties, many of them established by returning expatriates from the United States and France, also sprouted up. A total of twenty parties participated in the elections.

In mid-September 1992, the parties began opening offices. In authorizing the opening of these offices, I encountered two major problems. Although the electoral law required a separation between the property of the party and that of the government (this was the whole essence of control over civil administration), it was hard to separate the CPP from the SOC. And three of the new parties—FUNCINPEC, the BLDP, and the LDP—had until recently been archenemies of the CPP, which continued to label them the enemy.

Photo 7.3.   UN vehicles passing beneath a banner publicizing elections in Phnom Penh. Credit: UN Photo 120698/P. Sudhakaran.

The first problem arose when the CPP informed me by letter that they were opening offices at the commune level within each district in the entire province of Siem Reap. Since I knew how much office space cost, I wondered how they were going to pay for this and requested ownership information. The CPP replied that all these offices belonged to the CPP. But there was no separation of power between the SOC and the CPP. I reported this to Phnom Penh but was instructed not to do anything about it.

As for the second problem, FUNCINPEC was the most active in opening new offices, followed by BLDP. Lacking campaign funds, FUNCINPEC and BLDP opened offices that were often nothing but shacks with their flags in front. The offices were frequently attacked as soon as they opened because they were considered the enemy within SOC territory. I would then be called to mediate—under the protection of our CivPol—between FUNCINPEC activists and SOC police, who said they could not allow their "enemy within" to fly their flag. I would then patiently explain that in preparation for the elections all political parties, including former enemies of the SOC, had to be allowed to open offices and campaign. Nevertheless, attacks would sometimes continue at night.

During the preelection period, I chaired roundtables with members of the political parties on a biweekly basis. In one such meeting, BLDP and FUNCINPEC expressed concern that the CPP had already started campaigning, though the other parties were not yet allowed to start. They also voiced fear that people were being coerced into obtaining CPP registration cards and were being told that they must vote for the CPP. I assured them that the elections would be by secret ballot and that international monitors would guard against irregularities. I further explained that UNTAC would conduct a civic education campaign between now and the elections, which would counter all misleading tactics.

By the eve of the elections, the twenty political parties had opened 2,037 offices throughout Cambodia. FUNCINPEC (which controlled only a sliver of land) had 762 offices, the CPP 644, the BLDP 204, and the LDP 146.

UNTAC initiated its civic education campaign on 10 February, nearly two months before the start of the official campaign period. It intended to assure voters that their vote would be private and that they could vote for any party they chose. In Siem Reap the informational road shows that had started earlier were now directed toward the elections.

During the official six-week campaign period that started on 7 April, parties were allowed to hold public meetings and rallies. This was the first time in decades that Cambodians had been given the opportunity to participate in public political activity in a multiparty environment. It was quite extraordinary.

Sam Rainsy and Prince Sirivudh, the two main pillars of the FUNCINPEC party, came to Siem Reap twice to lead a rally. We provided them maximum security. As they did not have their own transportation, UNTAC helicoptered them from Phnom Penh to the rallies, which were well attended considering that they were by resistance factions. In general, however, the tense atmosphere ensured that attendance at rallies in Siem Reap was not very large. Those who came timidly huddled together as if they were doing something illegal. Even the CPP did not attract much attention. It had informed us that on the last day of the campaign it expected two hundred thousand at a rally, but only between four thousand and five thousand showed up. UNTAC held a combined rally for the eleven parties represented in Siem Reap on Friday, 14 May, attended by 2,500 people.

In their campaigning, the two largest parties, the CPP and FUNCINPEC, relied on strategies from the civil war days of the 1980s. The CPP emphasized its role in rescuing Cambodia from Pol Pot. It warned villagers against voting for parties that were playing games with Pol Pot. Mindful of the disillusionment of many Cambodians with two successive communist regimes, the CPP fashioned itself as a populist party. It took as its logo a Buddhist angel (*tevoda*).

FUNCINPEC repeatedly warned against Vietnamese infiltrators in Cambodia and claimed that a vote for FUNCINPEC was a vote for Sihanouk. Its claim was patently untrue, since as head of the Supreme National Council, Sihanouk was the father of all Cambodians. But it was a potent rallying cry for Cambodians, especially the uneducated farmers, who in spite of years of indoctrination against royalty still considered the king the supreme leader, with almost godlike powers.

FUNCINPEC also violated a rule not to use Sihanouk's image as a campaign tool. They wore T-shirts depicting Prince Ranariddh wearing a T-shirt with Prince Sihanouk's picture on it. FUNCINPEC had earlier broadcast an interview with Prince Ranariddh in which he had spoken of the benefit of having Sihanouk as president and stressed that Sihanouk was the key to national unity.

FINALLY THE ELECTIONS

The elections were held for an entire week, 23–28 May 1993. Since Siem Reap was considered a high-risk area, Yasushi Akashi phoned Colonel Kamal and me the week before to inform us that he was leaving it up to us to decide whether the elections should be held in the province. After discussing the question deep into the night with other senior UNTAC personnel, we recommended that they should.

We realized that we shouldered a heavy responsibility. Nobody knew exactly what the Khmer Rouge was up to. We were deciding matters of life and death for the three thousand UNTAC personnel and the Cambodians in the province. I argued that the Khmer Rouge would be committing suicide if, after all the coddling they had received, they attacked UNTAC's elections, let alone killed UNTACists. The Cambodian political parties and the people of Siem Reap applauded our decision.

I have seen elections in Indonesia, Thailand, and the United States, but I have never seen what unfolded on Sunday, 23 May. Cambodians thronged the

Photo 7.4. Crowds gathering near voting booth in Prey Veng province. Credit: UN Photo 120697/John Isaac.

voting booths. Dressed in their nicest clothes and beaming, they looked as if they were going to a carnival. Many came from up to twenty kilometers away—by foot, bicycle, or trucks provided by the SOC or private companies. Whole families came, from grandmothers to nursing babies carried by their mothers. Most carried picnic baskets in anticipation of a long wait.

To reduce costs, voting booths had been set up in schools and pagodas as much as practicable, with some of the bigger schools housing five booths. The Cambodians lined up in front of the booths, waiting patiently for hours while joking with each other. Security was provided by Bangbatt and CivPol, as no Cambodian security forces or other unauthorized people were allowed into the compounds where voting took place.

Inside the polling places, Cambodian electoral officers, the UNVs, and the 1,400 International Polling Station Observers (IPSOs) all played important roles. The electoral workers checked voters' United Nations–issued ID cards and dipped their fingers in invisible ink. They then handed voters a large, folded ballot with the symbols of the twenty political parties. The rate of invalid ballots was surprisingly low. (A number of people voted for UNTAC, on

Photo 7.5.   A woman receiving her ballot from UNTAC electoral staff. Credit: UN Photo 137768/P. Sudhakaran.

top of the ballot box.) Political agents from the major political parties were always present and watched our every move like hawks. They could question anything that they believed did not conform to the electoral law. But only a miniscule percentage of the registrants were challenged.

In the subsequent days, I went to the districts to observe the voting. Some of these trips I made by helicopter with Colonel Kamal. Sandbags and razor wire, provided by Bangbatt, surrounded the voting booths in most districts, reminders of the precarious security situation. But only one serious incident was reported, in the notorious district of Soth Nikhum, east of Siem Reap city. The Khmer Rouge attacked a mobile polling team there, wounding one Bangladeshi officer.[6]

Akashi and his senior staff wished to observe the voting in Siem Reap with high-level diplomats, but some staffers were apprehensive, and Dherm Wheelan, head of the electoral component, advised against it. I was adamant that a visit would boost morale in the province. Fortunately, the Khmer Rouge kept quiet. On the third day of balloting, Akashi arrived in three helicopters with an entourage that included many journalists from around the world.

In the province all the ballots were eventually brought back to the heavily guarded Bangladeshi battalion's main garrison in Siem Reap city, the ultimate "safe haven." The ballot boxes then had to be transported to the provincial capital for counting. At the end of the third day, an MI-17 helicopter touched down at an open space near the Bangbatt garrison. Catherine Pascal, a DES, drove up to the helicopter followed by a truck loaded with ballot boxes guarded by Bangladeshi soldiers. Other soldiers with their weapons drawn protected the perimeter. Within minutes, the soldiers loaded the ballot boxes into the helicopter, jumped back into their vehicles, and cleared the space of spectators so the helicopter could take off. "It's a relief to get the boxes out of here," Catherine sighed. "The Khmer Rouge are just over there." She pointed to a hill five kilometers away.[7]

Nationally, there were problems safeguarding and transporting the ballots. According to the electoral law, each political party could place its seal on every ballot box. But UNTAC had provided the wrong specifications to the box manufacturers, and the boxes did not have space for the seals. The law was then abruptly amended, but the CPP protested vehemently and questioned UNTAC's impartiality.[8] Also, because of the worsening security conditions, UNTAC's military component decided that the ballots would be moved to a secure site each night and then returned to the polling stations in the mornings. But the boxes had not been manufactured to withstand multiple moves. The plastic locks were flimsy, in spite of the expensive contract with the manufacturers.[9] And the ballots were transported by soldiers over bad roads and in hurried helicopter trips. The result was that in several cases the boxes burst open and spilled their contents, again inciting tremendous protests from the CPP.

On Friday, 21 May, the CPP and SOC even threatened to boycott the election. Their already strong suspicion that UNTAC was partial against the SOC had been fueled by the decision to move the ballot boxes from the polling stations—where their party agents were stationed—to the newly created safe havens at night. That the boxes would not be sealed by their party seal also convinced them that UNTAC could not be trusted.[10]

On 29 May, the process of vote counting began. Every international UNTAC and IPSO staffer participated. The Cambodian employees were excluded to prevent accusations of partiality. The pace was very slow, and most of the younger people spent almost twenty-four hours each day counting the ballots; I lasted only until midnight every night. Party agents scrutinized the counting carefully; many of them also stayed at the counting site overnight.

Photo 7.6.   A UN staff member counting the votes. Cambodians were excluded from participating in the counting process. Credit: UN Photo 137771/P. Sudhakaran.

Distribution of Seats in the Constituent Assembly

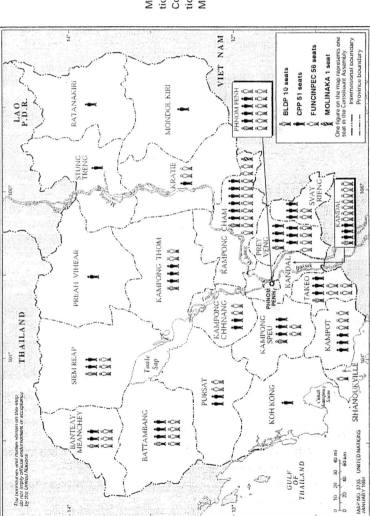

Map 7.2. Results of UNTAC elections: Distribution of seats in the Constituent Assembly. United Nations, Cartographic Section, UN Map no. 3735.

In Siem Reap province, 82 percent of the registered voters came out to vote. This was quite an achievement. Five of Siem Reap's fourteen districts were classified as "high risk" and two were completely inaccessible due to Khmer Rouge intransigence. In the entire country, 89.5 percent of the 4.7 million registered voters cast their votes. On the edges of Khmer Rouge strongholds, a few Khmer Rouge soldiers even trickled out to vote.

Radio UNTAC broadcast nationwide partial results twice a day. By 1 June it was clear that FUNCINPEC was winning in early returns, provoking CPP to demand that the broadcasting of the results be stopped. UNTAC ignored their protests.[11]

On 29 May, Akashi declared the voting free and fair at an SNC meeting. Four days later the UN Security Council adopted a resolution endorsing Akashi's statement. The resolution also called upon all parties to abide by the results.[12] The secretary-general and Sihanouk exchanged letters congratulating each other on the elections.

A CONSTITUTIONAL COUP?

But the situation in Cambodia was becoming tense. On 31 May, the CPP protested irregularities in the elections to Akashi and Reginald Austin, Director of the Electoral Component. Akashi reported that there had been no serious irregularities, however. Chea Sim, the chairman of the CPP, met with Sihanouk and requested that Sihanouk arrange a meeting with Ranariddh to effect national reconciliation and realize the popular will for peace. Chea Sim also wrote a letter to UNTAC declaring that the CPP would not accept the results of the electoral process unless new elections were held in four provinces—Battambang, Kompong Chhnang, Phnom Penh, and Prey Veng—where he alleged the irregularities were extensive.[13]

On 3 June, Chea Sim and Hun Sen met with Prince Sihanouk and requested that he assume all power. They also demanded equal power sharing with FUNCINPEC in the new cabinet. Sihanouk decided to act. On 3 June at 5 p.m., the royal palace and the CPP issued a communiqué announcing an agreement between FUNCINPEC and CPP to form a "Provisional National Government" with Sihanouk as head of state, prime minister, and supreme commander of the armed forces and police; Hun Sen and Prince Ranariddh would be vice presidents. The CPP and FUNCINPEC would share power fifty-fifty. Sihanouk, who later said that he had acted to prevent bloodshed and turmoil, informed Akashi of his move at 5:30 p.m.

Akashi issued a statement expressing appreciation of the vital role of Prince Sihanouk as the national conciliator and stating that "this new initiative to resolve the difficulties which face Cambodia after the elections is extremely important." He added, however, "I am assured by Prince Sihanouk that, within the Paris Agreements he, as President of the SNC, will continue his full cooperation with UNTAC in fulfilling its remaining responsibilities, until a new constitution is adopted."[14] While applauding Sihanouk's initiative, he had stopped short of recognizing the new government.

Apparently France, Japan, and Russia had encouraged Sihanouk to take this step, while the United States, China, the UK, and Australia had opposed it.[15] Ranariddh was surprised by his father's move, and from his headquarters in the small hamlet of Ampil he sent a fax to his "*Papa tres venere*" saying he would find it difficult to work with Hun Sen and the CPP. Sihanouk later confided to me with a chuckle that he told Ranariddh that if he did not want to cooperate, he could be relegated to serving as the prime minister of the hamlet of Ampil in the sliver of land controlled by FUNCINPEC, covering about 1 percent of Cambodia's territory.[16]

Reportedly, representatives from Japan and France had met secretly with Sihanouk in Beijing in May to propose the interim government. Sihanouk was said to have rejected the proposal then, but his latest move on 3 June had the support of both countries. Australia, the United States, China, and Britain are said to have worried that the interim government would become permanent and that it did not reflect FUNCINPEC's electoral victory.

The United States was wary of giving Sihanouk too much power. After all, it was the U.S. feud with Sihanouk in the 1960s that had started all the trouble Cambodia faced. A confidential U.S. "non-paper" distributed on 3 June at 5:30 p.m. said that the immediate formation of an interim coalition government in Cambodia may lead to a violation of the Paris accords and the spirit of the successful election. It warned that any attempts to forge a new government must adhere strictly to the process laid down by the Paris Agreements.[17]

The U.S. position, which reached Sihanouk within hours of his formation of the new government, outraged the prince, who still blamed the United States for his ouster from power twenty-three years earlier. But the next day Sihanouk, in a nationwide radio address, said that he had abandoned the idea of his government largely because of U.S. opposition. He alluded to the opposition within UNTAC, including of Tim Carney, who reportedly had called the prince's proclamation a "constitutional coup."

The U.S. "non-paper" escalated the crisis. Raoul Jennar, a Belgian Cambodia expert, claimed that "whilst CPP must bear responsibility for [the later secession led by dissidents in the CPP] . . . they are not alone. Those who sought to torpedo Sihanouk's initiative by calling it 'a constitutional coup' helped to push matters to this extreme situation."[18] Jennar said he overheard a senior U.S. official state, "In order to do what we want to do in Cambodia, we can do without Prince Sihanouk. We can do without the CPP. We have ninety million dollars to keep officials and soldiers of the SOC and to buy CPP Deputies necessary to get the 2/3 [majority] and then put in a coalition of our choice."[19]

These allegations had appeared earlier in a publication of the NGO coalition in Cambodia subtitled "A Dangerous Plot." The article referred to "American members of UNTAC" who allegedly spread the idea that "if the CPP wins, it will mean that the elections will not be free and fair." U.S. Ambassador Charles Twining, who later became my personal friend, denounced Jennar's allegations and their implication that "the United States is behind some sort of plot against the Cambodian People's Party." In a letter to the executive secretary of the NGO coalition, Twining continued, "Please let me make it clear on this, the eve of the elections, that my Government is absolutely neutral."[20]

According to the Paris Agreements, the elections were supposed to produce a Constituent Assembly that would draft and promulgate a new constitution within ninety days, after which the assembly would transform itself into a national assembly and legalize a permanent government. Then UNTAC would withdraw. Unfortunately there was no provision for the three-month power vacuum between June and September. Sihanouk had stepped in and acted to stabilize the situation only to be reprimanded by the United States.

To avoid the power vacuum, the diplomatic community and UNTAC had agreed to support some sort of Sihanouk-led government in the weeks after the elections.[21] They believed that would keep Hun Sen's forces in the SOC from staging a full-scale insurrection. "As long as it is interim, and does not interfere or curtail the activities of the Constituent Assembly to draft a constitution and form a new government, we are all in agreement," said one diplomat. "We need an interim arrangement to increase chances of stability during this transition period."[22]

The question was the amount of power to be given Sihanouk. Japan and France in particular, with the support of Russia, had long favored granting Sihanouk strong executive powers to preempt the long-simmering threat of a collapse of the Paris Agreements. It was France that had proposed holding early presidential elections in order to transfer real power to Sihanouk. Some diplomats say that France, Japan, and Russia were prepared to turn a blind eye should the interim government become permanent.

On 10 June, the vote counting was completed and the results declared by Akashi, who proclaimed that they accurately reflected the will of the Cambodian people. FUNCINPEC won; the CPP was close behind. BLDP came in third, with the rest of the parties not getting many votes. FUNCINPEC won in urban areas like Phnom Penh, but it also did well in such CPP strongholds as Kampong Cham and Siem Reap, which made my counterpart, Governor Nuo Som, very unhappy.

In a statement to the SNC before the counting was completed, Hun Sen had expressed his satisfaction with the "excellent" result of the electoral process. He also noted, however, rather ominously that the CPP had submitted observations to UNTAC on technical aspects of the electoral process, and that the party was awaiting the election results in the hope that the counting of the votes would proceed in strict conditions that would allow all parties to accept the results. The UN secretary-general, in his report of 10 June to the Security Council on the elections, reproduced Hun Sen's statement but included no quotes from the other factions. This was presumably to prevent further protests from the CPP.[23]

The UN Security Council passed Resolution 840 fully endorsing the results of the elections.[24] Completion of the process signaled the end of UNTAC's

Table 7.1.   Cambodian 1993 election results by party.

Party	Number of valid votes received	Percent of total valid votes	Number of seats obtained
FUNCINPEC	1,824,188	45.5	58
CPP	1,533,471	38.2	51
BLDP	152,764	3.8	10
Molinaka	55,107	1.4	1
Others*	466,101	11.1	0

Source: UNTAC.
*The Liberal Democratic Party, an offshoot of the BLDP, actually obtained 62,698 votes, or 1.6 percent more than Molinaka. However, because of the proportional system of elections, they did not obtain a seat in the assembly.

role in Cambodia. The country's remaining problems were now in the laps of the Cambodians.

SECESSION

On 10 June Hun Sen dropped a bombshell. He accused the United Nations and foreign countries of engineering a conspiracy of massive fraud. In protest, he announced, six eastern provinces—representing almost 40 percent of Cambodia's territory—had seceded from the nation. Their secession was led by "dissident figures" in the CPP including SOC Deputy Prime Minister Chakrapong, a half brother of Ranariddh, and Chakrapong's friend, General Sin Song.[25] They proclaimed these provinces a *Samdech Euv* (King father) autonomous zone. The secessionists ordered UNTAC to leave the area. UNTAC decided to withdraw its civilian personnel but left its military in place.[26] Although Hun Sen announced the secession, he did not officially endorse it.

This was a bizarre turn of events pitting two half brothers, descendants of Sihanouk, against each other. Chakrapong had always been something of a loose cannon and a rival of Ranariddh. The two brothers loathed each other. They had been inseparable growing up and had both studied in France and joined FUNCINPEC but had fallen out over politics. Chakrapong envied Ranariddh, who seemed to get all the plum positions. Their differences became irreconcilable. Chakrapong defected from FUNCINPEC and joined Hun Sen's CPP in early 1992. The CPP received him with open arms. It rewarded him with the post of deputy prime minister in charge of six ministries, made him a member of the politburo of the CPP, and gave him a sprawling residential villa.

General Sin Song had come to the CPP by way of the Khmer Rouge. After leaving the Pol Pot regime in 1977, Sin Song had fled to Vietnam and joined the Hun Sen group. He had become a member of the SNC. He was the unsavory minister of national security during UNTAC times.

The day after Chakrapong and Sin Song's secession, Hun Sen made a speech broadcast over government media bewailing the pain that UNTAC's handling of the elections had caused him:

> As for me, I have experienced suffering before, but never so much as now, because this pain, under unjust actions, doesn't affect the CPP (Cambodian People's Party) or me, but these unjust actions affect many millions of people, affect almost all of the political parties which participated in the election. Therefore,

this is a huge injury, five times bigger than when I had eye surgery, than when the doctor took my eye out. But the size of this injury is not equal to the pain. I have exhausted all my abilities but cannot protect the people from this injustice.[27]

Once again, Hun Sen had denounced the elections but without supporting the secession. Three days later, he traveled to Kampong Cham to quell the secession. Hun Sen later made it clear that he had not been part of the secession: "Prince Chakrapong and General Sin Song did it themselves. They arrested me on 2 June 1993 and tried to force me to resign as the prime minister so that they could hold power and oppose the results of the election. Afterwards they fled and formed the autonomous zone. It was I who solved these problems and prevented fighting."[28] Hun Sen also continued to harshly criticize UNTAC. The body had behaved like "armed robbers," he said in 2001. UNTAC held the distinction of presiding over "the worst elections in the 20th century."[29]

The secessionist movement quickly collapsed, and Chakrapong and Sin Song fled to Vietnam. Later, Chakrapong insisted that he had been made the fall guy by the CPP. "I was very surprised that the CPP was not standing with me."[30] As a reward for returning to Phnom Penh and abandoning the secession movement, he was later promoted to four-star general by Sihanouk! Such was the Byzantine politics of the country.

A TWO-HEADED GOVERNMENT

As the secession movement in the east was petering out, Sihanouk was inaugurating the constituent assembly, consisting of the newly elected deputies, on 14 June. Its first act was to annul the 1970 coup d'etat against Sihanouk, who was reaffirmed as head of state, with unspecified powers. The "constitutional coup" had now been confirmed. Realizing that some form of provisional government was important, the United States did not protest. Sihanouk proposed the establishment of an Interim Joint Administration that would rule until the constitution was completed, with Ranariddh and Hun Sen as coprime ministers. This time his son Ranariddh did not object. On 21 June, agreement was reached on a power-sharing formula; five days later, the assembly announced a provisional government. The CPP had accepted the election results.

In the Provisional National Government of Cambodia (PNGC), Prince Ranariddh and Hun Sen were cochairmen and coministers of defense, interior, and public security. The CPP got sixteen and FUNCINPEC thirteen positions in the new cabinet, with another three taken by BLDP and one going to Molinaka, an offshoot of FUNCINPEC. Each CPP minister would have a FUNCINPEC member as deputy and vice versa. FUNCINPEC gained the important ministries of foreign affairs and finance. Ranariddh and Hun Sen viewed each other with suspicion, but they soon developed a working relationship.[31]

Although the Paris Agreements had not spelled out a role for Akashi in the formation of the new government, he helped Sihanouk persuade Ranariddh to accept power sharing with the CPP while urging CPP leaders to refrain from taking reckless action.[32] The United Nations encouraged the two major parties to work together by providing emergency financial assistance from its UNAMIC Trust Fund to pay for the government's army, which, of course, was the same as the SOC army. At the provincial level, the new government remained the same SOC government, and in Siem Reap I continued to deal with my counterpart, SOC Governor Nuo Som. He was quite disillusioned with the CPP's failure to win the election in the province, for which he was blamed by Phnom Penh.

As we in UNTAC were winding down our operations, we took care of administrative matters such as handing over expensive communications equipment to the SOC administration. Provincial personnel of UNTAC were maintained until September. We spent most of our time consolidating the work we had performed during the previous year and a half.

A rash of thefts of expensive UNTAC vehicles and equipment meanwhile had broken out at night. The total loss included 1,898 vehicles at a residual value of $15,842,789, satellite equipment valued at $1,364,978, and computers and the like valued at $23,987,101.[33] Although many of the vehicles later showed up—repainted—at the homes of powerful generals in Phnom Penh and elsewhere, UNTAC could do nothing about it. The rest of the vehicles were shipped to Somalia and other United Nations peacekeeping operations.

Before UNTAC departed, General Sanderson managed to amalgamate the three Cambodian armies into a nominally united Royal Cambodian Armed Forces. But there was a problem: the small armies of FUNCINPEC and KPNLF had earlier promoted many of their officers to the rank of general. In Siem Reap, General Long So Pheap of the CPAF, after returning from a meeting with his counterparts in the two other factions, complained to me that there were too many stars at the meeting. The new Royal Cambodian Armed

Forces had no less than two thousand generals, each earning the princely sum of $30 a month!

A new Constitution of the Kingdom of Cambodia was ratified on 21 September, and the Constituent Assembly proclaimed a constitutional monarchy in which Sihanouk would become a king who reigned but did not rule. The assembly transformed itself into a legislative branch, and Sihanouk was crowned on 24 September. After having abdicated his crown in favor of his father in 1955, Sihanouk again found himself king of Cambodia.

His first act was to appoint Ranariddh first prime minister and Hun Sen second prime minister, with equal powers. The newly appointed government was essentially the same as the Provisional Government of Cambodia that had taken power on 26 June, belying the notion that the latter was a temporary arrangement. This would have far-reaching consequences.

With UNTAC's mandate ended, Akashi and Sanderson left on 26 September. I left a week later. We all felt sad to leave. After one and a half years of excitement and danger, it felt strange to return to work in the air-conditioned comfort of my offices on the thirty-first floor of the United Nations in New York. Little did I know that I would soon be returning to Camdodia albeit in a different capacity.

NOTES

1. Much smaller numbers were also repatriated from camps in Hong Kong, Indonesia, Malaysia, Singapore, and Vietnam.

2. Symbolically, it ended exactly one year later, with Ms. Sagato Ogata closing the Site Two camp, the largest border camp. The actual movement of refugees was completed the following month.

3. Although the Khmer Rouge held about 20 percent of Cambodia's territory, they controlled no more than 5 percent of its people.

4. "Confiscation of Registration Cards Will Not Deter Secret Balloting," *Free Choice*, UNTAC Electoral Newsletter, 26 February 1993, 6.

5. Kate Frieson, "The Politics of Getting the Vote in Cambodia," in Stephen Heder and Judy Ledgerwood, *Propaganda, Politics and Violence in Cambodia*, op. cit. 192.

6. Personal notes. See also "Siem Reap Braces for Final Weeks of Campaign," *Free Choice*, 30 April 1993, 14.

7. "Troubled Siem Reap Province Goes to Polls," *Free Choice*, 8 June 1993, 11.

8. Internal UNTAC sources. Ten years after UNTAC left Cambodia when I was invited to Phnom Penh for the celebrations of the tenth anniversary of the Paris Agreements, Hun Sen still emphasized this and other "irregularities" as showing UNTAC's bias against the CPP.

9. Obviously, someone had made a lot of money in kickbacks.

10. Reginald Austin, "Election Monitoring: Preparation and Conduct," in Azimi, ed., *The UN Transitional Authority in Cambodia (UNTAC)*, op. cit. 166.

11. *New York Times*, 1 June 1993.

12. UN document S/RES/835 (1993), Security Council resolution on the completion of the elections in Cambodia, 2 June 1993.

13. UPI, 1 June 1993.

14. UNTAC sources. See, for instance, UNTAC, *Brief*, no. 32, Information/Education Division, June 1993, 12.

15. Tim Carney and Tan Liang Choo, *Wither Cambodia: Beyond the Election*, Singapore: Institute for Southeast Asian Studies, 1993.

16. Personal information provided by Sihanouk.

17. Copies of this non-paper circulated widely in Phnom Penh at the time.

18. Raoul M. Jennar, "Chroniques Cambodgiennes (X) Samdech Preah Upayuvaraj Norodom Sihanouk," 29 June 1993, in Raoul M. Jennar, *Chroniques Cambodgiennes 1990–1994*, Rapports au Forum International des ONG au Cambodge, Paris: L'Harmattan, 1995, 466.

19. Jennar, Chroniques.

20. Copy of letter obtained by author.

21. Nate Thayer, "Split Emerges in Core Group," *Phnom Penh Post*, issue 2/13, 18 June–1 July 1993.

22. Thayer, "Split Emerges."

23. UN document S/25913, "Report of the Secretary-General on the Conduct and Results of the Elections," paragraph 9, New York: United Nations, 10 June 1993.

24. UN document S/RES/840 (1993), *Resolution on the Results of the Elections in Cambodia*, New York, 15 June 1993.

25. Nate Thayer, "Sihanouk Back at the Helm," *Phnom Penh Post*, issue 2/13, 18 June–1 July 1993, 1.

26. Thayer, "Sihanouk."

27. Hun Sen's speech over government media, 11 June 1993, then repeated many times a day. As quoted in Zhou Mei, *Radio UNTAC of Cambodia: Winning Hearts and Minds*, Bangkok: White Lotus, 1994, xxiii.

28. Hun Sen on several occasions to a gathering of diplomats during my second stay in Cambodia.

29. *Cambodia New Vision*, issue 45, October 2001.

30. Garish C. Mehta and Julie B. Mehta, *Hun Sen: Strongman of Cambodia*, Singapore: Graham Brash, 1999, 194.

31. Joint Communiqué on the Role and Duties of the PNGC, 16 August 1993.

32. Personal communication from Akashi. Akashi also publicly stated his role in lectures at Johns Hopkins University and Columbia University.

33. UN document A/53/340, "Losses of United Nations Property of Peacekeeping Operations," New York, 4 September 1998, table 2, 5.

II

A UN ENVOY IN PHNOM PENH, 1994–1997

8

Not Enough
Actors for the Play

NEITHER THE CARROT NOR THE STICK

After leaving Siem Reap in September 1993, I found it difficult to return to my desk job in New York. At night I often dreamt of artillery shells, whose sound used to lull me to sleep. I was now shuffling papers. My biggest thrills came from making sure I wouldn't miss the morning commuter train and the last train home.

Yasushi Akashi had moved on to become the UN secretary-general's special representative in Bosnia Herzegovina in the former Yugoslavia. Fortunately, my small staff at the Regional Commissions' New York office eased the pains of readjustment. Harriet Schmidt, my faithful deputy, had held down the fort while I was away. As the officer in charge of a complex office with five bosses from all the regions of the globe, she had earned the praise of all her superiors. With my return, she had to reassume the number two position. I assured her that I was looking for another position, preferably in the political field, because even though I was an economist, the taste of politics in Cambodia had whetted my appetite.

Suddenly, in November, things started picking up. In pursuance of a Security Council resolution,[1] and after a period of negotiations and uncertainty, the secretary-general of the UN appointed me his political representative to the new government in Cambodia, and the UN Security Council agreed to my appointment![2] I would be the highest UN official in post-UNTAC Cambodia.

I was delighted. To go back to Cambodia—the New Cambodia, whose people I had grown to love dearly—was more than I could have hoped for.

Because of opposition from the developing countries in the UN to a person who carried both a political mandate and an economic one of coordinating aid to Cambodia, economic coordination would be carried out by the United Nations Development Program (UNDP) resident coordinator. Thus, my position would be low-key: I would carry neither the stick nor the carrot but essentially be confined to monitoring the political situation. My main tasks would be maintaining a political dialogue with the government of Cambodia, monitoring political and security developments in the country, and reporting to the secretary-general through Marrack Goulding, the Undersecretary-General for Political Affairs. I would be allowed to bring my wife because Cambodia was now at peace (or so the security coordinator of the UN declared). During my UNTAC years, she had only visited me occasionally, traveling all the way from Connecticut.

In the same resolution that authorized my appointment, the UN Security Council also authorized the establishment of a UN military liaison team consisting of twenty officers. For a single period of six months, the team would deal with residual military matters relating to the Paris Agreements. The team was established in Phnom Penh on 25 November with another Bangladeshi colonel, Muniruz Zaman as its head.

I was later informed that the period of uncertainty was caused by a delay in Cambodia's approval of my appointment. The holdup, I found out, came from my former colleague Jacques Godfrin, a Belgian and former UNTAC provincial director of the obscure province of Stung Treng. He had applied intensive pressure to the government in Phnom Penh to keep me from securing the post. When UNTAC had left, Leon was the head of the UNTAC liquidation unit so that he could directly lobby the authorities including Foreign Minister Sirivudh through his wife, Princess Christine Norodom née Alfsen, to assume the post himself. Christine was a French national and former colleague of mine at the UN ESCAP in Bangkok. There was also a baseless rumor that my health was not very good. Little did Godfrin know that in New York the decision had already been made to appoint me. I had the backing of Akashi and other senior personalities inside the UN and that of important ambassadors of Security Council members.

After my appointment was cleared by everyone concerned including the Cambodians, I was ordered to depart immediately for Phnom Penh in order to be on hand when Sihanouk returned from a long absence in Beijing. My wife and I arrived in Phnom Penh on 7 April, one day before the king.

During the short flight from Bangkok, my heart pounded as I considered how lucky I was to return to beloved Cambodia. My fellow passengers were different now. In the old days they had been UNTAC colleagues, military types wearing uniforms from all parts of the world or civilian staff returning from leave or reporting for duty. This time they looked like businessmen, mostly young and adventurous ethnic Chinese from Malaysia, Taiwan, Indonesia, Singapore, and Thailand, searching for business opportunities in Cambodia. These were the intrepid ones; their more cautious and conservative peers from Japan and Korea would arrive much later, once law and order was more visibly restored.

Other passengers reflected other changes in Cambodia. In the first-class cabin, an obviously important person traveled with a sizeable entourage. At the Phnom Penh airport, staff from the royal palace and a girl with a bouquet of flowers eagerly welcomed him. Later I found out that he was Yuvaneath, the oldest son of Sihanouk who also had come to greet the king. Indeed, with the coronation of Sihanouk, many members of the royal family had returned from abroad, as if expecting that the giddy days of pomp and circumstance were again theirs for the taking.

Although no royal party came to greet us, my wife and I received a warm welcome all the same. I was officially met at the airport by Ms. Marina Pok, a FUNCINPEC member and able under secretary-general from the Cambodian Ministry of Foreign Affairs. Other senior officials of the ministry were also there, along with enthusiastic old friends on the residual UNTAC staff (minus Godfrin, who had discreetly left before my arrival).

Our drive on the road from the airport revealed how much Phnom Penh had changed. Peace had brought rapid economic progress to the city. On top of the high-tech garbage trucks that Paris had provided, Singapore had sent some shiny red fire engines. The city looked much cleaner. Other signs of economic growth were less aesthetically appealing, including row upon row of so-called Chinese shop houses similar to those found all over Southeast Asia. In these houses, a family lived in the two upper stories of a three-story apartment while the first floor housed a business such as a bicycle repair shop or a noodle restaurant. The construction industry was booming everywhere. In the elite neighborhoods of Norodom Boulevard and embassy row of Monivong Boulevard,[3] huge mansions were springing up to house new embassies and the Cambodian *nouveaux riches.*

We chose to stay one month at the Holiday International Hotel, a three-star hotel, rather than at the five-star Cambodiana where all of UNTAC's top brass except Akashi used to stay. Akashi had resided in a huge mansion, and now real estate brokers besieged me thinking that I had the same status, monetary means, and tastes. It was generally believed that the rich countries secretly provided rent subsidies for their senior officials.

I did not have any subsidies from my country, and so I lived more simply. After my one-month stay at the Holiday International, I moved into the Lucky Apartments, which were equipped with the same amenities one could get in Bangkok. They were comfortable but not extravagant and located on top of the only huge supermarket in town at the time. In the evening, the whole compound was closed and security was tight.

On the road from the airport, Marina Pok had briefed me about the grave security problems caused by intermittent attacks by the Khmer Rouge. She indicated that the government thus wanted to extend the term of the UN Military Liaison Team (UNMLT), which was expiring 25 May. I told her that the government should send a written request to the secretary-general.

The day after I arrived, I went to receive the king at the airport. He had spent a lot of time in Beijing for treatment of his many ailments, including prostate and bone marrow cancer and diabetes. Even during UNTAC times, and particularly during the electoral campaign period, Sihanouk had spent most of his time in Pyongyang or Beijing. Some SNC meetings had been conducted in Beijing to accommodate him. While abroad, he had sent a constant deluge of faxes and statements expressing his views on all and sundry matters.

Arriving in time for the all-important celebrations of the Khmer New Year starting on 13 April, he was greeted at the airport by the coprime ministers, the president and vice presidents of parliament, and all the cabinet ministers. The top brass of the military and police also turned out—a huge group allowing for the two thousand generals in the armed forces. Members of the diplomatic corps, which consisted of twenty-one ambassadors, were also present.

Photo 8.1. A typical Saturday afternoon family outing in the new Cambodia. Credit: UN Photo 137764/P. Sudhakaran.

As the political representative of the secretary-general, I was the only one from the United Nations invited. The Cambodian protocol officer was at a loss on how to treat me. As I did not replace Akashi, who was virtually the head of state of Cambodia, should I—at best—be given the courtesies of a diplomatic envoy? At the airport I was told by the nervous protocol officer to stand with the ambassadors, and both the king and queen greeted me warmly as the symbol of the continuing presence of the United Nations.

I am sure the king nostalgically remembered his triumphant return to Phnom Penh on 14 November 1991 from Beijing. He was welcomed by Hun Sen, prime minister of the SOC. For Hun Sen the return marked a rare and symbolic moment of triumph. If in January 1979 Sihanouk was persuaded by Pol Pot to flee the Vietnamese and the PRK, the king in 1991 returned to the Cambodia of the SOC, the successor of the PRK.

After their stormy relationship in the 1980s, Sihanouk's return to Phnom Penh in 1991 was the highlight of their relationship. It was before the arrival of UNTAC and Hun Sen spared no effort to welcome the king. Sihanouk had arrived in a China Air Boeing 707 chartered by the Chinese government—symbolically the same plane that had taken him and Pol Pot to Beijing when they had fled Phnom Penh in 1979. Hun Sen had ridden on the plane too, along with Queen Monineath and Ranariddh.

After landing, Sihanouk and Hun Sen had toured Phnom Penh in an art deco 1963 Chevrolet Impala convertible loaned by the Thai government for the occasion. As many as four hundred thousand people had lined the ten-kilometer route from the airport to the palace. Sihanouk had said that he was grateful to Heng Samrin, Chea Sim, and Hun Sen for allowing him to return home.[4] In the absence of TV, news of their triumphant ride had spread throughout the country. It had seemed to the Cambodian people a promise of things to come.

THE ROYALISTS ARE BACK

As it turned out, Yuvaneath and his entourage were also staying in the Holiday International, which I later found out was owned by Tony Tandiono, a fellow Indonesian and prominent businessman who would become a close associate of Hun Sen. The manager of the hotel, Cherry Tan, a jovial lady, was also Indonesian; she befriended us immediately. In the weeks to come, she would complain about the behavior of Yuvaneath's entourage, who consumed enormous quantities of beer and food, charging everything to their rooms and never paying their bills.

They were also spreading rumors that Yuvaneath could become the next king. In the hierarchy of the princes, he was number two. Ranariddh was the most senior, holding the rank of Samdech Krom Preah, or Leading Senior Prince.[5] Yuvaneath would soon simply disappear from public life. These were all members of the ruling House of Norodom, one of two dynasties in Cambodia's royalty. The other was the house of Sisowath who ruled until 1941 when King Sisowath Monivong died and the French denied the house of Sisowath the succession by appointing Norodom Sihanouk king instead.

In a few days I got a taste of the high living by the Royalists who had returned from exile ready to resume their glitzy life of the 1960s. At the airport Marina had handed me an invitation from the secretary-general of FUNCIN-PEC, Norodom Ranariddh, to attend a gala party to celebrate the Khmer New Year on 13 April. The party was at the large swimming pool of the posh Cambodiana Hotel. It was a surreal affair. A live band was playing popular Cambodian as well as American songs, the standard fare on such occasions. This was my first encounter with Ranariddh but certainly not my last. My wife and I were also introduced to other members of the FUNCINPEC elite, many of them princes and princesses but also commoners who came from exile abroad. Their wives, ethnic Khmer, wore Cambodian dresses of foreign design. These ladies hailed from Australia, New Zealand, the United States, and France to occupy high posts in the new government. They were very happy and much at ease on such occasions among the diplomatic corps. They were a new sight in Cambodia as the wives of the top brass of the Cambodian People's Party (CPP) during UNTAC days there wore very simple dresses. They also had less interaction with foreign wives, except those from Eastern Europe.

I spotted some familiar faces at the party, including Norodom Sirivudh and his best friend, Sam Rainsy. Both thanked me profusely for protecting them with UNTAC troops and police when campaigning in Siem Reap and welcomed me back to Cambodia. They had been the key to FUNCINPEC's success in the elections.

The unexpected triumph of FUNCINPEC had created many lucrative jobs for the party stalwarts, not only those of royal ancestry but also commoners who had returned from exile in the West. Returnees who promptly became cabinet members included You Hockry, allegedly a fast-food cook from New

York who became the cominister of the interior; Veng Sereyvuth, a taxi driver in New Zealand who became minister of tourism and the powerful cominister in the Council of Ministers; Pou Sothirak, who had worked in the Boeing factory in Seattle and thus was made minister of industries; and Ung Huot, an employee of the Post and Telecommunications Company of Australia who became minister of education. Except for Sam Rainsy, all had dual nationality. These key ministers of FUNCINPEC soon became wealthy, as did the ministers of the SOC, as the three fs—foreign aid, foreign investment, and foreign tourists—started to pour in, finally bringing needed foreign exchange.

While standing in line for the buffet dinner, I bumped into Princess Norodom Christine, then the wife of Prince Sirivudh. Having known her as a junior professional at ESCAP in Bangkok, I shouted, "Hey, Christine," only to be stared at coldly. So I said, "Hello, your Royal Highness Princess Norodom," and she shook my hand. But the cold stare remained. Obviously she was still smarting that her lobbying for Godfrin had not worked.[6]

THE DYNAMICS OF THE ROYAL GOVERNMENT

Almost one year after the UNTAC elections of May 1993, and half a year since the official inauguration of the Royal Coalition Government, one could best characterize the government as having muddled along in the right direction. This period is part of the "honeymoon" between the copremiers Ranariddh and Hun Sen.

The Royal Coalition Government was practically a continuation of the Provisional National Government of Cambodia established by Sihanouk in 1993. Of the twenty-three cabinet posts available under the copremiers, FUNCINPEC and CPP got eleven each and BLDP one, the Ministry of Information and Culture. Each CPP minister would have a FUNCINPEC member as a deputy with the title of secretary of state and vice versa. In addition, in all the ministries two undersecretaries of state belonging to each of the two major parties were appointed.[7]

The exceptions were the important defense and interior ministries, which were headed by coministers of equal rank from the two parties. The coministers of defense were Tea Banh, an ethnic Thai from the CPP and a close associate of Hun Sen, and Tea Chamrath from FUNCINPEC. Sar Kheng from the CPP, who was not so close to Hun Sen, and You Hockry from FUNCINPEC were the coministers of the interior. The powerful Council of Ministers was also headed by equal-ranking coministers: Sok An from the CPP, who was Hun Sen's right-hand man, and Veng Sereyvuth from FUNCINPEC. In spite of this sharing of top posts, I soon found out that the overall structure of the new administration clearly gave Second Premier Hun Sen most of the power.

At the provincial (khet) level, now half of the governorships were allocated to FUNCINPEC while the other half remained in the hands of the CPP. The vice governor always represented the other party. Again, however, most of the staff below the governor level remained the old staff, all of which belonged to the CPP. For example, in Siem Reap, Nuo Som, my former counterpart governor, was demoted to deputy governor, with newly appointed General Tuon Chay of FUNCINPEC taking his place. Two more deputy governors made up the top provincial leadership.

At the district (srok) level and below that at the commune (khum) level, the CPP retained practically all of the 172 district governor posts and the 1,140 commune heads. This gave the CPP overwhelming political dominance of the country. All the CPP ministers, vice ministers, governors, and lower-ranking leadership had long experience with Cambodian bureaucracy and were able to retain a system of networking, information, influence, and control developed over the years. Although the SOC had been officially dissolved with the formation of the Royal Government, structurally the SOC civil service machinery was never disbanded.

Although FUNCINPEC had won the 1993 elections, it was inserting only a few hundred people returning from exile or refugee camps in Thailand into the enormous civil service, which numbered more than one hundred thousand people. FUNCINPEC's homegrown supporters, who never went into exile, got few jobs and little power.[8] Of course, in a pluralistic democracy the winning party should not necessarily receive a proportionate number of civil service jobs. After all, the British civil service, emulated in such countries as India and Malaysia, is apolitical.

Ironically, the period of political isolation imposed on the PRK during the 1980s had allowed it to rule with an iron hand devoid of any scrutiny. While economic isolation had perpetuated the poverty of Cambodians, politically the PRK had grown very strong. It was now more than ready to face the handful of FUNCINPEC exiles intruding into its midst. All of the approximately 140,000 civil servants were members of the CPP and remained loyal to the party.[9] Its political power continued to reign supreme in all ministries, provinces, and districts. The provincial political structures that controlled the police, armed forces, tax collection, and civil service remained under the control of the CPP, which placed political loyalty above the directives of the central authority. The strict, secretive, discipline of its years in power during the era of isolation remained basically intact, at least during the first years of the Royal Government.

It became immediately clear to me upon returning to Cambodia that UNTAC's elections had been a necessary but not sufficient step in securing political stability, let alone democracy. In the new Cambodia, the SOC was still a principal actor: It had metastasized into a political party. The CPP, born out of the SOC, was the predominant component in the new coalition government.

Most FUNCINPEC bosses could not command the respect of their staffers from the CPP, whose dominance was perpetuated through patron-client relations.[10] Pierre Lizee argued that "social interaction in Cambodia has tended to be conceptualized in terms of personalized and localized relationships. So is the role of numerous networks of personal connections which present the main point of contact between the individual and society, and which, together with the superior interior framework linked to the Brahmanic influence, for the basis of the patronage structure essential to the Cambodian way of life."[11]

Known in Cambodia as *khsae roo-yia* (networks) or simply *khsae* (links), the patron-client relationship, in which clients are loyal to party leaders or bosses rather than the party itself, still dictated political relationships.[12] Of course, the CPP, with its hold over most of the powerful jobs, had an advantage in nurturing patron-client relationships, thereby fortifying its already strong power base. Political supporters as well as sons and daughters of senior CPP officials got lucrative jobs and contracts in the private sector, which also perpetuated its dominance.

The position of the CPP in Cambodia reminded me of GOLKAR's position in Indonesia during Suharto's rule from 1966 to 1998. GOLKAR (Golongan Karya), the all-powerful and ubiquitous party founded by Suharto, was the only show in town. Although it later lost to the Partai Demokrasi Indonesia Perjuangan (PDIP) led by President Megawati in elections in 1999, the civil service continued to be dominated by GOLKAR and most of the senior positions in the government continued to be occupied by GOLKAR or ex-GOLKAR members. In fact, Hun Sen later confided to me that he had been emulating the organization of GOLKAR and the United Malays National Organization (UMNO) in Malaysia. Of course, unlike GOLKAR and UMNO, Hun Sen had to deal with a king and a Royalist party. FUNCINPEC not only commanded a majority in parliament but had informal members in the palace, including the king himself.

But FUNCINPEC's position was much worse than the PDIP's in Indonesia. FUNCINPEC was not only the electoral opposition but the former enemy. While all of the PDIP's cadres in Indonesia were homegrown, FUNCINPEC's cadres had returned from exile. And whereas GOLKAR had been decapitated with the removal of Suharto, Hun Sen remained in power at the helm of the CPP.

The late Om Rasdy, a highly respected FUNCINPEC member of parliament (who for still unknown reasons was assassinated in 2003 before that year's elections), told me that Cambodia resembled a play that lacked enough actors. Consequently, each of the main players had to assume many roles. One doesn't have to look too closely at Sihanouk's political odyssey to see that he was a primary example.

In the new Cambodia, the National Assembly and the judiciary were supposed to provide checks and balances on the conduct of the coalition government, rather than serving merely as rubber stamps as before. The Royal Cambodian Armed Forces (RCAF) and the police were also important wings of the government. The RCAF was an amalgamation of the powerful and huge Cambodian People's Armed Forces (the former SOC army) and the minuscule armies of FUNCINPEC and KPNLF. However, their individual units had never been disbanded, and they continued to be commanded by generals from their factions.

The low pay of the many generals forced them to seek means of income, including from casinos, hotels, nightclubs, karaoke bars, and other lucrative concessions such as forestry. The new Cambodian army also reminded me of Indonesia, where all the generals have other jobs in the private sector and own hotels, restaurants, nightclubs, and other profitable concessions.

With the premiers united, the executive branch held the bulk of the power. During its first four years, the National Assembly was dominated by the two premiers. Because of the coalition of the major parties, there was no opposition in parliament. It did, however, serve as a debating society on key issues, and its members learned to critically assess government policy (which was unheard of during the previous regime). But many times parliament had to be adjourned for lack of a full quorum. This was shameful: parliament members received $2,000 a month in salary, about one hundred times the average salary at the time.

The judicial system, inherited from the previous regime, was very weak. Moreover, with judges' salaries all of $20 a month, it was incredibly corrupt. Judges condemned journalists and editors who, to the annoyance of both premiers, became increasingly vocal in their criticisms of the government. An unusually liberal press emerged, with a proliferation of newspapers and radios. FUNCINPEC was as uneasy as the CPP with the unbridled criticism.

THE FOREIGN PLAYERS

Then there was the international community, consisting of the diplomatic corps, the whole array of United Nations, other international agencies, and the ever-growing community of NGOs. Gone were the days when the Expanded Perm Five or UNTAC could breathe down the necks of Cambodians. In sovereign Cambodia, we, the foreign community, were essentially relegated to being observers. However, one group of countries and international agencies continued to wield considerable clout: the donor community. Their role will be discussed in greater detail later.

ASEAN also found a way to wield influence. It strove to achieve the goal of ASEAN 10 to include Cambodia, Vietnam, Laos, and Myanmar among its members. Cambodia was keen to join ASEAN, which was a powerful economic bloc. The diplomats from ASEAN countries promoted private foreign investment in Cambodia as the top investors were from ASEAN countries.

Other relationships also changed. The most incredible and dramatic transformation took place with China. Since the Chinese ambassador and thousands of advisors had been ousted with the Khmer Rouge in January 1979, China had gradually regained a foothold in Cambodia and become its most influential trade and political partner. Despite its former strong support for the Khmer Rouge, China now became one of the closest allies of the coalition government, which was dominated more and more by Hun Sen, China's erstwhile adversary. Cambodia was important in China's new strategy to become the most important player in Asia. Chinese schools and clinics as well as hotels sprouted up everywhere. Meanwhile the Eastern European countries, the key partners of the PRK in the 1980s, declined in importance, though they continued to occupy the most imposing embassies in Phnom Penh.[13]

THE FIRST TIME BOMB EXPLODES

April is symbolically very significant in the Cambodian calendar. It marks the important festival of the Cambodian New Year.[14] Back in 1975, the Khmer Rouge had entered Phnom Penh on 17 April. Now, almost two decades later, on 13–17 April 1994, the Khmer Rouge again made their presence felt. They launched a successful counterattack against an RCAF offensive, and one of their tanks appeared on the doorsteps of Battambang, Cambodia's second largest city. In the disastrous RCAF dry-season offensive in March that had precipitated this bold move, the RCAF had managed to capture Pailin, headquarters of the Khmer Rouge, only to abandon it a few days later when their commanders went back to Battambang to celebrate the Khmer New Year. The commanders' departure left the army rank and file without leadership, and the Khmer Rouge took advantage of it.

The fighting was the heaviest since the final contingent of Vietnamese troops had withdrawn from Cambodia in 1989. The country was alarmed. But the Khmer Rouge's appearance at Battambang was a fluke, and they were slowly but surely sent back to their headquarters at Pailin. Such was the situation when I arrived in April.

NOTES

1. United Nations Security Council Resolution 880 on transitional period in Cambodia following the withdrawal of UNTAC, 4 November 1993, paragraph 13.

2. UN document S/1994/389, letter dated 29 March 1994 from the secretary-general to the Security Council.

3. One of the first signs of regime change was the restoration of the use of names of royalty for major streets. The two main arteries of Phnom Penh would once again be named Norodom and Monivong Boulevards. During UNTAC times, we had known them as Tousamuth and Achar Mean Boulevards. Tousamuth and Achar Mean were communist heroes. The names had earlier been used during PRK/SOC times. It took me some time to absorb the new names.

4. Harish C. Mehta, *Warrior Prince: Norodom Ranariddh, son of King Sihanouk of Cambodia*, Singapore: Graham Brash, 2001, 85

5. Julio A. Jeldres, *The Royal House of Cambodia*, Phnom Penh: Monument Books, 2003, 17.

6. Fate would seem to bring us together all the time, albeit in different capacities. Later I met her often in the corridors of the United Nations in New York. No longer a princess, as she and Prince Sirivudh divorced, she was an official of UNESCO living in New York.

7. See appendix 2 for the composition of the cabinet as of November 1993.

8. J. McAuliffe, "Welcome to Cambodia, Where Nothing Is Ever as It Seems," *Indochina Interchange*, September 1997, 3.

9. Because nobody knew how many government officials there were, the new government found it necessary to take a census of all civil servants, which established this total around 140,000. The census took place on 7 February 1995, when every civil servant had to show up in his or her office to be counted and reregistered. Because of their low pay, averaging $13 a month, many civil servants ordinarily did not bother to show up at work or only came occasionally. In December 1994, a total of 146,311 civil servants were paid. The February 1995 census yielded 137,604 civil servants, with 8,707 absentees, of whom 5,220 gave explanations for their absence. Many more showed up for the census than actually worked throughout the year, and thus the census did not reveal the number of "ghost employees." Personal notes.

10. David P. Chandler, *Facing the Cambodian Past, Selected Essays, 1971–1984*, Chiengmai, Thailand: Silkworm, 1996.

11. Pierre P. Lizee, *Peace, Power, and Resistance in Cambodia*, New York: St. Martin's Press, 2000, 30.

12. Kate G. Frieson, "The Cambodian Elections of 1993: A Case for Power to the People," in R. H. Taylor, *The Politics of Elections in Southeast Asia*, Cambridge, MA: Harvard University Press, 1996, 231. The following discussion draws heavily from this source.

13. Later important countries such as Japan and Thailand built impressive new embassies to prove their commitment to the country. And at the time of this writing in January 2005, the United States was building a massive embassy complex, which reflected its commitment to be an important player in Cambodia over the long haul.

14. The Cambodian New Year is celebrated in Theravada Buddhist countries like Thailand, Myanmar, and Laos as well.

9

The King Reigns but Does Not Rule

In contrast to my earlier tour, when I was stationed in Siem Reap, I was now in the heart of the power game. I witnessed firsthand the unfolding drama of the new Cambodia. I found it quite sobering: Cambodia was now governed by Cambodians for Cambodians. Things were different: the intricate dance of governance between UNTAC, the SNC, and the SOC had ended. The drama of post-UNTAC Cambodia was like a high-stakes poker game. The game was first played by Hun Sen and King Sihanouk, and later by Hun Sen and Ranariddh, the coprime ministers, with the king lurking in the background. Though the game was outwardly friendly, everyone was playing to win. It was fascinating and tragic at the same time.

HUN SEN

Hun Sen was the longest continually serving head of government in Cambodia. He had been born into poverty on 4 April 1952 in Kompong Cham province. In response to a call from Sihanouk after the 1970 coup that deposed the king, he had joined the maquis[1] to fight General Lon Nol. He quickly rose in rank to company commander, battalion commander, chief of the general staff, and then deputy commander of a regiment. During the resistance he met and fell in love with Bun Rany, a sixteen-year-old girl who had joined the maquis as a nurse. But romance was prohibited during the era of the Khmer Rouge, and Hun Sen and Bun Rany could only exchange glances and secret letters. Hun Sen also had to ask *Angkar*, the Khmer Rouge top leaders, for permission to marry her. After several requests, permission was granted.

On 20 June 1977, Hun Sen fled to Vietnam to avoid being executed by Pol Pot's regime during the great purge of the eastern zone by Khmer Rouge forces. Together with Heng Samrin, he established the UFNSK (United Front for the National Salvation of Kampuchea). He later became foreign minister at the age of twenty-nine and shortly thereafter the prime minister of the People's Republic of Kampuchea (PRK).

Hun Sen's years at the helm of the Ministry of Foreign Affairs well exemplify his leadership style. After returning from guerrilla warfare in the jungle, he had a lot to learn about the bureaucracy. Unlike Ranariddh, Hun Sen quickly picked up information from his staff and advisers. A major ingredient of his success was his ability to select first-class adjutants and advisers and to reward them well. They were as loyal to him as he was to them. Rarely did any of them defect.[2]

The foreign ministry was a good learning laboratory. In the Cambodia then isolated from the outside world, ministry officials implemented foreign policy and wielded day-to-day power over Cambodians by controlling their contacts with foreigners and foreign organizations. In 1984 the ministry also began regulating tourism, which became an important source of foreign exchange for the PRK.

More importantly, the ministry needed educated, literate Cambodians to read and draft diplomatic documents and English and French speakers to interpret and translate. Hun Sen made personal appeals to intellectuals to join the ministry. The first former Khmer Rouge leader to extend such an invitation, he offered noncommunist intellectuals a career opportunity. His pragmatism paid off handsomely.

Diplomacy gave these Cambodians a chance to demonstrate political loyalty as well as to advance their technical and administrative competence. Later, after Hun Sen became prime minister, several former foreign ministry officials became powerful ministers in an increasingly noncommunist regime.[3]

Hun Sen, like all the ministers of the PRK, maintained close relations with Ambassador Ngo Dien of Vietnam. As the senior diplomat from Vietnam, Ngo Dien was also the chief adviser to the foreign ministry. Hun Sen learned a great deal about global politics and basic diplomacy from Ngo Dien, who admired the young minister's intelligence and aptitude.[4]

Hun Sen's ability to attract and make effective use of the skills of competent people was also evident in his position as coprime minister. His leadership was admired by the diplomatic community, both from the West and ASEAN. The Vietnamese, Russians, and other Eastern Europeans had long supported Hun Sen. The Chinese quickly learned to deal with him effectively. One Western ambassador recalled: "We, the western diplomats, shared the view that with Hun Sen things got done. We knew that when he promised something it would happen, whether it was dealing with western hostages held by the Khmer Rouge, business deals or foreign aid projects." It was also common knowledge that he worked deep into the night, chain-smoking his 555-brand cigarettes.

Hun Sen had waited a long time for the moment of truth in postelection Cambodia. After the elections he had two options: continue fighting or seek a solution based on the Paris Agreements. In other words, he could reject the election results or accept them and create conditions for national reconciliation. By 1994, he did not need to fight anymore. And Hun Sen and his CPP continued to control the government, as we've seen, most importantly the security apparatus.

RANARIDDH

Ranariddh was born on 2 January 1944 in Phnom Penh. His mother was a ballet dancer, a commoner, and one of Sihanouk's six wives. Unlike Hun Sen, he had led a charmed life. He was born into wealth in a royal house with a sprawling garden; under the PRK, the house was later given in perpetuity to the ambassador of the Soviet Union. When Ranariddh became prime minister, he tried to get the house back but failed. I went there many times, invited by the Russian ambassador for lunch and vodka. Ranariddh was brought up and adopted by his father's aunt, Princess Rasmi Sobhana.

He studied in Phnom Penh at the prestigious Lycée Descartes where many Cambodian leaders were schooled in their youth and attended high school in Marseilles, France. He married Marie Eng, a very sedate and beautiful woman of Cham (Muslim) descent, in Cambodia in 1968. He then returned to France, where he received law degrees from the University of Aix-en-Provence. During the turbulent years of 1979 to 1983 in Cambodia, he taught courses on political regimes of Southeast Asia and the Far East at Aix-en-Provence. In 1983, he was appointed personal representative of Sihanouk in Cambodia and Asia and coordinated FUNCINPEC's activities. In 1986, as a general, he was appointed commander in chief and chief of staff of the Armée Nationale Sihanoukienne (ANS), which later became the Armée Nationale pour un Kampuchea Independent (ANKI), the armed wing of FUNCINPEC. In 1989 Ranariddh became secretary-general of FUNCINPEC, and in 1990 he joined the SNC.

When Sihanouk resigned from FUNCINPEC in February 1992 to become the supposedly neutral head of the SNC, Ranariddh took over as president of the movement. In 1993 he became copremier of the Provisional Government and later of the Royal Government.

Ranariddh had grown up as a royal prince even during his exile in the French academy. Now, back as a Royalist premier, he enjoyed his office immensely and brazenly. After spending the 1980s as a beleaguered French junior professor, he reveled in the perks he received as prime minister. He loved the sumptuous receptions, gala dinners, airplanes, fast cars, and his game of golf back in Bangkok and later in Phnom Penh, which opened its first golf course in 1996. Ranariddh showed less interest in the affairs of state. Diplomats as well as foreign visitors considered him self-centered and boastful. It was rumored that he would put a few impressive-looking folders on his empty desk just before a diplomat would visit him. His style and mannerisms resembled that of his father, but there the resemblance ended. He left the thinking about politics to his copremier, Hun Sen, rubber-stamping most of the things Hun Sen proposed.[5]

Ranariddh's leadership style left a lot to be desired. Even though he brought with him a number of competent and highly educated aides who had taken relatively low-level jobs in Western countries, they lacked the experience of governance accumulated by their SOC counterparts. Furthermore, Ranariddh's lack of effective leadership made this group less efficient than the group assembled by Hun Sen. In fact, some of the key personalities among them, Sam Rainsy, Norodom Sirivudh, and Ung Huot, soon left him for one reason or another. The notable exception was Veng Sereyvudh, who cleverly walked a tightrope and continued with FUNCINPEC while maneuvering his way through the CPP bureaucracy. As minister of tourism he did quite well both professionally and financially. At the secretary of state level there was Ly Tuch, and at the under-secretary level Marina Pok; both remained trusted aides in his inner cabinet until the bitter end. His charming personal assistant, Christine Penn, who became my friend, also stayed to the end and beyond.

AN AUDIENCE WITH THE TWO PREMIERS

On 16 April 1994, eight days after my arrival in Cambodia, I was granted my first audience with the coprime ministers. We met in the Council of Ministers building. This was where they held cabinet meetings and where the powerful coministers attached to the council, Sok An from the CPP and Veng Sereyvuth from FUNCINPEC, held office.

It was a solemn occasion. The prime ministers were sitting on a dais. Ranariddh was to my right, Hun Sen to my left; Hun Sen was accompanied by his interpreter, Bun Sambo, whom I got to know very well later. Perpendicular to the dais were two rows of chairs. According to protocol, I was seated to the right. Colonel Muniruz Zaman, head of the UN Military Liaison Team, accompanied me. Across from us sat the principal aides of the two prime ministers whose faces I did not yet recognize. This was the first of many occasions on which I met the two premiers; later there would be private dinners, private audiences, and outings to open this or that project.

My first impression told me a great deal. In general, during those early days, for the outside world the copremiers presented a picture of complementary resolve on the major issues of the day. Ranariddh, the first prime minister, did most of the talking and listened to his own voice with delight. Hun Sen, the second prime minister, sat slumped in his chair, but he was keenly observing everything that went on. He did not say much. While this was the first time that we had met face to face, I felt sure that he had done his homework and received reports on my performance in Siem Reap during UNTAC times, including on my protection of Sam Rainsy and Sirivudh, the two key FUNCINPEC personalities, from attacks while campaigning. He also responded to my questions. Ranariddh, on the other hand, resumed his monologue as soon as I conveyed greetings from the secretary-general.

The conversation was dominated by talk of the disastrous Khmer Rouge counterattack to the government's dry-season offensive. Both premiers insinuated that Thai support for the Khmer Rouge had allowed the guerrillas to retake their nominal base on the northwestern border. Relations with Thailand had already soured because of the thriving trade of Thai businessmen with the Khmer Rouge.

The copremiers never mentioned Thailand by name, but Hun Sen later lashed out against Thailand in Battambang when the Khmer Rouge came within a doorstep of that city. Ranariddh and Hun Sen wanted the UN Military

Liaison Team (UNMLT) to monitor all of Cambodia's land and sea borders. But as far as the UN was concerned, I explained to them, it had no obligation under the Paris Peace Agreements to guarantee the borders of Cambodia without an official complaint of violations lodged with the Security Council. And with the rising cost of UN peacekeeping operations around the world, to go back to the General Assembly and ask for more money for the UNMLT, let alone authority to expand its functions, would be like pulling teeth.

At a welcome breakfast thrown for me by Taufik Sudarbo, the Indonesian ambassador, another ambassador from a powerful country suggested that instead of extending the twenty-person UNMLT to secure the Cambodian borders, three military observers should be assigned to me as advisers.

During the diplomatic corps's discussions at my welcome breakfast, it was clear that the ambassadors felt the Khmer Rouge's counterattacks did not merit an escalation of the UN security presence. The king's assertion that they were threatening the Paris Agreements was obviously taken with a grain of salt. Henceforth, three liaison officers from the UNMLT were detailed to work with me.

My capacity to assess the deteriorating security problems facing Cambodia was greatly enhanced with their attachment. Major Harbans Singh from Malaysia, Major Jan Wanderstein from Belgium, and Major Herve Gourmellon from France provided invaluable aid in the military work that continued to be crucial to postconflict peacebuilding.

All three were excellent. Major Gourmellon was a particularly wily and capable intelligence officer. He would chat with the still powerful contingent of French military advisers in the country and then report to me amazing intelligence details. Later I found out that in exchange, he reported to the French the contents of the confidential reports I sent to New York. These reports were sent by crypto fax machine and could not be intercepted, but the French seemed to know everything I said. Major Singh had good relations with the ASEAN military attachés from whom he also gathered invaluable intelligence, whereas Cambodian military officers from both factions provided Major Wanderstein important information on troop movements and their intentions. Wanderstein was invaluable when the general security and political situation of the country deteriorated.

During my audience with the copremiers, they elevated my status to the equivalent of an ambassador. Instructions were given to the foreign minister present to include me in the list of the diplomatic corps as number twenty-two.[6] I was, of course, very pleased with this elevation in status, which allowed me to perform my mandate with greater efficiency and enabled me to gather invaluable inside knowledge through constant interaction with the Cambodian leadership and the diplomatic corps.

Most, if not all, ambassadors accepted me as an adopted member of the corps, and soon I received invitations to diplomatic dinners and lunches welcoming me to Phnom Penh. At many of these gatherings I learned a great deal about the political landscape emerging in post-UNTAC Cambodia. I maintained very close relations with most of the ambassadors throughout my stay. During turbulent times we would huddle together to discuss events.

AN AUDIENCE WITH THE KING

On 1 May, three weeks after being received by the two premiers, I was granted an audience by King Sihanouk. I was, of course, not a stranger to Sihanouk. I had first met the flamboyant and versatile prince in the 1980s, when he had undertaken his annual pilgrimage to the General Assembly of the UN. Then he had come to the UN as head of the exiled Coalition Government of Democratic Kampuchea (CGDK) to condemn the Vietnamese occupation of Cambodia and promote the continued presence of the CGDK in the General Assembly.[7]

He had done so in a typical Sihanouk way, hosting popular singing-and-dancing parties at the Helmsley Hotel, within a stone's throw of the United Nations, to lobby for the CGDK. Invitations to them were much coveted. Featuring a Cambodian band playing western dance music and the prince himself singing old standbys like "That's What Friends Are For," the parties were a refreshing change from the dull UN cocktail circuit. The Khmer Rouge leaders, senior partners in the CGDK, also attended these parties but maintained a stoic silence. Led by Khieu Samphan, they acted as self-proclaimed minders of the king, watching his every move from the opposite side of the room. Unlike in 1979, when Sihanouk had tried to defect to the United States while under the watchful eyes of the Khmer Rouge, he was no longer under their control. I was fascinated by the interplay between the charming king and the dour Khmer Rouge.[8] At around the same time, I had also met Sihanouk at lavish ASEAN annual dinners at the nearby Hyatt hotel, where he had again campaigned for the CGDK. And, as we have seen, I had met the king twice in Siem Reap during UNTAC times.

Now I was being received in the Preah Tineang Tevea Vinicchay, or Throne Hall, where royal coronations, audiences for the prime ministers and senior ministers, and other ceremonies were normally held. The hall was also used for the formal presentation of credentials of foreign envoys to the king, an honor usually bestowed on plenipotentiary envoys.

This magnificent part of the palace complex was built in the traditional Khmer style and designed in the shape of a Roman cross. The hall was sixty meters long and thirty meters wide. It stood on a high base of approximately seven meters that constituted a kind of ground floor. The hall had a tiered roof, covered in the traditional orange and green tiles, and a fifty-nine-meter spire, which was said to have been influenced by the Bayon Temple on Angkor Wat.[9]

In September 1993, just before UNTAC left Cambodia, we had witnessed the solemn coronation of King Sihanouk in this same hall in a ceremony that recalled ancient customs. Heralds had blown conch shells as Sihanouk and Princess Monineath, his wife, entered the beautifully decorated hall. I felt deeply honored to be received in a building with so grand a history.

That morning I was accompanied by Colonel Munir, head of the UNMLT. Sihanouk greeted me warmly and welcomed me for the second time to Cambodia, where I had served earlier successfully, he said. He conveyed his regards to UN Secretary-General Boutros Boutros-Ghali and his gratitude for sending me as a sign of the continuing UN interest in Cambodia despite the ascension of a new government. Champagne and petit fours were served.

After exchanging formalities, we were led to a smaller room with a huge map of Cambodia. Here the king went into great detail in outlining the crisis caused by the Khmer Rouge's counteroffensive, which now dominated the conversation. In a highly animated fashion, he predicted that the Khmer Rouge, buoyed by its recent successes, would try to take Poipet, Sisophon, Thmar Puok, Sam Raong, and Tbeng Mean Chey, and that they would proclaim a separate state in an outer northern crescent bordering on Thailand. He said that if the Khmer Rouge succeeded they could conquer the large crescent containing Battambang and Siem Reap cities, but that if they did not they could be contained in a smaller outer arc of Poipet and Preah Vihear (see map 1.1 in chapter 1). According to the king, their success would provoke the hill tribe minorities in Ratanakiri, Mondulkiri, and Stung Treng to demand autonomy. He was thinking aloud about what to do next to save Cambodia. He

Photo 9.1.   My first audience with the king. Author's personal collection.

complained that the Royal Government did not take him seriously, and he was very pessimistic about the outcome of the peace negotiations. Not for the first time, he presented a picture of gloom and doom for Cambodia, as if the misery of the past twenty years were not enough.

Outwardly, the king appeared to be very sad. He confided to me and Munir that he was thinking only of saving Cambodia and no longer of saving the Royal Government! His lack of confidence in the two premiers was striking. He drew a comparison with the last years of Lon Nol, when Lon Nol had refused to see that he was losing against the Khmer Rouge until it was too late. Strangely, his eyes appeared to gleam when he said this. Sihanouk told me that he had always contended that the Khmer Rouge was still strong but that nobody listened to him. But I wondered: was he exaggerating the Khmer Rouge threat to assume control once again? Turning to me, he almost whispered, "Cambodia will be divided into two, your Excellency: the Royal Government and the Khmer Rouge–controlled areas."

AN AMBITION REDUCED TO ASHES

Why would the king's eyes brighten when predicting disaster for the Royal Government? For one thing, he had a fatherly feeling of superiority over the "young and inexperienced" copremiers, whom he considered greenhorns. "I told you so" was his mentality. And the copremiers had chosen to attack the Khmer Rouge rather than negotiate with them as he had suggested from Beijing. Moreover, it was quite evident that Sihanouk was unhappy with his position as a king who reigned but did not rule. He resented it.

Behind Sihanouk's resentment was, I believe, an unfilled lifelong ambition. Ever since he had been crowned king by the French in 1941, he had dreamed that he would one day be the executive head of government (be it as a king or president) with full powers of an independent, prosperous, and strong Cambodia in an era of peace and progress. An accomplished filmmaker, he liked to shoot movies, many of which were thinly veiled autobiographies. One of them, made in 1995, was tellingly titled *An Ambition Reduced to Ashes.*[10]

Even during the UNTAC period he had made three attempts to take the reins of power, but he had met with persistent American opposition. In January 1993, he had made a feeble attempt to lobby for presidential elections that would make him head of state with full executive powers.[11] The United States had strongly opposed his effort. In November 1992, Sihanouk had rushed to

Beijing for medical attention and threatened to resign from the presidency of the SNC. When Akashi, Hun Sen, and others had attempted to persuade him to stay on, Sihanouk had proposed that he be made the overlord of Cambodia until legislative elections were held and a new constitution was adopted. UNTAC rejected this idea. Then, in June 1993, Sihanouk had again attempted to assume power by forming a national government of reconciliation but had abandoned his attempts after the Americans had protested.[12]

After the UNTAC elections he had appeared to be within reach of his dream. Alas, in the constitution of September 1993, true power had gone to two young people: his son Ranariddh, whom he never particularly liked, and Hun Sen, whom he respected despite regarding him as his true nemesis. On many private occasions, he said that Hun Sen resembled him.[13]

A few months after our conversation that morning in May at the palace, at a farewell private dinner for the departing Indonesian ambassador, Sihanouk clearly expressed to me his discontent with his position of nominal king. He recounted that after the Constituent Assembly finalized the constitution in September 1993, the copremiers flew to Pyongyang to present him with two versions of the constitution. Despite their pretense of offering an alternative, he said, the two had already made up their minds to strip him of all but ceremonial power. He lamented that they persuaded him to sign the version favoring a constitutional monarchy. "They wanted me to be somewhere up in the sky above Cambodia," he complained to us at the dinner.

According to my notes, that was not exactly what happened in September 1993. Indeed, two versions of the constitution had emerged from the drafting exercise of the constituent assembly: one written by the drafting committee consisting of members of FUNCINPEC, CPP, and BLDB, and a so-called FUNCINPEC draft already available to the committee. The first draft, called a republican draft, stipulated that the head of state and the assembly would be elected, while the FUNCINPEC draft described a monarchy. When Hun Sen and Ranariddh flew to Pyongyang with the two drafts, Sihanouk made extensive annotations on both drafts but evidently made clear that he preferred the monarchial draft to the republican draft. Upon their return to Phnom Penh, both Hun Sen and Ranariddh reported that Sihanouk would be king. But the king apparently reversed himself the next day, and there were conflicting reports over the weekend about what Sihanouk had or had not said.[14]

This was vintage Sihanouk. Just like in 1955, he vacillated between reigning as a king who the peasants would worship as a God King or serving as a head of state whose authority the people would not question.

On 21 April 1994, ten days before he met with me, the king made public a secret letter he received from Khieu Samphan requesting that he leave the country on the first available commercial flight to Bangkok in order to avoid Khmer Rouge disturbances. In response to Samphan's letter, the king called for a roundtable discussion in his presence at the royal palace. It would involve the coprime ministers, Khieu Samphan, and Chea Sim of the CPP, who was president of the National Assembly. All four parties quickly agreed to attend the roundtable, thereby defusing a potentially dangerous situation. The National Assembly cancelled its Monday session, and a threat to outlaw the Khmer Rouge—a priority for the CPP—was shelved. Unfortunately, despite Khieu Samphan's pledge to take part in the roundtable discussions, the Khmer Rouge once again pulled out of the negotiations.

SHOWDOWN OF THE PEN

In June 1994 Sihanouk unveiled yet another plan to retake the reins of power. From his self-exile in Beijing, he summoned veteran journalist Nate Thayer for a long interview.[15] In it, he accused the coalition government of being incapable of halting the deterioration of the country's politics. "How can I avoid intervening in a few months' time or one year's time if the situation continues to deteriorate?" he asked rhetorically. He had no plan to take power right away, he said, as "the situation is not desperate enough." But if the situation became "desperate," he would "have to take power for one or two years." He added, "I did it in 1952 and 1953 to put an end to the anarchy of the kingdom . . . so why not now before I die, the last mission?"[16]

Sihanouk said his plan for a new government of national unity was very simple. He would be "not just the Head of State, but also the head of government. This means my own Prime Minister." The regime would have four vice presidents: Ranariddh, Hun Sen, Finance Minister Sam Rainsy (a maverick FUNCINPEC member), and Khmer Rouge leader Khieu Samphan. He would also give important portfolios to the Khmer Rouge. Anticipating objections from the copremiers, he said that he did not wish to replace them. He would do so, he continued, only if the need arose and parliament asked for him to take over. And only with their consent.

Sihanouk expressed confidence that his son Ranariddh would not betray him. But he anticipated a different reaction from the other premier. "Mr. Hun Sen will be red in the face. . . . when he will read your article," Sihanouk chuckled. "He will say that 'we were absolutely wrong to elect Sihanouk as King, it is extremely bad, extremely dangerous, and now he wants to retake power and to take the Khmer Rouge again in his government. It will be a catastrophe.' Mr. Hun Sen will attack me very, very violently. I know that." He knew also that his bid for power would be doomed without the acquiescence of Hun Sen and the CPP, however. "If he does not support me, it is useless to go back to Cambodia, because I don't want to shed blood to fight a secession led by Hun Sen." His wife, Queen Monineath, strongly opposed the idea of resuming power, Sihanouk said. "But to lose my wife, to lose Mr. Hun Sen, is nothing compared to Cambodia. For me Cambodia is my life. If Cambodia sinks, I have no reason to survive."[17] In a weekend radio broadcast, the Khmer Rouge put forward a plan for power sharing similar to the one offered by Sihanouk.

Thayer's interview revealed Sihanouk's absolute conviction that only he could save Cambodia from catastrophe. He ignored the fact that his support of the Khmer Rouge in 1970 had helped create the catastrophe in the first place. The king thrived on crises and had resorted to hyperbole to make a case for his return to power.

Hun Sen's reaction was swift. In an unprecedented step, he wrote a long and pointed open letter to the king in which he pointed out that such a move would be unconstitutional. Responding to allegations that he posed the major obstacle to reaching a solution with the Khmer Rouge, Hun Sen claimed that he had "done nothing but conform myself to the Constitution." The Khmer Rouge was not interested in peace or stability, he said. "Now they oppose your Majesty's initiative of national reconciliation. . . . They even dare to demand that a new government be formed, which is tantamount to the dissolution of the legitimate institutions resulting from the elections and to nullifying all the efforts jointly exerted by the whole Cambodian people and the international community in implementing the Paris Agreements." He added, "To accept the Khmer Rouge demands is equivalent to a . . . coup d'etat."[18]

According to Hun Sen, the coalition government had no choice but to pursue the military option against the Khmer Rouge. The Khmer Rouge had sabotaged two rounds of talks, he emphasized. The copremier also flatly rejected the idea of giving the Khmer Rouge seats in the government.

On 18 May, Chea Sim and Hun Sen accompanied Sihanouk from the royal palace to the Pochentong airport. "There are people who accuse me of wanting to take power," Sihanouk remarked, according to Hun Sen. "But I am too old. What do I want the power for?" Sihanouk later denied again that he wanted to resume power. But his interview with Nate Thayer indicated that Sihanouk intended to take direct state power, Hun Sen observed. He complained that the interview portrayed the copremiers as another obstacle to conferring power to Sihanouk.[19] In his meeting with me and in subsequent interviews, the king repeatedly predicted an impending catastrophe which Hun Sen and Ranariddh would not be able to handle. But Hun Sen, a military general, did not consider the Khmer Rouge's threat a potential national catastrophe.

Sihanouk's reaction to Hun Sen's open letter to him was rather predictable. He sulked and said that he now wanted to withdraw from political life. In a handwritten fax to the *Phnom Penh Post*, Sihanouk wrote, "His Excellency Hun Sen and others want me to remain powerless." He vowed that he would "no longer intervene in the affairs of the Royal Government of Cambodia."[20] Instead, he would remain in Beijing to undergo further treatment for cancer.

In the meantime the failure of Sihanouk-instigated talks in mid-June between the government and the Khmer Rouge had ground the peace process to a halt. The Khmer Rouge representatives in the capital were subsequently ejected by the government, and their compound closed. When asked about the way forward for the country, Sihanouk replied, again predictably, that reconciliation between the Khmer Rouge and the government was now "impossible . . . for reasons which everyone knows and in spite of all my efforts." He ended his latest attempt to retake power. After his pronouncement, he spent a great deal of time in Beijing.

But although officially without power, Sihanouk maintained his influence through frequent meetings of the royal family in the palace. And in the countryside, where FUNCINPEC had won the elections because many illiterate peasants thought they were voting for him, Sihanouk remained popular. What's more, he could still advise the two premiers, appoint cabinet ministers and ambassadors, and grant amnesty. Plus he could delay or refuse an appointment if he so chose. Despite his ceremonial position, Norodom Sihanouk remained a factor to be reckoned with in Cambodia.

The words traded between the two leaders revealed their different conceptions of Cambodian politics and underscored their complementary places in the nation's destiny. Sihanouk, having played the power game since 1941, was a figure from the past, with a symbolic role. But Hun Sen embodied power in the future. The king lost their war of words. He had lost his grip on the present and remained nostalgic for the past. He overestimated his popularity with the people he used to control. Hun Sen knew the National Assembly would not support his bid for power.

I wish to emphasize that the showdown of the pen was but one incident in a long love-hate relationship between the king and Hun Sen. Deep inside, the king was full of respect and admiration for Hun Sen, who had come far since his days as a fugitive from the Khmer Rouge in the late 1970s. Sihanouk had said in private that he wished Hun Sen was his son. In moments of rage, however, especially during the 1980s, Sihanouk did call Hun Sen all kinds of names, including "my bad son" and "lackey of the Vietnamese," etc.

THE EMERGENCE OF A "STRONGMAN"

During the early days of the Royal Government, Hun Sen began to slowly but surely emerge as the "strongman," as the king frequently dubbed him. He knew that he had a solid power base. Armed with a constitution and National Assembly created with help from the United Nations, he had figured out how to outmaneuver the king. He had also learned to use the Western concepts of constitutionalism and democracy to legitimate himself to the international community and keep aid flowing in.

Perhaps only Sihanouk's devoted wife and close adviser could fully understand the king's thoughts on Hun Sen's political ascent. Ranariddh certainly could not and often misread his father's thinking, though he attended the frequent family gatherings at the palace, where Sihanouk reigned supreme and often castigated Ranariddh.

Ranariddh's frame of reference, having returned from exile, was his father's *Sangkom Reastr Niyom* regime of 1955–1970. It had been no pillar of democracy and had killed and tortured opponents like its successor Lon Nol government. Throughout the postelection honeymoon period, which lasted until March 1996, Hun Sen, on the other hand, extolled the virtues of the coalition government with FUNCINPEC. It "should continue for decades to come," he said many times. The top FUNCINPEC ministers cooperated with the CPP as they shared in the spoils of the foreign aid bonanza and bonuses paid by the many foreign investment projects. Hun Sen bet that Ranariddh would not be willing to forego the spoils, and he turned out to be correct.

Before the elections, Sihanouk, while flying in a North Korean aircraft, had reportedly tried to convince Ranariddh not to run in them but to merge FUNCINPEC with CPP instead. According to Harish Mehta, Sihanouk stated that the CPP was "very powerful. They have been running Cambodia since 1979. They have everything in place. You will not win the elections. . . . It is better to join them, and work together for Cambodia, but within the framework of the CPP." Ranariddh reportedly only smiled.[21]

Sihanouk knew very well that the SOC's machinery was there to stay. Hun Sen had determinedly built it up in the 1980s. For his part, Hun Sen realized that Sihanouk was still a powerful symbol among the Cambodian people, particularly the peasants, but also among the urban population who had been isolated from the world. Hun Sen and Sihanouk complemented each other, and both realized it. Hun Sen had roundly supported Sihanouk's two or three bids to become the president of Cambodia during UNTAC times. The ever-flexible Sihanouk figured that if he could work with the Khmer Rouge, why not with the SOC too?

Clad in the cloak of the Royal Government, Hun Sen was respected by the entire world. The donor community no longer shunned him. On the contrary, aid had begun pouring in at a rapid pace. Foreign aid financed the entire development budget of the Royal Government and provided a compelling reason for Ranariddh to stay with the new regime.

Outwardly at least, the two prime ministers were increasingly speaking with one voice. But while Ranariddh continued to play the role of first prime minister and spokesman, making his marathon speeches, most of us in the international community soon noticed that Hun Sen really held the power. At ceremonies where we sat next to the podium, we observed the two premiers whispering to each other all the time. Hun Sen would do most of the whispering, while Ranariddh would vigorously nod his head. Clearly, the terms "first" and "second" prime minister did not signify seniority.

Of course, Hun Sen had to pay a price for holding the power. He had to unconditionally pursue the path of pluralistic democracy dictated by the constitution and the Paris Agreements. Nobody could define exactly what that meant, but translated into specific terms it meant he had to safeguard his coalition with Ranariddh and FUNCINPEC. Failing to do so could provoke the Western countries to cry foul, as they would three years later.

RUOM RITH IN THE PYRENEES

Sihanouk was never fully gone. Throughout the post-UNTAC period, while nestled in his preferred retreats of Beijing and Pyongyang (and occasionally Siem Reap), he continued to stay in touch through his unique way of governing by his sharp tongue and pen. He often handwrote biting letters, commentaries, and annotations to newspaper and magazine articles on Cambodia in English and French, lavishly decorated by multiple exclamation marks and underlinings. He published his writings in his *Bulletin Mensual de Documentation* (*Monthly Bulletin*), which was widely distributed around the world by airmail to three hundred researchers on Cambodia, including myself.

The bulletin allowed him to wield influence by providing him with a vehicle to criticize the governance of the copremiers. He could blame them for lack of direction while maintaining his official dignity as king. The last part of the bulletin always contained a selection of photo souvenirs from his reign during 1955–1970, many depicting hotels, factories, or other buildings in Phnom Penh and other big cities from this era, as if to tell people that only he could bring back prosperity to Cambodia. Ironically, these old buildings from the 1960s were not impressive.

Outwardly, the king continued to be extremely polite and circumspect in his criticism of the two prime ministers. In fact, he was often more critical of his son Ranariddh, who shared his mannerisms and even his high-pitched cackle but not his extraordinary brains, than he was of Hun Sen. However, when the coalition government began to grow more and more strained, the writings of a man called Ruom Rith suddenly appeared in his bulletin. Ostensibly, Ruom Rith was an old friend of the king; he was his exact age and living somewhere in the French Pyrenees. They shared identical writing styles, alive with exclamation points and multiple—up to four or five in a row—question marks. They also shared anger and despair over the way things were going in Cambodia in the post-UNTAC era. But whereas the king was restrained in criticizing Hun Sen, Ruom Rith was outspoken.

Apparently, this extraordinary Ruom Rith was like a "big brother" to Hun Sen, with X-ray vision, and was watching Hun Sen's every move. And he was sending caustic comments addressed to the king that Sihanouk then published in the bulletin.

But it was commonly known in Phnom Penh that there was no such Ruom Rith, that he was, of course, the king himself. The king absolutely denied this. Later, during tense periods in Phnom Penh, other alter egos of the king appeared in the bulletin. They began to argue with each other. The king appeared to enjoy the role of puppet master, choreographing his own private puppet show.

Obviously, Hun Sen was not happy at all, but he was powerless against this imaginary figure. The biting "Dear Sire" letters must have annoyed him immensely. In 1998, when Hun Sen would win the Cambodian elections, he demanded justice and asked for Ruom Rith's address. The king then quietly shelved Ruom Rith for a while. However, Ruom Rith did not stay gone for long. In June 2003, Hun Sen again demanded a halt to his writings, saying that "Ruom Rith has insulted me and the government for half a decade." He asked, "Who is Ruom Rith? How does he know to write such smart letters, as if he lived here and knew everything that goes on?"[22]

Hun Sen had a similar way of attacking the king—through pro-CPP newspapers. Meanwhile, using the constitution as a weapon, he continued to diminish Sihanouk's power. Symbols of Sihanouk's stature slowly began to fade.

In the early days, we in the diplomatic corps had always come out in force to the airport to greet the king and queen when they arrived from Beijing. A royal welcome replete with red carpet and an army band had awaited them, and schoolchildren had lined the route from the airport for hours in the hot sun. Now, suddenly, at one of Sihanouk's arrivals, there was no such welcome. Tired of being reminded of his symbolic status, the king had ordered the ceremonies halted.

NOTES

1. *Maquis* was a term borrowed from the French resistance. They were named after the underbrush and thickets called maquis. The term was used in Cambodia to denote the resistance who allied behind Sihanouk against Lon Nol. They were dominated by the Khmer Rouge.

2. The following several paragraphs draw heavily from Evan Gottesman, *Cambodia After the Khmer Rouge, Inside the Politics of Nation Building*, New Haven: Yale University Press, 2003, chapter 9.

3. One was Cham Prasidh, who attracted the attention of Roger Lawrence during UNTAC times as a person in the Ministry of Finance of the SOC who was eager and willing to learn the internationally accepted principles of budgeting. He would later become the successful minister of trade after the cabinet reshuffle of October 1994.

4. Gottesman, *Cambodia After the Khmer*, 206.

5. In May 2004, newspaper reports from Cambodia indicated that history was repeating itself. Ranariddh, who steadfastly aligned himself with Sam Rainsy to oppose the implementation of the 2003 election results, with Hun Sen the head of the winning party, had signed a joint letter with Hun Sen refusing an invitation from the king for the two to go to Pyongyang to settle their differences under the auspices of dear papa.

6. There were twenty-one ambassadors resident in Phnom Penh, and protocol informed me that invitations to official functions would henceforth always be given to those twenty-one plus myself. My car bore the plate "CMD, Chef de Mission Diplomatique" and the vehicles in my component all bore CD plates.

7. See chapter 2.

8. I was privileged to be invited to Sihanouk's grand soirees as a representative of Mr. Sams Kibria, the under-secretary-general of the UN Economic and Social Commission for Asia and the Pacific and the secretary-general's representative for humanitarian matters in Cambodia.

9. Julio A. Jeldres and Somkid Chaijitvanit, *The Royal Palace of Phnom Penh and Cambodian Royal Life 1999*, Bangkok: Bangkok Post Publishers, 1999, 63.

10. His website, www.norodomsihanouk.org, informs readers of the movies he has produced and the music CDs of his compositions. His movies may be ordered from www.meridianvideo.com.

11. In an interview with Nayan Chanda of the *Far Eastern Economic Review*, he claimed to have the support of the Chinese for this move. Nayan Chanda, "I Want to Retake Power," *Far Eastern Economic Review*, 1 February 1993, 20.

12. See chapter 7.

13. Unpublished letter from Hun Sen to Sihanouk dated 18 June 1994.

14. John C. Brown and Ker Munthit, "Sihanouk Backs Royalist Charter," *Phnom Penh Post*, issue 2/19, 10–23 September 1993.

15. Nate Thayer, "Last Act: Sihanouk's Plan to Retake the Reins of Power," *Far Eastern Economic Review*, 23 June 1994, 16. See also Nate Thayer, "King Talks of Taking Power," *Phnom Penh Post*, issue 3/12, June 1994.

16. Thayer, "Last Act."

17. This section draws heavily from Thayer, "Last Act," and Thayer, "King."

18. Unofficial translation of a letter dated 18 June 1994, from Hun Sen to Sihanouk as circulated to diplomats in Phnom Penh by Hun Sen aides. This English version also appeared in the *Phnom Penh Post*, issue 3/13, 1–14 July 1994, but, oddly, the words "cool coup d'etat" appeared in brackets.

19. I have a transcript of tapes of the three-hour interview, and the words Thayer attributed to Sihanouk were indeed the king's.

20. John Ogden, "King Washes His Hands of Politics," *Phnom Penh Post*, issue 3/13, 1–14 July 1994.

21. Harish C. Mehta, *Warrior Prince: Norodom Ranariddh, Son of King Sihanouk of Cambodia*, Singapore: Graham Brash, 2001, 95.

22. Seth Mydans, "The Royal Alter Ego Wields a Poison Pen in Cambodia," *New York Times*, 29 June 2003.

10

A Mysterious Coup Attempt

WHO WAS THE MASTERMIND?

After the showdown of the pen between the king and Hun Sen in June 1994, rumors flooded Phnom Penh about planned large-scale demonstrations to support a return of the king to power. Truong Mealy, the chef de cabinet of Sihanouk, went on television to discourage people from demonstrating. However, our intelligence in the diplomatic community and the press did not detect plans for any large-scale demonstrations, and the rumor quickly fizzled out. Were the rumors deliberately sown to heighten the tension?

Suddenly, around dusk on Saturday night, 2 July, government troops took up positions at the homes of major government leaders in Phnom Penh. I received several phone calls from ambassadors, my military advisers, and government sources that a coup attempt was taking place. We were warned to stay home. According to rumors, unidentified troops from the east were marching on the capital. I discussed this on the phone with my good friend Deva Mohd. Ridzam, the Malaysian ambassador. "Why from the east?" we wondered. The Khmer Rouge strongholds were in the west, bordering on Thailand. To the east lay Vietnam, and it was quite impossible that Vietnamese troops would march on Phnom Penh.

We found out later that a clumsy coup d'etat had been swiftly quelled. At 5 p.m. that day, twelve armored personnel carriers (APCs) and close to three hundred police forces, said to be loyal to the secretary of the interior, CPP's

Sin Song, had left the eastern province of Prey Veng and headed for the capital. After crossing the broad Mekong River by slow vehicle ferry at Neak Luang mysteriously unhindered, they were finally stopped by loyalist forces twenty-five kilometers from Phnom Penh at Dei Eth, three hours after the coup attempt began. There was no confrontation, and the would-be rebels were eventually allowed to return to their barracks unpunished.

The government officially declared the duo Chakrapong and Sin Song, the leaders of the short-lived secession movement, as the coup plotters. This time Chakrapong narrowly escaped death and landed in exile. He was the first of what would eventually be three Norodoms to go in as many years.

Chakrapong, the second son of Sihanouk, led a very active political life, switching back and forth between FUNCINPEC and CPP. Born 21 October 1945, he and his half brother Ranariddh grew up together and were inseparable. They both went to France to study. Both joined FUNCINPEC, but they fell out over politics. Chakrapong envied Ranariddh who seemed to get all the plum positions. Following irreconcilable differences with Ranariddh, including denial of his request to get equal status, Chakrapong defected from FUNCINPEC and joined Hun Sen's CPP in early 1992. The CPP received him with open arms, rewarded him with the post of vice prime minister in charge of six ministries, and gave him a sprawling residential villa.

Born in Prey Veng, Sin Song became a supporter and aide to Chea Sim in 1970 at the age of twenty-three. In 1977 he fled to Vietnam and joined the UFNSK and returned to Cambodia with Hun Sen. He was the dreaded minister of national security during UNTAC times. UNTAC accused him of instigating criminal irregularities during the 1993 elections. Relieved from his position as head of national security after the secession attempt in June 1993, he still commanded some respect among the police forces. Sin Song landed in jail but escaped to Thailand. But everyone seemed to agree that there were bigger fish behind the coup attempt.

We were subsequently informed that Hun Sen had become aware of a coup attempt at 1 p.m. Acting on a tip, he summoned the secretary of state of the defense ministry, General Chhay Sang Yun (CPP). The latter admitted that acting on orders of General Sin Song (CPP), he was trying to arrest three top generals in the army. Allegedly the objective of the arrests was to prevent the CPP army from mobilizing opposition to the coup plotters. The plotters ostensibly relied heavily on the highly politicized and fully armed police forces.

Hun Sen began making plans to suppress the rebellion. He did not notify Ranariddh until 5 p.m., four hours later, and Sar Kheng, the CPP cointerior minister, until 6 p.m. We in the diplomatic corps surmised that initially Hun Sen had suspected Sar Kheng of involvement in the coup attempt, although he never officially accused him.

In the aftermath of the coup attempt, accusations and counteraccusations resounded throughout the government about the identity of the plotters, including the mastermind. Because of the clumsy execution of the coup attempt, most of us in the diplomatic community believed that it was more political theater than a realistic bid to seize power. Yet the theater had some far-reaching consequences for the balance of power, particularly within the CPP.

On 11 June in Beijing, Sihanouk had told reporters that Chakrapong and General Sin Song were furious because they had not been rewarded for leading the 1993 secession movement. Though the secession had quickly fizzled out, many seasoned observers credited it with forcing FUNCINPEC to include their CPP rivals in the coalition government. Sihanouk quoted Chakrapong as saying, "Papa, it is unacceptable. They used us as their instrument to remain in power." The king never said, however, whether Chakrapong informed him of his coup intentions or if he had promised to turn the country over to the king if the coup had succeeded. However Sar Kheng later asserted that "according to intercepted telephone conversations," Chakrapong was involved in the coup and his objective was to give power to the king.

Yet another theory of the coup emerged when it became known that all the officials implicated had close links to the faction within the CPP led by party president Chea Sim and his brother-in-law, Sar Kheng. In those early years, Hun Sen had to face challenges within his own party. Persistent rumors surfaced on and off in our diplomatic circle of an impending rift between the so-called Chea Sim wing and the Hun Sen wing.[1]

When the chips were down, however, the CPP always managed to close ranks, and rumors about an impending split disappeared as fast as they surfaced—attesting to the increasing power and grip of Hun Sen over the party and his ability to maintain party unity.

Sar Kheng, who categorically denied involvement in the coup, had been born on 15 January 1951 in a village in the eastern province of Prey Veng. During the Khmer Rouge period he had been the Khmer Rouge's permanent secretary of the northeast zone. In 1977 he had fled to Vietnam and joined the UFNSK front. He had been minister of the interior of the SOC government during UNTAC times. In the Royal Government of Cambodia, he became deputy prime minister, cominister of the interior and national security. In the last capacity he controlled the forty-thousand-strong and well-armed police force.[2]

When interviewed by the journalist Nate Thayer, Sar Kheng could or would not say why Hun Sen was late to tell him of the coup attempt. He asserted that it was he who had ordered the rebel police forces technically under his command to retire to their barracks.[3]

Chakrapong and Sin Song's involvement in the coup attempt was in all likelihood merely the tip of the iceberg. Senior government sources involved in the interrogation of Sin Song claimed that he had "threatened to reveal very high government officials who supported him." Despite Sar Kheng's denials, suspicion of his involvement persisted. Some also suspected that Chea Sim, the acting head of state, must have at least been aware that a coup plot was brewing.

The operation to put down the coup was commanded from Hun Sen's house. We in the diplomatic corps were surprised by Hun Sen's highly unusual move to use FUNCINPEC forces—Cominister of the Interior You Hockry and his FUNCINPEC associates—and those of former KPNLF General Pan Thai to thwart the coup, as if he was not sure which CPP troops were loyal to him. According to senior officials, Hun Sen met other CPP officials, including Chea Sim, at a dinner on 7 July and agreed, as angrily demanded by Chea Sim, not to push for more arrests. Apparently, he was convinced that further arrests would result in armed conflict and turmoil within the party.

On 8 and 9 July top government leaders made their first show of unity since the events began. They issued strong joint warnings to the media and officials against "spreading rumors" that could cause "divisions among the leadership." It was their attempt to stifle what was by then an open secret: that powerful figures in the government were deeply embroiled in a power struggle. Who was the ultimate mastermind? The coup attempt was a mystery that will probably go down in history unresolved. It was quite clear though that Hun Sen and probably Ranariddh with him were the main targets of the coup. Hun Sen then was not yet in full control over the security apparatus, especially the police forces.

Whoever was behind the coup attempt, Cambodian officials and diplomats acknowledged that there had been serious talk of a coup for several months among CPP officials upset with recent political developments. The United States had specifically informed government officials in recent weeks— including Sin Song and Sar Kheng—that the United States would refuse to support any government that emerged from a putsch.[4]

At a gathering of the diplomatic community to explain the coup attempt, Hun Sen told us, with fondness, that he would protect Ranariddh, who was like a "weaker brother." Hun Sen, the experienced statesman, was obviously the dominant of the two, leading Ranariddh by the hand along the arduous path of governing Cambodia. But Ranariddh, on the other hand, taught Hun Sen the ways of the Western world: how to cope with international recognition and aid and with the international scrutiny of journalists, diplomats, and NGOs. For a time, they worked well together.

THE KHMER ROUGE ARE FINALLY OUTLAWED

While the shock waves of the failed coup attempt of 2 July were still reverberating in Phnom Penh, on 7 July the CPP spurred the Royal Government to pass a bill in parliament to officially outlaw the Khmer Rouge. The coddling of this faction would finally cease. There was unconfirmed speculation that the mysterious coup attempt might have been linked to efforts, perhaps very high up, to stop this outlawing of the Khmer Rouge.

The bill revealed deep divisions within the National Assembly. Many opposition figures feared that it could be used to quash legitimate dissent. After all, it would be easy to accuse someone of being pro–Khmer Rouge since all of the leaders were at one point or another associated with the Khmer Rouge. After debating for two and a half days and adding two articles to the bill concerning the safeguarding of human rights and the protection of innocent people, the National Assembly unanimously approved it on 7 July. The bill provided a six-month grace period during which the government would be amenable to negotiations and the king could grant amnesty to Khmer Rouge members. The king, who was always in favor of reconciliation rather than outlawing the Khmer Rouge, refused to sign the bill and deferred it to Chea Sim, who as president of the National Assembly had the constitutional right to act on behalf of the king in his absence.

The promulgation of the bill put pressure on Thailand and other countries to prevent free passage of Khmer Rouge personalities through Bangkok. Until now, they had traveled under the Coalition Government of Democratic Cambodia passport, which the bill declared invalid. Khmer Rouge assets at home and abroad became subject to confiscation by the government. The United States and Thailand made statements backing the bill. The Khmer Rouge radio greeted the outlawing of its organization by announcing the formation of a new government. The Royal Government, it proclaimed, was a Vietnamese puppet.

THE HOLLOWAY CABLE

At the end of his two-and-a-half-year term, on 9 June 1994, John Holloway, the ambassador of Australia, ended his mission in Cambodia. But he remained in Cambodia, paid by his government, as an adviser to Foreign Minister Norodom Sirivudh.

On 5 October 1994, all hell broke loose in Phnom Penh when the *Sydney Morning Herald* in Australia published an edited version of Holloway's "Protected" end-of-mission report that he had sent in June. It had been leaked to the press by a rival in the Australian government. In his cable, Holloway scathingly disparaged the Royal Government and the king. It was, even by Western standards, quite harsh in its criticisms.[5]

Holloway asserted that "the two Prime Ministers . . . are unable to exercise leadership, even when they are in the country. Most government ministries are barely working and civil servants are only motivated to attend their offices at all by the possibility of making some extra money." As a result, "corruption reaches to the highest ranks of government. Every business deal must have a cut for the relevant Minister (or Prime Minister)."[6]

Holloway drew a sharp contrast between the troubled administration in Phnom Penh, with its "out of control army," and the Khmer Rouge, whom he characterized as "well disciplined, committed and not engaged in petty corruption." Unlike the motivated guerillas, people "join the [RCAF] army to use their uniforms and weapons as a meal ticket." And "as government forces move through the countryside, unpaid and out of control, looting and committing a wide range of crimes, the Khmer Rouge get more potential support." His remarks reminded me of what I had observed when traveling with General Long So Pheap in Siem Reap province.

For ambassadors, and for myself, protection of our cables was crucial. I sent my confidential cables to New York by way of a crypto fax machine, which I inherited from UNTAC. Even though I was assured by the UNTAC operator before he left that this channel was absolutely secure, I sometimes had an uneasy feeling that some cables might have been leaked, for instance to the king. During an audience with me, Sihanouk had once pointed to all the columns surrounding us and proclaimed that there were no secrets in the palace. Sensing that the walls had ears and that the king had informers everywhere was an eerie feeling. That same feeling usually came over me on ceremonial occasions when the king glanced at me as if he knew what was in my crypto faxes. But at least I knew that FUNCINPEC could not decipher my coded messages. At his birthday party on 1 January 1995, Foreign Minister Ung Huot kept asking me in an arrogant tone about the contents of my cables to New York, even though I kept stating that these cables were confidential. The CPP, which had a long history of eavesdropping on its citizens, may have had the skills to decipher my crypto faxes. I never knew.

Later in the year, there was another leak involving Indonesian military aid. Apparently, behind the back of the Indonesian ambassador, Taufik, the powerful and often renegade Indonesian military had been delivering large quantities of ammunition through its own channels to the Cambodian military from its Pindat factory in Bandung, Indonesia. This was leaked to the consternation of Taufik, who scolded the military attaché. The attaché, who maintained his own office in Phnom Penh, was stoically silent. Taufik complained that "now *Pak* Benny Widyono and other civilian Indonesians will be targeted for kidnapping and even death by the Khmer Rouge."

In Canberra, Holloway's cable landed in the middle of a debate over whether Australia should provide military aid to the Cambodian government. The Khmer Rouge had repeatedly threatened to kill and kidnap citizens of countries who provided such aid; most countries therefore gave it surreptitiously.

In his cable, Holloway had been most critical of Sihanouk, who had never been a favorite of Australian or American policymakers. "The antics of the King have also been disruptive—still pathetically pursuing power although riddled with cancer," Holloway wrote bluntly. "He has belittled the government, tried to cause splits in the ruling groups and thrown aside government strategy to outlaw the Khmer Rouge (a firm precedent in Thailand, Malaysia and the Philippines)." Like a Broadway star in a high school play, Sihanouk had "strutted around his small stage, erratic and emotive, continuing the negative influence he has wielded over the last two years."[7]

While not accusing Holloway of committing "lese Majesty,"[8] which the king could have done according to the constitution, the king's private cabinet expressed outrage over Holloway's "slanderous and baseless attacks." "Everyone recognized the pivotal role played by the king in ensuring the success of Cambodia's recent UN supervised peace process," the cabinet's statement continued. "His majesty is a stabilizing factor for the kingdom. Throughout his life, he has worked to reconcile the Cambodian people." "As regards power, our king has never dreamed for a single second of retaking it and has sworn in front of the throne to respect the constitution," the statement concluded.[9]

In the end, Holloway did not lose his job. Despite his criticisms of the government, he had recommended that Australia continue to help fight the Khmer Rouge. Moreover, by the time the cable was leaked, the tumult he described had pretty much subsided, as the copremiers had largely come together in the wake of the mysterious but clumsy attempt.

EXIT SAM RAINSY

Sam Rainsy and Norodom Sirivudh, the able and most effective campaign managers for FUNCINPEC, had been rewarded for their efforts with two powerful posts in the Royal Government. Sirivudh became deputy prime minister and minister of foreign affairs, while Sam Rainsy became the minister of economics and finance.

However, from the word go, Sam Rainsy was in trouble, not only with Hun Sen but most apparently with his own boss in FUNCINPEC, Ranariddh. After taking office, Rainsy had introduced economic reforms and commenced a fight against the crooked businessmen who laundered money and lined the pockets of Cambodian politicians. To the dismay and embarrassment of both Hun Sen and Ranariddh, he often aired the government's secrets in public, making points by relying on confidential documents that he obtained in his capacity as minister. He was an original enfant terrible. His determination to root out corruption made many enemies in the government, the private sector, and the armed forces, though he was popular among urban and educated young Cambodians and NGOs.

Even friends of Rainsy conceded that the French-trained minister often found it hard to communicate his ideas and strategies. Not a team player, he often made decisions on his own, without checking with his peers or superiors, let alone the Council of Ministers. For instance, the week before his removal, he promoted, transferred, or recruited 106 customs officials in his ministry. His rebellious attitude, and maybe his popularity, alarmed Ranariddh and his close supporters.

Technically competent, Sam Rainsy had attended schools in Paris and London and the elite Lycees Sisowath and Descartes in Phnom Penh. His father, Sam Sary, had achieved prominence as a civil servant in Sihanouk's government. After a disagreement with Sihanouk, Sam Sary had mysteriously disappeared, presumably killed by government assassins. Rainsy studied political science, economics, and accountancy in France and worked in several investment banks in Paris, the United States, and the Middle East before running his own accountancy practice in Paris.

He had been a founding member of FUNCINPEC in 1981, and in 1989 he had become Ranariddh's representative in Europe. During UNTAC times, Sam Rainsy had been a member of the SNC and campaigned effectively for FUNCINPEC, including in Siem Reap, where I hosted him several times.

Rainsy married the brilliant Tioulong Saumura, the future vice governor of the Central Bank and the daughter of Nhiek Tioulong, an adviser of the king. The pair became a formidable and outspoken voice of the opposition, with Saumura as the brain. Rainsy's efforts to clean up what he called Cambodia's "jungle economy" were much appreciated by the donor community but hated by certain businessmen who benefited from shady deals. Indeed, Rainsy lost his job just four weeks after the opening of a market owned by businessman Teng Bun Ma, who was embroiled in a fight with Rainsy over the exorbitant prices he charged poor stallholders. Teng Bun Ma, a murky figure with plenty of cash, was banned from the United States for his alleged involvement in the drug business.

In October 1994, after a long feud with the prime ministers, Sam Rainsy was sacked and his firing announced in a long-awaited cabinet reshuffle. Ranariddh, his boss in FUNCINPEC, fully agreed with Hun Sen's decision to remove Rainsy from office. The cabinet reshuffle was approved by parliament on 20 October. The most important changes were the removal of Rainsy and the resignation of his friend Sirivudh.[10] FUNCINPEC, already weak because of institutional and personal factors, thus became seriously marginalized politically. According to most of the Western press, Sirivudh resigned in sympathy with Sam Rainsy. Sirivudh denied this and cited two reasons for his resignation: the government's marginalization of the king and its refusal to make peace with the Khmer Rouge.

After his sacking, and to the immense annoyance of Ranariddh, Sam Rainsy used his position as a member of parliament to continue criticizing the government. To stop him, on 22 June 1995 Ranariddh introduced a motion to expel Rainsy from the National Assembly. A sizable crowd turned out for the occasion. The public gallery was full of journalists, members of NGOs, and other young supporters of Rainsy who had scrambled for seats to watch the spectacle. It was as if he were on trial. We in the diplomatic corps were seated in our reserved seats on the left-hand side of the hall. There was no sign of the country's top leaders—Ranariddh, Hun Sen, or Chea Sim. But the rest of the members of parliament (MPs) from both parties filled up their usual seats.

Sam Rainsy gave a broad V sign of victory when he entered and smiled at us. It was quite a strange sight as he walked very slowly into a room where the verdict against him was already in. He glanced at us as if to say, are you not going to say anything? National Assembly Vice Presidents Loy Sim Cheang (FUNCINPEC) and Son Soubert (BLDP) took their seats. According to an aide, Chea Sim refused to attend because he was "embarrassed" by the whole affair. Finally, Loy Sim Cheang was given the task of announcing the removal of Rainsy based on a petition from FUNCINPEC. Officially, then, Rainsy had been sacked by his own party, and parliament only confirmed the decision. Most people agreed that something was not right, but nobody dared to speak up, as technically everything seemed to have followed "the letter of the law."

Sam Rainsy and a friend, BLDP member Khem Sokha, raised their hands to speak, but Loy Sim Cheang quickly banged the gavel indicating that the session had adjourned. The MPs filed out the door quickly and only Khem Sokha and Ahmed Yahya, two other friends of Rainsy, remained to hear Rainsy speak. Ahmed Yahya also spoke. Later he and Sirivudh denied that they signed a petition to support Rainsy's expulsion from the National Assembly. Yahya contended that the so-called petition was in fact a list of attendees at a FUNCINPEC meeting called by Ranariddh to discuss Rainsy. Son Soubert, the vice president of BLDP, complained that Ranariddh had imposed his will on the National Assembly. Although this shady affair was condemned by a number of Western countries, the international community refrained from taking action on what was considered an internal matter.

After his expulsion, Rainsy toured the United States, Canada, Australia, and New Zealand for months to gather support for a new party he was launching: the Khmer Nation Party (KNP). Young people critical of government policy who had increasingly lost confidence in FUNCINPEC (Ranariddh had become no more than a fellow traveler of the CPP) flocked to the KNP, later renamed the Sam Rainsy party.

Rainsy also lobbied donor governments as he thought the diplomatic corps in Phnom Penh was too soft on the premiers. Domestically, he became a champion of the rights of female textile workers in this fast-growing export industry. Sihanouk told me that these girls were very poor farmers' daughters who had never earned a single dollar before they joined the textile factories. Wages of $50 a month were competitive in the region, Sihanouk said, and increasing them would make footloose textile industries leave the country for Bangladesh or Sri Lanka. Then the king, with a mischievous chuckle, said that Sam Rainsy was slicing the prime ministers like salami. They could not kill him as he would turn into a martyr, but to let him remain in the National Assembly would allow him to continue his vigorous campaign against them.

Sirivudh wanted to move a FUNCINPEC congress, scheduled for November 1995, forward to July in order to reconsider Rainsy's expulsion. Rumors circulated that Norodom Sirivudh, Ahmed Yahya, and other dissidents within FUNCINPEC planned to embarrass Prince Ranariddh with difficult questions about Rainsy's expulsion at the congress. But they did not succeed. Later, Ranariddh managed to postpone the congress further, to March 1996. He, it seemed, had learned how to play the political game.

THE SECOND NORODOM TO GO

Dusk was settling in Phnom Penh and the cocktail hour starting for us in the diplomatic world on the night of 17 November 1995 as we were bidding farewell to popular Bob Porter, the number two man in the U.S. embassy. Bob was throwing the party in the beautiful front garden of his home on street number 240 in the elite neighborhood of Phnom Penh that housed many prominent personalities, including Norodom Sirivudh, the conspicuously absent foreign minister. At nine my wife and I bade goodbye to Bob. Little did we know that the drive home, which normally took not more than five to ten minutes, would last over half an hour.

Now heavily armed soldiers and APCs blocked the entire neighborhood as if an attack by the Khmer Rouge were imminent. Three tanks guarded the city home of Hun Sen, located on the rotunda surrounding the Democracy Monument two blocks away.

Our driver tried to navigate through the quiet streets, but we had to make an extensive detour toward the center of town and double back to our home. I called my friend, Hun Sen's neighbor Deva Mohd. Ridzam, to compare notes. He told me nervously that one of the tanks had its nose trained on his residence, which was separated from Hun Sen's home by the embassy of the Democratic People's Republic of Korea. Deva and I were close; we met at least once a week. That evening, we did not have the slightest idea what was happening. Another coup attempt? Was it the Khmer Rouge?

Later we found out that Foreign Minister Sirivudh had been arrested. We surmised that his arrest was the culmination of incidents that had started on 23 October during a celebration commemorating the signing of the Paris Agreements. The celebration, which Sirivudh had hosted, had taken place in the library of the Cambodian Institute for Cooperation and Peace, a think tank he chaired. Diplomats and journalists had been present; as the representative of the United Nations secretary-general, I had been the guest of honor. While I had engaged in small talk with some diplomats, Sirivudh had been laughing and joking with Cambodian journalists at the far end of the room. Perhaps under the influence of beer, he had made some unguarded remarks to two journalists, So Naro, the secretary-general of the Khmer Journalists Association (KJA) and the political director of the *Angkor Thmei* newspaper, and Cheam Phary, the KJA's advertising director. He had said something about shooting Hun Sen.[11]

So Naro was convinced he had a scoop, so three days later the two journalists went to see Sirivudh. The topic of their conversation had allegedly turned to plots to kill Hun Sen. Two weeks later, the 11 November issue of the *Angkor Thmei* had carried an article praising Sirivudh for "effectively obstructing" a plot to kill Hun Sen—who immediately flew home from Siem Reap and summoned the two journalists. Soon thereafter, Sirivudh had been put under house arrest.

Later, So Naro's statements to us in the diplomatic corps were even more revealing than the *Angkor Thmei* article. Sirivudh had apparently told the two journalists that some military people had asked his permission to kill Hun

Sen. They had presented him with a detailed plan to ambush Hun Sen's car with B40 rockets. But, Sirivudh said, he had not given them his approval. So Naro recalled, "He said he had not given the green light—he used the words 'green light' in English—but would wait until 1996." But if Hun Sen gave any trouble to Sam Rainsy or the Khmer Journalists Association, Sirivudh had said, he would take action. He could go "to the Royal Palace . . . I am a member of the Royal family, so no one will check me," he had told the two journalists. "I could take a shotgun." He had then pretended to put a gun under his jacket, elaborating, "And when I get close to Hun Sen, I will shoot him." Sirivudh had also told So Naro, "It does not matter what happens to me, if I can change the pages of history."[12]

Then came the real bombshell. Apparently on 6 November, after Sirivudh's conversation with So Naro and Cheam Phary but before the publication of the *Angkor Thmei* article, Ung Phan, a shady and controversial FUNCINPEC cabinet minister, had taped a phone conversation with Sirivudh about accusations of corruption in a passport deal involving Sam Rainsy and Sirivudh.[13] Allegedly, Sirivudh and Rainsy had received a kickback from Thomas de la Rue in London for the lucrative deal of printing Cambodian passports. Sirivudh had denied the charges, which had been lodged by Hun Sen, over the phone, and in a fit of anger had made threats against Hun Sen's life. A FUNCINPEC person close to Ung Phan apparently gave the tape of the phone conversation to Sar Kheng. Hun Sen eventually got hold of the tape, and in his own fit of anger and show of force had brought out the tanks, APCs, and heavily armed soldiers.

Although the armies of the three Cambodian factions had been integrated into the RCAF, their individual units, as we have seen, continued to be commanded by generals from their factions. Since the phone conversation had taken place between two FUNCINPEC cabinet ministers, Hun Sen felt, FUNCINPEC police should handle Sirivudh. You Hockry, FUNCINPEC's co-minister of the interior, supported by heavily armed security forces under his command, worked all through that night to extract a confession from Sirivudh that the voice on the tape was his. They also tried to get Sirivudh to agree to go abroad. But he refused to relent on either count and declared that he would defend his innocence in court.

On Saturday, 18 November, Ranariddh urgently summoned the diplomatic corps to his house to brief us confidentially on the events leading to Sirivudh's house arrest. "It was connected to the plot to assassinate Mr. Hun Sen," he whispered to us. Ranariddh then played a tape recording of about one and a half minutes allegedly featuring the voice of Prince Sirivudh. The voice said, "As I told you, Your Excellency, if he continues with these problems, I will shoot him." The voice then added, "I warn you, please tell Hun Sen clearly, I am not afraid of him. If he wants violence, he will sure get it. I always keep my word." We agreed that the speaker seemed extremely agitated and did not sound as if he were joking.

The tape only featured one voice, as the other person's voice had been expunged. It appeared that Ranariddh was trying to convince us that Sirivudh was indeed guilty of threatening to kill Hun Sen. Later, we learned that the other voice was that of Ung Phan. Ranariddh told us, again in a whisper, that the king had confirmed that the voice we heard was Sirivudh's. The king congratulated the Royal Government for discovering the threat and gave his imprimatur to the government "to do whatever was necessary," including arresting his brother, Sirivudh. The prince then accepted house arrest. Publicly, Ranariddh in the next few days patted himself on the back for having saved Sirivudh's life. But if Ranariddh really wanted to protect Sirivudh, whose life he claimed had been threatened, why did he not take him into his house?

Sirivudh's formal arrest followed a unanimous National Assembly vote to strip him of his parliamentary immunity in a closed-door session on 21 November. Later, Ranariddh described the votes by FUNCINPEC MPs as a symbol of "unity." Democracy had been expressed, Ranariddh seemed to be saying.

Sirivudh was put into the notorious T3 prison, where the guards were astonished and kneeled before him. After the king's intervention, he was moved to detention in the Ministry of the Interior. The king told us privately that he was convinced that at T3 there would be a sudden explosion to destroy the prison in which Sirivudh would die. The king, again, knows everything in Cambodia.

On Thursday, 30 November, the CPP and FUNCINPEC issued a joint statement signed by Chea Sim and Ranariddh saying that the assassination plot that led to the arrest of the king's half-brother was an individual case, not a political one.

Ranariddh, in encounters with the diplomatic corps, now assured everyone that the bond between the two parties was as strong as ever. And, indeed, the two premiers were seen in their usual whispering-consultations mode. Probably to ease his conscience, Ranariddh now took the line that there was ample evidence that Sirivudh had threatened to kill Hun Sen. "In all civilized countries you cannot just go around saying that you want to kill someone without going to jail or being committed to an asylum," he said over and over again to a group of diplomats, including myself, as if to convince himself.

There were strong indications that Sihanouk was thoroughly annoyed with events and had even threatened to leave for Beijing after Sirivudh was sent to T3 prison. However, his three public statements after Sirivudh's imprisonment did not express public support for the prince. Sihanouk said it was better for Sirivudh to be detained in the Ministry of the Interior than out in the street since there were many "anti-Sirivudhs" roaming the streets. In a second statement, he suggested that some analysts, who had accused him of being unable to intervene on behalf of Sirivudh, ought to go out and find another, better king, and he offered to abdicate if they could find one. This was his favorite refrain.

While the king had managed to broker Sirivudh's transfer from T3 prison to the Ministry of the Interior, he still suspected that Sirivudh's life was in danger. This prompted another exchange of letters between the king and Hun Sen. Sihanouk wrote Hun Sen humbly:

> My younger brother Norodom Sirivudh has said against Your Excellency some words completely unjust, unjustified and unpardonable. But as Your Excellency is a great pillar following nobly Buddhism of which the Dharma encourages us to be tolerant and to give pardons to offenders, permit me to solicit from Your Excellency Samdech your compassion to the three young children of Norodom Sirivudh and a semi-pardon for my younger brother Norodom Sirivudh in the form of being expelled from Cambodia and being sent into exile to France.[14]

The king's obsequious letter amounted to an offer that Hun Sen could not refuse. The king did not normally write such letters. Hun Sen had no choice but to agree to the king's solution and pledged eternal loyalty to the monarchy. Sirivudh thus became the second Norodom to be exiled in as many years.[15] Both Hun Sen and Ranariddh saved face by getting him out of the country alive. Before his departure, Sirivudh wrote two letters to the co-premiers thanking them for their clemency and promising not to engage in Cambodian politics anymore. The prince underlined that he made this oath to His Majesty the King (who, rumors had it, had drafted his letters). Hun Sen thanked Sirivudh for his "good words" and wished the best of health and happiness for his family. And Ranariddh praised Sirivudh for being a prominent member of the royal family and for having done so much for the FUNCINPEC party.

Opinion on the affair differed between Western and Asian diplomats. I remember vividly an incident at the airport when we were invited to see Hun Sen off on an official trip abroad. We were huddled in a small circle on the tarmac when Tony Kevin, the new Australian ambassador, moved angrily toward the Vietnamese ambassador, Tran Huy Chuong, then the dean of the corps. Gesticulating angrily and moving closer and closer until he almost touched his breast, Tony demanded that Tran, on behalf of the corps, make a demarche to the prime ministers to protest what he said was "unjust treatment" of Sirivudh. Tran replied that he was certainly not going to interfere in Cambodia's internal affairs and suggested that Tony go visit Hun Sen himself, maybe accompanied by like-minded ambassadors.[16] As for me, my superiors in New York said that it was not proper for the United Nations to make a demarche.

Sirivudh arrived in Paris on Sunday, 24 December, at 7 a.m. This brought to an end, at least temporarily, what many believed was the most severe crisis of the Cambodian government since the 1993 elections. Several journalists had even predicted that it would be the deathblow to FUNCINPEC.

Was Norodom Sirivudh a threat to Hun Sen? A smooth politician and diplomat, he was a popular dinner guest, and privately many friends and acquaintances had heard his jokes about "killing Hun Sen" and planning a coup. Most dismissed them because he did not fit the profile of a killer. Since his resignation as foreign minister, Sirivudh had publicly spearheaded the movement within FUNCINPEC to try to keep it from being completely usurped by the CPP. He therefore became an embarrassment in the eyes of Ranariddh, who was probably satisfied with the status quo.

The bizarre Sirivudh affair removed any lingering doubt as to who actually controlled the country. The use of tanks to arrest Sirivudh made clearer than ever how far the CPP had succeeded in marginalizing FUNCINPEC. It had occurred under the nose of Ranariddh, who with his advisers and ministers was busily cutting deals and signing business contracts while his copremier, Hun Sen, quietly consolidated his grip over the military, the police, and other apparatuses of the state, especially in the provinces. By demanding the cochairmanship of the Cambodian Development Council, Hun Sen also assured his grip over the business aspects of governance. Hun Sen's success could be attributed to sheer hard work, perseverance, good advisers, and the cunning that allowed him to always keep two or three steps ahead of any potential adversary.

NOTES

1. In the party hierarchy, Hun Sen was Chea Sim's vice chairman.

2. Inherited from the PRK/SOC communist regime, the police force was quite powerful and fully armed.

3. Nate Thayer, "Sar Kheng: 'We Can Survive This,'" *Phnom Penh Post*, issue 3/14, 15–28 July 1994.

4. Nate Thayer, "Coup Plot Thickens," *Phnom Penh Post*, issue 3/14, 15–26 July 1994.

5. John Holloway, "Cambodia: The Government and the Khmer Rouge," edited version, published as "Guerrillas to Exploit Deepening Crisis," *Sydney Morning Herald*, 5 October 1994. The cable was reproduced in edited form as "Australian Diplomat's Cambodia Analysis," *Phnom Penh Post*, issue 3/22, 4–17 November 1994.

6. Holloway, "Cambodia."

7. Holloway, "Cambodia."

8. The crime of violating majesty is an offense against the dignity of a reigning sovereign or state.

9. Holloway's cable was written before the king's interview with the *Far Eastern Economic Review* proposing his resumption of power under certain circumstances.

10. Other important changes resulting from the October 1994 cabinet reshuffle include the following (F stands for FUNCINPEC, C for CPP):
    a. Ing Kieth (F), minister of public works and transport, replaced Norodom Sirivudh (F) as deputy prime minister.
    b. Ung Huot (F), minister of education, replaced Norodom Sirivudh as minister of the Ministry of Foreign Affairs and International Cooperation.
    c. Keat Chhon (C), vice chairman of the Cambodian Development Council (CDC), replaced Sam Rainsy (F) as minister of economics and finance.
    d. Chantol Sun (independent), secretary general of CDC, replaced Cham Prasidh (C) as secretary of state, economics, and finance.

    e. Cham Prasidh (C), secretary of state, economics, and finance, replaced Var Huot (C) as minister of commerce. The latter became ambassador to Australia.

    f. Tao Bun Lor (F), secretary of state and agriculture, replaced his boss, Kong Sam Ol (C), as minister of agriculture. Kong Sam Ol joined the king's cabinet.

    g. General Tol Lah (F), secretary general of the National Assembly, replaced Ung Huot (F) as minister of education.

    h. Four secretaries of state were promoted to ministers to reflect the increased priority of their ministries: Veng Sereyvuth (F), Tourism; Hong Sun Huot (F), Rural Development; Mok Mareth (C), Environment; and Nut Narang (C), Culture and Fine Arts.

11. He later claimed that any such remarks he made were a joke.

12. Jason Barber and Ker Munthit, "From Calendars to Killing—the Reporter's Tale," *Phnom Penh Post*, issue 4/24, 1–14 December 1995.

13. Ung Phan had switched back and forth between the CPP and FUNCINPEC. As a Khmer Rouge cadre, he had fled with Hun Sen to Vietnam. He had become head of the office of Heng Samrin between 1979 and 1981 and director of Hun Sen's office in 1985. In 1990 he had been arrested for trying to form a political party under the PRPK's one-party system. After his release he had again tried to establish a political party. On 29 January 1992, he had survived an assassination attempt after Hun Sen had rescued him and hid him in his home. In 1992 he had joined FUNCINPEC and been appointed adviser to Ranariddh. He became minister of state in the Royal Government and in that capacity was questioning Sirivudh on the phone.

14. Personal copy of an unofficial translation of the letter.

15. Later, during his open dispute with Ranariddh in 1996–1997, Hun Sen boasted that he had already exiled two Norodoms, in 1994 and 1995, and that he would not hesitate to exile the third Norodom.

16. In an ironic twist, Tony Kevin would later become one of Hun Sen's staunchest supporters.

11

Is There an Asian Model for Development?

POST CONFLICT PEACE BUILDING

My mandate in Phnom Penh fell within what the UN calls Post Conflict Peace Building (PCPB). PCPB involves identifying and supporting structures that will tend to strengthen and solidify peace. Thus, although I was not in charge of coordinating aid to Cambodia, a job ably performed by Eduardo Wattez, the United Nations Development Program (UNDP) resident coordinator, I maintained a close watch on the impact of economic development on political relationships and tensions.

If there was a clear winner in post-UNTAC Cambodia, it had to be the economy. Many Cambodians, especially in urban centers, were in 1995 far better off than in any year since 1970. Unfortunately, rapid economic development had created its own tensions. On the one hand, the swiftly growing economy spawned friction between the two partners in the government who competed for the spoils. On the other hand, development united the two premiers in confronting their critics—the donor community, the UN special representative on human rights, and the NGOs—in their pursuit of what they called the "Asian model for development," which emphasized economic growth over human rights and democracy.

At the same time, the transition from socialism to market liberalism, dictated by the constitution, was proceeding relatively smoothly. The technocratic economic approach adopted by the coalition government was possible because the CPP leadership willingly dismantled the stifling Eastern

European–style of governance, which still dominated many rural areas, so that the reinvigorated party could become an agent for change.

During the first half of the 1990s, the gross domestic product (GDP) had expanded at an annual rate of 6 percent, while inflation had dramatically declined from an average of 140 percent per annum in 1990–1992 to 3.5 percent in 1995.[1] The main reasons were the elimination of domestic bank financing and a substantial inflow of external assistance. By the mid-1990s, the entire development budget was financed from foreign aid.[2]

Cambodia benefited from two important circumstances. It was located in the center of Southeast Asia's economic "miracle" and could not help but share in the dynamic growth that continued unabated in the region until the regional financial crisis of July 1997. And the establishment of a broadly recognized legitimate government had opened up the floodgates of international aid.

The favorable economic situation was a boon to the Cambodian people. After twenty years of war and devastation, Cambodians finally had some hope for the future. Compared to the recent past, the Royal Government of Cambodia (RGC) had achieved a great deal. There was evidence of recovery everywhere. Tourism was rapidly making a comeback, especially at Angkor Wat in Siem Reap, with new hotels and restaurants springing up all over the place. The garment industry, located mainly in Phnom Penh, was booming.

Aid agencies, foreign businessmen, and foreign investors kept cabinet ministers busy, especially those dealing with the economy in finance, industry, agriculture, and public works. Cambodia's budding new elite continued to enjoy their exorbitant windfall revenues by renting out houses vacated by UNTAC types to newly arrived diplomats and businessmen.

Unfortunately, aid and foreign investment projects mostly benefited Phnom Penh and, to a lesser extent, the three designated growth areas of Battambang, Siem Reap, and Sihanoukville (Cambodia's only oceanic port). Even in rural areas, however, there were many new houses being built by farmers and increasing motor-vehicle traffic that indicated peace and economic progress. People traveled from hamlet to hamlet by motorcycle, commercial pickup truck, or "*remoks*," the open wagons pulled by a motorcycle that had begun to replace traveling on foot. Schoolchildren everywhere, in urban and rural areas alike, who used to walk around in bare feet and rags, now wore sandals or shoes and neat blue-and-white uniforms like kids in neighboring countries.

Of course, a daunting task still lay ahead. Poverty continued to be rampant in rural areas. Most people still lacked access to health and educational facilities, potable water, electricity, and serviceable roads. Land mines remained prevalent in many parts of the country, making valuable agricultural land unusable. Most importantly, Cambodia had lost human resources through genocide and an exodus of its most educated citizens between 1975 and 1979. Per capita income remained low, at around $260, whereas in several other countries in the region it had risen by a factor of seven or more since the late 1960s. Rehabilitation needs were massive, and Cambodia's administrative capacity remained weak. Under these circumstances, the trickle-down effect of economic growth was slow—much too slow.

The cabinet reshuffle of October 1994 had reflected the pragmatic approach to development adopted by the government.[3] The changes had been carefully crafted behind closed doors. Prince Ranariddh, who had been heavily criticized within his party for getting rid of Sam Rainsy and Norodom Sirivudh, had tried to justify these inexplicable moves by claiming that putting the Ministries of Economics and Finance and Commerce in the hands of one party, the CPP, would promote harmony in decision-making. In the past, he said, there had been difficulties between Commerce, the Cambodian Development Council, and Economics and Finance.[4]

The new government had little experience in economic policy and no tested institutional arrangements to rely on. Though its Cambodian Development Council (CDC) had two wings dealing with external assistance and foreign investments respectively, the final power to approve large foreign aid and private investment projects was vested in the coministers of the Council of Ministers, Sok An of the CPP and Veng Sereyvuth of FUNCINPEC. They, especially Sok An, were the real power behind approval of foreign investment projects, as any businessman trying to invest in Cambodia could testify. It soon became an open secret among shrewd businessmen, mostly ethnic Chinese from neighboring countries, that the CPP channel of influence through Minister Sok An to Hun Sen was more effective in getting things done than going through FUNCINPEC's Veng Sereyvuth to Ranariddh. However, they made sure that they did not ignore either channel.

After the reshuffle, FUNCINPEC continued to control some of the lucrative ministries, and some of its top members became quite wealthy. It was the party's rank and file, especially in areas outside Phnom Penh, who felt increasingly duped and marginalized. Despite Ranariddh's laconic remarks, tensions were brewing.

Jobs in the Cambodia of 1993 were hard to come by. But although the average pay for the civil service was only $30 a month, there were perks such as subsidized rice and other essential goods that helped families survive. Some of the middle-level and more senior jobs also provided opportunities for accruing fabulous riches from distributing licenses and concessions to the private sector. In the heavily aid-dependent economy, the most highly educated people supplemented their salaries by assignment to donors' projects as counterparts, often with much-coveted access to foreign travel and per diems. The CPP, with enough influence to mete out these jobs, gained power through its patronage.

Many international Cambodia watchers hailed the appointments of CPP technocrats like Keat Chhon (who now controlled the Ministry of Economics and Finance) and Cham Prasidh in the reshuffled cabinet as signs that the CPP really wanted to change. The two men turned out to be truly committed to the sound economic policies required by the donor community. Years after the reshuffle, the donor community continued to laud the economic performance of the country at the annual donor coordination meetings on Cambodia organized by the World Bank.

AN ASIAN MODEL FOR DEVELOPMENT?

The government's vacillation between complying with Western demands for democratization and clinging to political power produced a picture in contrasts. Encouraged by such international bodies as the World Bank and the Asian Development Bank, Hun Sen and Ranariddh had agreed to emphasize economic development while relegating the expansion of democracy and human rights to a later stage. They declared that Cambodia was following the Asian model exemplified by Malaysia, Singapore, and Indonesia (until the fall of Suharto in 1998) rather than the path of Western liberal democracy. "When the stomach is hungry, discipline and stability comes first, before democratic rights," Ranariddh said in August 1995. He went on: "Democracy means food for the people's stomachs, shelter, education, medical facilities, and basic amenities and the freedom to express and move freely. This is democracy in the Cambodian sense . . . To millions of poor rural people democracy is just a phrase to be talked about in idle gossip. It does not ensure food for their stomach nor an end to their plight." Ranariddh anticipated that "when the rural poor people have sufficient food, shelter, education and basic amenities, then democracy can be preached and installed in abundance."[5]

What Ranariddh failed to mention is that in a number of East and Southeast Asian countries, rates of growth were impressive in an atmosphere in which democracy was introduced, renewed, or consolidated, including South Korea, Taiwan, the Philippines, and Thailand.[6] Yet a third "Asian" model for growth is provided by the spectacular rise of authoritarian capitalism in China, which tops the world in rates of growth year after year, and equally impressive Vietnam. Although officially still driven by one party, the communist party rule, which at one time vowed to bury capitalism, rapid economic growth in these two countries is driven by a sprawling private sector and a wide open-door foreign investment policy. CPP has adopted liberal democracy and in 1995, Ranariddh and Hun Sen obviously chose the Asian model of Malaysia, Singapore, and Indonesia.

Ranariddh did support the idea of a free, self-regulated press but said that the "western brand of democracy and freedom of the press is not applicable to Cambodia." He compared democracy and a free press to a suit that "we have to redo or trim in order to fit ourselves." But Lao Mong Hay, president of the Khmer Institute of Democracy (KID), a respected Cambodian think tank and NGO, declared "Ranariddh's defense of the 'food-first-democracy-later'" concept "a dangerous departure from the government's commitment to uphold democratic values" as stipulated in the Paris Agreements, the International Covenant and Convention on Human Rights, and the Cambodian Constitution.[7]

Sam Rainsy, after his ouster from the government and parliament, became Ranariddh and Hun Sen's most outspoken opponent. He did not believe there was such a thing as an Asian way to democracy. Constantly lobbying in state capitals like Paris and Washington, he lamented that Cambodia was moving further and further from democracy as practiced in the Western countries and argued that donor countries should refrain from giving aid to the RGC. While his campaigning resonated with some U.S. and French lawmakers, donor countries continued to support the RGC.

THE DONORS' RESPONSE

But because of Cambodia's massive dependence on foreign aid, wide support around the world for NGOs focusing on human rights and the presence in

Cambodia of the world's only field office of the Center on Human Rights, human rights abuses and lack of democracy came under close scrutiny.

Aid was given by bilateral donors, multilateral donors (e.g., UN agencies), and NGOs. This was a far cry from the 1980s, when development aid had not been allowed in Cambodia. Now, all UN agencies, including the Bretton Woods Institutions, the World Bank, the IMF, and the Asian Development Bank, returned to Cambodia.

The Cambodian economy was highly dependent on foreign aid. By 1998, total external assistance was 14 percent of the GDP, 57 percent of the value of exports, 167 percent of government revenue, and 169 percent of government expenditures.[8] The top bilateral donors were Japan, France, the United States, and Australia. The United States also channeled a lot of aid through NGOs. The UN agencies, the World Bank, and the Asian Development Bank were important sources of aid too.

As the Cambodian government quickly learned, there was no such thing as a free lunch, however. The "Asian model" may work for countries like Malaysia and Singapore that do not depend on foreign aid, but the massive amounts of aid so generously given by donors came with strings attached, some overt, others covert. The donors, of course, had substantial leverage to promote broader political participation in Cambodia and sound economic growth. Annually, aid meetings were held to coordinate both bilateral and multilateral aid, rotating between Tokyo and Paris.

At the annual aid coordination meetings, donors castigated the government for wrongdoings, including corruption, the destruction of Cambodia's forests, and human rights abuses. But in spite of these protests, Cambodia's main donors still granted largely unconditional aid to the Royal Government. They obviously put a high priority on stability in this postconflict country.

Donors adopted a two-pronged approach. Ambassadors of donor countries generally went along, albeit reluctantly, with the "Asian model" followed by the copremiers and continued to dispense aid despite the many strange internal power struggles. At the same time, some donor countries supported institutions, NGOs, and opposition politicians who engaged in prodemocracy and human rights activities.

The NGOs had become a significant conduit of foreign aid. A system of subcontracting between major aid agencies and NGOs had developed. Many of the NGOs were engaged in projects to foster democracy and human rights, including by providing assistance to parliament, trained judges, and experienced defense attorneys. The aim was to create a firm respect for the rule of law, which involved building an independent, functioning judiciary and nurturing the Cambodian human rights movement.

Notably, the United States channeled most of its technical assistance through the Asia Foundation, to be parceled out to NGOs. The Asia Foundation financed numerous NGOs, including the International Republican Institute and the National Democratic Institute (affiliated with the two American political parties) to help in subsequent elections.

I personally felt the influence of one NGO, the Defenders Project, which was financed by the U.S. AID. One day I stated in a press interview that I believed the Khmer Rouge had grown weak and no longer posed a threat to the country. The next day, while I was away from my office, a Khmer Rouge messenger delivered a sheet of paper to my secretary with the threat: "Mr. Benny, U-N Chief, I'll blow your head off." It was signed, "From, suffer victim." As I was the UN secretary-general's envoy, the government then provided me with military-police bodyguards who followed me everywhere, even to the men's room.

Photo 11.1. Death threat from the Khmer Rouge delivered to my office by a Khmer Rouge messenger. Note the mixture of colloquial with flawed English. Author's personal collection.

The person delivering the message, who thought I was a tall Frenchman, returned to my office again and again. Finally, the police arrested him. When he stood trial, he was defended by a bright young Cambodian law student engaged by the Defenders Project. This young man managed to declare my stalker insane and gain his release. The stalker promptly tried to see me again in my office but was prevented by security guards. Of course, in the United States, defendants who are declared criminally insane are sent to asylums, not set loose on the street. The experience made me consider how establishing piecemeal institutions to promote justice might have unforeseen consequences. It almost cost me my life. Yet I realized that the architects of democratic processes had to start somewhere.

In the post-UNTAC period, the scale of aid to Cambodia was so huge that it distorted the economy. In an aid-related version of "Dutch disease," a high proportion of Cambodia's scarcest resources, educated people, is pulled toward employment in donor agencies and international nongovernmental organizations (NGOs) or attached to projects as salary-supplemented counterparts. At the same time donors and NGOs virtually take over the funding of education, health care, social welfare, rural development, and so on, while the government spends most of its funds on defense and security.[9] The "Dutch disease" effect was observed in the Netherlands in the 1960s when large reserves of natural gas were first exploited. It refers to the massive inflow of foreign exchange that deindustrialized the Dutch economy. In the Cambodian case, aid crowds out other sectors becoming a tradable sector financed by "revenues" in the form of aid.[10]

In addition, donor funding eased pressure on the government to increase the collection of revenue and to raise the salaries of government employees because so many top and middle-level officials received salary supplements for working as project counterparts. Foreign aid did a great deal to help Cambodian citizens, but it also altered the ways their own government proved willing to work for them.

Because donor funding became such a critical component of the economy, the threat of suspension of aid became a potent and effective weapon in the hands of donor countries. However, it worked only as long as the government submitted to it. The clash between sovereignty and foreign interference became vividly apparent in the aftermath of the Sirivudh affair. Increasingly irritated by Western criticisms of his handling of it, Hun Sen sent a blunt message to Western countries not to tie aid to human rights. In speeches in early December 1995, he appealed for a Cambodian "patriotic movement" to protect Cambodian sovereignty. "If you're happy, give aid, but if you're not, don't talk about our affairs," the second prime minister said. He singled out the United States and France for particular criticism.

But Hun Sen added that the United States should still pay "compensation" of at least $20 billion for its past bombings of Cambodia. "You created war in Cambodia. . . . You investigate Pol Pot's crimes—you must investigate the beginning when you created Pol Pot." Noting that he himself had lost an eye during the American bombing of Cambodia in the 1970s, Hun Sen stated pointedly: "You are now talking about human rights but when you bombed Cambodia you did not think in what state Khmer lives were."

As far as I know, this was the only time Hun Sen spoke publicly about the Nixon bombings of Cambodia. It was a bold step, especially since Vietnam, which had suffered more from U.S. actions than Cambodia, was then completely silent on these issues. Of France, Hun Sen said: "They have interfered in Cambodian affairs too much; it's impossible to remain patient." He called for demonstrations at embassies of foreign countries which "interfered" in Cambodia's affairs. His comments made the Westerners in the foreign community nervous.

Hun Sen also stated that Minister of Commerce Cham Prasidh had telephoned him to talk about delays in U.S. granting of most-favored-nation (MFN) trading status to Cambodia because of its human rights record. "I said, 'Your Excellency, you and I used to eat rice porridge together. Be patient, we're used to difficulty.'" (This reminded me of Sukarno's "Go to hell with your foreign aid" statement to the United States back in 1963, and of Sihanouk's rejection of American aid in 1965.) "We're not going to die if they give MFN or not," Hun Sen said in his speeches. "During the State of Cambodia era, we lived in a time when they attacked us, they surrounded us, and they imposed sanctions against us. We survived [then] and why can't we survive now?" He made no complaint against Asian nations and specifically praised Japanese aid to Cambodia. "Don't protest against Japan, it does not interfere, it is very good," he said to the applause of villagers. "Japanese assistance is the only one which does not have conditions attached to it."

Ranariddh was oddly silent but appeared to be in complete agreement with Hun Sen. Before Hun Sen's speeches, Ranariddh had approached the diplomatic bench on several ceremonial occasions and warned us against making harsh criticisms of the Sirivudh affair as the Cambodians would then "close ranks." Ranariddh muttered to us that French action against Cambodia would be unfair, particularly since the French had approved ten times as much aid to Vietnam as to Cambodia. He added with a chuckle that he would refrain from commenting on Vietnam's human rights record as his father was about to visit Vietnam. From Paris, Sam Rainsy criticized Hun Sen's statements, saying that in their tone and content they revealed the communist training of the speaker. Rainsy claimed to find the "approving silence of Prince Ranariddh" even more surprising.

Back in Cambodia, following internal meetings of the CPP, Hun Sen expressed some remorse for his fit of temper. He complained that he had been misquoted as advocating the "storming" of foreign embassies in Phnom Penh. Frank Huffman, the director of AID and an expert in the Khmer language, confirmed to me that Hun Sen had used the word "enter," not "storm." Hun Sen assured diplomats, "Don't worry. I'm not against you."

This was a rather unusual situation. Whereas Ranariddh was seen on TV making speeches all the time, in those days Hun Sen seldom appeared in public. Privately, he told a small group of ambassadors and me that he did not like to make speeches that were meaningless, but that if he felt the need, he could speak for eight hours without feeling tired. He also said that he tended to speak off the cuff—which probably explained his retraction of some of his more extreme remarks.

THE FLAMBOYANT PRIVATE SECTOR

Since both prime ministers were fully committed to private entrepreneurship and the market, a liberal investment law was promulgated, and in all major cities and towns the hustle and bustle of economic rehabilitation and rapid growth pointed to an increasingly vibrant private sector. In *Psar Thmei*, Phnom Penh's central market and the barometer of all progress, which I had earlier visited the first morning of my arrival in Cambodia in April 1992, the transformation was complete. Shops were full of consumer durables imported from Thailand, cameras, motorcycles, refrigerators, TVs, computers, and the ubiquitous pirated CDs and videocassettes. Often top hit CDs were available in Phnom Penh at two or three dollars prior to their release in the United States.

The goods overflowed onto the sidewalks. Items that UNTAC had once imported were now readily available. The lady who had refused to sell me lobsters in 1992 because she had thought I was Cambodian smiled as she recognized me. Now, she sold to anybody, Cambodian or foreign, as long as they brought cash. In fact, the nouveau riche Cambodians were more often the buyers of lobster than the backpackers and NGO foreigners who had replaced the big spenders of UNTAC.

A vibrant two-way flow of traffic and trade with Thailand and Vietnam—legal and illegal—became the cornerstone of a revived private sector. On the highway from Poi Pet on the Thai border through Battambang and on to Phnom Penh, there was a steady flow of lorries, and in the rainy season frequent breakdowns occurred, especially on the still-rudimentary bridges. An equally buoyant trade took place between Phnom Penh and Ho Chi Minh City (formerly Saigon), although Vietnamese goods were considered inferior to their Thai equivalents. Thai goods were often carried across the long, porous border between Thailand and Cambodia and then transported through Cambodia to Vietnam. As a result, illegal trade in cigarettes to supply the much bigger market of Vietnam was thriving.

Foreign private investment continued to flow into Cambodia. The country was surrounded by nations with high-growth economies who saw in Cambodia abundant forests (their own countries had often been almost completely denuded) and other business opportunities. Intrepid investors from these countries, dominated by Thailand before the UNTAC elections, and by Malaysia and Singapore afterward, rushed in. Ethnic Chinese who forged links with the ethnic Chinese of Cambodia—the top of the business pyramid—dominated. Logging, hotel, entertainment, and services were the most prevalent industries.

Malaysia led the pack of foreign investors. My friend Deva Mohd. Ridzam, the Malaysian ambassador to Cambodia, played a major role in attracting Malaysian investments. He told me that back home Mahathir, the Malaysian prime minister, took a personal interest in persuading top Malaysian companies to invest in Cambodia. Deva said that Malaysians understood Cambodia and sympathized with the country's plight. "We have not forgotten that thirty years ago Cambodia was ahead of us [economically] and so we have nothing to be arrogant about."

The $1.3 billion investment package pledged by the Malaysian company Ariston Berhad was a perfect example of how unscrupulous foreign businessmen could take Cambodia for a ride. On 2 January, Ranariddh's birthday, in 1995, Ranariddh flew to Kuala Lumpur for a birthday lunch with a host of royal government officials and ambassadors. In Kuala Lumpur, Ranariddh signed the deal with Ariston Berhad. It was Cambodia's largest contract to date with a foreign investor. Ariston ostensibly agreed to develop a resort complex in Sihanoukville as well as power plants, infrastructure, and improvements in the town's airport. Ariston was owned by FAHD Berhad, a Malaysian conglomerate reportedly worth $2.3 billion, which in turn was owned by Tan Sri Chen Lip Kiong. The signing was a joyous occasion. The prince was beaming.

Unfortunately, apart from a casino deal, this mammoth investment contract turned out to be a giant hoax. None of the promised investments materialized. And even the casino contract raised the eyebrows of MPs and the press. Back in December 1994, while driving to work at the Cambodiana Hotel located on the Tonle Sap River, I had passed a large crowd looking at the giant cruise liner *Heritage* moored to the shore. I soon found out that it was going to be a floating casino owned by Chen Lip Kiong.

Like everything else surrounding "Chen's Enterprises," including his shady lottery operation in Phnom Penh (in which nobody ever won the first prize), the casino contracts were shrouded in secrecy. The presence of the ship had indicated that Chen had been the successful bidder for the Naga Island casino off Sihanoukville. Under the terms of the tender, the preferred bidder was given the right to temporarily operate a floating casino in Phnom Penh while the multimillion-dollar Naga Island resort off Sihanoukville was supposedly being built.[11]

On 4 January, eight MPs led by Son Chhay sent a letter to National Assembly Chairman Chea Sim questioning the deals with Ariston/Chen Lip Kiong. The MPs also wished to examine a logging deal with another Malaysian company, Samling, granting a sixty-nine-year logging concession on 800,000 hectares of forests, about 4 percent of the entire country. That deal was also signed in Ranariddh's presence in Kuala Lumpur. Not surprisingly, the MPs' requests were ignored.

The larger concerns were whether the deals would stick and whether the investments would actually materialize. Chen Lip Kiong was immensely chagrined, and in response to critics who asked why he did not go ahead with the Sihanoukville plans, he stated that in the secret contract he had been given the sole concession for operating casinos in Cambodia. The subsequent proliferation of casinos in Phnom Penh had caused revenues to fall way below expectations, he said. As a result, the Sihanoukville projects would have to be "postponed." As time passed, his postponement became permanent.

In 1996 You Hockry, the cominister of interior, ordered all casinos closed to comply with gaming laws passed by parliament. Because all of the casinos were backed by powerful military figures and had their own heavily armed bodyguards, he had to use military armored vehicles and police armed with automatic rifles to close them. Only the Naga and Holiday International casinos, the latter owned by the Indonesian Tony Tandiono, which operated under an earlier SOC license, remained. But still Chen Lip Kiong refused to go ahead with his Sihanoukville plans. In a few weeks, I saw that other casinos quietly reopened.

That year General Prabowo Subyanto, the son-in-law of Suharto and head of Indonesia's Special Forces (KOPASSUS), got a lucrative forest concession in Cambodia. Although he pursued the concession as a private citizen, he got it in exchange for the training of a Cambodian military battalion by KOPASSUS in Indonesia. I was present when the Cambodian battalion returned to Phnom Penh wearing KOPASSUS uniforms and red berets; they were also given sidearms which were shipped in secret so as not to draw the attention of the Khmer Rouge, who had threatened to behead nationals from countries supplying weapons to the government. But apparently the deal with Prabowo fell through because he was given land in Khmer Rouge territory unsuitable for forestry operations.

The rehabilitation of infrastructure in Cambodia was normally not very lucrative for private business and continued to depend predominantly on foreign aid from Western and multilateral donors. But there were exceptions. The Built Operate Transfer (BOT) projects were one, including the airport expansion that was worth $250 million to the Dumez Company of France. The project was linked to French foreign aid and thus Dumez was able to oust a Malaysian company, Muhibbah-Masterson, which originally had received approval to build a new runway and terminal. Dumez was given a monopoly on collecting all proceeds from airport taxes and was ostensibly promised that there would be no direct flights between Siem Reap, the city of Angkor Wat, and Bangkok.[12]

The revival of Cambodian domestic entrepreneurship was even more fascinating, and I witnessed it firsthand. Living in the apartment owned by Lucky

Enterprises in Phnom Penh, I extracted, bit by bit, the extraordinary story of Mr. Heng Hang Meng (Keo Sophy), the owner.

Like every Cambodian during the Khmer Rouge period, Mr. Heng had then been a faceless and penniless person dressed in black, slaving in the fields to serve the glorious *Angkar*. After the liberation of Cambodia, this remarkable man had somehow managed to ride a bicycle the entire length of Cambodia, from the Thai border to the Vietnamese border, a distance of approximately 575 kilometers. He had carried goods such as cigarette papers, which brought him exorbitant profits, upwards of 1,000 percent, in Vietnam. Soon he traded his bicycle for a motorcycle so that he could carry more goods. This was followed by his opening of a trading store in Phnom Penh, which became a small grocery store that bore the name Lucky. Cashing in on the UNTAC miniboom, he then continued to expand. I remembered during my Siem Reap period always stopping at the Lucky store in Phnom Penh for supplies of imported items unavailable in Siem Reap.

When UNTAC left, many in Phnom Penh had predicted that the boom was over. But, advised by his two younger brothers, David and Roger, who had returned to Cambodia from California, Mr. Heng had bet the opposite. He had predicted that with the return of peace and political legitimacy, economic prosperity would also return. He had been right. Instead of slowing down like most of his competitors, he had expanded robustly. Completely overhauling his mom-and-pop store of UNTAC times, he invested in the first full-scale American-style supermarket in Phnom Penh. Anticipating that parking would be a problem in the future, he also built Phnom Penh's first multistoried parking garage. Simultaneously he built the apartment complex above the store, which became our home for the next three years.

David told me how they built up the inventory for the supermarket. Mr. Heng, David, and Roger went to a well-established supermarket in Singapore with plenty of U.S. dollars. They bought one of every item in the store, noting its price and where it was made. Then they contacted the manufacturer in Singapore and developed a business relationship. Although Mr. Heng was a good friend of the minister of planning of the SOC Chea Chanto, later of the coalition government, who went on to become the Central Bank governor, he never asked for facilities or loans. Lucky Enterprises was self-financing.

Mr. Heng and his brothers then kept forging ahead. After the supermarket, garage, and apartment complex, they built the first U.S.-style hamburger place in Phnom Penh, the Lucky Burger. Surprisingly, the clientele was all Cambodians as the economic boom after UNTAC had produced a new and growing middle class in Cambodia. When my wife and I returned to Phnom Penh to be observers for the elections in July 2003, David and Roger took us proudly to the four different Lucky Burger locations and the two more Lucky supermarkets sprawled all over Phnom Penh.[13] While the story of Lucky Enterprises was replicated over and over again by other businessmen, none of them could match the tenacity of Mr. Heng, who worked without getting special deals or facilities from powerful government officials.

If Mr. Heng's story was a shining example of success based on sheer perseverance, entrepreneurship, and hard work, some of the better-known business ventures only succeeded through often secretive deals between the businessmen and their patrons in the government. The businessmen soon discovered their best patrons were in the Hun Sen wing of the government. The unlucky backroom dealer who chose the Ranariddh wing could get stuck with empty promises. The rather adventurous entrepreneurs from neighboring countries were not constrained by the rudimentary rule of law in Cambodia; they were used to benefiting from special relationships and deals struck with the powers that be in their own countries.

Let's look at the experience of the late Oknha Teng Bun Ma, a most controversial entrepreneur.[14] Teng Bun Ma owned the Thai Boonrong Company and was, like all top businessmen, a Sino-Khmer. He held a massive property portfolio in Cambodia and was involved in several highly controversial development projects. He was allegedly wanted in the United States for suspected links to drug dealings, though this was never proven. In June 1994, he opened the Cambodia Mekong Bank, reportedly the country's richest bank, with capital of $20 million. In November, a gleaming four-star Sharaton (not Sheraton) Hotel that he owned opened in Phnom Penh. In 1997, his 372-room, five-star Intercontinental Hotel (the first five-star hotel in Cambodia) also opened, reputedly financed fully from his private funds.

Prior to that, in March 1994, Finance Minister Sam Rainsy had railed, "There are some so-called investors in Cambodia who were in fact the representatives of the mafia established in Hong Kong and Thailand. . . . These mafias are big businessmen from Thailand and Hong Kong involved in gambling, narcotics and money laundering." He was referring to criminal gangs known in Asia as triads. Rainsy, who had received several death threats, described the banking situation in Cambodia as a "facade." A combination of lax financial regulation of banking and a booming cash economy made ideal conditions for money laundering. In Rainsy's estimation, "the whole of Cambodia is a big casino." Then Rainsy had attacked Teng Bun Ma directly.

Other successful ethnic Chinese tycoons in Cambodia at that time included Okhna Kong Triv, owner of the Cambodian Tobacco Company; Pho Kok An, managing director of Anco Brothers, who would emerge in the late 1990s as the czar of Poi Pet, a casino city; and Srey Leang Chheang, general-director of the Chimex Import-Export company.

THERE IS A PEBBLE IN MY SHOE

Hun Sen's bluster aside, there were many signs of significant change in the government's approach to human rights in the post-UNTAC period. Up to a point the Cambodian government displayed a willingness to acknowledge problems and to cooperate with international human rights and humanitarian bodies. But, overall, progress was slow. The strongest criticism of the government's progress toward democracy came from Michael Kirby, the United Nations secretary-general's special representative on human rights in Cambodia, who was like a pebble in the shoes of the premiers.

Michael Kirby had been appointed in pursuance of a resolution of the United Nations High Commission on Human Rights adopted in 1993. The resolution had asked the secretary-general to ensure continued human rights progress in Cambodia after UNTAC departed through the presence of the Center for Human Rights and the appointment of a special representative. The Center was the first field presence of the United Nations High Commission on Human Rights, which was headquartered in Geneva. At the time there had been objections from Asian countries to singling out Cambodia for special scrutiny, but they had been outvoted.[15] At the 25 June 1993 World Conference on Human Rights in Vienna, the Khmer Rouge atrocities in 1975–1979 had been cited as the overriding reason for singling out Cambodia,[16] although ironically it was the Phnom Penh government—which in its earlier form had ousted the Khmer Rouge—that would now bear the brunt of this special scrutiny.

Some scholars and others, including the former prime minister of Singapore Lee Kuan Yew, maintain that Asians prefer a different standard for human rights than Westerners do. According to the Kenyan legal scholar Yash

Ghai, among developing regions only Southeast and East Asia are in an economic position to challenge the West's widely perceived attempt to assert its hegemony over the rest of the world through its emphasis on Western-oriented rights.[17] As Yash Ghai asserts, making aid dependent on human rights and democracy has politicized (and polarized) the discourse on human rights. "Many Asian governments argue that rights are relative, contingent on culture and religion, and those priorities among them are based on the level of economic development, not some general notion of the nature of rights," Yash Ghai writes.[18] But Sidney Jones of the International Crisis Group, drawing upon an abundance of data on East Asia, charges that such relativist and "growth first" arguments are motivated by authoritarian governments' interest in maintaining power.[19]

The United Nations Human Rights office in Phnom Penh was established with a twofold mandate: to manage the implementation of educational and technical assistance and advisory programs in the area of human rights and to provide support to the special representative of the secretary-general for human rights in Cambodia.[20] In practice, the work of monitoring progress in human rights was carried out by a highly efficient officer, Christophe Peschoux, an UNTAC official who had stayed behind. To the considerable embarrassment of the government, Christophe discovered, among other things, that members of the B-2 military intelligence units in Battambang provinces, which had been authorized to arrest and interrogate resistance fighters, had turned in 1993 and 1994 to abducting civilians, extorting ransom from their families, and often murdering the victims. A report by the UN Center for Human Rights drafted by him estimated that the group murdered at least thirty-five individuals between late June and November 1993 and held others captive in secret locations in Battambang and a remote village called Che K'mau. Some of the victims had never been located and were believed to still be detained. Among the others was one man who allegedly died while his captors ate his liver and another who lost a limb and an eye when forced to perform demining, according to the report. Although the crimes of these B-2 units were privately reported to political leaders during the UNTAC period, the new government was slow to take action.

An investigation by the Ministry of Defense corroborated most of the details of the Center's report, but investigators from the prime ministers' office initially denied the findings. Details of the investigations were then leaked to the press in August 1994, and pressure from both within the country and abroad forced the government to continue its inquiry. In October 1994, Ranariddh and Interior Minister You Hockry, both of FUNCINPEC, suggested that all the abuses had occurred prior to the May 1993 elections. It was an attempt to absolve the new government of responsibility. The prime ministers' office continued to investigate, inviting the UN Center to participate as an observer.

The public exposure in Cambodia and abroad of military atrocities demonstrated the power of the press and the local human rights movement to mobilize public opinion, which raised the specter of retaliation. An early danger signal was the inadequately investigated death of Tou Chhom Mongkol, editor-in-chief of the newspaper *Antarakhum* (*Intervention*), on 11 June 1994. His death followed a 24 March grenade attack on the newspaper's office by perpetrators never identified by the police. Suspicions of official retribution were fueled by the paper's articles condemning corruption among government authorities.

Retaliation for the investigations by the UN Center for Human Rights hit home when the daughter of my secretary, Marilou Velilla, from the Philippines was kidnapped and shot in the thigh. Her husband was Oscar Oliveros, the Spanish administrative officer of the Center. It was a dark night and Christophe Peschoux and other members of the Center were in Battambang following a lead to yet another secret detention center. Oliveros had been left alone to man the office in Phnom Penh. As he was coming home from a meeting at 10 p.m., he was forced to relinquish his four-wheeler Toyota to two gunmen in front of his house. His twelve-year-old son followed him swiftly out of the car. As the two gunmen sped away, Oliveros suddenly realized that his nine-year-old daughter was sleeping in the back of the car. My secretary and I held vigil while Oliveros and other friends roamed the city for leads. In those days it was not possible to report a crime to the local police and ask for their help—not after 10 p.m., anyway, as the police stations were all closed.

Then, at 2 a.m., we received word that the little girl had been admitted to Calmette Hospital owned by the government. Apparently a Khmer lady had found her crying and bleeding profusely while wandering the streets. She spoke no Khmer and the lady suspected her to be Vietnamese. Like a Good Samaritan, she brought the girl in a slow cyclo (tricycle) to the hospital where her identity was established. The child had been punished for the investigations by her father's office by being shot and thrown out of the car by unidentified elements linked to the military. She was shipped out to Bangkok, and her mother, Marilou, went with her, vowing never to return. I lost a good secretary.[21]

The discovery of the secret detention center was reportedly the reason the copremiers wrote a letter to the United Nations secretary-general in March 1995 requesting that the office of the Center for Human Rights be closed when its term ended a year later. This was a serious matter: seldom anywhere in the world does a member state demand that the United Nations close an office which ostensibly is there to provide technical assistance free of charge.

The secretary-general appointed a senior representative, Marrack Goulding, the under-secretary-general for political affairs based in New York and my direct boss, to resolve the issue. That he appointed Goulding rather than the high commissioner of human rights in Geneva, who holds the same rank, indicated that the secretary-general considered the issue to go beyond human rights.

In May 1995 Marrack Goulding arrived in Phnom Penh. I was in charge of his program. At a meeting with the premiers, Ranariddh roundly criticized the Center for Human Rights, fully supporting Hun Sen's insistence that it be closed. The copremiers complained that the Center engaged in serious monitoring rather than technical cooperation (its main mandate). At the end it was agreed that the Center would remain open under four conditions: that "informal confidential consultative meetings" be held between the copremiers and the office's leadership every few months; that a more formal meeting be held once a year, before the UN Commission on Human Rights meetings, to ensure a "full exchange of views"; that the office take a more "pro-active" approach when writing reports on Cambodia, submitting draft versions to the government for attention and comment; and that seminars on the office's work be run for government officials and that one or two officials visit the UN Commission's Geneva headquarters each year.[22]

Ung Huot, the foreign minister (FUNCINPEC), who held Australian as well as Cambodian nationality, had a different opinion than the premiers.[23] If the United Nations wanted the office to continue, Ung Huot told a journalist, he would not object. I was present at a dinner in honor of Marrack Goulding in his house when some ASEAN ambassadors took Ung Huot aside and admonished him, saying that he should be tough on this issue. Cambodia's field office of the Center could spread to other ASEAN countries, they fretted.[24]

Goulding had stated to me that he wanted to keep one day free in Phnom Penh to attend to personal matters. As the security situation was still raw in the country, I relayed his wish to the government. I remembered Goulding's hobby was bird watching, so I told the government security officers that he did not want the government's armed vehicle to follow my car, as it would scare the birds away. They were quite puzzled. I learned later that they had an internal discussion about what bird watching was. The government insisted on providing a military vehicle escort. Goulding was furious. As a compromise, the military was kept a good distance away. Later Goulding said that the half-day bird watching exercise added a half-year to his life.

Although the Center for Human Rights continued to operate, the co-premiers remained annoyed with the reports of Michael Kirby. In November 1995, the government sent another thinly veiled warning to the Center accusing Kirby of making inappropriate, unclear, and unfounded assertions and of acting like a policeman. After giving up his job upon his appointment to the Australian Federal Supreme Court, he was replaced by Thomas Hammarberg from Sweden, a former head of Amnesty International who arrived in Phnom Penh on 10 June 1996. But he had the same trouble, and for the same reasons, with the copremiers as Kirby did. From the beginning he was a strong advocate for establishing an international tribunal to put the Khmer Rouge on trial.

NOTES

1. In the recent past, Cambodia had twice experienced hyperinflation: the first time was when the riel depreciated by 2,300 percent between 1968 and 1974; the second was between 1989, when Soviet aid was withdrawn, and 1994/1995, when the value of the riel dropped 1,300 percent. See K. P. Kannan, *Economic Reform, Structural Adjustment and Development in Cambodia*, Phnom Penh: Cambodian Development Resource Institute, 1996, 2.

2. World Bank, *Cambodia: From Recovery to Sustained Development*, World Bank: Washington, 31 May 1996, ii.

3. See chapter 10 for details of the reshuffle.

4. The resignation of Sirivudh had been an unexpected bonus for Hun Sen, who disliked both him and Sam Rainsy.

5. Ranariddh, "Vital Issues," a widely distributed eight-page policy statement issued on 3 August 1995 addressing a wide range of criticisms made of the Royal Government.

6. Ian Marsh, Jean Blondel, and Takashi Inoguchi, eds., *Democracy, Governance and Economic Performance; East and Southeast Asia*, Tokyo: United Nations University Press, 1999, 3.

7. KID was founded by Julio Jeldres, a self-proclaimed champion of human rights hailing from Chile and an official biographer of the king.

8. Martin Godfrey et al., "Technical Assistance and Capacity Development in an Aid-Dependent Economy: The Experience of Cambodia," *Working Paper no. 15*, Phnom Penh: Cambodian Development Resource Institute, August 2000, table 2.1, 11.

9. Martin Godfrey et al., "Technical Assistance," 123.

10. Sophal Ear, "The Political Economy of Aid and Governance in Cambodia," *Asian Journal of Political Science*, Vol. 15, No. 1, April 2007, 77.

11. At the time of writing, in 2007, this "temporary" casino still operates in Phnom Penh albeit now housed in permanent buildings near its former river location.

12. In 1997, this monopoly was broken by the open-skies policy adopted by Hun Sen, and tourism was considerably boosted by direct flights to Siem Reap, the site of Angkor Wat, from Bangkok, Singapore, and other Asian hubs. The French company was furious but could not do much.

13. In 2005, Lucky Enterprises consisted of three supermarkets, four Lucky Burgers, one Lucky Seven ministore, and one Lucky bakery. Communications provided by Lucky Enterprises.

14. *Oknha*, or nobleman, is the highest title bestowed on civilians (no royalty) by the king.

15. Asian countries had objected to Cambodia's special treatment in a regional preparatory meeting for the conference in Bangkok where the Bangkok Declaration on Human Rights was issued in 1993. At the meeting there was a standoff between human rights advocates and several East Asian governments.

16. United Nations High Commission on Human Rights, Official Records of the Vienna Conference.

17. Yash Ghai, "Human Rights and Governance: The Asia Debate," *Asia Pacific Journal on Human Rights and the Law*, vol. I, no.1, 1 January 2000, 9.

18. Ghai, "Human Rights," 10. Ironically, in 2005 Yash Ghai became the UN secretary-general's special representative on human rights in Cambodia. Like Kirby and his other predecessor, he got into trouble with Hun Sen, who in 2005 was the sole premier of Cambodia.

19. Sidney Jones, "The Impact of Asian Economic Growth on Human Rights," New York, Council on Foreign Relations, Asia Project Working Papers, January 1995.

20. The emphasis—in fact, 90 percent of the office's work—was in the area of technical cooperation. Only about 10 percent was supposed to be in the area of monitoring human rights conditions.

21. I recruited another Filipina, Helen Recto, who was not only a good secretary but an accountant. In Cambodia as elsewhere, there were many Filipinos working for various businesses and sending their money home. Helen's three children were studying in the Philippines.

22. Personal records of the meeting.

23. Many FUNCINPEC members held dual nationality, which often led to conflicts of interest.

24. Indeed, at the time of this writing in 2005, there were a total of thirty-four field presences of the United Nations High Commission for Human Rights in the world, five full-scale offices besides the one in Cambodia, twelve in which human rights were part of the United Nations mission, and sixteen technical cooperation projects on human rights.

A Puppet Prime Minister?

LIBERATION OR INVASION?

The Sirivudh affair in 1995 had been a harbinger of things to come. In early 1996, when both FUNCINPEC and the CPP began rehashing arguments deliberately set aside by the Peace Agreements, the gloves came off. Two issues in particular rekindled antagonisms: the reintroduction of 7 January as a public holiday and the uproar over the alleged Vietnamese "invasion" of 1996.

January 7 marked the anniversary of the ouster of the Khmer Rouge regime by Vietnamese forces in 1979. Hun Sen proposed reviving the holiday. He obviously was testing his consolidation of power. Was the time right to redress what the CPP felt was a grave injustice: the negative UN reaction to the liberation of Cambodia from Pol Pot? To FUNCINPEC and others, the date also marked the start of the decade-long occupation of Cambodia by Vietnamese troops.

In a marathon speaking tour kicked off on 4 January in Svay Rieng, the first province liberated from the Khmer Rouge seventeen years earlier, Hun Sen visited town after town on the same days they were liberated in 1979, culminating in a visit to Phnom Penh on 7 January. He thanked the Vietnamese profusely for their help and urged Cambodians not to forget it. He indicated that the holiday's revival would be endorsed by a royal decree.

The holiday, which had not been recognized in Cambodia for four years, was renewed by a 5 January government circular signed by both Hun Sen and, surprisingly, Ranariddh. Sihanouk balked at signing a decree and asked them to declare the holiday themselves. To angry FUNCINPEC supporters, the docile Ranariddh defended his signing of the circular by saying that he was only following orders from the king. It was apparently too much for senior FUNCINPEC members to swallow. In a rare move, twelve of them, all generally known to be staunch supporters of Ranariddh's policies, issued a strong protest to the king. While they agreed that the liberation from Pol Pot was a cause for celebration, they wrote, the day also commemorated the invasion of Cambodia by 250,000 Vietnamese, or *yuon*. *Yuon* was a derogatory term for Vietnamese that had been banned during the entire PRK/SOC period but liberally used by coalition partner FUNCINPEC, Prince Ranariddh included, in his speeches.

On 7 January we in the diplomatic corps were all invited to the inauguration ceremony of a new park bearing Hun Sen's name beside the Phnom Penh riverfront. While addressing the crowd of fifteen thousand, Hun Sen paid special attention to ambassadors from countries who had not recognized the PRK and SOC, namely many Western and ASEAN ambassadors and myself from the United Nations. But he welcomed me now as the representative of the UN secretary-general. "Had it not been for 7 January [1979], there wouldn't have been the Paris Peace Agreement, nor UNTAC in Cambodia and everything we have today," he stated.

Apparently to counterbalance the Victory Day proclamation, Ranariddh, in his usual haphazard way of handling even important affairs, accused Vietnam of "invading" three or four [sic] provinces. International observers, including myself, saw Ranariddh's outburst as an attempt to force Hun Sen's hand, just like Hun Sen had challenged Ranariddh on the Sirivudh affair and the 7 January holiday. However, if Hun Sen had made demands on those issues that were rather difficult, if not impossible, for the prince to refuse, Hun Sen could conveniently remain quiet on the alleged Vietnamese "invasion." And as with many of Ranariddh's other bombshells, Ranariddh failed to follow up on his claim.

For its part, Vietnam vehemently denied this latest "slander" and proposed that border problems be solved through peaceful negotiations. Unlike the border with Thailand, which was stipulated by a 1907 treaty between French Indochina and Cambodia, the borders between Laos, Vietnam, and Cambodia had been established by French decrees. The only treaties between Cambodia and Vietnam were signed in the 1980s when the PRK was under Vietnamese domination and were advantageous to the latter.

Ranariddh certainly had no monopoly on playing the *yuon* card. His outbursts against Vietnamese invasions received strong support from traditionally anti-*yuon* Sam Rainsy and Son Sann, head of the BLDP.[1] Ironically, clandestine Khmer Rouge radio, the most vehement anti-*yuon* element, maintained that Ranariddh was "clowning around." While stating that *yuon* incursions had indeed taken place (in six provinces, no less), Khmer Rouge radio claimed that the whole episode was a charade by Ranariddh to fool the West into thinking that he was still powerful so as to keep foreign aid flowing in.

Actually, Ranariddh's anti-Vietnam rhetoric was mainly meant for domestic consumption. Indeed, National Assembly MPs from BLDP and FUNCINPEC as well as Khmer Nation Party (KNP) members outside parliament rallied behind him. Although Sam Rainsy, founder of the KNP, was closer to FUNCINPEC than the CPP ideologically, he often criticized FUNCINPEC harshly on issues of corruption and for toeing Hun Sen's line. Rainsy's KNP had never registered nor been recognized by the government. But despite continuous harassment by the government, especially by FUNCINPEC Cominister of the Interior You Hockry, who was in charge of political parties, the KNP continued to grow rapidly. A petition circulated among MPs applauding Ranariddh's "brave ideas in defending territorial integrity and having pity on suffering people along the borders caused by invasions made by foreign people."

On Sunday, 28 January, my friend Tran Huy Chuong, the Vietnamese ambassador to Cambodia, informed me that the previous day he had been summoned to the foreign ministry by Secretary of State Uch Kim An of the CPP (the number two man in the ministry). Both had agreed that some formula should be found to resolve the controversy through negotiations.

A MEETING BEHIND CLOSED DOORS

As Hun Sen was consolidating his power, it was provoking increasingly militant reactions from FUNCINPEC. On 20–21 January 1996, FUNCINPEC held a closed-door seminar in the beach resort of Sihanoukville attended only by two hundred invited members of the party—those that still believed in Ranariddh's leadership. The seminar was intended to restore unity and support for Ranariddh. No journalists were allowed. From eyewitness reports, I learned that the discussions often turned into heated attacks on Hun Sen and the CPP. But Ranariddh was also robustly criticized for being Hun Sen's yes man. It was resolved that the party should insist more firmly on the implementation of the principles of cooperation adopted when the coalition government was formed.

Publicly, a relatively mild statement was issued dealing with the next elections in 1998. However, the most important resolution adopted at Sihanoukville was not made public. It called for FUNCINPEC to strive for military balance with the CPP. Military balance meant parity between the FUNCINPEC and CPP wings of the army. FUNCINPEC underscored the well-known fact that while it had won the elections, the amalgamation of the minuscule armies of FUNCINPEC and KPNLF into the Royal Cambodian Armed Forces that had been accomplished by UNTAC was ineffective, as the CPP army dominated everything. FUNCINPEC resolved to build up its wing of the RCAF, which in effect would nullify UNTAC's efforts to amalgamate the armies.

On Saturday, 27 January, Ranariddh gleefully took off for Burma, India, and Europe while the king left on the same day for Beijing, where he would stay until late March. It was as if they wanted to give the ill-tempered Hun Sen—who did not care for FUNCINPEC's statement on the next elections and who would have learned about its resolution on military balance—free rein to vent his anger and do something he would later regret. Apparently, the idea of provoking him had been discussed at Sihanoukville.

Ranariddh Drops a Bombshell

After two months of relative calm, Ranariddh surprised everybody when he virtually exploded. On 21–22 March, he attended a long-awaited FUNCINPEC congress, held in their new, shiny, huge headquarters in Phnom Penh next to the equally new, shiny, and huge French embassy. The date marked the fifteenth anniversary of Sihanouk's formation of FUNCINPEC. And in March of 1970, Sihanouk had established the Royal Government of National Union of Kampuchea (GRUNK) to fight Lon Nol.

Until recently, Ranariddh had echoed Hun Sen's enthusiasm for the coalition government. Together they had shared the glory, the lucrative contracts, and at least formally the power as well. And together they had ridiculed, sabotaged, and attacked critics like journalists and Sam Rainsy. At the

FUNCINPEC congress, Hun Sen attended as a special guest and was welcomed with huge banners proclaiming "Long live the FUNCINPEC-CPP alliance." After Hun Sen gave his speech and departed along with the journalists who had come to cover him, Ranariddh fired off his fusillade—a forthright indictment of the CPP, later broadcast on FUNCINPEC television and radio. Ranariddh peevishly described his role as "first puppet prime minister" and the roles of other FUNCINPEC members as "puppet vice-prime minister, puppet ministers, puppet governors and deputy governors, and soon-to-be puppet chiefs of districts." The prince declared himself "absolutely not happy" after two years as a first prime minister but second banana and asserted that FUNCINPEC would rather withdraw than continue to "betray" the government and the Khmer people. "Being a puppet," he told the assembled party, "is not so good."

To Ranariddh, FUNCINPEC representatives in government ministries had been denied appropriate roles. He complained of forced delays in appointments of FUNCINPEC members as district-level officials. But FUNCINPEC had been victorious in the 1993 national election, he pointed out. The coalition government was nothing but a "slogan," he said, an "empty bucket." "Our FUNCINPEC also beats it and says that this bucket has water . . . I think after this congress we should stop beating that empty bucket."

Ranariddh warned that if the CPP did not take note of his comments, FUNCINPEC might choose not to wait for the next election to take action. It could vote to dissolve the National Assembly, establish itself as an opposition party, and have an election "before the end of 1996." Phnom Penh was aghast. Submissive Ranariddh, who hitherto had always echoed Hun Sen, suddenly had lashed out. For all practical purposes, the honeymoon between the two premiers was indeed over.

What had caused Ranariddh's sudden metamorphosis? Frustrated by Hun Sen's growing power, FUNCINPEC party members had been criticizing Ranariddh for being too soft on the CPP. At the congress the crowd of thousands of FUNCINPEC supporters had been whipped into a frenzy denouncing the CPP and loudly calling for change. It was obvious that Ranariddh had been influenced by this frenzied crowd. They had goaded him to rebel.

Ranariddh's speech made it clear that despite his blistering attacks on the alleged Vietnamese invasion and the controversy over the 7 January holiday, the cause of his outbursts lay in the perceived inequities in power sharing.

FUNCINPEC's rank and file resented the fact that their bosses had fewer jobs to distribute to their clients than the CPP did. In Sihanoukville and at the party congress, I was told, many party members who had campaigned hard for FUNCINPEC during the 1993 elections but who by 1996 still had received no jobs were very angry at Ranariddh. I knew of at least one person in Siem Reap who had sold his house to help finance FUNCINPEC's campaign but got nothing after the elections. Tensions consequently ran high at the congress.

Naturally, Ranariddh and You Hockry diverted the blame to the CPP. At the congress, to avoid being blamed by an angry constituency, Hockry deceptively claimed that the CPP was stalling on power sharing at the district-chief level. Sirivudh had been working hard on this but went into exile before completing it. Before his departure, he had indicated that Sar Kheng had arranged for the districts to be handed over to FUNCINPEC. Sar Kheng of the CPP, Hockry's cominister of the interior, also told journalists that he had already submitted a list of district-chief positions to be handed over to FUNCINPEC and that FUNCINPEC was responsible for the delay. It was obvious that Hockry lied to the congress. He later admitted that was indeed the case, since FUNCINPEC did not have enough people to fill these posts. It was also rumored that Hockry was busily selling back the posts to CPP incumbents.

Some senior FUNCINPEC officials came running to me as the UN representative to look for clauses in the Paris Agreements on power sharing. I told them there was nothing in the agreement about it. Obviously the framers of the agreement had not envisaged such a power-sharing arrangement between the two parties. It was the king who had engineered the master plan of power sharing, with coprime ministers. The sharing of ministers and governors had been accepted and implemented at the beginning of the coalition; corule at the district level had been agreed upon orally but never implemented.

Hun Sen initially reacted coolly to Ranariddh's comments, urging CPP members to remain calm in the face of "some regrettable events." In two speeches in late March, Hun Sen said the loudest voices he could hear were those of poor farmers, students, and workers "asking for peace, national reconciliation and development." An apology was in order from FUNCINPEC for its television broadcast of Ranariddh's statements, he added.

Hun Sen's reserve was ominous. It felt like the calm before a storm. I suspected that he was mapping out strategy with his aides. For three weeks, Hun Sen went into seclusion in his country home in Takhmau, a suburb of Phnom

Penh, dubbed his "tiger's lair" by foreign journalists. He appeared in his Ph- nom Penh villa only long enough to see the king off to Paris on 18 April. That night, four tanks and two truckloads of soldiers came to protect him in his villa; it reminded observers of the Sirivudh affair and gave us all the creeps. Except for passing references in several of his speeches, he did not officially re- ply to Prince Ranariddh's ultimatum, which made Ranariddh—and everyone else—very nervous. The calm in Phnom Penh lulled some people into believ- ing that the situation was cooling down, what with senior members from both parties meeting over French wine and food.

But the CPP did not keep quiet. On 26 March, the CPP's Central Commit- tee issued a statement that it was "obliged to base its position on principle and law" and thus would not discuss the issue of power sharing anymore. Hun Sen and other party officials said that they had met their legal obligations to FUNCINPEC and would not give it anything else. The CPP argued that the Paris Peace Agreements required the sharing of power only in senior political positions, which had been done. The CPP, "in the spirit of compromise," it said, had integrated more than eleven thousand members of FUNCINPEC into government and provincial positions.

AN INVITATION TO TAKHMAU

I saw the coming storm when Hun Sen invited me in my capacity as the UN secretary-general's representative to his Takhmau hideout to explain his view of the crisis and prepare me for things to come. I was the first among the diplomatic corps to be granted an audience by Hun Sen and as a result was be- sieged afterwards by diplomats and journalists.

The road to Hun Sen's Takhmau fortress had all the appearances of a pro- tocol road leading to the residence of the ruler of the country. It wound for perhaps two kilometers down from the main road and was in the process of being paved. Its path was carved through forests. The whole complex was de- signed to provide maximum security, with new houses to the left and right in- habited by his close associates. Hidden behind trees and bushes were his personal bodyguards and their tanks. These elite bodyguards were reportedly paid $300 per month, far above the normal soldier's salary of $13.

Hun Sen appeared quite comfortable in his modest farm-style house whose surrounding flowery gardens made for a rare sight in Phnom Penh. From here he planned to patiently probe Ranariddh's weaknesses and wait for the opportunity to strike swiftly and aggressively, as he had done with Sirivudh. Like a good chess player, he had not only mapped out his moves but speculated on Ranariddh's options.

In a rare two-hour tête-à-tête, Hun Sen spoke through his interpreter, Bun Sambo, a jovial man who loved his gin tonics after strenuous interpretation. Bun translated in a monotonous voice that contrasted sharply with Hun Sen's passionate intonation. Hun Sen, whose English had improved steadily, often corrected Bun when he missed nuances in his speech. He was obviously incensed with Ranariddh's "folly" and with rumors of FUNCINPEC "extremists" gathering weapons for a resurgent FUNCINPEC army. Hun Sen unleashed a constant barrage of criticism of Ranariddh, which diverged markedly from his assurances until recently that the coalition worked and that the two got along well. At one point he claimed that the prince was operating behind a thin curtain that was now completely exposed. Always savvier than his coprime minister, Hun Sen outlined the prince's tactical errors in speaking out against the Vietnamese and the CPP and sketched his response to possible outcomes.

With his statements, Hun Sen said, Ranariddh had unleashed the extremist forces within his own party and crossed a point of no return. Hun Sen saw only three options available to the prince. He could swallow his pride and continue with business as usual. He could follow through on his threat, withdraw from the National Assembly, and call for new elections. Or he could engage in armed conflict. Hun Sen claimed that Ranariddh stood to lose no matter what option he chose. The first option—to engage in business as usual—was the lesser of three evils for Ranariddh, Hun Sen concluded. FUNCINPEC would be weakened, but the prince would lose little more than his reputation and credibility. The second option—to withdraw from the National Assembly and call for new elections—was invalid because it would be unconstitutional. Still, Hun Sen assured me, he was fully prepared to counter Ranariddh should FUNCINPEC pursue this option. They were welcome to try to leave the National Assembly, Hun Sen said, but several senior "FUNCINPEC neutral forces" would refuse and continue in the government in cooperation with the CPP. Hun Sen calculated that Ranariddh's threat to dissolve parliament would fail. He claimed that fifty-one CPP MPs would oppose it. In addition, he confidently stated that the pro-CPP BLDP (Ieng Mouly) faction and National Movement for the Liberation of Kampuchea

(MOLINAKA) would also oppose such a move. FUNCINPEC members could just walk out and take a vacation.

As head of the CPP, Hun Sen also opposed Ranariddh's plan to hold early elections. He believed that Ranariddh wanted them so that he could again use the king as a draw, implying that the king was not neutral. To Hun Sen, it seemed unfair for the CPP to have to fight father and son yet again—once, during UNTAC times, had been enough. Hun Sen chuckled dryly that sooner or later Sihanouk would die and leave the parties to vie on their own terms.

Whenever the next elections took place, Hun Sen said, he absolutely opposed the substantial international supervision preferred by FUNCINPEC, favoring limited international observation. If major international supervision was imposed, he threatened, he would postpone the elections. He also insisted on a law banning dual nationality for senior positions. Such a ban would hurt FUNCINPEC and BLDP deeply, as many of their returned exiles also held French, Australian, United States, or Canadian nationality, whereas senior CPP people had never left the country. The final scenario sketched out by Hun Sen—that Ranariddh would employ force to counter the CPP—was the most dire, but he assured me that he would do everything possible to avoid a violent solution. He claimed to have a transcript of Ranariddh's speech at the FUNCINPEC meeting in Sihanoukville in which Ranariddh gave an order for FUNCINPEC forces to be organized for 1997 and 1998. Thus, Hun Sen concluded, the unleashing of extremist forces could be traced back to Ranariddh himself.

He also claimed to have intercepted a large quantity of arms that General Ho Sok of FUNCINPEC, the secretary of state of the interior, had distributed to FUNCINPEC border police forces, ostensibly to fight the Vietnamese. Further, he said, General Nhiek Bun Chhay of FUNCINPEC was helping himself to 2,000 pieces of arms from a Battambang garrison to be distributed to FUNCINPEC forces. Hun Sen said he had recovered 1,200 of these arms. Nhiek Bun Chhay, who was in charge of RCAF forces fighting the Khmer Rouge in the northern sector of the northwestern front, was also suspected of having ordered FUNCINPEC forces to withdraw. Hun Sen hinted that he might arrest these two generals on the grounds that they were committing treason. In addition, he said that FUNCINPEC's Ek Sereywath, the weapons procurer for RCAF, had failed to deliver the procurement order he was entrusted with, and that Ing Kiet had failed to purchase construction material with the $1 million allocated to him—implying that they might have used the money for buying arms for FUNCINPEC. Hun Sen said he would caution Ranariddh against opposing arrests of these four men. And if FUNCINPEC started armed attacks, he would destroy FUNCINPEC's machinery.

Hun Sen also made such accusations and others in meetings with ambassadors. To one, he claimed that there were indications that a FUNCINPEC/Khmer Rouge coalition might again try to capture Siem Reap and use it as a bargaining chip in discussions on power sharing. Such charges that FUNCINPEC was reviving an army independent of RCAF and possibly realigning with the Khmer Rouge were quite serious. After the UNTAC elections, it was neither acceptable nor normal to re-create individual armies, he asserted. Unlike Ranariddh, Hun Sen was obviously perfectly comfortable with the amalgamation of armies accomplished under UNTAC.

Hun Sen and top military leaders had disclosed privately to diplomats that the RCAF intended to retake rebel strongholds. Up to twenty thousand troops were committed (in private conversations Hun Sen talked of forty thousand), supported by more than sixty T-54 tanks; they would attack and take five important Khmer Rouge bases in the north and northwest. It was the biggest effort against the rebels since the ill-fated offensive of March–April 1994.

News from the battlefront was scarce, but there were soon indications that the RCAF had captured several Khmer Rouge outposts on the road to Pailin. However, the offensive seemed stalled, and the Khmer Rouge remained in their two strongholds. Many reasons were provided apart from the onset of the rains. In recent months there had been increasing reports that the government was beset with morale problems. Underpaid soldiers continued to sell their weapons to the Khmer Rouge army, which appeared to be much more disciplined.

During our interview, Hun Sen blamed FUNCINPEC generals for sabotaging the offensive. I had indeed heard rumors that FUNCINPEC forces under General Nhiek Bun Chhay were threatening to withdraw. Hun Sen maintained that the recent political difficulties had only benefited the Khmer Rouge and saved it from extinction. He had ordered a halt to the Pailin offensive and commanded ten thousand troops to return to protect Phnom Penh against any eventualities. He also confirmed something that the king had told me a year earlier: the purported Khmer Rouge defectors in Siem Reap were actually serving the Khmer Rouge inside the RCAF. Some time after my meeting, I was told that General Nhiek Bun Chhay had since apologized to Hun Sen, whose threat to arrest the generals and warning that Ranariddh not interfere were reminiscent of the Sirivudh case. Hun Sen, however, was angling for bigger fish than the two generals: he sought to catch Ranariddh himself.

Hun Sen hinted to me that he did not think it was a coincidence that Ranariddh's attacks against Vietnam and the CPP came as the drive against Pailin—led by predominantly CPP forces—reached its final stages. He insinuated that Ranariddh's outbursts might have been deliberate moves to sabotage the offensive or even to save the Khmer Rouge. He pointed out that, around the same time, Sihanouk had returned from Beijing and visited military hospitals.

Although Hun Sen did not trust Sihanouk, he did respect him. Reading the transcript of Ranariddh's speech in Sihanoukville, he had learned that the prince had accused him of wanting to do away with the monarchy. He disputed Ranariddh's claim to me and said that the reinstitution of the monarchy in 1993 would not have been possible without the CPP's imprimatur. He thought Sihanouk was right in predicting that FUNCINPEC would wither away once Sihanouk was gone.

Hun Sen's temper normally flashed and cooled off quickly. But when he was really annoyed, as he was at this time, he would go into hiding and nurse his grudge. He had done so against the coup plotters in 1994 and against other archenemies, such as Sirivudh and Pol Pot. He seemed to be doing it now with Ranariddh.

The situation was grave, primarily because the dispute this time affected some of the basic principles of the Paris Agreements and the amalgamation of armies by UNTAC. I left my meeting with the coprime minister unsure what to expect. The king also knew that the situation was precarious and had reprimanded Ranariddh in Paris for his thoughtless ultimatum. Two days after my interview with him, Hun Sen issued a public threat. In a speech to medical students, he warned that he would have no compunction about using military force against anyone moving to dissolve the National Assembly and the constitution. "And I have forces to do it, don't forget," he declared, alluding to the troops he had called in from Pailin to guard Phnom Penh. Rumors of military action ran rife in the capital; some government officials chose not to venture out at night, and royal palace staff were reportedly advised against it.

With the CPP's renewed ascendancy, Cambodian politics had turned full circle. But now Hun Sen had the legitimacy of the UNTAC elections behind him, and he seemed stronger than ever. For Ranariddh, the last straw appeared to have been a Beijing media interview with the king in which Sihanouk had ridiculed him as powerless and bullied by Hun Sen. In his excited state, it seems, Ranariddh had gone overboard in his attacks. But Hun Sen linked the prince's outbursts against Vietnam and the CPP to a sinister Royalist plot to save Ranariddh and use the Khmer Rouge as a powerful bargaining chip

APRIL IN PARIS

After Ranariddh's outbursts had provoked six weeks of unprecedented tension in Phnom Penh, FUNCINPEC fell silent. Ranariddh and other Royalists had nonchalantly taken off for a French vacation, and the king had followed his Paris trip with an extended stay in China. FUNCINPEC's rank and file were displeased. And the Chinese were uncomfortable. The Chinese deputy chief of mission in Phnom Penh lamented to me that his government, which had shown unlimited hospitality to Sihanouk during the Cold War, now was unhappily urging him to go back and see to matters in Phnom Penh.

Obviously enjoying the delights of Paris in the springtime, Sihanouk showed his sharp tongue in an interview published by *Le Monde* on 23 April 1996. He expressed a measure of admiration for Hun Sen when he said: "Our Second Prime Minister is very, very intelligent. I get along well with him. He is a very good tactician. He knows how to divide and conquer, as you would say. He pulled off two formidable moves which split the opposition in two."[2] Sihanouk said that Hun Sen was more than a strongman. But he described Ranariddh as full of illusions about his real power. The king also claimed that his telephones were bugged and that the royal palace was "packed with spies." He would not say who was responsible, except "some men in power."

In a fighting mood, the king told *Le Monde* that "I am ready to run for president, against Hun Sen, against my son Ranariddh, provided we have a presidential regime one day, of course. And I shall win: More than 80 percent of my people are still with me." Hun Sen did not deny this; he still had a lot of respect for the king's popularity.

Meanwhile, pro–Hun Sen newspapers in Phnom Penh began gossiping about a big royal family gathering taking place in Paris. They claimed that papa was presiding over Ranariddh as well as Chakrapong, Sirivudh, and Sihamoni (another son), who all lived in Paris. The gathering also purportedly included Veng Sereyvuth, Deputy Chairman of Parliament Loy Seam Cheang, and some lesser officials loyal to Ranariddh. Sam Rainsy revealed that he had met with the king, Sirivudh, and Ranariddh in Paris.

The royal family meeting along with provocative remarks by the king made Hun Sen even more suspicious of FUNCINPEC and the king. In another of his masterstrokes to save the day, Sihanouk stated in Paris on 27 April that they were not forming and would never form a group of anti–Hun Sen or anti-CPP "plotters"; that they had no intention or desire to contravene in any way the current Cambodian constitution; that his son Ranariddh and FUNC-INPEC had no intention or desire to quit the Royal Government or the National Assembly; and that he had no intention to enter the political arena.[3] The king went on to assure Hun Sen's government that neither he, Ranariddh, nor FUNCINPEC were with Sam Rainsy "or his kind" and that the royal family had much esteem for Hun Sen and the CPP. "We are not and will not be responsible for anti–Hun Sen, anti-CPP, anti-RGC demonstrations," Sihanouk stated.[4]

But Hun Sen did not bite. Instead, pro–Hun Sen papers, which often conveyed his thoughts, grew increasingly belligerent toward the royal family. They published attacks on FUNCINPEC, the king, and Ranariddh. After the king's declaration, Ranariddh left Paris for Aix-en-Provence, where he imperturbably went back to teaching law to safeguard his tenure. It was as if everything were under control.

On Sunday, 28 April, a group of overseas Cambodians organized a demonstration in front of the Cambodian embassy in Paris in opposition to Hun Sen. They advocated "respect for the Paris Peace Accords; the end of the war; and establishment of a state of law and national reconciliation," among other things. FUNCINPEC members and Sam Rainsy's KNP reportedly planned to organize a similar demonstration in Phnom Penh demanding power sharing and full powers to the king. Hun Sen warned that the demonstration would be met with a counterdemonstration. The king issued a communiqué expressing concern about the "unexpected crisis" in the coalition and suggesting that he would need to organize yet another roundtable if things were not resolved.

But Hun Sen went about his business in defiance of the king. Taking advantage of Sihanouk's absence, on 9 May the Council of Ministers decided to establish relations with South Korea. With Ranariddh in France, the decision was announced by Hun Sen. In a move sure to displease Sihanouk, who maintained a residence in Pyongyang, North Korea, Ranariddh endorsed the decision upon his return. Cambodia and South Korea agreed to establish diplomatic missions (which have a lesser status than embassies) in each other's countries. Diplomats and observers interpreted the announcement as a direct snub of Sihanouk. Henceforth the diplomatic corps consisted of twenty-one plus two, Widyono and the South Korean envoy.

AN INVITATION TO SAMDECH PANN ROAD

On Monday, 27 May, one month after seeing Hun Sen, I was granted an audience of one and a half hours with Ranariddh to hear his version of events to convey to the secretary-general of the United Nations. The prince received me in his unimposing Samdech Pann Road home in the elite neighborhood of Phnom Penh—quite a contrast with Hun Sen's Takhmau fortress. There were sandbags and troops at the entrances off the road, but security was a far cry from Takhmau. Yet these sandbags gave one a strange feeling that all was not well. They were certainly not there to protect against the Khmer Rouge, who were hundreds of miles away.

After the Peace Agreements were signed, Hun Sen had confidentially offered Ranariddh two residences, one near the national stadium and one in town. Ranariddh had refused the offer, demanding that he reobtain his old childhood house that had become the Soviet embassy. Hun Sen said that was impossible. Finally, Hun Sen gave him two adjacent villas in town on Samdech Pann Road then occupied by officials of the Ministry of the Interior, though Ranariddh's bodyguard unit was located on the road to the airport far away.

Ranariddh, who spoke English fluently, did not need an interpreter in our meeting. He covered much of the same ground as Hun Sen but with a starkly different interpretation of events. Ranariddh categorically denied accusations by Hun Sen that his attacks against Vietnamese border encroachments and his criticism of the CPP at the FUNCINPEC congress had undermined the RCAF's dry-season offensive. Long before then, he claimed, the offensive had run into great difficulties owing to a proliferation of Khmer Rouge land mines, inadequate logistical support and salaries, and the consequent low morale of RCAF soldiers. He had recommended that it be terminated after large units of RCAF troops were destroyed, he said. Besides, he pointed out, Hun Sen himself had stopped the offensive.

Ranariddh also took issue with Hun Sen's accusations that FUNCINPEC had tried to destroy the constitution. FUNCINPEC would always act within the framework of the constitution, he said. He denied that he had ever threatened to withdraw from the National Assembly. Through me, he invited Hun Sen to listen to his speech at the congress carefully to confirm this. While he admitted saying that FUNCINPEC might withdraw from the coalition government if necessary, he stated that if he left, Hun Sen would be unable to act or sign anything by himself. It would be in violation of the constitution, he said, which stipulated that there be two prime ministers during the first legislature. The government would thus be paralyzed, he continued, and the National Assembly would be affected as well, creating the need for early elections. The prince pointedly reminded me that the arrangement of dual premierships had been masterminded by his father, the king. FUNCINPEC had generously agreed to share power with the losers of the election, the CPP, he added.

Later, after returning to my office, I asked of my staff to be left alone to try to unravel what Ranariddh, the law professor, had said about the constitution. He was obviously engaged in a game of words. The FUNCINPEC press statement of 22 March had read: "If necessary FUNCINPEC will withdraw from the government and FUNCINPEC would support an election before 1998 if there is a dissolvement [sic] of the National Assembly." Thus, while he indeed had not said that FUNCINPEC would withdraw from the National Assembly, he had essentially admitted to me that his withdrawal from the coalition government would result in the dissolution of the assembly. The constitution stipulated that the government must represent a two-thirds majority in the assembly. Ranariddh did not specify a way out of this situation, only that Hun Sen would not be able to govern. To me, the problem appeared to be largely one of semantics.

Ranariddh denied the existence of the so-called FUNCINPEC neutralist forces that Hun Sen had claimed would remain in the cabinet even if the prince ordered FUNCINPEC's withdrawal. The only person who admitted promising neutrality was the uncanny State Minister Ung Phan, he said. Ung Phan claimed to have been threatened with death if he did not cooperate.

Ultimately, Ranariddh saw the present problems as rooted in the fundamental way in which the country was run. Proclaiming himself a liberal democrat, he said that he found Hun Sen's methods unpalatably close to

"Stalinism." He cited five disturbing examples during the previous eighteen months: a grenade attack against the BLDP office; the ruthless campaign against Sirivudh; Hun Sen's revival of the 7 January holiday; an attack on a newspaper office by Krangyov villagers; and the murder of journalist Thun Bun Ly. But only two of the five—Sirivudh and 7 January—could be laid directly at Hun Sen's feet.

The grenade attack had occurred on the night of 30 September 1995, when two people on a motorcycle had thrown hand grenades at the house of Son Sann, the founder and head of the Buddhist Liberal Democratic Party (BLDP). Another attack had taken place on a nearby Buddhist temple where many BLDP supporters were staying. The attacks, which injured at least thirty-five people, were apparently intended to prevent the BLDP from holding a congress the next day. They marked the culmination of a split in the BLDP. On 13 May the BLDP's Executive Committee had moved to expel Ieng Mouly, the minister for information and the only BLDP representative in the cabinet. Mouly, who enjoyed the support of Hun Sen, had swiftly struck back and convened a congress in which he took over the leadership of the party and passed a motion of no confidence against Son Sann and his followers. Son Sann never recognized this congress and convened his own congress on 1 October at the National Stadium. Roadblocks were set up by the government at all routes leading to the stadium to prevent people from attending. But despite the grenade attacks the previous night, the congress proceeded. An investigation never revealed the identities of the attackers. Yet Ranariddh pointed at Hun Sen.

Ranariddh also saw Hun Sen's hand in the Krangyov attack. Krangyov was a model commune near Phnom Penh. It had a Hun Sen Development Center and a small, concrete headquarters with a link to the outside world by a modern telephone/fax system connected to mobile telephone lines. It also boasted a smart new medical clinic and several schools. Life was undoubtedly better for the commune's 2,583 families and 12,000 people than they had ever dreamed of, and their gratitude bred fierce loyalty. The villagers called Hun Sen their father. When a pro–Sam Rainsy newspaper, the *Sereipheap Thmei* (*New Liberty*), criticized Hun Sen, its office was smashed to smithereens, allegedly by angry villagers.

Violence against the press had escalated when Thun Bun Ly, editor-in-chief of the *Udomkati Khmer* (*Khmer Ideal*), another pro-Rainsy paper, was murdered in May 1996. His newspaper had been closed down several times for insulting both prime ministers, saying that they should "stop barking." He had also declared that one of the prime ministers' faces was thicker than the blade of an ax. His funeral procession turned into a battle of his supporters and police when the former insisted on marching with the coffin past the National Assembly and the royal palace. Ranariddh accused Hun Sen of being behind Thun Bun Ly's killing too.

Ranariddh told me that Hun Sen's actions were not supported by most senior members of the CPP. He disclosed that on 30 April, one week after Hun Sen saw me, Hun Sen had proposed in a secret CPP meeting to take military action against FUNCINPEC's machinery. But his proposal had been opposed by everybody except two generals, Ranariddh said: Pol Sareoun and Long So Pheap. Ranariddh claimed that Hun Sen was increasingly isolated.

It appeared to me that just as Hun Sen was trying to capitalize on the perceived disunity in FUNCINPEC, Ranariddh was emphasizing the divisions in the CPP. This, I thought, could lead to dangerous miscalculations. Ranariddh was hoping for opposition to Hun Sen to grow and for a split between the Hun Sen and Chea Sim factions of the CPP to come into the open. But he was engaged in wishful thinking. What he failed to see was that the CPP continued to be a well-disciplined party and that its leaders had maintained an old boys' network since their days together in opposition to Pol Pot.

The lack of support in the CPP for Hun Sen's apparent proposal to annihilate FUNCINPEC did not mean that he was isolated in the party on other matters. He was clearly acting in the CPP's interests on many issues. The party, at least publicly, was still firmly united. Sar Kheng, in a rare political speech on 23 May, said that "the current tension between political parties is only benefiting the Khmer Rouge." He urged that it be resolved peacefully, warning that there would be no winners if the conflict became violent. Chea Sim echoed his remarks.

From my conversations with colleagues, it appeared that many diplomats, including Western ones, had come to emphasize stability over party alliances. Ranariddh, we felt, needed to realize that the Cold War was over and that a doctrinaire adherence to anticommunism was counterproductive.

Ranariddh assured me that his party did indeed want to settle matters amicably. He denied Hun Sen's accusations that some FUNCINPEC ministers and generals, including Ing Kiet, had illegally retrieved arms from warehouses for use by FUNCINPEC armed forces. "I am sure your Excellency agrees with me that Mr. Ing Kiet is most unlikely as an arms purchaser," he chuckled. Indeed, a gray-haired, nice, and diminutive civilian, Ing Kiet would probably not know an AK47 from an M16. Ranariddh said that FUNCINPEC was firmly opposed to armed conflict and civil war again.

I commented to the prince that in spite of refusals by General Ke Kim Yan and Sar Kheng to deploy the army and the police during the secret CPP meeting, Hun Sen still commanded his formidable Battalion B of bodyguards with tanks as well as the military police. Ranariddh brushed this off by replying that he had his own battalion of bodyguards and tanks, Battalion A, and that FUNCINPEC had units in the military police too. FUNCINPEC did not want to talk about its military power and thus provide a pretext for the other party to act, he added.

I knew from my military advisers that the military police, although theoretically under the direction of both prime ministers, were thoroughly controlled by Hun Sen. I believed that if Hun Sen felt pushed into a corner, he could strike back powerfully. But I kept this to myself.

During our meeting, Ranariddh said he felt confident that the elections would keep tensions from escalating into armed conflict. As he pondered his election strategy, the prince pointed out that during the UNTAC elections, despite the CPP's control of the army, police, and administrative structure and the $20 million in cash it received from the shady Teng Bun Ma, it had lost. Therefore, they would lose again, he predicted, with FUNCINPEC now entrenched in the system as a coalition partner.

I asked him why, then, did the king say that Hun Sen would definitely win the next elections and that FUNCINPEC was quite weak. He replied that one must always try to understand carefully what the king really meant. If he were to say that FUNCINPEC would definitely win, it would worry Hun Sen too much, Ranariddh argued. Now Hun Sen was very confident.

But what was Ranariddh going to do to reach out to Hun Sen? Knowing him, I thought, he would launch more blistering attacks—about the Vietnam border and other things—then simply resume his drifting mode, playing with his son's model airplanes on weekends or going to Bangkok for golf. Of course, though he did not say so, he probably hoped that moderate forces in the CPP, including Chea Sim and Sar Kheng, would prevail upon Hun Sen to abandon his scare tactics and threats of violence. Or, better still, that Hun Sen would get ousted as number two of the party, and eventually from his premiership, in the next CPP congress scheduled for June 1996.

Before traveling to Beijing in late May to visit Sihanouk, Ranariddh again attacked Vietnam for encroaching upon another province. And once more he deliberately used the derogatory word *yuon* to provoke the Vietnamese and Hun Sen. He also lashed out at CPP district chiefs, reminding them that he was still the first prime minister and should be treated as such.

Upon his return from Beijing, Ranariddh seemed much more conciliatory. He was optimistic about Sihanouk's health and predicted that the king could be back in two more weeks. He said that the king was buoyed by good news from Chea Sim, who had told him in Beijing that the two parties were really willing to work together to resolve all problems. Ranariddh himself felt that the two parties could resolve their differences peacefully. As with so many of his political calculations, however, the prince was quite mistaken.

NOTES

1. Son Sann is an ethnic Khmer hailing from South Vietnam, an area that was once part of Cambodia and that Cambodians still refer to as Kampuchea Krom.

2. Sihanouk was obviously referring to splits in the BLDP and KNP.

3. On the last point, Sihanouk later said that *Le Monde* had misquoted him. He had been referring to his desire to enter the political arena in 1993, not in 1996, he stated.

4. Sam Rainsy was also in Paris, coinciding with an openly anti–Hun Sen demonstration there on 28 April, which led Hun Sen to threaten his own demonstration in Phnom Penh.

13

Toward a Climax

THE DEFECTION OF IENG SARY

The days when the copremiers appeared unified and cordial in public were now gone. After the ill-fated FUNCINPEC congress of March 1996, they seldom, if ever, met face-to-face. This gave the population the strange sense of being ruled by two governments increasingly hostile to each other. As they approached the 1998 elections, both the CPP and FUNCINPEC intensified their efforts to undermine each other.

In the second half of 1996, though, tensions temporarily waned. On 9 August, Hun Sen stunningly announced that under the leadership of Ieng Sary, the majority of Khmer Rouge forces had defected and wished to enter the government. This was the best news about the Khmer Rouge since their ouster in January 1979. Hun Sen warmly welcomed Ieng Sary and his breakaway movement. Coming from the Khmer Rouge's most uncompromising opponent—he had successfully pushed for the passage of a law outlawing the Khmer Rouge in July 1994—Hun Sen's turnabout perplexed even the most seasoned Cambodia watcher.

Ieng Sary was the former deputy prime minister and foreign minister of Pol Pot's regime. He was one of the Khmer Rouge's top leaders and had been with Pol Pot since their Paris days. His Khmer Rouge troops were holed up in the so-called rich area of Pailin/Malai in Battambang province. I had met these troops in September 1992 and found them more liberal than the hardliners Pol Pot, Ta Mok, and Son Sann, who were based in An Long Veng in

Siem Reap province. With the Phnom Penh government receiving worldwide support, Ieng Sary probably realized that the game was up for the Khmer Rouge holdouts.

Khmer Rouge radio immediately denounced Ieng Sary as a traitor. He was also charged with embezzling money from the Khmer Rouge's gem mining and logging operations. It appeared that his defection signified a major split in the leadership of the Khmer Rouge between the "rich" and the "poor": Ieng Sary on the one side, and Pol Pot and company on the other. The mass defections were a heavy military and psychological blow to the hardliners in An Long Veng. Indeed, they indicated that the Khmer Rouge movement was on the brink of death.[1]

The 1994 law outlawing the Khmer Rouge contained a clause granting amnesty to those who voluntarily defected to the government. Since passage of the law, Khmer Rouge troops had been trickling in. But Ieng Sary's defection—without a single shot fired—was a milestone.

The battle against the remaining Khmer Rouge hardliners, in which the two prime ministers outwardly presented a united front, now grew more complex as the two competed to woo the defectors. This, in turn, encouraged splits within the Khmer Rouge between those who favored integration with the government and those who engaged in increasingly senseless struggle against it. It also pitted those forces who favored integration with Hun Sen against those who opted for the weaker FUNCINPEC, their former allies.

Hun Sen, who by now called all the shots, hailed the defection of Ieng Sary as a triumph for the Royal Cambodian Armed Forces and therefore a triumph for Cambodia. He tried to convince Ranariddh to see it this way, but, as usual, his copremier dithered. Ranariddh vacillated between agreeing that Ieng Sary's defection was a major coup and assessing it less enthusiastically in light of his "military balance" doctrine.

The wily Ieng Sary was well aware of the power struggle between the two premiers. Thus, instead of accepting Hun Sen's olive branch, he sent the nation on a roller-coaster ride with on-again, off-again negotiations about the terms of his defection, demanding first amnesty, then autonomy, and then retention of his military units and their Beijing-style uniforms—in which, he claimed, his men felt "more comfortable."

At a press conference on 9 September held in his territory, Phnom Malai, just nine kilometers from Thailand, and attended by many journalists from around the world, Ieng Sary established what he called the Democratic National Union Movement (DNUM). It was never clear whether the DNUM would become a new political party vying in the next elections or some kind of cover for an autonomous zone. What became evident was that while Ieng Sary wanted to break away from the hardliners in An Long Veng, he was not yet ready to fully surrender to the government.

On 14 September, at a reception, Ranariddh informed the ASEAN ambassadors and me that the king, at the urging of the two prime ministers, had signed a letter pardoning Ieng Sary. The decree relieved Ieng Sary from a death sentence that had been handed down to him in absentia by the People's Republic of Kampuchea in 1979 and gave him amnesty from the 1994 legislation outlawing the Khmer Rouge. Significantly, it said nothing about future trials for genocide and crimes against humanity during the Pol Pot regime.

The international diplomatic community in Phnom Penh reacted to the pardon with mixed feelings. The Chinese agreed with it, but some Western ambassadors considered Ieng Sary beyond the pale. Nevertheless, no foreign country officially criticized it. Even the United States resisted making any statement, except to say the issue was a "Cambodian affair." Finally, in September, the rebels accepted Hun Sen's overture to join the government.

MY SECOND TRIP TO PAILIN

Both copremiers visited Ieng Sary's stronghold of Pailin. Ranariddh's visit, on 11 October, was a low-key affair. Hun Sen, on the other hand, went to Pailin with much fanfare. He arrived as a soldier in his glittering four-star army uniform "to meet with the people." As the United Nations secretary-general's representative, I and some other diplomats were asked to accompany him. In contrast to my earlier trip with Sihanouk to Pailin in September 1992 in a small six-seat helicopter, I accompanied Hun Sen in a huge M26 Russian-made helicopter. It was reportedly a gift from the tycoon Teng Bun Ma, at that time perhaps the richest man in Cambodia, who joined us. I had the distinct feeling that the helicopter was the same one that took me and my land cruiser when I was deployed to Siem Reap the first time.[2]

Because he was venturing into the lion's den of his archenemy, the Khmer Rouge, Hun Sen needed protection. The helicopter thus contained three hundred of the most trusted and heavily armed crack troops from the 911 paracommando brigade, trained by Indonesia's special forces (KOPASSUS). They came in their shiny KOPASSUS uniforms and red berets. They sang an Indonesian KOPASSUS song, "Dari Bandung ke Cilacap" ("From Bandung to Cilacap"), which made me feel completely at home. I was reminded of a trip during UNTAC times from Battambang to Siem Reap when my wife and I were the sole passengers on this giant helicopter. My colleague in Battambang, the provincial director Enrique Aguilar, had simply ordered the helicopter to fly us back. A rare sign of UNTAC power.

When the huge helicopter landed, we were greeted by the commander of Pailin, General Y Chhean, who was protected by around four hundred armed Khmer Rouge troops in uniforms identical to those of the People's Liberation Army (PLA) of China. It was a bizarre but heartrending moment when the troops from the 911 brigade and Khmer Rouge embraced. It looked like a reconciliation between Indonesian and Chinese troops, two countries estranged from each other since the abortive coup by leftists in Indonesia in 1965, which Suharto had blamed on Beijing until 1990.

The Khmer Rouge troops, AK-47s over their shoulders, had lost their mystique. They turned out to be ordinary people, with ordinary wants and needs. When I had accompanied Sihanouk to Pailin earlier, everybody had carried

Photo 13.1.   Hun Sen, left, meeting Ieng Sary in Pailin. Author's personal collection.

small Supreme National Council flags, as the Khmer Rouge had insisted that the SNC be fully empowered to replace Hun Sen's government. Now, there were no flags. While the SNC flag had lost its legitimacy, Ieng Sary did not want the old Khmer Rouge flag to fly again. Nor was he ready to fly the Royal Government of Cambodia flag.

Later the two groups of soldiers stood side by side in pairs at intervals of ten meters. They guarded the entire road from the helipad to the Kao Kang pagoda in the center of town where the welcoming ceremonies and, later that night, a party took place. Ieng Sary welcomed Hun Sen at the helipad. Both walked, followed by the rest of us, to the beautiful Kao Kang pagoda. The two leaders prostrated and prayed in front of a chapter of monks apparently flown in from Battambang to replace the Khmer Rouge monks. It was a surreal scene: two leaders of opposing communist factions praying together in full deference of the monks. "A peaceful opportunity is now available, so go now and take care of your livelihood, your crops," Hun Sen later told a crowd of some 3,500 Khmer Rouge soldiers and their families crammed into the pagoda's courtyard.

That afternoon, as Hun Sen began to trust the Khmer Rouge, most of the 911 brigade left, although journalists told me that many government soldiers from Battambang remained to attend the party that evening in the temple grounds. Ostensibly a "gift" from Hun Sen, the party was actually financed by Teng Bun Ma and Malaysian tycoon Andrew Yo, who also accompanied Hun Sen. A rock band had been flown in from Battambang that morning complete with scantily clad singers. The Khmer Rouge soldiers, together with the government soldiers and the population of Pailin, danced the night away to traditional Khmer *ramvong* tunes, Cambodian rock songs, standard Western tunes like the ubiquitous "Lambada," and Indonesia's evergreen "Bengawan Solo," which was enormously popular in Cambodia at the time. There was plenty of roast chicken, papaya salad, and rice, and Tiger-brand beer flowed unabatedly.

Teng Bun Ma benefited greatly from his "generosity": he was reportedly given exclusive rights to establish casinos and nightclubs in the area, mainly to entertain Thais from just across the border, where gambling was prohibited. Journalists saw government soldiers, together with their newfound Khmer Rouge friends, digging and finding sapphires while Thai mining companies were working around the clock to take out the gems.

To assure their loyalty, Hun Sen gave Y Chhean and Phnom Malai leader Sok Pheap diplomatic passports and promised to build schools and roads in Pailin and Malai. CPP sources said Hun Sen was prepared to let soldiers, police, and village and commune leaders keep their jobs and guns, and even to give Chhean and Pheap generalships within the RCAF. The Khmer Rouge leaders recognized who was the real boss in Phnom Penh, regardless of overtures of all kinds from FUNCINPEC or indeed from the king himself. They made their willingness to negotiate with Hun Sen quite clear.

A few months later, on Saturday, 8 February 1997, Hun Sen, an entourage of ambassadors including myself, Teng Bun Ma, journalists, security troops, and the top brass and ministers of the CPP visited Phnom Malai, another of Ieng Sary's Khmer Rouge strongholds adjacent to Pailin. Walking next to him, I observed that Teng Bun Ma surreptitiously surveyed everywhere we went with a keen business eye.[3] Hun Sen's main purpose for this visit, as far as I could tell, was to remind the DNUM and other breakaway leaders that he held the power. The visit came in the wake of recent provocative announcements by Ranariddh that the DNUM was ready to join the National United Front (NUF), a loose alliance of former resistance forces touted by Ranariddh. The DNUM assured Hun Sen that it wanted to remain neutral. All the top leadership were on hand to welcome him, including Ieng Sary, his wife, and the commanders of the four strongholds.

After discussions at a sumptuous Cambodian lunch hosted by the DNUM, any idea that the DNUM ever had of joining NUF surely evaporated. As a reward for their refusal to join NUF, Hun Sen gave General Y Chhean authority to represent Cambodia in talks with Thailand on the border. The Khmer Rouge, like a fair maiden courted by two competing men, never had it so good!

COALITION AT THE BREAKING POINT

During the first half of 1997, relations between the coprime ministers worsened alarmingly against the backdrop of a protracted and hard-fought campaign for the 1998 elections. The battle greatly impaired the effectiveness of the government and raised questions about its ability to even hold the elections.

Feeling increasingly threatened, and outmaneuvered at every turn by Hun Sen, Ranariddh struck back. One of his strategies was to push Hun Sen over the brink and into rash action. FUNCINPEC had earlier decided in secret meetings that Hun Sen was the "bad apple" and should be isolated and targeted for removal. And Ranariddh had said publicly that the problem was not the CPP but Hun Sen himself. FUNCINPEC's newfound confidence in openly defying Hun Sen was based on, among other things, a presumption that he had lost support within his own party for his "Stalinist" behavior and that he had in effect become a "paper tiger" without much support in the regular army. Provoking Hun Sen, FUNCINPEC believed, would bring international condemnation of him and raise eyebrows in his own party.

But the CPP's congress on 24–27 January, its largest ever and first since 1992, pulled the rug out from under this strategy. Despite predictions to the contrary, widely circulated by FUNCINPEC and other adversaries, Hun Sen sailed through the congress relatively unscathed. There were intense, surprisingly frank, and at times acrimonious debates. And there was some resentment of Hun Sen for his popularity, his control of funds enabling him to build more than one thousand schools named after him and to buy off former Khmer Rouge generals and soldiers, and his handling of the Khmer Rouge generally. But there was no attempt whatsoever to oust him from his position of second prime minister. He and the other leader of the CPP, President Chea Sim, repeatedly stressed the importance of party unity.

The congress elected eighty-five new members of the Central Committee, in addition to the sixty-eight who were then serving. Hun Sen did suffer a serious setback when three of his most radical and loyal aides were rejected for the Central Committee: Om Yen Tieng, his media adviser; General Keo Pong, a Khmer Rouge defector; and Kun Kim, the vice governor of Kandal. However, the enlarged Central Committee included many pro–Hun Sen RCAF generals, including Police Chief General Hok Lundi, who would later emerge as one of the most feared men in Cambodia; the notorious head of the military police, Kieng Savuth; and the premier's military adviser, General Mol Roeup. Their selection seemed to contradict the premise that the military and police should remain neutral in the next elections.

The first armed confrontation between forces loyal to CPP and those loyal to FUNCINPEC erupted in Battambang province on 10 February, with sporadic fighting. This was a bad omen: it proved that the tensions could indeed lead to military skirmishes. It also proved that the integrated RCAF was splintering.

FUNCINPEC IMPLODES

In the week of 14 April, the crafty Ung Phan of FUNCINPEC showed up in the news again when he announced that a FUNCINPEC faction consisting of twelve MPs (reportedly with more to follow) had broken away from the party. The Ranariddh and Hun Sen sides then traded increasingly vitriolic insults over the split. A radio commentator from Ranariddh's camp blamed it on the "crazy Vietnamese" and Hun Sen's meddling. Ranariddh, for the first time, labeled Hun Sen a "Vietnamese puppet," echoing the language of the Khmer Rouge.

Ung Phan's announcement was immediately supported by Hun Sen and the CPP, and by Chea Sim as acting head of state in the absence of the king. While denying that he had a hand in it, Hun Sen immediately pledged support to any move within FUNCINPEC to oust Ranariddh as its leader.

Ranariddh was dealt a further crippling blow when a rebel FUNCINPEC congress was held on 1 June. Remarkably strong security surrounded the entire event. Attended by roughly eight hundred people, the congress overwhelmingly voted Toan Chye, governor of Siem Reap, the new president of FUNCINPEC. It also accused Ranariddh of gross incompetence. The congress selected a new Steering Committee and a new National Council as well.

There were now two rival FUNCINPECs, with all the attendant confusion. Toan Chye promised to rekindle the "spirit of cooperation" between FUNCINPEC and the CPP. Ranariddh's office subsequently issued a statement declaring the congress illegal and accusing the CPP of interfering in the party's internal affairs.

RANARIDDH'S OTHER STRATEGIES

As part of the effort to provoke Hun Sen, rumors of Sirivudh's imminent return from exile in France surfaced in the week prior to the Khmer New Year of 13–15 April. But this scheme was thwarted when the airlines, upon the advice of both prime ministers, refused to carry Sirivudh to Phnom Penh. While FUNCINPEC had staked a lot of pride on securing Sirivudh's safe return, Ranariddh had yielded to Hun Sen's wish not to allow it. The king had also advised against it following a conversation between Hun Sen and the queen.

Hun Sen generally remained quiet throughout these provocations. Always two or three steps ahead of his adversary, he was well aware of the strategy to isolate and provoke him. However, a statement by FUNCINPEC General Nhiek

Bun Chhay that he would bring three hundred troops to the airport to protect Sirivudh on his return was too much for Hun Sen. He threatened to bring forty-five tanks to the airport and shoot down any airplane that carried the prince. This threat, publicized around the world, damaged Hun Sen's image and that of the CPP. The heads of UN agencies huddled together to follow the news. I phoned my friend Paul Redicliffe, the British ambassador to Cambodia, who confirmed that though Sirivudh was at the Hong Kong airport (still under British control), no airline was willing to take him to Phnom Penh. Reassured, we all went back to work, even if the situation was still quite fluid.

Hun Sen's threat was followed two days later by a statement that he would welcome the prince at the airport provided that Sihanouk granted him amnesty first. He covered himself by circulating among diplomats and the press letters from the king and Sirivudh dated a year earlier in which both promised solemnly that Sirivudh would remain abroad and refrain from engaging in politics. The king did not grant amnesty to the prince.

The next provocation was the much-heralded inauguration ceremony of the National United Front on 27 February. NUF was intended to unite the opposition parties against the CPP. Before an enthusiastic crowd of 1,200, four parties—FUNCINPEC, Sam Rainsy's KNP, the Son Sann faction of the BLDP, and the small Khmer Neutral Party—signed a fourteen-point charter to establish the front.[4] Ranariddh was unanimously elected NUF's first president. Beaming, he declared that the chance of the alliance winning the elections was strong.

NUF's political platform seemed to include many of the old arguments against Vietnam and the CPP. Holding up NUF's charter, Ranariddh defiantly proclaimed in a shrill voice to the diplomatic corps in the front row that he would send the charter to An Long Veng. An audible gasp of incredulity arose from our row. Here was a prime minister openly inviting the archenemy in An Long Veng to join a coalition against his copremier, Hun Sen. It was vintage Ranariddh.[5]

On 28 January, Sam Rainsy's KNP had issued a statement explaining that the alliance of all patriotic forces in NUF was intended to address national issues of vital importance. They included violations of Cambodia's territorial integrity and increasing Vietnamese illegal immigration; the dictatorial power of the pro-Vietnamese and communist CPP, which operated against fundamental democratic principles, oppressed the people, and continuously violated human rights; and rampant corruption, which was the main cause of bad governance and social injustices. Sam Rainsy organized demonstrations against deforestation and oppressive conditions in garment factories, which, ironically, involved two industries controlled by FUNCINPEC ministers in the government. Corruption was certainly not a monopoly of the CPP.

The day after NUF's inaugural ceremony, the CPP predictably issued a terse statement condemning the formation of NUF. In a thinly veiled reference to the opposition Khmer Nation Party, the CPP said, "This front is a strange one in which a governing political party includes an anti-government party that regards the government as a mafia and provokes regular unrest in Cambodia. It is [like] closing the door and opening the door again to let thieves come in and steal." By then, the CPP had signed up seven small parties, which ironically included the anticommunist, antimonarchist Republican party consisting of remnants of the Lon Nol Republicans.

In his next provocation, Ranariddh moved to win the remaining Khmer Rouge to his side. The Khmer Rouge hardliners, in turn, used this as a bargaining tool with Ranariddh. To make the negotiations more palatable, FUNCINPEC attempted to exile notorious Khmer Rouge leaders Pol Pot, Ta Mok, and Son Sann and to negotiate with the more acceptable "intellectual" leaders such as Khieu Samphan and Tep Kunnal. But this plan collapsed because no country wanted to take in these criminals.

Officially, Ranariddh would deny entering into secret negotiations with the hardliners, claiming that he simply did what Hun Sen had done with Ieng Sary and others—woo the remaining Khmer Rouge back to the government. Yet in interviews on Khmer Rouge radio, Khieu Samphan and Chan Youran praised NUF profusely as an alternative to the CPP alliance, which they condemned, and heartily welcomed the opportunity to ally with Ranariddh against Hun Sen.[6]

Then, on 21 May, Khieu Samphan officially pledged the support of his Khmer National Solidarity Party—read Khmer Rouge—for NUF. The timing of his provocative declaration raised some eyebrows, aimed as it was at increasing tension between FUNCINPEC and the CPP. Hun Sen already had warned against allowing the hardliners a way into politics. But Ranariddh and Khieu Samphan went ahead with their alliance, hammering out a secret joint statement that endorsed NUF and pledged mutual support. Incredibly, the deal in effect amounted to re-creating the earlier Coalition Government of Democratic Kampuchea (CGDK).[7]

Ranariddh was completely misreading political realities. Fifteen years after the establishment of the CGDK, with the Cold War over and with the international community invested in peace, any attempt to re-create the old alliance to fight the Royal Government was bound to fail. Absurdly, Ranariddh was fighting the government while still its first prime minister. Given that captured Khmer Rouge documents indicated that the Khmer Rouge desired to join FUNCINPEC "to continue the struggle against the Vietnamese and its puppets," any idea that the hard-line leaders were prepared to go in peace, exile, or amnesty was laughable.[8]

RELINQUISH THE THRONE YET AGAIN?

Adding fuel to the already volatile situation, on 26 February the king stated once again that he was ready to abdicate the throne. He gave as his reason the surge in antiroyalist sentiment in Cambodia, which he said threatened to turn the country into a republic. He blamed Republicans and other anti-Sihanoukists for an upsurge in antiroyalist articles in the press.[9]

On Friday and Saturday, 14 and 15 March, Hun Sen launched an attack on the monarchy in two hard-hitting speeches. He claimed Ranariddh supported the king's threat to abdicate, and warned that if the king did give up his throne he would initiate an amendment to the constitution to force all members of the royal family from politics. "If they want to be involved in politics, they have to quit from the royal family forever," he said. "If they want to continue the kingdom, the country must be ruled by a king. Thus we must be clear whether we want to continue to be a kingdom or turn the country into a republic."

Hun Sen's attack on the monarchy came as a complete surprise. Meanwhile criticism of the king's plan to abdicate continued unabated in Republican and pro–Hun Sen newspapers. One alleged that the plan was a prelude for the king to enter politics, as without political power he would not stay quiet. It ominously predicted that war in Cambodia would not end before the king died. The attacks in the press reflected a deep-seated fear on Hun Sen's part: that the king would abdicate and, as in 1955, enter politics as a citizen and win the elections. The wily king was well aware of Hun Sen's fears and must have chuckled about this one in his palace.

Hun Sen's attack on the monarchy was clever. He knew it would weaken and split FUNCINPEC, as the party contained many people who were not necessarily monarchists. He may even have hinted to these people secretly that they could continue in the party once it was cleansed of Royalists.

On 18 March, FUNCINPEC made its move. It issued a statement to the effect that any attempt to change Cambodia from a constitutional monarchy would amount to a coup d'etat and cited Article 134 of the constitution (which prohibited amendments affecting the country's status) in support of its case. The statement called upon the two parties to issue a joint statement promising to respect the constitution. On the same day, Ranariddh attacked the "dictatorial" nature of Hun Sen's proposals. Both Sam Rainsy and Son Sann made similar statements.

Then, in a curious move on the first day of yet another FUNCINPEC congress held on 19–21 March, Ranariddh stated that he intended to file a complaint with the Commission on Human Rights against Hun Sen. He called Hun Sen's attack on the royal family "racial discrimination" and pointed out that all Cambodians had a constitutional right to participate in government. Son Sann and Sam Rainsy, he stated, would join his complaint, which would be open to signature by all members of FUNCINPEC. But, predictably, nothing came of Ranariddh's latest threat.

A HORRIBLE GRENADE ATTACK

On 30 March, in the worst incident since the 1993 elections, at least nineteen people—including three children, young female textile workers who had demonstrated with Sam Rainsy against low wages the year before, and two journalists—were killed when four grenades exploded outside the National Assembly at a Sam Rainsy–led demonstration against the judiciary's lack of independence. One hundred and fifty people were wounded, including the American Ron Abney. Sam Rainsy's voice on the bullhorn was quickly drowned out by screams as the scene descended into mayhem. Blood was everywhere. The blasts blew off arms and legs, and a shortage of ambulances in Phnom Penh left many bleeding on the sidewalk for more than an hour.

I was attending an ecumenical Easter Sunday service in the ballroom of the Cambodiana Hotel where I also had my office, a block from the grenade attack when Major Wanderstein, my military adviser who had been observing the demonstration, whispered the details in my ear. I told the congregation what had happened and then sped to the scene.

Because of the wounded American, the FBI conducted its own investigation, but it was inconclusive. Eyewitness accounts varied widely, with some observers claiming that people in a white speeding car threw the grenades while others insisted that people in the crowd did. Some claimed that the perpetrators in the crowd fled in the direction of the heavily guarded nearby CPP compound behind Hun Sen's house. Sam Rainsy, protected by his bodyguard, escaped injury, but the bodyguard died. After the first pair of blasts, a person allegedly shouted that they had missed Sam Rainsy, after which two other blasts followed. Theories on who was responsible abounded. The CPP, FUNC-INPEC, and the king all issued statements condemning the attack.

FUTILE BIPARTISAN EFFORTS

The dreadful attack occurred just one week after appeals for calm from bipartisan defense officials and Chea Sim. On 21 March, Minister of Defense Tea Banh, his cominister Tea Chamrath, and top generals Ke Kim Yan and Nhiek Bun Chhay had ordered troops to remain neutral amid continuing political tension between the two prime ministers. The orders, broadcast on national television and radio, had proclaimed that the Royal Cambodian Armed Forces were neutral and did not belong to any political party.

The grenade attack came in the wake of rapidly escalating tensions in the capital. The causes: the building up of the bodyguard units of both premiers, attempts by Sirivudh to return, and persistent rumors of a coup. In the midst of the tension, Hun Sen and Ranariddh took great pains to woo the diplomatic corps. In explaining their positions to us, each prime minister accused the other of destabilizing the country. Hun Sen alleged that Ranariddh was employing Khmer Rouge forces, while Ranariddh claimed that Hun Sen was relying on Vietnamese troops. Despite the receding possibility of armed conflict, the underlying problems that had generated the coup rumors remained: the government was still frozen and the copremiers' relationship remained in tatters. And numerous critical elements in the electoral preparations were still unsettled.

In a move to reduce tensions, the Bipartisan Joint Commission for Abnormal Conflict Resolution, established after the Battambang clashes and comprising the cointerior and defense ministers, the chiefs of staff, and the police, addressed the nation's provincial governors and security chiefs on 29 April. In an eight-point declaration, it repeated the order for the armed forces to remain neutral. In addition, Co-Interior Minister Sar Kheng of the CPP and Co-Defense Minister Tea Chamrath of FUNCINPEC reportedly wrote a joint letter to the coprime ministers requesting that they not resort to violence and assuring them that the armed forces would remain neutral.

The joint letter and the meetings of the Commission appeared to be attempts to signal that the problems that had afflicted Phnom Penh in recent weeks lay with the coprime ministers alone, not with their parties. The Commission was hoping to keep the situation from turning violent. But the critical wounds afflicting the government remained untreated. Moreover, it was overly simplistic to see the coprime ministers as the sole disputants in either party. The actions of the parties can more accurately be seen as intended to bring the greatest political gain to the parties themselves.

Despite the overall calm that had descended upon Phnom Penh, rumors of unusual troop movements persisted, and the highly partisan local press continued to make much of them. Particularly worrying were the continuing accusations in the FUNCINPEC press that the CPP was secretly deploying Vietnamese troops around the capital. There was some concern in the diplomatic and NGO communities that these accusations could fuel harassment of Cambodia's Vietnamese community. Also, Hun Sen's assertion that the army would remain neutral did not pertain to its stance toward what he called ex-Khmer Rouge "illegal forces" recruited by Ranariddh. There remained the specter of attacks on those forces, which formed part of Ranariddh's bodyguard structure. That Cambodia's coalition government was in its death throes was increasingly evident as ongoing conflicts worsened, and new ones arose.

RANARIDDH'S "ILLEGAL" WEAPONS IMPORTATION

On 26 May, senior government officials discovered an alleged clandestine arms shipment to Ranariddh. That day, military authorities seized a two-to-three-ton shipment of arms—including AK-47 assault rifles, handguns, rocket launchers, and ammunition—addressed to Ranariddh and labeled as spare parts. Senior government officials from the CPP who were considered moderate compared to Hun Sen, including the chief of staff of the armed forces, Ke Kim Yan, and Co-Interior Minister Sar Kheng, immediately deemed the shipment illegal. But government officials belonging to FUNCINPEC, including Ranariddh himself and the secretary of state of defense, Ek Sereywath, who was in charge of arms purchases for the Royal Government, said the weapons were intended for Ranariddh's bodyguard unit, whom he had the right to arm. But, of course, one has to ask: Why did he hide the weapons by labeling them spare parts?

Upon their discovery, the weapons were taken to a military base near Pochentong airport. Under guard of both FUNCINPEC and the CPP, an inventory was taken. Reports indicated that the inventory was extremely tense, highlighting the partisanship of military units. Subsequently, the dispute appeared to be resolved with a plan to allocate the light arms to FUNCINPEC and integrate the heavy antitank arms into the RCAF. Demands to put Ranariddh on trial began to appear in the CPP-dominated press.

The situation worsened on 31 May when Hun Sen's cabinet denounced Ranariddh, reiterated that the arms shipment was illegal, and said legal recourse should be pursued. The cabinet's statement went on to claim that Hun Sen's bodyguard unit belonged to the government and that he had the right to use it against whoever opposed the government and damaged national security. The statement rejected Ranariddh's proposal to reduce the number of bodyguards and return the weapons to the Ministry of Defense on the grounds that Ranariddh could not be trusted to keep from covertly building up a private arsenal.

The argument over the legality of the shipment and the explicit manner in which both prime ministers justified the need to maintain private armies graphically underlined the depth of their mutual mistrust. Ranariddh appeared to be increasingly boxed into a corner.

THE BODYGUARD BATTALIONS

The most dangerous aspect of the escalating confrontation between the two prime ministers was undoubtedly the growth of their bodyguard units. Of course, many authoritarian governments have bodyguard units to protect the leader against internal dissent. Such units are often the elite crack troops in the country. Sukarno of Indonesia had his handsome Cakra Birawa regiment, from which came Colonel Untung, leader of the 1965 aborted coup d'etat in that country. What made Cambodia unique was that there were two premiers with separate elite bodyguard units. Originally created after the abortive coup d'etat of July 1994, these units had grown into menacing miniarmies under the direct command of each prime minister and followed them everywhere.

It became common in Phnom Penh to see long columns of military-type vehicles escorting the premiers or indeed any high-ranking military or civilian official. They had replaced UNTAC's white cars. It was a game for bystanders, including children, to guess who was passing by. The longer the convoy of shiny new black cars and policemen in sharp uniforms with their motorcycle sirens wailing—with the longest reaching fifteen to twenty vehicles—the higher the rank of the person being escorted. My driver, the wily and very intelligent Samet who never missed a beat, commenting on these convoys, would identify without fail Ranariddh, Hun Sen, Sar Kheng, or Hok Lundi. In the diplomatic community, we became acutely aware of the menace posed by these bodyguard units when in April both prime ministers gave us a grand tour of them.

Hun Sen briefed the diplomatic corps on 25 April at Takhmau, his suburban fortress. His briefing was undoubtedly meant to give us ample opportunity to view his formidable and heavily defended complex, which appeared to be the largest military base in the country, encompassing an area of one square kilometer. One week earlier, on 19 April, he had given a two-hour press conference there. It was obvious that his arsenal was not directed against faraway Khmer Rouge redoubts but against threats from his copremier. His message was clear: Don't try anything silly. Rumors of an impending coup d'etat had started to swirl around the capital about this time.

As a layman, I could detect the considerable changes that had been made to the compound since my private briefing by Hun Sen a year previously. Elevated guard posts manned by troops in full combat gear with machine guns were spaced along the outer walls. Some of the soldiers in the compound had patches on their sleeves with "Hun Sen Body Guard" in English on them. Hun Sen's bodyguards, whom the Khmer Rouge called Vietnamese Dac Cong sappers, were carefully selected and well trained, and while they were Khmer, they could very well have been trained by real Dac Cong. They were also ruthless. Ranariddh's forces were not half as effective. Overall, the bodyguard units of both prime ministers were better and more regularly paid than RCAF troops, although few people knew where the funds came from or their amounts.

Outside the hall where our briefing was held, twenty-eight Russian-made military trucks were parked in tight order. Most of them looked new. Six others with artillery pieces attached to the rear were parked nearby. Across an open parade ground were six tanks and ten armored personnel carriers

(APCs) lined up in an open-air garage. Farther back was a helipad with a huge Russian-made MI-26 helicopter painted in camouflage colors sitting on it. Two antennae, one of which was over eighty meters tall, could be seen in the distance, indicating that the compound had ample communications equipment to keep in touch with the entire country.

An aide to Hun Sen said that one battalion, or 600–800 troops, was based in the compound; he called it a "rapid intervention force." He added that the compound had its own water supply, pumping equipment, and even a rice field. However, my friend General Cunanan, a graduate of West Point and the ambassador of the Philippines, whispered to me that the numbers were probably higher, perhaps in the 1,000–1,400 range, and that there was enough equipment for two battalions, one of which was undoubtedly an armored unit.

Hun Sen had another bodyguard unit based behind his house in Phnom Penh—known as "the CPP compound"—near the Independence Monument. While the premier rarely stayed at this residence, these troops—numbering around 100–150—were permanently stationed there and equipped with at least two APCs. Hun Sen's house had a helipad on top of the back annex. Technically, Ranariddh's and Hun Sen's bodyguard units were Battalions A and B, respectively, of the 70th Brigade, which was based on the road to Takeo province past Pochentong airport. Military analysts said that the base had about 300 to 400 soldiers, five tanks, and several APCs. It was believed that the forces there reported directly to Hun Sen.

My military adviser, Wanderstein, went to a similar briefing offered by General Nhiek Bun Chhay of FUNCINPEC for military attachés. The bulk of Ranariddh's bodyguard unit was based at Tang Krasang, a military compound just beyond the entrance to Pochentong airport, far away from his residence in town. There were 300–900 troops, three tanks, and three APCs. Ranariddh's Samdech Pan residence also boasted a bodyguard unit, comprising another 200–250 soldiers. Beyond Tang Krasang, Ranariddh had troops on the military side of Pochentong, where three tanks and three APCs were based, as well as a smaller bodyguard unit based permanently at the home of General Nhiek Bun Chhay.

It was not known where, precisely, Ranariddh's troops came from. Some could have come from Division 3 in Siem Reap province, which included Khmer Rouge defectors who had joined the government. And some could have been drawn from former FUNCINPEC units that had been demobilized several years earlier.

Analysts did agree that, given FUNCINPEC's minuscule army to begin with, the only place Ranariddh and his FUNCINPEC generals could obtain reinforcements was the Khmer Rouge, their former allies. Defenders of Ranariddh argued that his courting of the Khmer Rouge in An Long Veng was no different than what Hun Sen was doing with Ieng Sary. But to his critics, Ranariddh's secret meetings with Khmer Rouge leaders, and their open declaration of support for NUF, were not only illegal but designed with the dissolution of the coalition government in mind.

While all the right things had been said about main line RCAF soldiers and police remaining neutral, the issue of who would fight for whom was further complicated by the existence of units with historically well-defined alignments. For example, apart from the bodyguard units, the gendarmerie, or military police, had about seven thousand well-armed soldiers with jeeps and trucks spread out in almost every province. Created with support from the French government, they had been set up in theory to provide a separate police force with powers to arrest both civilians and military. While on the payroll of the Ministry of Defense, they had a channel of command that bypassed the chiefs of staff, reporting directly to the coprime ministers. However, the senior officer in charge of the gendarmerie was Kieng Savuth, who was a known Hun Sen loyalist. How these troops would respond in a crisis could only be guessed at. Further, human rights workers speculated that there were a number of secret military and police units loyal to the CPP. During UNTAC times, a number of such units—known as A groups—had been responsible for political intimidation directed against both the BLDP and FUNCINPEC. The exact number and status of these groups could not be determined.

According to defense analysts, Wanderstein related to me, there were at the time about ten thousand military officers and soldiers in Phnom Penh, including three thousand on the General Staff, another three thousand in the Ministry of Defense, and others at the headquarters of the special forces, the navy, and the air force. The question was how long would all these people remain neutral in the event of an armed clash? When asked, several Cambodians hesitated, laughed, and then said, "About five minutes."[10] Indeed, as long as there were two separate bodyguard units, the potential for confrontation remained.

A PERSONAL NOTE

At the end of May 1997, I officially left Cambodia and entered retirement. The United Nations mandates that career staffers should retire at the age of sixty, which I had reached the previous October. However, as I occupied a post that was political in nature, my term had been extended until April to complete my three-year assignment as the secretary-general's representative. Then, on 7 April, Hun Sen had written a letter to Secretary-General Kofi Annan asking him to extend my appointment until the 1998 elections. Describing me as an "old hand" in Cambodia, Hun Sen wrote that "any replacement of Mr. Widyono at this juncture of Cambodia's democratic progress may be regarded as an attempt to derail it."

Ranariddh, on the other hand, ostensibly concerned with my old age and health, wrote to Kofi Annan on 22 April asking that a replacement for me be appointed since I had reached retirement age. I suspected that he had been tipped off by someone in the UN Secretariat about Hun Sen's letter, which had been kept confidential. He claimed that Hun Sen's request was made without his knowledge. Ranariddh wrote that he "very much" welcomed "the nomination by the United Nations of a **new** [his boldface] Special Representative in Cambodia at the expiration of . . . Mr. Benny Widyono's term of office." He asked his faithful ambassador in New York, Prince Sisowath Sirirath, to circulate his letter as an official United Nations document in six languages.

I suspected that Ranariddh and FUNCINPEC would have preferred that I had indirectly helped them during my term, as UNTAC had done in the 1980s because Ranariddh was then the "liberal democrat" and Hun Sen the "communist dictator." Ranariddh forgot that the end of the Cold War had marked the end of these overly simplistic labels. Throughout my posting, I had tried to remain neutral, attending functions of both sides, if invited. In my reporting to New York, I had to be very balanced; otherwise, two secretary-generals, Boutros Boutros-Ghali and Kofi Annan, would not have kept me on for three years.

Because of the disagreement between the premiers, Kofi Annan sent a special envoy to Phnom Penh on 3 May to discuss my replacement. The UN envoy, Assistant Secretary-General Alvaro de Soto, met separately with Ranariddh, Hun Sen, and Foreign Minister Ung Huot, explaining that according to UN rules I was due to retire. He proposed to replace me with Lakhan Mehrotra from India. Hun Sen noted with a chuckle that, at age sixty-seven, Mehrotra was even older than me. There they go again, he probably thought—he had long felt that the United Nations was biased against the CPP. (According to UN staff rules, Mehrotra was a political appointment and his age did not matter.) Hun Sen explained to me later that he accepted Lakhan Mehrotra because India had stood by the PRK during the dark years of the 1980s.[11]

Before I left Cambodia at the end of May, both Hun Sen and Ranariddh hosted dinners for me. Ranariddh thanked me and assured me that he had nothing against me personally; the king also sent me a very nice letter. Although Ranariddh said that my age was the only reason he supported my departure, I wondered about his other motivations. Hun Sen toasted me as a true friend of Cambodia. Sadly, I had to watch the inevitable endgame of the power struggle in Phnom Penh from faraway New York.

NOTES

1. Nayan Chanda, "The Enemy Within," *Far Eastern Economic Review*, vol. 159, no. 34, 14.

2. Indeed it was as UNTAC had leased these helicopters from Aeroflot and after UNTAC left, Aeroflot reportedly sold two of these helicopters to Teng Bun Ma, one of which he kept for his own operations.

3. By 2005 Phnom Malai had become a bustling frontier town where Thai gamblers and pleasure seekers flocked to the casinos and karaoke bars which had sprung up there. It looked like Teng Bun Ma was plotting to cash in.

4. Ieng Mouly, minister of information and leader of the pro–Hun Sen breakaway faction of BLDP, totally rejected NUF. He said that Son Sann could join anything he wanted but could not use the BLDP banner and logo since he had already been ousted from the party. Thus, after lying dormant for more than a year, Ieng Mouly had now come alive as leader of the BLDP.

5. Matthew Lee, the AP journalist, later confided in me that the contingent of expatriate journalists were more interested in watching the body language of us, the diplomats, rather than Ranariddh on stage.

6. Jason Barber and Christine Chaumeau, "Power Struggle Shatters KR Leadership," *Phnom Penh Post*, issue 6/13, 27 June–10 July 1997.

7. English translation of joint statement between Ranariddh and Khieu Samphan in Royal Government of Cambodia, *Crisis in July. Report on the Armed Insurrection: Its*

Origins, History and Aftermath, Phnom Penh: Ministry of Foreign Affairs, 22 September 1997, Annex N. This document, produced after the 5–6 July military showdown in Phnom Penh that sent Ranariddh into exile, was issued by the Ministry of Foreign Affairs, whose minister was a pro–Hun Sen FUNCINPEC official, Ung Huot.

8. David Ashley, "KR Papers Show Rebels Still Living in the Past," *Phnom Penh Post*, issue 7/13, 3–16 July 1998.

9. Republicans in Cambodia are remnants of the anticommunist party of Lon Nol, who overthrew Sihanouk in 1970.

10. Michael Hayes, "All Eyes on the PMs' Bodyguard Units," *Phnom Penh Post*, issue 6/9, 2–15 May 1997.

11. Mehrotra was lucky, as two months before I left I had recruited from New York Jonathan Prentice, a very able young British officer, to my office. He was an excellent writer. Later Jonathan went to East Timor and became special assistant to the late Sergio de Mello, who subsequently brought Jonathan with him to Geneva and then Baghdad. Jonathan narrowly escaped death when on the day of the bomb attack that killed Sergio de Mello he asked for a one-day leave to visit his wife in Lebanon to celebrate their wedding anniversary.

14

The Final Showdown

After I left Cambodia at the end of May 1997, I returned home to Stamford, Connecticut, though I still regularly went to the UN to complete my final report. I was now part of the Department of Political Affairs, the lead unit for Cambodian political affairs in the UN. I held almost daily discussions with Francesc Vendrell, head of the Asia Pacific Division, on the deteriorating situation in Cambodia. We read the excellent reports written by Jonathan Prentice, Mehrotra's assistant. It became quite clear to us that events were heading toward a climax and that the endgame would only conclude with the defeat of one or the other faction, this time without interference from outside powers.

5–6 JULY IN PHNOM PENH

With troop movements on both sides continuing around the capital in the last weeks of June, the city became increasingly militarized. Then, on 17 June, fighting broke out between bodyguard units of Ranariddh and those of his neighbor Hok Lundi, the feared director-general of the National Police and a staunch supporter of Hun Sen. The incident, which resulted in several deaths, occurred near the residences of these two. Both the CPP and FUNCINPEC had repositioned their forces to strategic points around Phnom Penh in the days prior to the showdown, revealing the depth of the mistrust between the coprime ministers. Ranariddh had admitted to secretly meeting Khieu Samphan, leader of the Khmer Rouge, on 4 June in the remote Khmer Rouge

stronghold of Preah Vihear. Hun Sen's response was to issue Ranariddh an ultimatum on 18 June: The first prime minister, he said, "must choose to join
the Khmer Rouge or [remain in] the Royal Government."[1]

On 2 July, pro-CPP military units blocked a twenty-truck FUNCINPEC
convoy near Prek Taten naval base, twenty-five kilometers north of Phnom
Penh. They were ostensibly searching for illegal Khmer Rouge forces that had
infiltrated into the city. The following day, two hundred pro-CPP military police disarmed members of Ranariddh's motorcade in Kompong Cham
province north of Phnom Penh.

These small skirmishes culminated in the final showdown. It unfolded on
5–6 July in Phnom Penh, with fierce fighting between forces loyal to Ranariddh and those loyal to Hun Sen. Armored personnel carriers and tanks
rumbled through Phnom Penh's streets. Eyewitnesses claimed that troops often fired indiscriminately; mortars, rocket-propelled grenades, and machine
gunfire sent thousands of residents fleeing on foot, bicycle, and motorcycles.
The fighting caused a great deal of property damage and numerous casualties.
There was also widespread looting, mostly by soldiers but also by others. At
the end of the two days, the CPP's forces had gained the upper hand, with the
remnants of FUNCINPEC's forces fleeing to their stronghold in O Smach at
the border of Thailand and Siem Reap province.

Many Western journalists and authors, echoing Ranariddh,[2] immediately
condemned the fighting as a bloody coup d'etat by Hun Sen.[3] CNN and other
television networks showed a devastated Phnom Penh but offered no details
on who had started the fighting. Those who saw Ranariddh as the victim of a
"coup" ignored the build-up to the showdown. Western academics were divided: one group called the confrontation a coup d'etat, others simply labeled
it an armed conflict.[4]

Cries of a coup were not echoed by the United Nations. Secretary-General
Kofi Annan refrained from blaming either side. On 7 July, Alvaro de Soto, the
assistant secretary-general in the UN Department of Political Affairs, gave the
following account of the showdown to the Security Council. It was, in my
view, an objective rendition and is reproduced in toto below. The word "coup
d'etat" was never mentioned:

> This weekend's fighting erupted after weeks of rising tension as both sides of the
> coalition tried to take advantage of the disintegration of the Khmer Rouge

(KR). Both sides publicly threatened to use force against the other, and fighting did break out briefly on 17 June in Phnom Penh between PM Ranariddh's and PM Hun Sen's body guard units. Both CPP and FUNCINPEC have been seen repositioning their forces to strategic points around Phnom Penh in recent days, which reflected the degree of near absolute mistrust between the co-PMs.

First Prime Minister Prince Ranariddh was negotiating with the remainder of the Khmer Rouge led by Khieu Samphan . . . In this process, the FUNCINPEC side seemed to hope that the re-integrated Khmer Rouge would bolster their strength vis-a-vis Second Prime Minister Hun Sen's CPP in the run up to the elections, which was announced as scheduled for 23 May next year.

CPP had accused FUNCINPEC of deploying Khmer Rouge in the city and threatened force to prevent such occurrences. . . . PM Hun Sen's forces seemed to have [carried out this threat] on Saturday, 5 July. Fighting between military forces loyal to Hun Sen and those of PM Ranariddh took place over the weekend . . . Fighting was reported most heavy around Ranariddh's town residence, the airport, the base controlled by FUNCINPEC General Nhiek Bun Chhay and FUNCINPEC HQ. After two days of fighting, Hun Sen's forces were in total control of the city. A state of emergency had been declared in the city to prevent the large-scale looting.

There were also unconfirmed reports of fighting in other areas of the country . . . Main FUNCINPEC military and security leaders are believed to be in northwest Cambodia and possibly regrouping with Khmer Rouge forces to fight forces loyal to PM Hun Sen—a return to the pre–Paris Peace Accord configuration.

First PM Ranariddh was in France when the fighting broke out in Phnom Penh. In an interview with *Le Monde*, he reportedly said that he left for France under the advice of his military advisors who suspected a coup by PM Hun Sen to take place shortly and who thought it better to have the Prince overseas to mobilize international support against PM Hun Sen. The Prince stated that Hun Sen had launched a coup against him and he should now be considered as the sole Prime Minister of Cambodia.

Meanwhile, Second PM Hun Sen in a radio address on Sunday branded PM Ranariddh as a "traitor" who no longer held the post of First PM and called for his arrest along with four other FUNCINPEC leaders (General Nhiek Bun Chhay, Serey Kosal, Hor Sok and Chao Sambath). He also called on FUNCIN-PEC to choose a new person as First PM and denied he wanted to take over the post himself. PM Hun Sen also denied that he was leading a coup attempt and [said] that his action was a pre-emptive move against what he called a plot by Ranariddh to attack his forces using disaffected Khmer Rouge rebels.

The persistent CPP line seemed to be that "mixed" Government forces are engaged in "mopping up" operations against illegal elements, namely Khmer Rouge that had supposedly infiltrated the city, with the assistance from Ranariddh and his close aides. To deflect accusations of attempting a coup, Hun Sen seemed to be attempting only to oust Ranariddh and some of his close aides, but not "overthrow" the Government, and assured other FUNCINPEC members that they would "not be punished". . . .

While fighting in Phnom Penh seems to have subsided for the moment, the situation in other parts of the country remains unclear, with potential of similar outbreaks of fighting present. It is difficult to see how the coalition Government could re-emerge from these developments, but the international community and the Cambodians would have to find a way to restore peace under the Constitution and to hold free and fair elections next year.[5]

Eerily, all three top leaders—Hun Sen, Ranariddh, and Sihanouk—were away on that fateful day of 5 July. Hun Sen was on vacation with his family in Vungtao, Vietnam; Ranariddh was in his abrupt self-exile in France; and the king was in Beijing for more of his increasingly frequent medical treatments and rest. Hun Sen had earlier boasted that he could send off one Norodom every year: Chakrapong in 1994, Sirivuddh in 1995, and now Ranariddh in 1997. Only Ranariddh had left voluntarily.

THE GOVERNMENT'S VIEW

On 9 July, the Ministry of Foreign Affairs, headed by Ung Huot from FUNCINPEC, who supported Hun Sen, issued a "White Paper."[6] Later an expanded and somewhat revised version entitled "Crisis in July" appeared on 22 September.[7] The "White Paper," published just days after the military showdown, admitted that "the visit of Government authorities to check and disarm suspected illegal troops, including Khmer Rouge soldiers," had "triggered the fighting as the camps under suspicion fired on authorities."[8] The document stated that the FUNCINPEC barracks at Wat Phniet in Kompong Speu "were established without the authorization of the Ministry of Defense and [were] one of the objects of the search which led to the fighting on 5 July."[9]

Hun Sen himself confirmed on national television and radio at 1 p.m. on 5 July that government troops had launched an offensive to stop the infiltration into the city of "irregular troops." In a 8 July letter to the UN secretary-general, Chea Sim explained that "regular" government forces had been "urgently dispatched to disarm and disband those illegal forces in order to prevent any activities aiming at disrupting public security and destabilizing the Royal Government."[10]

However, the revised "Crisis in July" paper and other subsequent documents, including an undated government report entitled "July 5–6?!,"[11] emphasized the element of surprise. They pointed out that upon hearing a Voice of America broadcast the morning of 5 July in which Ranariddh accused him of initiating a coup d'etat, Hun Sen had immediately returned from Vietnam to his Takhmau residence by helicopter, arriving at 10 a.m. These later documents blamed Ranariddh for provoking the clash by issuing a call to arms. They claimed that he had ordered the use of force and that the government had been caught woefully by surprise. They were mirrored in Hun Sen's subsequent speeches and in a published government aide-mémoire.[12]

According to the "Crisis in July" paper, by the time of Hun Sen's arrival from Vietnam on 5 July, FUNCINPEC forces were already moving tanks from the military airport, which they controlled, to the nearby Pochentong airport. And just as Hun Sen's helicopter was about to land, the document stated, six military aircraft had taken off from the military base to the north, almost hitting his helicopter. According to this document (and Hun Sen's voice was in it), the conflict started when Ranariddh deployed his forces to "topple the Government," not after government forces had commenced searches for illegal troops.

In later accounts, Hun Sen confirmed his surprise at the extent and timing of FUNCINPEC's attacks. He alleged that at the time of Ranariddh's "attempted coup" the government only had police and military police forces in the vicinity of the capital. Government forces, he said, had not been ordered to retaliate until 1:30 a.m. on 6 July. Later that day, these accounts stated, it was at the house of General Chao Sambath of FUNCINPEC that government troops, who had come to negotiate the surrender of illegal troops and weapons at 3 p.m., were fired upon. That firing, according to the "Crisis in July" paper, initiated the two-day fighting.[13]

Ranariddh's forces gained the upper hand, the paper recounted. At 4 a.m. the morning of 6 July, two columns of tanks and soldiers loyal to Ranariddh moved out of Taing Krasang Barracks heading north toward the capital. By 8 a.m. the forces of Nhiek Bun Chhay (FUNCINPEC) had reached the Buddhist hospital, and fighting was fierce. Realizing the perilous situation, Hun Sen ordered his bodyguard unit from Takhmau to quickly join the line of defense at 9:30 a.m. The fighting continued until late afternoon, but by early evening Hun Sen's forces were in full control.[14]

While it is inconceivable that Hun Sen was caught completely off guard, the extent of the preparations for combat by Ranariddh's forces may indeed have surprised him. The revision in the government's account was reportedly due to secret documents found at Nhiek Bun Chhay's and Chao Sambath's houses on 10 July that talked of a plot to kill Hun Sen.[15] Rather than Ranariddh being the victim of a coup d'etat, now it was the other way around.

But the truth, I believe, lies somewhere in the middle. The CPP's actions were a sequel to Ranariddh's alliance with the Khmer Rouge. Ranariddh had planned for a military confrontation as much as Hun Sen's forces had. In short, both leaders were clearly willing to draw swords for political ends. It is difficult to say who is most to blame.

EXPATRIATE EYEWITNESSES

Two expatriate Westerners, journalist Christine Chaumeax and former UN-TAC peacekeeper Judith Ledgerwood, were eyewitnesses to events and adhered to the earlier "White Papers'" version.[16] Ledgerwood claimed that the CPP's version in the "July 5–6?!" document—which stated that "the Government did not have any plan to disarm either Taing Krasang military base or Pochentong airport nor send troops to surround them"[17]—was clearly inaccurate. It was the CPP who started the fighting, she argued, noting that journalists' accounts directly contradicted the government.[18] She said that CPP forces were on the move before dawn on 5 July and by first light had surrounded the airport and the military base at Taing Krasang, where they demanded that FUNCINPEC's forces disarm. But General Nhiek Bun Chhay ordered his troops to resist and the fighting soon engulfed the city itself.[19]

Human Rights Watch reported that the CPP deployed several units, equipped with tanks and armored personnel carriers, in strategic locations throughout the city. It claimed that the key units did not belong to the regular army but to armored forces commanded by Hun Sen confidantes: the interior police, led by Police Chief Hok Lundi; the military police under Kean Savudh; Hun Sen's personal bodyguard battalion led by Nat Saveun; and former Khmer Rouge fighters commanded by Keo Pong and Pon Pheap.[20]

The UNCHR reported that forty-one FUNCINPEC military officials were killed, with another sixty missing. They were executed after the fighting, according to UNCHR. They included senior FUNCINPEC officers Ho Sok, Chao Sambath, and Kroch Yoeum, all of whom I knew personally. General Nhiek Bun Chhay, the top FUNCINPEC commander, escaped death by fleeing through back roads to the Thai border. There was evidence of torture of prisoners by the crack 911 battalion.[21]

AFTERMATH

Ranariddh denied to Kofi Annan that he had brought so-called Khmer Rouge forces into Phnom Penh to launch an attack against Hun Sen.[22] And UNCHR did not find evidence of significant infiltration of Khmer Rouge forces into Phnom Penh.[23] In an interview with Nate Thayer of the *Far Eastern Economic Review*, Ranariddh stated that Hun Sen "says I have hidden Khmer Rouge forces in the city, but it is a lie, just a pretext. . . . I think there will be fighting everywhere. We have our forces everywhere in the country and they will not surrender."[24]

While Ranariddh toured Asian capitals and visited the United Nations attempting to drum up condemnation of the alleged coup against him, his father, Sihanouk, declined to cast judgment on the events in Phnom Penh. The king called on both prime ministers and Chea Sim, the acting head of state and president of parliament, to meet him in Beijing to hammer out a solution. But Hun Sen dismissed Sihanouk's move as "too late."

On 12 and 14 July, Sihanouk did give interviews to his own *Monthly Bulletin*. His statements generally reflected disapproval of Hun Sen's actions, as did his unwillingness to return to Phnom Penh to sign decrees concerning the composition of the Royal Government. But his failure to mention Ranariddh showed that at this stage he was not inclined to come out in support of his son. He refused to label the military showdown a coup. And once again he did not rule out a political role for himself in Cambodia.[25] According to a number of ambassadors in Phnom Penh, the king might not have been keen to see Ranariddh return to Cambodian politics given his clumsy handling of the situation.

Meanwhile, back in Cambodia, an uneasy calm prevailed, but the situation quickly returned to normal. Many FUNCINPEC and other politicians who had been forced into hiding right after the showdown slowly reemerged, especially after Hun Sen on 4 August called on members of the National Assembly and Royal Government, civil servants, military and police officials, and members of FUNCINPEC and other political parties "who are in fear, whether outside or inside the country, to come forward and resume your positions as before."[26] The FUNCINPEC military elements still loyal to the prince were concentrated in O Smach and did not pose any major threat to stability.

Apart from twenty-nine staunch supporters of Ranariddh who were also in self-exile, FUNCINPEC cabinet ministers, members of parliament, and lower officials continued with their daily work. They included Ung Huot, who had returned from Paris; Loy Sim Cheang, the vice chairman of the National Assembly; Pou Sothirak, the minister of industries; and Nady Tan, the secretary-general of the Council of Ministers. Some Western journalists were quick to condemn them as quislings, although when they had returned to Cambodia after 1991 when the Paris Peace Agreements were signed they had been hailed as the best of their party.[27]

Some senior members of parliament who were opposed to the reorganized government did issue strong declarations. Son Soubert, leader of the BLDP and vice president of the National Assembly, stated that "Mr. Hun Sen led a barbaric and undemocratic coup d'etat."[28] Several other senior members of parliament also condemned the so-called coup.[29]

Meanwhile the National Assembly, which had been stalled for seven months, resumed its work on 28 July. The opening session was attended by 90 out of 120 members, surpassing the quorum of eighty-four. As the CPP had only fifty-one members, the rest were from FUNCINPEC. The reopening boosted Hun Sen's efforts to legitimize the government without Ranariddh and his supporters. On 6 August, in a secret ballot, the National Assembly elected FUNCINPEC's Ung Huot the first prime minister.[30] After receiving the green light from Sihanouk in Beijing, Chea Sim signed a royal decree replacing Ranariddh with Ung Huot.[31]

THE INTERNATIONAL REACTION

Most members of the international diplomatic community, especially those with embassies in Phnom Penh, did not agree with Ranariddh's claim of a coup. Like Kofi Annan, many of the ambassadors in Phnom Penh, including Mehrotra, my successor, refrained from ascribing blame for the fighting to either side. Everybody had witnessed the military buildup on both sides during 1996 and 1997 and had heard both factions publicly threaten to use force. The resident ambassadors had a clear appreciation of the complex background to the fighting. The word "coup," they knew, was too simplistic to describe the situation. Privately, many diplomats from key donor nations downplayed the seriousness of events and seemed eager to get on with a new political equation.

Sometimes the ambassadors' views of the conflict clashed with those of their capitals. As a result, some found themselves in trouble at home. In particular, U.S. Ambassador to Cambodia Kenneth Quinn came under attack for a variety of alleged offenses including being "pro–Hun Sen," failing to encourage or protect opposition politicians, reporting inaccurately to the State Department on the lead up to the coup, and refusing protection to those who felt threatened after the fighting.

The assault against Quinn was led by U.S. Congressman Dana Rohrabacher, a Republican from California whose constituency included America's largest Cambodian community in Long Beach. Rohrabacher's legislative assistant Al Santoli used even harsher language to criticize U.S. policy. "For the U.S. to kowtow to a little murderous dictator who's dependent on our money—that's not America's role," Santoli said in Washington. Quinn, for his part, said in a prepared statement that in mid-1996 he had first warned of the danger of a return to violence and the threat to the fragile democracy that had been established. Echoing Rohrabacher, Ron Abney, the former Cambodian director of the International Republican Institute who was wounded in the 30 March grenade attack, testified at a House hearing that Quinn was less supportive of the Cambodian opposition than his predecessor, Ambassador Charles Twining. Quinn responded that there was only one school of thought within the State Department on Cambodia: "The U.S. does not favor any person or party, but rather supports the democratic process."[32]

The United States refrained from labeling Hun Sen's action a coup d'état—a charge that legally would have required axing all aid to Cambodia. U.S. intelligence had reported that Ranariddh was also engaged in a power grab and that both sides were guilty of courting the Khmer Rouge. "There are no heroes in Cambodia," a senior Clinton administration official said. "Nobody's black or white; they are all a shade of grey."[33]

However, the U.S. response hardened with the announcement of a thirty-day suspension of aid to Cambodia. While the State Department expected that "programs providing humanitarian aid" would resume after that period, "depending on circumstances," it said, the Department did not "anticipate a resumption of aid programs at current levels."

Australia suspended its $1.5 million annual military aid program to Cambodia but did not touch its $32 million civil aid package. Two of Cambodia's biggest donors, Japan and France, refrained from expressing disapproval of Hun Sen.

Despite being the strongest supporter of the Khmer Rouge in the 1980s, and by implication of Ranariddh, the Chinese now adopted a sympathetic attitude toward Hun Sen. In fact, Hun Sen delighted Beijing by closing down the Taiwan representative's office in Phnom Penh after accusing Taiwanese elements of financing Ranariddh's adventures. Ties between Beijing and Hun Sen grew stronger as mainland Chinese business investments and aid projects increased. Hun Sen's favorable attitude toward the Chinese, including Cambodia's ethnic Chinese population, was in evidence everywhere. Phnom Penh boasted the largest Chinese elementary school in the world outside China.

As in the 1980s, ASEAN was called upon to play an important role in Cambodia. Meeting in Kuala Lumpur, ASEAN issued a statement on 8 July expressing dismay and deep regret at the unfortunate turn of events in Cambodia that resulted in the loss of innocent lives. However, it did not blame either side and called on the copremiers to settle their differences peacefully.[34]

Malaysian Foreign Minister Badawi, the chairman of ASEAN, viewed political developments in Cambodia following the reconvening of the National Assembly favorably.[35] However, Cambodia suffered a setback when ASEAN, which had agreed a few months earlier to admit Cambodia, rescinded its offer. At its summit meeting scheduled for the end of July it reasoned, Cambodia would not be represented by either of its premiers.

A delegation of three ASEAN foreign ministers led by veteran Cambodia specialist Ali Alatas of Indonesia visited Hun Sen in Phnom Penh on 2 August. Hun Sen told them that the "normal" situation in Phnom Penh and the reopening of the National Assembly demonstrated that Cambodia had sufficient capacity to resolve its internal problems by itself. While holding ASEAN to its principle of noninterference in the internal affairs of other countries, he politely rejected ASEAN's offer to mediate between him and Ranariddh.

ASEAN argued that all politicians and government officials should be allowed to return to Cambodia without fear of intimidation and under a full guarantee of safety. Hun Sen replied that all were indeed free to return to their former positions—except those who had been indicted for treason, including Ranariddh and four of his generals. However, he said, amnesty could be given Ranariddh after he had been tried and found guilty. The ASEAN delegation also urged that the election to select a new prime minister be held only after the MPs still outside the country had returned. Hun Sen replied that if they did not return, the National Assembly would proceed with the election of a new prime minister on 6 August, which it did. Ali Alatas, the Indonesian foreign minister, was hoping Ranariddh could return before the 1998 elections.

THE BATTLE MOVED TO NEW YORK

Meanwhile the battle quickly shifted to the United Nations headquarters in New York. Ranariddh, of course, told everybody at the UN that the whole episode was a bloody coup d'etat by Hun Sen. In a press conference he predicted a return to the situation of 1975, when Pol Pot took Phnom Penh, and said that there would be fighting everywhere.[36] But this time nobody took him seriously. He also appealed to all nations to condemn Hun Sen and withhold recognition of the Phnom Penh government, as they had fifteen years before. But not one single country broke off diplomatic relations with Cambodia, and their ambassadors remained in Phnom Penh.

Neither Kofi Annan nor the Security Council called the military showdown a coup d'etat.[37] Ranariddh asked that the Cambodian question be put on the Council's agenda, as his father had in 1979. But the president of the Security Council refused. Rather, he issued a statement of concern calling upon all parties to respect fully their commitments under the Paris Agreements.[38] Obviously, in 1997, developments in Cambodia were considered minor issues in global politics.

Thomas Hammarberg, the UN human rights representative, was the exception. He managed to slip the word "coup d'etat" in a rather oblique fashion into a report to the General Assembly. When describing a visit to Phnom Penh in his report, he said that he had used the term "coup d'etat" during a meeting with Hun Sen on 4 September and that Hun Sen had objected to it, contending that forces loyal to Ranariddh had started movements for a coup themselves but had been halted.[39] In a joint letter to Hammarberg, Prime Ministers Ung Huot and Hun Sen objected to his "mischaracterization" of events.[40]

Cambodia had two representatives at the United Nations at the time: Ambassador Prince Sisowath Sirirath from FUNCINPEC and his deputy, Ambassador Ouch Borith from the CPP, a trusted aide of Hun Sen. While Ambassador Sirirath launched a propaganda campaign against Hun Sen and the Phnom Penh government, Ambassador Borith defended them. The situation, with dueling ambassadors, was bizarre, to say the least.[41]

In July, Chea Sim sent a note verbale to the United Nations stating that Ambassador Sisowath was being recalled to Phnom Penh. A letter from Foreign Minister Ung Huot appointing Ouch Borith chargé d'affaires of the Cambodian mission with full plenipotentiary powers followed. But Sisowath balked. In a circular letter to all ambassadors dated 21 July, Sisowath claimed that Ambassador Borith had illegally tried to make appointments with the diplomatic corps in New York. Since the king had appointed him, Sisowath asserted, only the king could recall him.

On 24 July, Ranariddh sent a letter to Kofi Annan from France confirming Sisowath's continuation as ambassador. As the number one man in the mission, Sisowath barred Ouch Borith and other CPP diplomats from entering the premises by changing the locks of the building. Ambassador Borith now had to run the permanent mission, the only one recognized by Phnom Penh, from his house. Thus the Byzantine atmosphere of Phnom Penh extended to midtown Manhattan, where in effect there were two permanent missions of Cambodia. The United Nations vacillated and ignored the letters from Chea Sim and Ung Huot. The befuddled United Nations legal office decided to continue corresponding with both ambassadors at the different addresses.

In a letter to the UN secretary-general dated 18 July, Ranariddh denied again that he had infiltrated the capital with hard-line Khmer Rouge soldiers.[42] On the same day, Sisowath issued another circular to all UN ambassadors informing them that "a violent coup d'etat was staged by Hun Sen to wrestle total power from his coalition partner Norodom Ranariddh." Hun Sen was now working to consolidate his power by illegally appointing new cabinet ministers and a new puppet first prime minister from among renegade FUNCINPEC members, he said. Sisowath urged the ambassadors not to recognize any new government installed by the "coup" leaders.

The battle of words between the two factions intensified with the opening of the General Assembly in September 1997. According to the rules of procedure of the General Assembly, the delegation of each country must be communicated to the Assembly by the head of state, in this case Sihanouk. The king, who had meanwhile returned to Cambodia, sent a note verbale to the Assembly conveying the composition of the Cambodian delegation, which was headed by Ung Huot and Hun Sen and their wives. This provoked complaints from Ranariddh. The king later wrote Ranariddh that he still considered him first prime minister but that he had felt obliged to sign the note verbale. However, the next day, I was told, the king, who on his return resided in Siem Reap to avoid Hun Sen, summoned U.S. Ambassador Kenneth Quinn to see him. There was widespread speculation among journalists and diplomats that Sihanouk told Quinn not to take his note verbale seriously. During one of my many visits to Phnom Penh later, at a dinner in my honor hosted by Singapore Ambassador Mushahid Ali, Associated Press journalist Matthew Lee asked Quinn point blank whether this was the case. Quinn declined to comment. Meanwhile, a shadow delegation headed by Ranariddh and consisting of renegade FUNCINPEC members also vied to gain recognition by the General Assembly.

The rumor that Sihanouk told Quinn that the United States should ignore his note verbale gained credibility in New York when the United States strongly opposed the credentials of the Cambodian delegation. It was as if September 1979 was being replayed on 17 September 1997, when the UN Credentials Committee met for the first time to consider Cambodia's seat, and the United States took a strong anti–Hun Sen line. "The United States will not be in a position to concur in the seating of a Cambodian delegation which represents a regime that seized power through undemocratic means," State Department spokesman James Rubin told reporters.

In the Credentials Committee, the United States and Norway were widely reported to have backed Ranariddh's bid to name his own delegation, while the Russian Federation and China supported the Ung Huot-Hun Sen nomination. The committee postponed making a decision for two days, prompting furious lobbying by Ranariddh's delegation and by a rival advance team representing Ung Huot and Hun Sen. Although China and Russia endorsed the delegation of Ung Huot and Hun Sen officially sent by Sihanouk, the Credentials Committee, in which there was no veto power, decided to leave the seat vacant.

Razali Ismael, the Malaysian president of the General Assembly, tried to broker a compromise solution. He called Ouch Borith, who was legally still the

Cambodian ambassador, into his office. Razali asked Borith if he would agree to be seated with Sisowath. No, Borith responded, as Sisowath had been legally recalled by the acting head of state. So Razali said the Cambodian seat had to be left vacant.[43]

Hun Sen and Ung Huot, of course, reacted strongly to this rejection. Hun Sen lashed out at the United States for "severely violating the sovereignty" of his nation. "It is the seat of the Cambodians . . . not the Americans," he said on 22 September in Thailand, en route to New York. Ung Huot, speaking at Pochentong airport on 21 September as he left for New York, also expressed anger at the United States. The Credentials Committee's decision was "an insult to Cambodia and to His Majesty King Sihanouk," Ung Huot said.[44]

As neither Ranariddh nor Hun Sen were admitted to the General Assembly, Kofi Annan met separately with them in New York to discuss preparations for the Cambodian elections scheduled for 1998. He also discussed the return, under United Nations protection, of FUNCINPEC ministers and members of parliament who were still in self-exile abroad. Hun Sen reiterated that everyone was free to return, but that Ranariddh had to face a trial. As a result of Kofi Annan's discussion with the two premiers in New York, Lakhan Mehrotra, my successor, was given an expanded mandate and manpower to monitor the return of self-exiled politicians to Cambodia.

STABILITY AT LAST

Bowing to enormous international pressure, Hun Sen allowed Ranariddh to return and be pardoned for his "crimes." By the time of Ranariddh's return, practically all exiles had come back. The 1998 elections, with limited United Nations assistance, went ahead as scheduled.

Thirty-nine parties participated, almost double the number that had competed in the UNTAC elections in 1993. Some senior FUNCINPEC renegades who had alienated Ranariddh by siding with Hun Sen established their own parties. Loy Sim Cheang and Om Rasdy, for example, established the *Sangkom Thmei* (New Society) party, and Ung Huot created the *Reastr Niyom* (populist) party.

At the crest of his power, First Prime Minister Ung Huot boasted at a press conference that his party would get fifty seats in the new parliament. His portrait was now everywhere in Phnom Penh. But in the elections he received a negligible number of votes, and his party did not get a single seat. There were more portraits of him than votes for him, everyone chuckled. Before his defeat, Ung Huot spotted me one day and invited me to his new residence, which had been given to him in his capacity as first prime minister. I was received at poolside and served champagne at 10 in the morning. "Your excellency, those Western papers call me a puppet of Hun Sen, but, as you can see, I am not a puppet, I am the first prime minister," he said while sipping his champagne.

The elections, held on Sunday, 26 July, were monitored by both international and national observers. I had returned to Cambodia as a member of the official Indonesian observer delegation. The international observers, led by the European Union and the UN-coordinated Joint International Observer Group (JIOG), to which I belonged, judged the elections credible and observed that the polling officers—all Cambodians this time—were conscientious, well prepared, and proficient at their tasks. Many had gained experience in the UNTAC elections. They were also courteous toward the observers. The U.S.-based National Democratic Institute (NDI) and the International Republican Institute (IRI), however, issued rather critical statements on the elections. So did the Asian Network for Free Elections, consisting of nationals of election-monitoring groups in Asia. They believed that the CPP had intimidated some voters.

Three parties emerged victorious: the CPP came out first this time, with 41.4 percent of the vote, followed by FUNCINPEC with 31.7 percent, and the Sam Rainsy Party, surprisingly, with 14.3 percent. The Sam Rainsy Party, formerly the Khmer Nation Party, another offshoot of FUNCINPEC, attracted widespread support from disillusioned FUNCINPEC supporters and educated urban youth, many of whom were disappointed with both the CPP and FUNCINPEC. It had become a formidable third party. None of the other thirty-six parties, including offshoots of BLDP and FUNCINPEC, gained even a single seat.

Both FUNCINPEC and the Sam Rainsy Party claimed fraud and staged widespread demonstrations. Mehrotra had his hands full protecting dissident politicians. At one point Sam Rainsy took refuge in Mehrotra's office, where Mehrotra had diplomatic immunity, and coordinated his followers from there, which elicited a strong protest from Hun Sen.

On 25 November 1998, the National Assembly was reconvened, promising a new era of political stability. The reopening was achieved after Ranariddh had struck a deal with Hun Sen: because the CPP had not obtained a two-thirds majority in the elections, a second coalition government between the CPP and FUNCINPEC was established, with one prime minister, Hun Sen. Sam Rainsy's party became the opposition. Ranariddh became the new president of the Assembly. He was also given a newly built grand mansion, as his old residence had been ransacked during the military showdown. In order to accommodate the former president of the Assembly, Chea Sim of the CPP, an appointive Senate was established, of which he became the president.

But the CPP controlled the key ministries of trade, finance, and information. FUNCINPEC got tourism, education, health, culture, and women's and veterans' affairs. Defense and interior were shared by coministers like before, but now the FUNCINPEC ministers had much less power. Those who remained loyal to Ranariddh got posts in the new cabinet, including Veng Sereyvuth, who returned as minister of tourism, and Sisowath Sirirath, who became cominister of defense.

The FUNCINPEC renegades whose parties were completely defeated got nothing. Many of them, including Pou Sothirak, tried to return to the fold by

Photo 14.1. Cambodian Prime Minister Hun Sen, left, talks with Ranariddh, former prime minister and the new president of the National Assembly, on Human Rights Day, 10 December 1998. AP Photo/Ou Neakiri.

asking for pardons from Ranariddh. Many received them. However, it took a long time before Ung Huot, who frequently ridiculed Ranariddh, was rehabilitated. No longer needed as first prime minister, he just disappeared from Cambodian politics. He had to return his residence to the government, which turned his short-lived swimming pool into a parking lot. Hun Sen, in his speech at the reopening of the Assembly, promised that his government would uphold the principle of multiparty democracy and respect human rights. He stressed that they were a recipe and foundation for social stability and development. He also recognized the role of the opposition.

In New York at the UN, Cambodia's seat was again legally occupied. Two ambassadors, both from the CPP, Ouch Borith and Sun Suon, manned the only permanent mission of the country. And Cambodia was finally admitted to ASEAN as its tenth member.

One dominant lesson can be learned from the United Nations' experience in Cambodia: the progress of democracy cannot be measured only in terms of elections. Nevertheless, in 1998, after decades of civil war and turmoil, there was finally peace and stability throughout Cambodia. Economic progress and development, of course, benefited. What UNTAC could not accomplish was achieved in 1998 by the Cambodians themselves. With the apparent end of the power struggle between the CPP and FUNCINPEC, Cambodia could finally get on with the business of combating the real enemy: poverty.

NOTES

1. Nate Thayer, "Ambiguous Alliances: Can the Khmer Rouge Survive Pol Pot," *Far Eastern Economic Review*, 3 July 1997, 25. Nate Thayer "The Deal That Died," *Far Eastern Economic Review*, 21 August 1997, 15.

2. Norodom Ranariddh, "Communiqué," 5 July 1997.

3. See, for instance, Nate Thayer, "Law of the Gun: Hun Sen's Power Grab Puts Cambodia in a Precarious Bind," *Far Eastern Economic Review*, 17 July 1997, 14 ff; Nate Thayer, "The Deal That Died," *Far Eastern Economic Review*, 21 August 1997, 14ff; Ron Moreau, "Asia's New Boss," *Newsweek*, 21 July 1997. See also Henry Kamm's *Cambodia: Report from a Stricken Land*, New York: Arcade Publishing, 1998.

4. For academic sources that argue Hun Sen staged a coup d'etat, see, for instance, McAlister Brown and Joseph J. Zasloff, *Cambodia Confounds the Peacemakers, 1979–1998*, Ithaca and London: Cornell University Press, 1998; Sorpong Peou,

Intervention and Change in Cambodia: Towards Democracy, Singapore: Institute of Southeast Asian Studies, 2000. For accounts by academics who do not call it a coup d'etat, see, for instance, John McAuliff, "Welcome to Cambodia: Where Nothing Is Ever As It Seems," *Indochina Interchange*, vol. 7, no. 2, September 1997; Michael Vickery, "A Non-Standard View of the 'Coup,'" *Phnom Penh Post*, issue 6/17, 29 August–11 September 1997; Raoul Jennar, "The Political Situation in Cambodia after the Events of July 5–6, 1997," unpublished memorandum, Phnom Penh, 17 July 1997; David Roberts, *Political Transition in Cambodia 1991–99*, Richmond, Surrey: Curzon, 2001; Grant Curtis, *Cambodia Reborn*, Geneva: United Nations Research Institute for Social Development, 1998. Called it a coup de force but not a coup d'etat.

5. Briefing by Assistant Secretary General Alvaro de Soto, UN Department of Political Affairs to the United Nations Security Council, 7 July 1997. Personal copy.

6. Kingdom of Cambodia, Ministry of Foreign Affairs and International Cooperation, *White Paper: Background on the July 1997 Crisis: Prince Ranariddh's Strategy of Provocation*, Phnom Penh, 9 July 1997, hereinafter cited as the "White Paper."

7. Kingdom of Cambodia, Ministry of Foreign Affairs and International Cooperation, *Crisis in July. Report on the Armed Insurrection: Its Origins, History and Aftermath*, Phnom Penh, 22 September 1997, hereinafter cited as "Crisis in July."

8. "White Paper," summary.

9. "White Paper," 7.

10. Letter from Chea Sim to Kofi Annan, 8 July 1997.

11. Royal Government of Cambodia, "July 5-6?!" undated, presumably 1997.

12. Government of Cambodia, "Aide Memoire," 2 August 1997.

13. "Crisis in July," 8 and 9. According to Raoul Jennar, heavy fighting had already occurred at the Wat Phniet incident. See Raoul Jennar, *op.cit.*

14. "Crisis in July," 11.

15. "The Preparation of the War Clash on 15 July 1997," *Rasmey Kampuchea* (a pro-CPP daily in Khmer), as quoted in Annex I of "Crisis in July."

16. Christine Chaumeau, "Two Days That Shook the Capital," *Phnom Penh Post*, issue 6/14, 12–14 July 1997.

17. "July 5–6?!," 55.

18. Judith Ledgerwood, "The July 5–6 'Events': When Is a Coup Not a Coup?" in Judith Ledgerwood, "Cambodian Recent History and Contemporary Society: An Introductory Course," Department of Anthropology and Center for Southeast Asian Studies, Northern Illinois University, www.seasite.niu.edu/khmer/ledgerwood/contents.htm.

19. Ledgerwood, "The July," 4.

20. Human Rights Watch interviews with Cambodian parliamentarians who fled to Bangkok, 13 and 17 July 1997.

21. United Nations Center on Human Rights, "Evidence of Summary Executions, Torture and Missing Persons since 2–7 July 1997," memorandum to the Royal Government of Cambodia, 21 August 1997.

22. Letter from Ranariddh to Kofi Annan, 18 July 1997.

23. United Nations Center on Human Rights, "Evidence."

24. United Nations, Department of Public Information, "Press Conference by First Prime Minister of Cambodia," New York, 10 July 1997; Norodom Ranariddh, Press Communiqué, 5 July 1997; Nate Thayer, "Ranariddh Warns of War," *Far Eastern Economic Review*, vol. 6/14, 12–24 July 1997.

25. Interviews of the king by a team from *Bulletin Mensual de Documentation*, his monthly bulletin, Beijing, 12 and 14 July 1997.

26. Royal Government of Cambodia, "The Appeal of the Royal Government of Cambodia," signed by Hun Sen, 4 August 1997.

27. Michael Vickery, "A Non-Standard View of the 'Coup.'"

28. Declaration by Son Soubert, dated 16 July 1997.

29. Statement by Son Soubert, Khem Sokha, Pol Ham, and Son Chhay, 15 July 1997.

30. Letter from Nady Tan, dean of the Steering Committee of FUNCINPEC, to Loy Sim Chheang, acting president of the National Assembly, 18 July 1997.

31. Royal decree of Norodom Sihanouk, dated 7 August 1997, signed by Chea Sim; letter from the king to Chea Sim, dated 7 August 1997, authorizing Chea Sim to sign the decree. Two influential U.S. NGOs, the International Republican Institute and the National Democratic Institute, claimed that Ung Huot's nomination was

illegitimate. He already had been dismissed by Ranariddh, the president of the party, they argued, and the steering committee of the party who nominated him lacked a quorum. Chea Sim, Hun Sen, and Ung Huot then visited the king in Beijing, who addressed Ung Huot as Excellency (which he deserved as foreign minister anyway) but never as prime minister, a post that the king believed still belonged to his son Ranariddh. See International Republican Institute (IRI) and National Democratic Institute for International Affairs (NDI), "Restoring Democracy in Cambodia: The Difficult Road Ahead," 5. This was the report of a joint fact-finding mission launched by the two NGOs.

32. Elizabeth Moorthy, "Ambassador under Fire from DC," *Phnom Penh Post*, issue 6/17, 29 August–11 September 1997.

33. *Newsweek*, 21 July 1997, 15.

34. Statement by the chairman of the ASEAN Standing Committee on behalf of ASEAN, Kuala Lumpur, 8 July 1997.

35. "Malaysia Optimistic after Assembly Reconvenes in Cambodia," Kuala Lumpur, AFP, 7 August 1997.

36. Internal United Nations document, "Press Conference by First Prime Minister of Cambodia," 10 July 1997.

37. Kofi Annan did issue a statement in which he expressed grave concern about events, in particular about the death of General Ho Sok of FUNCINPEC, who had allegedly been shot point blank while in custody. Letters from Kofi Annan, dated 6 August 1997, to King Sihanouk and Prime Ministers Ranariddh and Hun Sen.

38. United Nations Security Council, S/PRST/1997/37, "Presidential Statement on Cambodia," New York, 12 July 1997. Such a statement carried less weight than a resolution and was often issued in minor crises of member states.

39. United Nations document A/52/489, "Report of the Secretary-General on the Situation of Human Rights in Cambodia," 17 October 1997, 9. This report was written by Hammarberg, but all reports from the UN were issued under the name of the secretary-general. Hence, one scholar, Sorpong Peou, quoted this oblique reference as proof that Kofi Annan called the fighting a coup. Sorpong Peou, *Intervention and Change in Cambodia: Towards Democracy?*, Bangkok: Silkworm, 2000, 303. Quoting Peou, Judith Ledgerwood then also claimed that Kofi Annan called it a coup. Judith Ledgerwood, *op. cit.*

40. Letter from Prime Ministers Ung Huot and Hun Sen to Thomas Hammarberg, 18 November 1997, 4.

41. Because of the volume and complexity of work in the United Nations, it is customary for countries to have more than one ambassador accredited to the United Nations in New York.

42. Letter from Ranariddh, in his capacity as first prime minister, to Kofi Annan, dated 18 July 1997.

43. Personal conversations with Borith.

44. Jason Barber and Hew Watkin, "Hun Sen Left Seatless at UN," *Phnom Penh Post*, issue 6/19, 26 September–9 October 1997.

Epilogue

My five years in Cambodia were life changing for me and the highlight of my lifelong career with the United Nations. After leaving my post as the UN secretary-general's representative in Cambodia, I frequently returned to the country, for I had grown to love it like my own. After observing the national elections of 1998, I returned to observe the communal elections of 2002 and the national elections of 2003. I also went to Cambodia to attend seminars and other meetings whenever invited. I last traveled to Siem Reap and Phnom Penh in July 2006.

The country's post-UNTAC record is a mixed one. On the one hand, Cambodia has made remarkable progress in a number of areas; signs of recovery are everywhere. Governmental institutions have resumed functioning, and democratic ones have emerged. Civil society has spread throughout Cambodia, and the nation's undeveloped media have grown. A tentative but impressive effort to spread democracy to local governments has been gaining momentum as a result of the communal elections of 2002.

The 1998 elections finally brought political stability, and those in 2002 and 2003 were relatively peaceful and fair. The Khmer Rouge movement has finally dissolved. One could say that Cambodia has rapidly turned from a postconflict country into a normal developing country with standard problems. On the other hand, however, its new government still faces several serious challenges; Cambodia's turbulent past still plagues the country. Its high poverty levels continue to be a serious concern, and governance remains a major challenge; corruption runs rampant while progress toward genuine democracy is uneven.

Politically, I am struck by the continued relevance of the late Om Rasdy's remark to me that Cambodia is like a play without enough actors. Except for Pol Pot and Son Sann, who have passed away, all the major actors from the 1980s are still there, in ever-changing roles.

In March 2006, it was as if history repeated itself when the troika of Hun Sen, Heng Samrin, and Chea Sim—who established the People's Republic of Cambodia in January 1979—again assumed the helm of the government. Hun Sen was once more prime minister, Heng Samrin was president of the National Assembly, and Chea Sim was president of the Senate. It was as if Cambodia went back to square one and nothing had ever happened in between. However, no longer shunned by the world, this time the three were the leaders of a triumphant Royal Government recognized by the whole world that had just pocketed an astounding pledge of $601 million from the annual meeting of the World Bank–organized Consultative Group of donors to Cambodia meeting in Paris. The government had requested $513 million. The top pledges came from Japan, $114 million; United States, $61.8 million; France, $38.1 million; and Australia, $31.8 million. At the meeting, the donors and the World Bank praised the government for its achievements.[1] They obviously valued political stability highly.

This was proven once again on 19 June 2007, when the annual donors' meeting in Phnom Penh pledged $689 million in aid—15 percent above the 2006 figure—and again exceeded the request made by the government.[2] For the first time the figure included a pledge of $91.1 million from China, even though it had in recent years become an increasingly significant donor. This time the conference was organized entirely by the Cambodian government through its newly established Cambodian Development Cooperation Forum (CDCF), which replaced the World Bank–organized Consultative Group (CG). While praising Hun Sen's government, donors had called for a swift enactment of the anticorruption law, which had been in the drafting stages for years.

The reemergence of the troika was made possible when on 2 March 2006, the National Assembly voted to amend the constitution to require only a simple majority (i.e., 50 percent plus one) to form a government rather than a two-thirds majority laid down in the Constitution that was adopted after the UNTAC elections. The two-thirds majority rule had been a constant thorn in Hun Sen's side, whose party never reached the two-thirds majority in parliament requiring a perpetual coalition with FUNCINPEC.

This was perhaps the single most important political development since the UNTAC elections. It was a major triumph for the CPP. Finally free from this constraint, on 3 March 2006, Hun Sen sacked the Cominister of National Defense Nhiek Bun Chhay and the Cominister of Interior Norodom Sirivudh, both members of FUNCINPEC. That left the old CPP stalwarts Sar Kheng and Tea Banh as the sole ministers of defense and interior, respectively. The National Assembly promptly removed Sirivudh as deputy prime minister, and Ranariddh resigned as president of the National Assembly, a post he had held since the 1998 elections. He was promptly replaced by Heng Samrin.

Prior to the amendment, the political fortunes of Ranariddh had continued to decline. Ranariddh had dragged FUNCINPEC down with him. The party lost National Assembly seats in the national elections in 1998 and 2003 and was soundly thrashed in the commune elections of 2002. It had gone from holding fifty-eight seats in the National Assembly in 1993 to forty-three in 1998 and to twenty-six in 2003. Its decline benefited both the CPP and the rapidly growing Sam Rainsy Party. In 2003 the CPP gained seventy-three seats, and the Sam Rainsy Party gained twenty-four.

After the 2003 elections, Ranariddh made one final defiant move against Hun Sen when he and Sam Rainsy united in yet another front, the Alliance for Democracy. The front refused to join a coalition government as long as Hun Sen remained prime minister. Despite the CPP's increasing strength, it still lacked the two-thirds majority required to form a government. An almost yearlong parliamentary and governmental paralysis followed. In the end, however, Ranariddh again succumbed to overtures from the CPP and agreed to form, for the third time, a coalition government between FUNCINPEC and the CPP. Sam Rainsy, that enfant terrible of Cambodian politics, accused Ranariddh of accepting an offer he could not refuse: bribes allegedly amounting to $30 million from pro-CPP businessmen in exchange for FUNCINPEC's participation in the coalition government with Hun Sen. Ranariddh promptly filed a defamation lawsuit against Sam Rainsy.

During the year of paralysis, Hun Sen simply continued to run the caretaker government. The deadlock was only broken when parliament voted to endorse the new government based on a controversial constitutional amendment that allowed for the simultaneous swearing-in of Hun Sen as prime minister and Ranariddh as president of the National Assembly. Previously, Ranariddh would have been sworn in first and then would have appointed the prime minister. Subsequently, on 17 July 2004, a gargantuan new government emerged in which Prime Minister Hun Sen led a team of 7 deputy prime ministers, 15 senior ministers, 28 ministers, and 135 secretaries of state, comprising a 186-member cabinet. The structure was necessary to accommodate not only FUNCINPEC but also the two informal factions in the CPP, the Chea Sim and Hun Sen wings. Hun Sen justified the size as he wanted to create a lot of rent-seeking positions for everyone.

Ranariddh's exit in March 2006 came amid thinly veiled public accusations by Hun Sen that Ranariddh was making political appointments of unqualified individuals and that his mistress, Ouk Phalla, was a moral embarrassment. Since his departure as president of the National Assembly, Ranariddh has spent most of his time out of the country; he announced that he and his wife of thirty-eight years, Princess Marie, would divorce.[3]

To add insult to injury, in October 2006 FUNCINPEC voted to expel Ranariddh as party chairman. He was replaced by Keo Puth Reasmy, who though not a Norodom himself was married to one, Sihanouk's youngest daughter, Norodom Arunrasmy. Unfazed, Ranariddh formed his own party, the Norodom Ranariddh Party; he was obviously trying to emulate the ascendant and successful Sam Rainsy Party. But his move backfired when on 12 December 2006 Heng Samrin, as president of the National Assembly, presided over the removal of Ranariddh and his supporter Chhim Seak Leng from the Assembly. Their removals were justified by pointing out that they no longer represented FUNCINPEC. At the same time, Ranariddh's half brother, Norodom Chakrapong, was removed from the Senate, as he too had formed his own party and no longer represented FUNCINPEC. Thus the three Norodoms who had been forced to leave the country in the turbulent 1990s were again expelled, this time from the government.

In the commune elections of 1 April 2007, only two parties emerged victorious: the CPP with 61.1 percent of the vote and surprisingly the Sam Rainsy Party, which emerged as the new second party in Cambodia, with 25.5 percent of the vote. In most communes SRP is now the only opposition party; FUNCINPEC's vote declined precipitously, and the so-called Prince Ranariddh Party was nowhere in sight.[4]

His political misfortunes did not prevent Ranariddh from enjoying the spoils of the flourishing economy. He now resides in a huge multistory mansion many times bigger than his Samdech Pann Road residence I had frequently visited, which was destroyed in the July 1997 showdown.

Most Ranariddh loyalists, including former renegades, had agreed to work in the third coalition government.[5] When I visited Cambodia in January 2005, I interviewed senior FUNCINPEC officials, including Norodom Sirivudh, who had come back and was then deputy prime minister. He unexpectedly expressed strong support for Hun Sen and argued that Cambodians must look forward, not backward.

Sihanouk had finally abdicated on 7 October 2004. It did not seem to much interest the general public. Norodom Sihamoni, a son of Sihanouk and Queen Monineath, was nominated by Sihanouk and chosen unanimously by the throne council to succeed him as king.

Sihamoni's selection was a surprise, for the modest, classical dance teacher and ambassador of Cambodia to UNESCO in Paris had up to that point taken no part in Cambodian politics and was considered reluctant to take the throne. He had lived for many years out of a modest apartment in Paris, where he took the metro train to work and led a quiet, almost reclusive existence. Because of Sihamoni's distance from political squabbling, both Sihanouk and especially Hun Sen saw him as the ideal candidate to succeed to the throne. Sihamoni arrived from Beijing on 20 October and was welcomed at the airport by an enthusiastic crowd of one hundred thousand. He was crowned in a simple ceremony on 29 October.

When I visited Cambodia in January 2005, Sihamoni had just visited two provinces where he had been enthusiastically welcomed by the people. They seemed very happy that the new king appeared simple and mild mannered. Their warm welcome also implied that Cambodia still wanted a king. Unlike his father, Sihamoni did not complain about being a king who reigned but did not rule.

The changeover from Sihanouk to Sihamoni came amidst some dramatic changes in Asia's Buddhist monarchies. On 9 December 2006, the Bhutanese King Jigme Singye Wangchuck abdicated in favor of his twenty-seven-year-old popular son Jigme Khesar Namgyai Wangchuk. In neighboring Nepal, popular uprisings last April 2006 culminated in a drastic turnaround that stripped the king of all power, titles, and privileges. This in turn paved the way for a Nepalese vote whether to do away with the monarchy in favor of a republic.[6]

In June 2006 the Thai King Bhumibol Adulyadet celebrated his sixtieth anniversary as Thailand's monarch in a grand way by inviting royal visitors from twenty-six countries. He is the longest reigning monarch in the world.

There was no tension between Hun Sen and Sihamoni, but strain persisted between Hun Sen and Sihanouk, even though most of the time Sihanouk resided in exile in his palaces in Beijing and Pyongyang. He now held the ominous title of king-father. When I visited Cambodia, I saw portraits of the king-father and the new king displayed side by side in Phnom Penh and Siem Reap. In Cambodia, everything comes in pairs, even prime ministers and kings, people commented.

Sihanouk repeatedly expressed frustration at the bizarre developments in Cambodia's governance, at first through his alter ego, Ruom Rith. Now Ruom Rith spoke from Sihanouk's blog visited by thousands of people instead of to the meager three hundred on the mailing list for his airmailed *Bulletin Mensual*. Letters by Ruom Rith that were very critical of the Hun Sen government appeared regularly on the blog. Obviously annoyed, Hun Sen reacted strongly. In a speech on his birthday, 4 April 2006, Hun Sen warned Ruom Rith that if he persisted in criticizing the government, he would order the Bayon TV station to air footage of summary executions of opposition leaders during Sihanouk's Sangkum Reastr Niyum regime prior to 1970.[7] The next day, Sihanouk said that he would no longer post political articles on his website. However, as of April 2006, Ruom Rith was still active on Sihanouk's blog. It will be difficult for Sihanouk to remain quiet or appear unaffected by political developments in his country.

In May 2005, tensions surfaced again between Hun Sen, who was then fully supported by the submissive Ranariddh and Sihanouk. Playing the anti-Vietnamese card, Sihanouk revived the touchy problem of the border with Vietnam. He denounced Vietnamese land grabbing. He also willingly became chairman of the Supreme National Council on Border Affairs (SNCBI). The SNCBI was short-lived, however, and even Sihanouk called it a joke. Hun Sen took it upon himself to deal with the border issue, and in October 2005 he signed a border treaty with Vietnam.

While activists in the NGO community widely denounced the treaty, it did not provoke much criticism from the population at large, suggesting that the Vietnam card had lost some of its potency or that people were afraid to express their opinion or both. Four NGO activists who protested the treaty were arrested for defamation of the regime: Mam Sonando, a popular radio talk show host; Kem Sokha, the president of the Cambodian Center for Human Rights (CCHR); his deputy director, Pa Nguon Teang; and Rong Chhun of the Cambodian Independent Teachers Union. At the rank-and-file level, there is still a great deal of resentment of *yuon* in Cambodia, but at the governmental level ties between Vietnam and Cambodia were boosted considerably by the reciprocal visits by heads of state in March 2006.

As the Sam Rainsy Party continued to grow stronger, tension developed between Hun Sen and Sam Rainsy, especially over judicial issues in the country. And Sam Rainsy continued to express his opposition to the government, especially to Hun Sen. He accused Hun Sen of masterminding the murder of union leader Chea Vichea on 22 January 2004 and of being involved in the grenade attack on 30 March 1997. Hun Sen, in turn, filed a defamation suit against Sam Rainsy.

The country has meanwhile had difficulty developing a separation of powers and therefore independent roles for the legislative and judicial branches of government. UNTAC's mandate did not include reform of the judiciary. Under the PRK and SOC, the judiciary had continued to be dependent on the executive branch. Exhortations to establish an independent judiciary and the appointment of a prosecutor general by UNTAC had redressed this problem in only a token way. Some of the problems continue until this day.

In the post-UNTAC period, various donor countries had assisted the institutions of the judiciary and the legislative branch in a piecemeal fashion, but the institutional framework remained fundamentally flawed. Although the National Assembly adopted legislative, judicial, military, and police reforms, they have not yet been fully implemented. The dominance of the executive branch inherited from the previous regime has continued.

On 3 February 2005, Sam Rainsy and two of his colleagues, Chea Channy and Chea Poch, were stripped of their parliamentary immunity by the National Assembly in a closed-door session. Both colleagues also faced defamation charges for accusing Ranariddh of accepting bribes to join the coalition government led by Hun Sen. Sam Rainsy went abroad. The stripping of the parliamentary immunity of Sam Rainsy and the others prompted an outcry in the legislative bodies of Europe and the United States, as well as from the kingfather, NGOs, and the UN secretary-general's representative on human rights, Peter Leuprecht. In 2005 Leuprecht was replaced by Yash Ghai.[8]

Then, in a complete about-face, in January 2006 Hun Sen told reporters that he was dropping all charges against the four NGO activists who had protested the border treaty with Vietnam. The wave of international criticism that had followed their arrests may have influenced his decision. On 5 February, Rainsy was issued a royal pardon by Sihamoni, nullifying his eighteen-month prison sentence. The pardon came after Rainsy had written apologetic letters to both Sihamoni and Hun Sen. Rainsy publicly withdrew his accusations that Hun Sen had orchestrated the March 1997 grenade attack and that Ranariddh had accepted millions of dollars in bribes.

Encouraged by the government's "new spirit" of clemency toward its critics, Sam Rainsy said he was hopeful and excited about his return to Cambodia and that he planned an immediate overhaul of his party.[9] In May, Hun Sen's about-face was extended to the human rights officials of the UNCHR when Hun Sen pledged to be more accessible to them. However, Yash Ghai suffered the same fate as his predecessors with Hun Sen calling him rude and refusing to see him during his last visit to Cambodia.[10]

Meanwhile, after twenty-seven years of international amnesia since the Khmer Rouge leadership was driven from power, the long-awaited Khmer Rouge trials were finally becoming a reality. On 13 May 2003, the United Nations had adopted resolution 57/228B endorsing an agreement between the Cambodian government and the UN to hold the trials. They will be essentially a Cambodian process, held in a Cambodian court, with the United Nations only providing an international input.[11] Seventeen Cambodians and twelve foreigners took office as judges and prosecutors in July 2006. As a hybrid tribunal, the Extraordinary Chambers in the Courts of Cambodia (ECCC) is staffed by international and Cambodian judges, investigating judges, and prosecutors. There are three international judges and two Cambodian judges, but under the supermajority rule, decisions will have to be approved by at least four of them, guaranteeing that at least one international judge will be involved.

Progress in the trials has been stalled since November 2006 due to wrangling over the internal rules, which govern every aspect of the court's operations. Fortunately the infighting at the ECCC came to an end on 12 June 2007 when a panel of Cambodian and international judges approved rules that clear the way for the court to finally put suspects on trial.[12] No date has yet been set for the trials, although the end of 2007 is now considered a realistic target. The potential defendants are either dead or in their seventies, and in 2006 only one was in custody, Kang Khech Ieu alias Duch, former head of the notorious S-21 prison, with the rest of the potential defendants living freely in Cambodia. It is expected that Duch will be the first to be tried.

ASEAN's resolve to adopt a charter, articulated in declarations at its eleventh and twelfth ASEAN Summits in Kuala Lumpur in December 2005 and in Cebu, the Philippines, in January 2007 will give this organization a legal basis. So far, the thirty-eight-year-old Association of Southeast Asian Nations (ASEAN) has found it healthier to treat politics lightly while concentrating on concerns over economics, trade, and development in the region.

As noted in this book, Cambodia was an exception to this rule. The then anticommunist ASEAN Six members played a key role in supporting U.S. and Chinese policies on Cambodia in the UN in the 1980s. Today, ASEAN realizes that without a common problem, their cooperation could be sluggish or put in the freezer. Therefore, ASEAN needs a charter to ensure the membership's compliance on all issues upon which they have agreed. Now, a rule-based organization is much more important than an issue-based organization.[13]

With the demise of the Soviet Union, and thus the end of the Cold War, in the early 1990s, and the accumulated confidence that had been built among them, ASEAN was more and more able to turn to collaborating in the political and security fields. It is in these fields that ASEAN now needs to accelerate its efforts in order to provide a solid base from which collaboration could be intensified to eventually form an entity such as the European Union.[14]

Meanwhile, according to the World Bank, Cambodia's real GDP grew by 10.4 percent in 2006, the third year in a row of double-digit growth rates. The average growth rate was 8.2 percent between 1993 and 2004. The stellar performance was driven by solid garment exports which now accounts for 91 percent of exports, strong tourism receipts, significant growth in Foreign Direct Investment, the continuing construction boom, and record crops in agriculture. Agriculture remained a crucial sector for the economy, accounting for 38 percent of GDP growth and some 60 percent of total employment in 2005. Consumer price inflation was projected to fall to around 5 percent in 2006, down from 6.7 percent in 2005. "A sound macroeconomic framework has helped underpin success in 2006," noted Robert Taliercio, World Bank country economist for Cambodia.[15]

Unfortunately, outside growing cities like Phnom Penh and Siem Reap, Cambodia presented an entirely different picture. Even though according to the World Bank the population living below the poverty line has been reduced from 47 percent in 1992–1993 to 35 percent in 2004, grinding poverty was still pervasive in much of the country.[16] Cambodia's impressive economic growth reflected the transformation from a conflict nation to a normal developing country, and most of it had not reached the nation's poor. Child mortality rates were high, almost three times the average in East and Southeast Asia. Moreover, the World Bank poverty reduction figures have been challenged recently by Sophal Ear, a young Cambodian economist, who claimed that the reduction in the poverty line published by the Bank was exaggerated.[17]

According to reports from the United Nations, the World Bank, and Harvard University, Cambodia is poised to become a major new global energy exporter, with a fossil-fuel windfall that promises to double the country's current gross domestic product (GDP) and potentially lift millions of Cambodians out of poverty. U.S. oil giant Chevron has indicated a huge oil-and-gas find off Cambodia's south coast, which could contain as much as seven hundred million barrels of oil, or nearly twice the earlier four hundred-million-barrel estimate.

Foreign investment in Cambodia hit $3.97 billion in 2006, nearly quadrupling the 2005 figure of $1.05 billion, the Council for the Development of Cambodia announced. More than $2.6 billion was invested in tourism, mining, energy, and construction. An amount of $552 million was invested in the industry sector, including garments; and agro-industry received more than $481 million, the report said.

When I came to Siem Reap city in January 2005, I thought I had arrived in a different city than the one I had previously known. The one-building airport that UNTAC had controlled in 1992–1993 was now a bustling international airport. As a result of the open-sky policy instituted after the showdown of July 1997, I saw planes disgorging tourists nonstop from many Asian capitals, including Bangkok, Seoul, Singapore, and Kuala Lumpur. On the vast stretches of fallow land, which had lined the long road from the airport during my UNTAC days, stood scores of gigantic four-star luxury hotels and restaurants offering mostly Asian food. Korean restaurants dominated because Koreans topped the list of foreign tourists; one restaurant was even owned by the Pyongyang government. The Grand Hotel where I had stayed had been torn down. In its place stood the five-star Grand Hotel d'Angkor; only the old iron-caged elevator—one of the hotel's tourist attractions—remained. Owned by the Raffles Group of Singapore, the Grand Hotel d'Angkor charged $250 per night for a single room, a bargain compared to the Amansari boutique hotel next door, owned by an Indonesian Chinese now living in Singapore, which charged $400 a night. Riem Sunsoley, my former interpreter, who had started a successful NGO to help educate poor children, explained that of the Cambodian-owned hotels, all except one now belonged to prominent members of parliament from the CPP, thus perpetuating the patronage system.

Most everyone in the city was smiling, as times were good. My former landlady was in California, but her daughter Aileen, who had lived in a wooden shack before, had built two Western-style bungalows on their property. My old wooden residence stuck out like a sore thumb and was rented out to a water bottling company.

The changes in Phnom Penh were not as striking to me as those in Siem Reap, as I had frequently visited Phnom Penh and had been there as recently as 2004. But the *Psar Thmei* (new market) was now dominated by shops dealing in computers, pirated PC software, music CDs, and DVDs, just like in neighboring Southeast Asian countries. The idyllic riverside Ranariddh Park (nobody ever calls it that anymore) was lined with restaurants and bars feeding the booming tourist industry and local expatriates. Three-wheeled "taxis" known in Thai slang as "Tuk tuks" supplemented the ubiquitous *motordops* and *cyclos* of the past, and across the Japanese bridge a dozen or more riverside restaurants featuring Khmer food catered to the new Cambodian middle class. Gigantic, freshly built villas housed the Cambodian elite, while less luxurious villas, many also newly built, were rented out to the expatriates, diplomats, and businesspeople who had settled everywhere in the city. Many private universities had also sprung up.

An issue of great concern was that the country's rapid growth in recent years has meant that land, hitherto of no economic value, has risen astronomically in value. Small farmers usually have no proof that they own their land or homes. Land grabbers, including powerful politicians and companies, take their land arbitrarily. It has been estimated that the poorest 40 percent own only 45 percent while the richest 10 percent own 70 percent of the land in the country.[18] On 5 March 2006, Hun Sen angrily distanced himself from those among the elite of his own party CPP and gave them a last chance to stop their land deals or be sacked.[19] Civil rights groups, including Thus Saray of ADHOC NGO, strongly issued statements in the same vein.

I fervently hope that the political stability and peace that Cambodia has finally achieved will prove long lasting and that the country will make additional strides toward democracy, human rights, and prosperity for its long-suffering people. May Cambodia soon fully experience the Southeast Asian miracle enjoyed by small and not-so-small tigers of the region.

NOTES

1. Source: World Bank, Consultative Group on Cambodia, Proceedings of the 8th Annual Consultative Group meeting in Phnom Penh, Cambodia, March 2006. Ironically, the government is still called the Royal Government although the Royalists are increasingly marginalized.

2. Reuters, "Donors Pledge $690 million to Cambodia," 20 June 2007. See also Hannah Beech, "Cambodia Keeps Taking, Gives Little," *Times*, 1 July 2007.

3. Vong Sokheng, "FUNCINPEC Dismisses Ranariddh," *Phnom Penh Post*, issue 15/21, 20 October–2 November 2006.

4. "2007 Commune Election Results versus 2002" *Phnom Penh Post*, issue 16/07, 6–19 April 2007.

5. A notable exception was Mu Sokhua, the minister of women's affairs, who resigned her post and joined Sam Rainsy's opposition party.

6. Kavi Chongkittavorn, "A New King and New Perspectives in Bhutan," *The Nation*, Bangkok, December 2006.

7. During Sihanouk's reign in the 1960s, it was required to show this footage before every movie as a warning to dissidents.

8. Like his three predecessors, Yash Ghai soon got into a bitter dispute with Hun Sen.

9. Vong Sokheng, "Rainsy to Return, Pledges SRP Overhaul," *Phnom Penh Post*, issue 15/03, 10–23 February 2006.

10. Cat Barton, "Cool Reception for UN Special Representative," *Phnom Penh Post*, issue 16/11, 1–14 June 2007, 6.

11. "The Extraordinary Chambers," *Justice Initiatives*, New York: Open Society Institute, Spring 2006.

12. Cat Barton, "Extraordinarily Troubled Chambers," *Phnom Penh Post*, issue 15/24, 1–14 December 2006, and Cat Barton and Vong Sokheng, "KRT Climbs Over Major Rules Hurdle," *Phnom Penh Post*, issue 16/12, 15–28 June 2007. See also Seth Mydans, "Rules Dispute Imperils Khmer Rouge Trial," *New York Times*, 26 January 2007.

13. E-mail conversation with Kavi Chongkittavorn of the *The Nation* newspaper in Bangkok, 2 February 2007.

14. Omar Halim, "ASEAN: Regional Approach to Conflict Resolution," unpublished.

15. World Bank, Cambodia, "Cambodia Achieves Continued High Growth in 2006," *Cambodia: The World Bank Newsletter*, volume 4, no. 12, December 2006.

16. World Bank, *Cambodia, Halving Poverty by 2015?*, Poverty Assessment 2006, Report No. 35213, Washington, DC, 7 February 2006.

17. Sophal Ear, "The Political Economy of Aid," 77.

18. Allister Hayman, "The Rich, the Poor and the Income Gap," *Phnom Penh Post*, issue 16/11, 1–14 June 2007.

19. Sue-Lyn Moyle and Aun Pheap, "Prime Minister Talks Tough on Land-Grabbing Issues," *Phnom Penh Post*, issue 16/07, 6–19 April 2007.

Chronology

1969	U.S. President Richard Nixon launches secret bombing of Cambodia.
18 March 1970	Sihanouk, head of state, is deposed in a coup d'etat by his prime minister, pro-American General Lon Nol. Sihanouk establishes a government in exile in Beijing—the Royal Government of National Union of Kampuchea (GRUNK)—aligning himself with the Khmer Rouge to fight Lon Nol.
30 April 1970	President Nixon announces that South Vietnamese and U.S. troops have entered Cambodia to destroy communist sanctuaries.
1970–1975	The U.S. bombings and the king's embrace radicalize and strengthen the Khmer Rouge, who become a formidable fighting force armed by China.
17 April 1975	The Khmer Rouge enter Phnom Penh, rename the country Democratic Kampuchea, and start their reign of terror.
9 September 1975	Sihanouk returns to Phnom Penh and assumes his position as head of state of the Khmer Rouge.
2 April 1976	Sihanouk resigns as head of state and is replaced by Khieu Samphan. The real leader, however, is the

shadowy Pol Pot. Sihanouk becomes a virtual prisoner of the Khmer Rouge.

2 December 1978   Following purges against Khmer Rouge cadres by Pol Pot, disaffected cadres under Chea Sim, Heng Samrin, and Hun Sen flee to Vietnam and create the United Front for the National Salvation of Kampuchea (UFNSK) just inside Cambodia.

25 December 1978   In retaliation for Khmer Rouge incursions and massacres of Vietnamese villagers, Vietnamese troops, with the help of UFNSK cadres, intervened in Cambodia. The Third Indochinese War begins.

7 January 1979   Vietnamese and UFNSK troops enter Phnom Penh and end the reign of the Khmer Rouge. The Khmer Rouge flee to sanctuaries along the Thai border.

12 January 1979   In Phnom Penh, the People's Republic of Cambodia (PRK) is proclaimed with Heng Samrin as prime minister and Hun Sen as foreign minister. It gains control of over 90 percent of the country, including all provincial capitals. The ruling party is named the People's Revolutionary Party of Kampuchea (PRPK).

9 October 1979   Son Sann, Dien Dell, and Sak Suthsakhan found the anticommunist Khmer People's National Liberation Front (KPNLF) to fight the PRK.

14 November 1979   The United Nations General Assembly adopts the first of a series of resolutions calling for the withdrawal of all foreign forces from Cambodia. The General Assembly does not recognize the People's Republic of Cambodia and instead allows Democratic Kampuchea, the Khmer Rouge government in exile, to retain Cambodia's seat in the General Assembly.

March 1981   In Paris, Sihanouk creates the National United Front for an Independent, Neutral, Peaceful and Cooperative Cambodia (known by the French acronym FUNCINPEC) to fight the PRK and the Vietnamese forces in Cambodia.

22 June 1982	Sihanouk establishes the Coalition Government of Democratic Kampuchea (CGDK) in exile, consisting of the Khmer Rouge (Party of Democratic Kampuchea, or PDK), FUNCINPEC, and KPNLF. The government in exile occupies the seat reserved for Cambodia in the United Nations.
1979–1991	Cambodia has two governments, each recognized by a different set of countries: The People's Republic of Cambodia (PRK), with de facto control over Cambodia, recognized by the Soviet bloc and India; and the Coalition Government of Democratic Kampuchea (CGDK), a government in exile dominated by the Khmer Rouge and recognized by the West, China, and most nonaligned countries. It has no territory but retains the United Nations seat for Cambodia.
14 January 1986	Hun Sen becomes prime minister of the PRK.
2–4 December 1987	Hun Sen and Sihanouk hold talks in Fer en Tardenois, France, followed by a second meeting at St-Germain-en-Laye, France, 20–21 January 1988.
June–July 1988	The United Nations Secretary-General Perez de Cuellar sends his representative, Rafeeuddin Ahmed, to the region to relay to the four factions a set of proposals for a comprehensive settlement plan.
25–28 July 1988	First Jakarta Informal Meeting (JIM) brings together for the first time the four warring factions to talk peace. This is followed by the second JIM (19–21 February 1989).
30 April 1989	The name People's Republic of Kampuchea is changed to State of Cambodia (SOC) to shed the image of communism.
30 August 1989	The Paris Conference on Cambodia is attended by the four Cambodian factions and nineteen countries, including France and Indonesia as its cochairs and the United Nations secretary-general's representative. It maps out a broad strategy for peace but is suspended

	without achieving agreement on a comprehensive settlement.
26 September 1989	All Vietnamese troops and advisers officially withdraw from Cambodia.
27–28 August 1990	At talks in New York, the five permanent members of the Security Council reach a breakthrough agreement on a framework for a comprehensive political settlement involving, inter alia, a principal role for the United Nations.
9–10 September 1990	Third Jakarta Informal Meeting accepts the framework and agrees to form a Supreme National Council (SNC) consisting of the four warring factions, with Sihanouk, who resigned from FUNCINPEC, as neutral head. The SNC is enshrined as the sole source of power in Cambodia.
September 1991	The SNC is given Cambodia's seat in the General Assembly in New York.
17 October 1991	The party of the SOC/PRK, the People's Revolutionary Party of Kampuchea (PRPK), adopts a new platform, renounces communism, adopts free-market policies, and changes its name to the Cambodian People's Party (CPP).
23 October 1991	The resumed session of the Paris Conference on Cambodia adopts the Paris Agreements on a Comprehensive Settlement of the Cambodian Conflict, proposing the creation of the United Nations Transitional Authority in Cambodia (UNTAC).
28 February 1992	The Security Council establishes UNTAC.
15 March 1992	The Special Representative of the Secretary-General Yasushi Akashi (Japan) and the UNTAC force commander Lieutenant General John M. Sanderson (Australia) arrive in Cambodia. The United Nations starts the deployment of UNTAC with 22,000 soldiers and civilians.
30 March 1992	The Office of the United Nations High Commissioner for Refugees (UNHCR) and UNTAC begin the repa-

	triation of 360,000 refugees and displaced persons from camps in Thailand.
30 May 1992	Akashi and General Sanderson are denied entry into Khmer Rouge territory by a bamboo pole held across a road by a young unarmed Khmer Rouge soldier.
12 June 1992	General Sanderson declares the beginning of the regroupment, cantonment, disarmament, and demobilization of the four armies of the warring factions despite the refusal by the Khmer Rouge to participate.
10 September 1992	Because of continuing sabotage by the Khmer Rouge, the process of demobilization of the four armies is halted. UNTAC's military component is restructured, with a principal task providing security for the elections.
30 November 1992	The Security Council confirms that elections will be held no later than May 1993.
December 1992	UNTAC's electoral component completes the registration of 4.7 million potential Cambodian voters, approximately 90 percent of those eligible.
11 March 1993	The Khmer Rouge slaughter ethnic Vietnamese in a floating village ten kilometers south of Siem Reap town. Encouraged by UNTAC's human rights component, an exodus of boats carry ethnic Vietnamese toward Vietnam.
April 1993	The Khmer Rouge pull out of Phnom Penh. Violence escalates throughout the country, including election-related intimidation and killings involving other factions.
3 May 1993	Major Khmer Rouge attack on Siem Reap town lasting six hours.
23–28 May 1993	National elections held by UNTAC with a 90 percent voter turnout, producing a Constituent Assembly.
15 June 1993	The UN Security Council endorses the results of the elections.
26 June 1993	Sihanouk establishes an interim government with Ranariddh and Hun Sen as coprime ministers. The CPP accepts the election results.

24 September 1993	A new Cambodian constitution is promulgated. Sihanouk is elected king and names Ranariddh and Hun Sen first and second premiers, respectively, with equal power.
8 April 1994	King Sihanouk arrives in Cambodia from Beijing.
13–17 April 1994	After a disastrous dry-season offensive by the Royal Cambodian Armed Forces, Khmer Rouge troops briefly reach the doorstep of Battambang, the second largest city in the country. They are quickly turned back to their sanctuary in Pailin.
June 1994	To solve the Khmer Rouge problem, the king proposes a government in which he would be the head of state, with four vice presidents: Ranariddh, Hun Sen, Sam Rainsy, and Khieu Samphan of the Khmer Rouge.
18 June 1994	Hun Sen writes a letter to the king rejecting his plan for a new government. This marks the beginning of a standoff between these two top leaders of Cambodia.
2 July 1994	Norodom Chakrapong and Sin Song attempt yet another coup against the government. The coup is aborted, and Chakrapong is exiled—the first Norodom to go.
7 July 1994	The Khmer Rouge are outlawed.
20 October 1994	The cabinet is reshuffled: Sam Rainsy and Norodom Sirivudh, two strong figures in FUNCINPEC, leave the cabinet.
August 1995	Sam Rainsy is ousted from FUNCINPEC and parliament.
October 1995	Norodom Sirivudh is arrested and exiled on charges of threatening to kill Hun Sen—the second Norodom to go.
7 January 1996	Hun Sen revives January 7 as a holiday marking the anniversary of the ouster of the Khmer Rouge regime by Vietnamese forces in 1979.
21–22 March 1996	FUNCINPEC holds a congress at which Ranariddh openly repudiates his role as a "puppet prime minister." This marks the beginning of open confrontation between the two coalition partners.

9 August 1996	Ieng Sary, a top Khmer Rouge leader, announces his defection to the government and those of the majority of Khmer Rouge troops stationed in the Pailin area of Battambang province.
14 September 1996	Sihanouk grants amnesty to Ieng Sary.
27 February 1997	Ranariddh inaugurates NUF (the National United Front consisting of FUNCINPEC, Sam Rainsy's KNP, the Son Sann faction of the BLDP, and the small Khmer Neutral Party) to fight the CPP in the 1998 elections.
30 March 1997	In the worst incident of violence since the 1993 elections, four grenades explode at a rally led by Sam Rainsy against the judiciary's lack of independence. At least 19 people are killed and 150 wounded, many of them seriously.
5–6 July 1997	A violent showdown takes place between forces loyal to Ranariddh and those loyal to Hun Sen.
31 July 1997	ASEAN postpones the acceptance of Cambodia as its tenth member.
September 1997	Once again, the Cambodian seat at the United Nations is left vacant.
26 July 1998	Cambodia holds its second elections.
1 December 1998	A new coalition government is established with one prime minister, Hun Sen of the CPP. Ranariddh becomes the president of the National Assembly. Cambodia is finally admitted as the tenth member of ASEAN.

Appendix 1
Deployment of UNTAC

UNTAC consisted of more than 22,874 peacekeepers from over one hundred countries, including:

1. 15,900 military personnel from thirty-four countries: 485 UN military observers, 12 enlarged infantry battalions totaling 10,200 soldiers, as well as logistics, signal, medical, and other units. The military would eventually be deployed to 270 locations throughout Cambodia. Indonesia had the largest contingent, with two battalions totaling 1,779 soldiers, followed by France and India with 1,350 and 1,336, respectively. The military was the most visible presence of UNTAC, and its conduct was watched closely by Cambodians of all factions.
2. 3,349 civilian police from forty-six countries.
3. 1,000 international civilians as well as 5,113 local Cambodian staff.
4. 450 low-paid UN volunteers (UNVs) who would later play an important role in the electoral process.
5. 1,400 international election monitors and 56,000 Cambodians recruited locally who would join UNTAC at election time in 1993.[1]

UNTAC differed from traditional peacekeeping operations in two aspects:

1. UNTAC was given wide-ranging powers in the realm of peace building, which went far beyond traditional peacekeeping.

2. As an "interim government" under the Paris Agreements, it was vested with
a number of executive powers of governance.

NOTE

1. See UN, *The UN and Cambodia, 1991–1995*, New York: UN Department of Public
Information, 1995, 12 and 23. For the countries represented, see *UN Chronicle*, June
1993, 23.

Appendix 2
The Royal Government of Cambodia, November 1993

Note: C refers to CPP, F to FUNCINPEC

First Prime Minister	Norodom Ranariddh (F)
Second Prime Minister	Hun Sen (C)
Vice Premier	Norodom Sirivudh (F)
Vice Premier	Sar Kheng (C)

Cabinet of the Council of Ministers:
Minister	Veng Sereyvuth (F)
Minister	Sok An (C)

Ministry of Foreign Affairs and International Cooperation:
Minister	Norodom Sirivudh (F)
Secretary of State	Uch Kim An (C)

Ministry of National Defense:
Minister	Tea Banh (C)
Minister	Tea Chamrat (F)

Ministry of the Interior:
Minister	Sar Kheng (C)
Minister	You Hockry (F)

Ministry of the Economy and Finance:
Minister   Sam Rainsy (F)
Secretary of State   Cham Prasidh (C)

Ministry of Information:
Minister   Ieng Mouly (B)
Secretary of State   Khieu Kanharith (C)

Minister of Public Works
    and Transportation   Ing Kieth (F)
Minister of Agriculture, Forests
    and Fisheries   Kong Sam Ol (C)
Minister of Justice   Chem Sanguan (C)
Minister of Education, Youth and Sports   Ung Huot (F)
Minister of Commerce   Var Huot (C)
Ministry of Industry, Energy and Mines   Pou Sothirak (F)
Minister of Planning   Chea Chanto (C)
Minister of Health   Chea Thaing (C)
Governor of the Central Bank   Thor Peng Leat (C)
Vice Governor of the Central Bank   Mme Sam Tioulong Saumura (F)

Note: All ministries have secretaries of state from the other party, but for the sake of brevity only the important ones are listed here. In addition, there were several offices headed by secretaries of state that were elevated to ministries in subsequent cabinets, including tourism, religions and culture, and fine arts and women's affairs.

Bibliography

PRIMARY SOURCES

This book is based mainly on my extensive notes on my observations, conversations, and interviews in Cambodia during my five years there.

Unpublished United Nations Documents

United Nations, *Report of the United Nations Fact Finding Mission on Present Structures and United Nations Practices of Administration in Cambodia, 24 April to 9 May 1990*, June 1990.

UNTAC, *Electoral Law of Cambodia*, August 1992.

Other resolutions and documents of the UN General Assembly and Security Council were consulted when relevant.

Published United Nations Documents

A/34/PV. Official Records of the 34th session of the UN General Assembly, nos. 3 and 4, 21 September 1979.

A/34/500. First report of the Credentials Committee of the General Assembly, New York: 34th session, September 1979.

A/46/608-S/23177. Letter from Cochairmen Indonesia and France attaching the Agreement on a Comprehensive Political Settlement of the Cambodia Conflict, Paris, 23 October 1991 (also known as the Paris Peace Agreements).

S/RES/745 91992. Security Council Resolution approving the UNTAC plan presented by the Secretary-General in S/23613.

S/23613. Report of the Secretary-General on Cambodia containing his proposed implementation of plan for UNTAC, 19 February 1992.

A/46/903. Financing of the UN Advance Mission on Cambodia, and Financing of the UN Transitional Authority in Cambodia, 7 May 1992.

SECONDARY SOURCES

Books, Dissertations, and Online Sources

Achariya, Amitav, et al., eds. *Cambodia—the 1989 Paris Peace Conference, Background Analysis and Documents.* Toronto: Center for International Strategic Studies, York University, 1991.

Alatas, Ali. *A Voice for a Just Peace: A Collection of Speeches,* Jakarta: Gramedia Press, 2001.

Anderson, Benedict R., and Ruth T. McVey. *A Preliminary Analysis of the October 1, 1965 Coup in Indonesia.* Ithaca, NY: Cornell University, 1971.

Azimi, Nassarine, ed. *The UN Transitional Authority in Cambodia (UNTAC), Debriefing and Lessons.* London: Kluwer International, 1996.

Barrett, Keith Nicholas Spencer. *Major Power Intervention in Cambodia, the Destruction of a Neutralist Country, 1969 to 1975.* MA thesis, The University of Hull, UK: November 1984.

Bartu, Peter. *The Fifth Faction: The United Nations Transitional Authority in Cambodia.* PhD dissertation, Monash University: 1998.

Basu, Sanghamitra. *Kampuchea as a Factor in the Sino-Soviet Conflict 1975–1984.* Calcutta: Firma KLM, 1987.

Becker, Elizabeth. *When the War Was Over: Cambodia and the Khmer Rouge Revolution.* New York: Public Affairs, 1998.

Berry, Ken. *Cambodia from Red to Blue: Australia's Initiative for Peace.* Canberra: Allen Unwin, 1997.

Boutros-Ghali, Boutros. *An Agenda for Peace,* UN document A/47/277- S/24111. New York: 17 June 1992.

———. Introduction to *The UN and Cambodia, 1991–1995.* New York: United Nations, 1995.

————. *Supplement to the Agenda for Peace,* UN Document A/50/60- S/1995/1. New York: 3 January 1995.

Brown, Frederick Z., and David G. Timberman. *Cambodia and the International Community: The Quest for Peace, Development and Democracy.* Singapore: Institute for Southeast Asian Studies, 1998.

Brown, MacAlister, and Joseph J. Zasloff, *Cambodia Confounds the Peacemakers, 1979–1998.* Ithaca, NY: Cornell University Press, 1998.

Carney, Tim, and Tan Liang Choo. *Whither Cambodia? Beyond the Elections.* Singapore: Institute of Southeast Asian Studies, 1993.

Chanda, Nayan. *Brother Enemy: The War after the War.* New York: Macmillan, 1986.

Chandler, David P. *Brother Number One: A Political Biography of Pol Pot.* St. Leonards, Australia: Allen and Unwin, 1992.

————. *Facing the Cambodian Past, Selected Essays, 1971–1984.* Chiengmai, Thailand: Silkworm, 1996.

————. *A History of Cambodia.* Chiengmai, Thailand: Silkworm, 1993.

————. *The Tragedy of Cambodian History: Politics, War and Revolution Since 1945.* New Haven: Yale University Press, 1991.

Coedes, George. *The Indianized States of Southeast Asia.* Honolulu: University of Hawaii Press, 1968.

Commonwealth of Australia. *Cambodia: An Australian Peace Proposal.* Canberra: Australian Government Publishing Service, 1990.

Cook, Susan, ed. *Genocide in Cambodia and Rwanda: New Perspectives.* Yale Center for International and Area Studies, Genocide Studies Program Monograph Series no. 1, 2004.

Cribb, Robert. *The Indonesian Killings of 1965–1966.* Clayton, Victoria, Australia: Centre of Southeast Asian Studies, Monash University, 1990.

Curtis, Grant. *Cambodia Reborn.* Geneva: UN Research Institute for Social Development, 1998.

De Nike, Howard J., John Quickley, and Kenneth J. Robinson. *Genocide in Cambodia: Documents from the Trial of Pol Pot and Ieng Sary.* Philadelphia: University of Pennsylvania Press, 2000.

Doyle, Michael. *UN Peacekeeping in Cambodia: UNTAC's Civil Mandate.* Boulder, CO: Lynne Rienner Publishers, 1995.

Etcheson, Craig. *After the Killing Field: Lessons from the Cambodian Genocide.* Portsmouth, NH: Praeger Publishers, 2005.

Fawthrop, Tom, and Helen Jarvis. *Getting Away with Genocide? Elusive Justice and the Khmer Rouge Tribunal.* London and Ann Arbor, MI: Pluto Books, 2004.

Frieson, Kate G. *The Impact of Revolution on Cambodian Peasants 1970–1975.* PhD dissertation, Department of Politics, Monash University, Australia: 1991.

Godfrey, Martin, et al. "Technical Assistance and Capacity Development in an Aid-Dependent Economy: The Experience of Cambodia," *Working Paper no. 15.* Phnom Penh: Cambodian Resource Institute, August 2000.

Gottesman, Evan. *Cambodia after the Khmer Rouge: Inside the Politics of Nation Building.* New Haven: Yale University Press, 2003.

Goulding, Marrack. *Peacemonger.* London: John Murray, 2002.

Group of Cambodian Jurists. *People's Revolutionary Tribunal Held in Phnom Penh for the Trial of the Genocide Crime of the Pol Pot-Ieng Sary Clique.* Phnom Penh: Foreign Languages Publishing House, 1990.

Heder, Stephen, and Judy Ledgerwood, eds. *Propaganda, Politics and Violence in Cambodia: Democratic Transition under United Nations Peacekeeping.* New York: M. E. Sharpe, 1996.

Hil, Hal, ed. *Indonesia's New Order.* St. Leonards, NSW Australia: Allen and Unwin, 1994.

Hitchens, Christopher. *The Trial of Henry Kissinger.* New York, London: Verso, 2001.

Hughes, Caroline. *The Political Economy of Cambodia's Transition, 1991–2001.* London and New York: Routledge Curzon, 2003.

Igout, Michael. *Phnom Penh Then and Now.* Bangkok: White Lotus, 1993.

Jeldres, Julio A. *The Royal House of Cambodia.* Phnom Penh: Monument Books, 2003.

Jeldres, Julio A., and Somkid Chaijitvanit. *The Royal Palace of Phnom Penh and Cambodian Royal Life.* Bangkok: Post Publishers, 1999.

Jennar, Raoul M. *Cambodian Chronicles. Volume I, Bungling the Peace Plan*. Bangkok: White Lotus, 1998.

———. *The Cambodian Constitutions 1953–93*. Bangkok: White Lotus, 1995.

———. *Chroniques Cambodgiennes 1990–1994, Rapports au Forum International des ONG au Cambodge*. Paris: L'Harmattan, 1995.

Jones, Sidney. "The Impact of Asian Economic Growth on Human Rights." New York, Council on Foreign Relations, Asia Project Working Papers, January 1995.

Kahin, George McTurnan. *Southeast Asia: A Testament*. London: Routledge Curzon, 2003.

Kamm, Henry. *Cambodia: Report from a Stricken Land*. New York: Arcade Publishing, 1998.

Kiernan, Ben, ed. *Genocide and Democracy in Cambodia: The Khmer Rouge, the UN and the International Community*. New Haven: Yale University Press, 1993.

———. *How Pol Pot Came to Power*. London: Verso, 1985.

———. *The Pol Pot Regime*. New Haven: Yale University Press, 1996.

Killjunen, Kimmo, ed. *Kampuchea: Decade of the Genocide: Report of a Finnish Inquiry Commission*. London: Zed Books, 1984.

Kingdom of Cambodia, Ministry of Foreign Affairs and International Cooperation. *White Paper: Background on the July 1997 Crisis: Prince Ranariddh's Strategy of Provocation*. Phnom Penh: 9 July 1997.

Kingdom of Cambodia, Ministry of Foreign Affairs and International Cooperation. *Crisis in July. Report on the Armed Insurrection: Its Origins, History and Aftermath*. Phnom Penh: 22 September 1997.

Kubes, Antonin. *Kampuchea*. Prague: Orbis Press Agency, 1982.

Ledgerwood, Judy. Cambodian Recent History and Contemporary Society: An Introductory Course, Department of Anthropology and Center for Southeast Asian Studies. Northern Illinois University, www.seasite.niu.edu/khmer/ ledgerwood/contents.htm.

Lizee, Pierre P. *Peace, Power and Resistance in Cambodia*. New York: St. Martin's Press, 2000.

Majumdar, R. C. *Kambuja-Desa*. Philadelphia: Institute for the Study of Human Rights Issues, 1980.

Marsh, Ian, Jean Blondel, and Takashi Inoguchi, eds. *Democracy, Governance and Economic Performance; East and Southeast Asia*. Tokyo: United Nations University Press, 1999.

Martin, Marie Alexandrine. *Cambodia: A Shattered Society*, translated from French by Mark McLeod. Los Angeles: University of California Press, 1994.

Mayal, James, ed. *The New Interventionism 1991–1994: United Nations Experience in Cambodia, Former Yugoslavia and Somalia*. Cambridge: University Press, 1996.

Mehta, Harish C., and Julie B. Mehta. *Hun Sen, Strong Man of Cambodia*. Singapore: Graham Brash, 1999.

———. *Warrior Prince, Norodom Ranariddh, Son of King Sihanouk of Cambodia*. Singapore: Graham Brash, 2001.

Mysliwiec, Eva. *Punishing the Poor: The International Isolation of Cambodia*. London: Oxfam, 1987.

Nasution, Nazaruddin, et al. *Pasang Surut Hubungan Diplomatik Indonesia Kambodha*. Phnom Penh: Indonesian Embassy, 2002. Also published in English as *Indonesia-Cambodia: Forging Ties through Thick and Thin*. Phnom Penh: Indonesian Embassy, 2002.

Osborne, Milton. *Sihanouk, Prince of Light, Prince of Darkness*. London: George Allen and Unwin, 1994.

Peou, Sorpong. *Intervention and Change in Cambodia: Towards Democracy?* Bangkok: Silkworm, 2000.

Ponchaud, Father. *Cambodia Year Zero*, translated from French by Nancy Amphoux. New York: Holt, Rinehart & Winston, 1978.

Power, Samantha. *A Problem from Hell: America and the Age of Genocide*. New York: Basic Books, 2002.

Prior, Marje, and Heide Smith. *Shooting at the Moon*. Australia: Ainslie Act, 1994.

Riddle, Tom. *Cambodian Interlude: Inside Cambodia's Peace Process*. Bangkok: White Orchid Press, 1997.

Roberts, David. *Political Transition in Cambodia, 1991–99*. Richmond, Surrey: Curzon Press, 2001.

Royal Government of Cambodia. "July 5–6?!" undated, presumably 1997.

Schoonoord, Dr. D. C. I. *The Koningklijke Marine in Actie voor de Verenigde Naties: Mariniers in Cambodia, 1992–1993.* The Hague: Ministerie van Defensie, 1993.

Schwarz, Adam. *A Nation in Waiting.* Boulder, CO: Westview Press, 2000.

Shawcross, William. *Cambodia's New Deal.* Washington, DC: Carnegie Endowment for International Peace, 1994.

———. *The Quality of Mercy: Cambodia, Holocaust and Modern Conscience.* New York: Simon and Schuster, 1984.

———. *Sideshow.* London: The Hogarth Press, 1991.

Sihanouk, Prince Norodom, as related to Wilfred Burchett. *My War with the CIA.* New York: Pantheon Books, 1972.

———. assisted by Simonne Lacoutere. *Prisonnier des Khmer Rouges.* Paris: Hachette, 1986.

———. *Sihanouk Reminisces.* Bangkok: D. K. Printing House, 1990.

———. *Souvenirs Doux at Amers.* Paris: Hachette, 1981.

———. *War and Hope: The Case for Cambodia.* New York: Pantheon Books, 1980.

Sihanouk, Prince Norodom. Personal website: www.norodomsihanouk.info.

Smith, Hugh, ed. *International Peace Keeping: Building on the Cambodian Experience.* Canberra: Australian Defense Studies Center, 1994.

Solomon, Richard H. *Exiting Indochina.* Washington, DC: United States Institute for Peace, 2000.

Taylor, R. H. *The Politics of Elections in Southeast Asia.* Cambridge: Cambridge University Press, 1996.

Tully, John. *A Short History of Cambodia.* Crow's Nest, NSH: Allen and Unwin, 2005.

United Nations. *The United Nations and Cambodia, 1991–1995.* New York: UN Department of Public Information, 1995.

———. "Agreement on A Comprehensive Political Settlement of the Cambodia Conflict." New York: United Nations, 1992.

World Bank. *Cambodia at the Crossroads: Strengthening Accountability to Reduce Poverty,* Report No. 30636-KH. Washington, DC: 15 November 2004.

———. *Cambodia, Halving Poverty by 2015?*, Poverty Assessment 2006, Report No. 35213. Washington, DC: 7 February 2006.

———. *Cambodia: Seizing the Global Opportunity: Investment Climate Assessment and Reform Strategy for Cambodia*, Report No. 27925-KH. Washington, DC: 12 August 2004.

Zhou, Mei. *Radio UNTAC of Cambodia: Winning Hearts and Minds.* Bangkok: White Lotus, 1994.

Articles

Akashi, Yasushi. "The Challenges Faced by UNTAC." *Japan Review of International Affairs*, vol. 7, no. 3.

Chanda, Nayan. "The Enemy Within." *Far Eastern Economic Review*, vol. 159, no. 34.

Crouch, Harold. "Another Look at the Indonesian Coup." *Indonesia*, Cornell University, April 1972.

Ear, Sophal. "The Political Economy of Aid and Governance in Cambodia." *Asian Journal of Political Science*, vol. 15, no. 1, April 2007, 68–96.

Esterline, John. "Vietnam in 1986: An Uncertain Tiger." *Asian Survey*, vol. 27, no. 1, January 1987.

Ghai, Yash. "Human Rights and Governance: The Asia Debate." *Asia Pacific Journal on Human Rights and the Law*, vol. I, no. 1, January 2000.

Hahn, Lorna. "No Deals with the Butchers of Cambodia." *Washington Post*, 9 January 1989, page A11.

Hughes, Helen. "Why Have East Asian Countries Led Economic Development?" *Economic Record*, 71 (212).

Kiernan, Ben. "The American Bombardment of Cambodia." *Vietnam Generation*, vol. 1, no. 1 (winter 1989).

———. "The Demography of Genocide in Southeast Asia." *Bulletin of Critical Asian Studies*, vol. 35, no. 4, 2003.

McAuliffe, John. "Welcome to Cambodia, Where Nothing Is Ever as It Seems." *Indochina Interchange*, September 1997.

McIntyre, Andrew J. "Interpreting Indonesia's Foreign Policy: The Case of Cambodia." *Asian Survey*, vol. XXVII, no. 5, May 1987.

Metzl, Jamie Frederic. "The Many Faces of UNTAC: A Review Article." *Contemporary Southeast Asia*, vol. 17, no. 1, June 1995.

Open Society. "The Extraordinary Chambers." *Justice Initiatives*, New York, spring 2006.

Pike, Douglas. "The Cambodian Peace Process: Summer of 1989." *Asian Survey*, vol. XXIX, no. 9, September 1989.

Prings, K. Viviane. "The Cambodian People's Party and Sihanouk." *Journal of Contemporary Asia*, vol. 25, no. 3, 1994.

Ratner, Stephen R. "The Cambodia Settlement Agreements." *American Journal of International Law*, vol. 87, no. 1, January 1993.

Scott, James C. "Patron-Client Politics and Political Change in Southeast Asia." *American Political Science Review*, vol. 66, March 1972.

Sihanouk, Prince Norodom. "Message and Solemn Declaration." Beijing, 23 March 1970.

Thayer, Nate. "Ambiguous Alliances: Can the Khmer Rouge Survive Pol Pot?" *Far Eastern Economic Review*, vol. 160, no. 27, 3 July 1997.

———. "Last Act: Sihanouk's Plan to Retake the Reigns of Power." *Far Eastern Economic Review*, vol. 160, no. 29, 23 June 1994.

———. "Law of the Gun: Hun Sen's Power Grab Puts Cambodia in a Precarious Bind." *Far Eastern Economic Review*, 17 July 1997.

Vickery, Michael. "Cambodia: A Political Survey," Discussion Paper no. 14, Research School of Pacific Studies, Australian National University, 1994.

———. "The Campaign Against Cambodia, 1990–1991." *Indochina Issues*, 93, August 1991.

Warner, Barbara. "Japan Views Leadership Opportunities through the United Nations." *Japan Economic Institute Report*, no. 10A, 13 March 1992.

Newspapers and Periodicals

Asian Survey

Asia Week

Bangkok Post

Brief (UNTAC internal periodical)

Cambodia Daily

Cambodia New Vision

Contemporary Southeast Asia

Far Eastern Economic Review

Foreign Affairs

Foreign Broadcast Information Service (FBIS)

Free Choice (UNTAC internal periodical)

Konflik Kambodia: Dokumentasi, Jakarta

New York Times

Phnom Penh Post

The Mirror (Phnom Penh)

The Nation (Bangkok)

UNTAC newsletters

Xinhua News Agency

Index